ANGRY ENGLISH
academic
VOCABULARY

Introduction

책의 대상 (Who should use this book)

최소한의 어휘만 외워도 문제를 풀 수 있다는 믿음은 틀리다. '아는 것이 힘'인 것 처럼, 단어는 많이 알면 알수록 좋다. 생전 가야 쓰지도 않는 걸 뭘 그렇게 힘들게 외우냐는 자칭 전문가들의 주장은 틀리다. 어느 지문에 어떤 단어들이 어떻게 나올지는 아무도 알 수 없기 때문이다.

아랫글은, 18년 9월 고2 모의고사 영어 영역 37번 지문이다.

[37~38] 글의 흐름으로 보아, 주어진 문장이 들어가기에 가장 적절한 곳을 고르시오.

37.

> However, when a bill was introduced in Congress to outlaw such rules, the credit card lobby turned its attention to language.

Framing matters in many domains. (①) When credit cards started to become popular forms of payment in the 1970s, some retail merchants wanted to charge different prices to their cash and credit card customers. (②) To prevent this, credit card companies adopted rules that forbade their retailers from charging different prices to cash and credit customers. (③) Its preference was that if a company charged different prices to cash and credit customers, the credit price should be considered the "normal" (default) price and the cash price a discount—rather than the alternative of making the cash price the usual price and charging a surcharge to credit card customers. (④) The credit card companies had a good intuitive understanding of what psychologists would come to call "framing." (⑤) The idea is that choices depend, in part, on the way in which problems are stated. [3점]

윗글의 출처는 *Nudge* (Richard H. Thaler and Cass R. Sunstein, 2009, p.36)이다. 다음의 문장 – 'Credit card companies typically charge retailers 1 percent of each sale.' – 이 생략된 것을 제외하고는 실제 원문과 동일하다. 심리학적 측면에서 경제학을 분석한 행동 경제학(behavioral economics)을 대표하는 책의 일부가 모의고사 지문에 나온 것인데 '수능을 공부하는 학생들은 토플과 같이 어려운 영어 시험에 나오는 단어들을 외울 필요가 없다'는 이들 전문가들의 주장은 옳지 않다. 예를 들면, 위의 *Nudge* 에서 나온 단어 '금지하다', '불법화하다'의 뜻인 'outlaw'는 수능 지문에 나올 것 같지 않은 단어로 보이지만 같은 지문에 나오는 'forbid(금지하다)'의 동의어이다. 'forbid 까지는 수능, outlaw는 토플' 이런 식으로 구분하고 나눌 수 있는지 궁금하다.

미국 대학에서 수업을 들을 수 있는지를 평가하는 영어 능력 시험인 토플 시험이나 *Nudge* 와 같은 영어 학술 도서, 그리고 그러한 영어 도서에서 필요한 부분을 가려 뽑아낸 수능 지문에 자주 나오는 이러한 아카데믹한 단어들은 수능을 준비하고 유학을 생각하는 학생이라면 반드시 알아야 하는 필수 어휘들이다. 또한 얼핏 초고난도로 여겨지는 이러한 빈출 단어들의 수준은 미국 초등학교 학생들이 알 만한 것들이다. 예를 들면, '에너지 고갈' 혹은 '자원 고갈'과 같은 환경 문제를 다루는 학술 논문이나 시사 주간지에 자주 등장하는 우리말의 '고갈'은 초등학교 6학년 생이면 누구나 알 수 있듯이 마찬가지로 같은 학년의 미국의 초등학생들도 자신들의 모국어인 영어 'depletion'로 어렵지 않게 접할 수 있는 단어이다. 바꾸어 말하면 outlaw, depletion 같은 단어들은 영어권의 초등학생들 모두가 알 만한 평범한 것들이다. 일례로 이 책에서 소개되는 많은 단어들이 미국 출판사 Scholastic(스콜라스틱)의 *Children's Dictionary*에 수록되어 있다

따라서 **idiosyncratic** 특이한, **grotesque** 기괴한, **salient** 두드러진(현저한), **inertia** 타성(불활발), **procrastinate** 미루다(연기하다), **municipal** 지방자치의, **volatile** 변덕스러운, **gigantic** 거대한 같은 *Nudge* 에 자주 나오는 이러한 단어들이 처음엔 생소하고 어렵게 느껴지지만 depletion처럼 아카데믹한 영어 시험을 준비하는 수험생이라면 꼭 암기해야 할 필수 단어(essential words)인 셈이다. 끝으로 이 책은 일상생활에서의 영어가 아닌 수능이나 토플과 같은 학문적 목적의 영어(Academic English) 능력을 키우고 또한 그런 유의 시험 대비에 필요한 필수 어휘들을 소개하는 것을 목적으로 집필되었다.

책의 구성과 특징 (How to use this book)

1. 구성

1) 본서
명동형부 명사/동사/형용사/부사 로 나뉜 약 50개의 단어를 하루치 양(Day 1)으로 총 60개의 Day로 구성하였고, 좀 더 세분화하여, 핵심편, 심화편, 주제별 어휘편 등 총 3개의 파트로 나누었다.

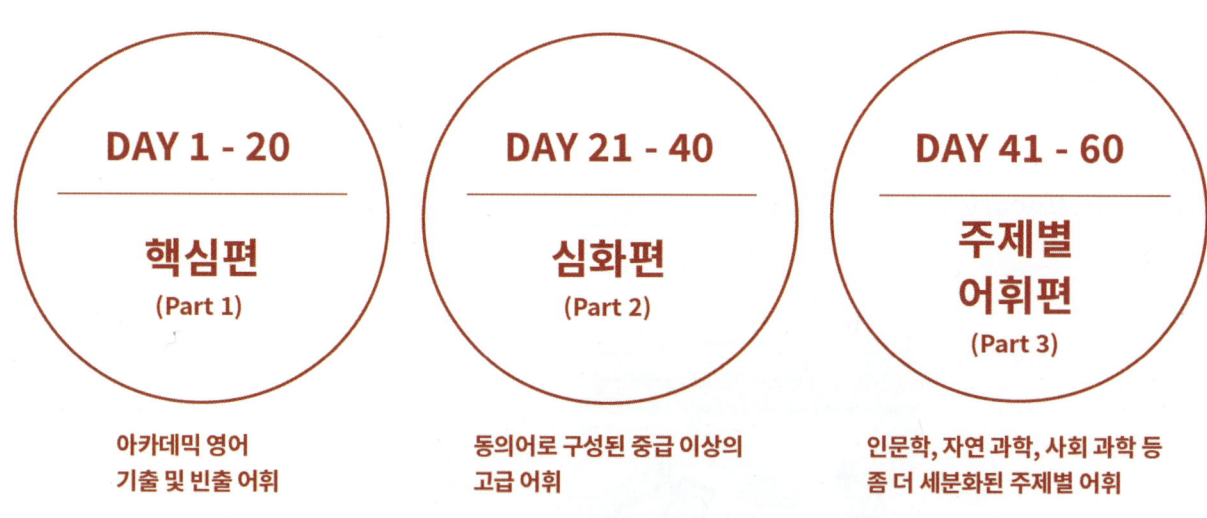

2) Workbook
학습한 어휘를 복습하기 위해 날짜별로 약 64개의 연습 문제로 구성, 총 3860개의 문제를 엮은 문제집(Workbook)을 별책으로 제작하였다.

2. 특징

1) 총 10,000개 어휘 (3,018 표제어 + 6,982 동의어(5,069), 반의어(419), 파생어(937), 연관어(557))
표제어 3,018개와 동의어, 반의어, 파생어, 연관어 등 표제어의 관련 단어 6,982개 – 총 10,000개의 어휘를 수록하였다.

2) 용례(usage)를 활용하는 암기법
용례를 들어 빈번하게 사용되는 표현들을 통으로 외우도록 하였다.

3) 인문학, 사회 과학, 자연 과학 등 20개의 세부 주제별 어휘
아카데믹한 어휘들을 문학, 건축, 음악, 영화, 미술사, 식물학, 동물학, 생물학, 보건학, 천문학, 지구과학, 지리학, 환경 과학, 고고학, 미국사, 세계사, 경제학, 심리학, 정치학, 법학, 경영학, 학창 생활 등 총 20개의 주제들로 분류하였다.

4) 총 3,860개의 연습 문제
여덟 가지의 다양한 문제 유형을 통해 단어를 자연스럽게 익히도록 하였다.

5) 시각적 자료 활용
의미를 시각적으로 쉽게 전달할 수 있는 단어들은 최대한 그림이나 지도로 설명하였다.

e.g. bay 만 바다가 육지 쪽으로 들어와 있는 형태의 지형

 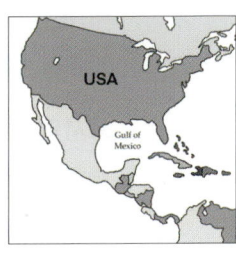

6) 실전과 동일한 수준의 지문을 통한 독해 연습
학술적인 주제를 다룬 지문에서 자주 보이는 도치와 강조 용법 등 반드시 익혀야 할 문법 내용들을 지문에 넣어 독해 연습을 할 수 있도록 했다.

7) 526개의 영작 문제
단어의 쓰임을 통문장으로 암기할 수 있도록 하기 위해서뿐만 아니라 문법 공부를 할 수 있도록 영작 문제를 추가하였다.

8) 원어민이 직접 녹음한 발음
큐알(QR) 코드로 단어를 원어민의 발음으로 손쉽게 들을 수 있도록 하였다.

Symbols & Abbreviations

1. 문법적인 설명과 같은 의미의 단어는 괄호 속에 넣었다.	e.g. reason (가산) e.g. bother (주로 부정문과 의문문에서 사용) e.g. hive 벌집 (=beehive)
2. 구체적인 부연 설명이 필요한 경우는 단어 뜻 앞에 괄호 속에 넣어 설명하였다.	e.g. serve (음식이나 음료 등을) 제공하다
3. 주로 쓰이는 형식 – 예를 들어 복수로 사용되거나 정관사와 함께 사용되는 단어들 – 은 단어 옆에 작게 표기하였다.	e.g. amenity amenities
4. 단어의 뜻을 부연 설명하는 경우는 단어 옆에 작게 표기하였다.	e.g. calligraphy 컬리그러피 글자를 아름답게 쓰는 기술
5. 타동사와 자동사의 구별은 ';'로 구별하였다. 단, 나눠서 설명해야 하는 경우는 단어 옆에 괄호 속에 넣었다.	e.g. shatter 박살내다; 박살나다 e.g. survive 살아남다 (자동사)
6. 발음은 영어 발음만 표기하는 것을 원칙으로 하였으나, 잘못 알고 있거나 발음하기 어려운 단어의 경우는 한국어 발음을 함께 기재하였다. 단, 한국어 발음 표기에서 장모음 구별은 따로 하지 않았다.	e.g. executive /igzékjutiv/ /이그제큐*티브/
7. 동사의 경우, 불규칙 과거와 과거 완료형은 표제어 아래 제시하였다.	e.g. burst *burst – burst – burst
8. 약자(abbreviation)와 부호(symbols)	1) ☺ : 다른 단어와 빈번하게 사용되는 표현(usage 용례)을 설명한다. 2) ◇ : 짧은 예시문이다. 3) ◦ : 주어와 동사로 이루어진 예시문이다. 참고: 예시문 번역은 직역을 원칙으로 하였고 필요한 부분에만 의역을 첨가하였다. 4) ▶ : 주어진 단어의 파생어 명사/동사/형용사/부사를 설명한다. 5) N : 표제어와 혼동하지 말아야 할 단어 혹은 표제어와 관련된 중요한 표현들을 설명한다. 6) S : 유의어 (synonym) 7) A : 반의어 (antonym) 8) sb : somebody 9) sth : something 10) 가산 : 가산 명사 11) 불가산 : 불가산 명사

CONTENTS

DAY 01	8
DAY 02	15
DAY 03	23
DAY 04	31
DAY 05	39
DAY 06	47
DAY 07	55
DAY 08	64
DAY 09	72
DAY 10	81
DAY 11	89
DAY 12	97
DAY 13	107
DAY 14	116
DAY 15	125
DAY 16	134
DAY 17	142
DAY 18	150
DAY 19	158
DAY 20	166
INDEX	175

DAY 01

ANGRY ENGLISH
ACADEMIC VOCABULARY

noun 명사
- [ ] acquisition
- [ ] barrier
- [ ] consumption
- [ ] debris
- [ ] efficacy
- [ ] flavor
- [ ] function
- [ ] host
- [ ] incursion
- [ ] offspring
- [ ] reservoir
- [ ] satire
- [ ] vicinity

verb 동사
- [ ] accomplish
- [ ] block
- [ ] cremate
- [ ] decay
- [ ] encroach
- [ ] form
- [ ] indicate
- [ ] mediate
- [ ] obliterate
- [ ] prosper
- [ ] rebel
- [ ] reserve
- [ ] reveal
- [ ] spur
- [ ] store
- [ ] trespass
- [ ] vanish
- [ ] wipe out

adjective 형용사
- [ ] abnormal
- [ ] analogous
- [ ] asymmetric
- [ ] bare
- [ ] common
- [ ] devoid
- [ ] huge
- [ ] imperative
- [ ] legendary
- [ ] martial
- [ ] obscure
- [ ] plausible
- [ ] reasonable
- [ ] sedentary

adverb 부사
- [ ] approximately
- [ ] clockwise
- [ ] slightly
- [ ] strangely enough

MP3 파일 다운

noun 명사

0001 acquisition
/ækwizíʃən/

1. 습득
- the acquisition of sth ~의 습득
- The older you get, the more challenging **the acquisition of** a new language is.

2. 기업 인수
- mergers and acquisitions (M&A) 기업 인수 합병

0002 barrier
/bǽriər/
/배리어/

장애(물), 장벽
- barrier to sth ~에 장애물
- trade barriers / barriers to trade 무역 장벽
- The main **barrier to** entry is the cost.

[S] obstacle

0003 consumption
/kənsʌ́mpʃən/

(에너지 또는 식품의) 소비, (상품의) 소비, 이용(활용)
- alcohol consumption 술 소비
- It is necessary to reduce the consumption of gasoline.

[S] use, utilization

0004 debris
/dəbríː/

잔해, 파편
- the scattered debris from the car crash 자동차 추돌 사고에서 나온 흩어진 잔해
- They had to close down the restaurant when they found insect debris inside the refrigerator.

[S] pieces, carcass 동물의 시체

0005 efficacy
/éfikəsi/

(약 등의) 효험, 효능
- Laboratory tests proved the efficacy and safety of the drug.

[N] efficiency (명사) 효율, 능률

[S] effectiveness

0006 flavor
/fléivər/

맛
- 31 different flavors of ice cream 31가지 다양한 맛의 아이스크림
- When people today prepare meals, they often consider only flavor rather than nutritional value.

[S] taste, savor 좋은 맛이나 냄새

0007 function
/fʌ́ŋkʃən/

1. 기능, 역할
- serve a function as sth ~로서 역할을 하다
- "Do" and "be" **serve a function as** auxiliary verbs in a sentence.
- The functions of pottery in Native American cultures vary.

2. 행사, 의식
- official functions 공식 행사

[S] purpose, role

0008 host
/hóust/
/호우스트/

1. 주인 (hostess 여주인)
- The hostess took a perverse pleasure in baffling her guests.

2. 주최측, 주최국
- the host country for the next Olympic Games 다음 올림픽 주최국
- The host city for the 2024 Summer Olympics is Paris.

3. 많음
- a (whole) host of sth (대단히) 많은
- Alcohol can cause **a** whole **host of** problems.

[S] a multitude of sth

0001 나이가 들수록 새로운 언어의 습득은 더 도전적이다.　0002 들어가는 데 주된 장벽은 비용이다.　0003 휘발유의 소비를 줄일 필요가 있다.　0004 그들이 냉장고 안에서 곤충의 잔해를 발견했을 때 그들은 식당을 닫아야 했다.　0005 실험실 실험이 그 약의 효험과 안전을 입증했다.　0006 오늘날 사람들이 음식을 준비할 때 그들은 종종 영양가보다는 맛만을 고려한다.　0007 'Do'와 'be'는 문장에서 조동사로서 기능을 한다. / 미국 원주민 문화에서 도기의 기능은 다양하다.　0008 그 여주인은 손님들을 당황하게 하는 데서 심술궂은 즐거움을 느꼈다. / 2024년 하계 올림픽 주최 도시는 파리이다. / 술은 대단히 많은 문제를 일으킬 수 있다.

0009
incursion
/inkə́ːrʒən/

급습
- an incursion into ~을 급습
- Gonzalo Pizarro made **incursions into** Vilcabamba, an ancient Inca city, which is now Peru.

[s] invasion, raid

0010
offspring
/ɔ́ːfspriŋ/

자식, (동물의) 새끼
- There wouldn't be any offspring to worry about.

[s] young

0011
reservoir
/rézərvwɑːr/
/레저브와/

(물을 저장해 두는 인공적인) 호수, 저수지
- In 1964, the Glen Canyon Dam, one of the largest dams in the United States, was constructed on the Colorado River in northern Arizona, and its reservoir, Lake Powell, which is 299 kilometers long, was also created.

0012
satire
/sǽtaiər/
/새*타이어/

풍자
- a stinging / biting / cruel satire on sth ~에 대한 신랄한 풍자
- He wrote a hip-hop song, **a stinging satire on** a society that always sides with the rich as the poor get poorer.

[s] sarcasm

0013
vicinity
/visíniti/
/비시*니티/

부근, 인근, 주변
- in the immediate vicinity of sth ~의 바로 인근에
- There are many small lodges in the vicinity where you camp on the island.

[s] locality, proximity

verb 동사

0014
accomplish
/əkɑ́mpliʃ/

성취하다, 달성하다, 완수하다, 이루어 내다
- Mission accomplished.
- Jesus said, "It is accomplished."

[s] achieve

0015
block
/blɑ́k/

1. (도로 또는 파이프 등을) 막다
- When the drainage pipes get blocked, it will create a water leak.

2. 시야를 가리다
- He sued his neighbor who is building a three-story building for blocking his view of the Han River.

3. (SNS 등에서 ~을) 차단하다
- I blocked him on Twitter.

[s] obstruct

0016
cremate
/kríːmeit/

(시체를) 화장하다
- His body was cremated and his ashes were thrown in a river.

0017
decay
/dikéi/

썩다
- Farmers add a chemical to their produce to prevent fruit and vegetables that they grow from decaying.

▶ decaying (형용사) 썩는

[s] rot, decompose

[s] rotting

0009 곤잘로 피사로는 지금의 페루인 고대 잉카 도시인 빌카밤바를 급습했다. 0010 걱정해야 하는 동물의 새끼들이 없을 것이다. 0011 1964년 미국에서 가장 커다란 댐 중의 하나인 글렌캐니언 댐은 아리조나 북쪽에 콜로라도강에 만들어졌고 그것의 인공 호수인 길이가 299킬로미터나 되는 파월호도 만들어졌다. 0012 그는 가난한 사람들이 점점 더 가난해지는 동안 언제나 부자 편에선 사회에 대해 신랄한 풍자인 한 힙합 곡을 썼다. 0013 당신이 야영하는 그 섬 주변에 많은 소형 오두막들이 있다. 0014 임무 완수. / 예수께서 가라사대, '다 이루었다.' 0015 배수관이 막혔을 때 그것은 누수를 일으킬 것이다. / 그는 3층짜리 건물을 짓고 있는 그의 이웃을 한강 조망을 막는다는 이유로 고소했다. / 나는 Twitter에서 그를 차단했다. 0016 그의 시신은 화장되었고 재는 강에 던져졌다. 0017 농부들은 그들이 재배하는 과일과 채소가 썩는 것을 막기 위해 그들의 농산물에 화학 물질을 첨가한다.

0018 encroach
/inkróutʃ/
/인*크로우취/

(남의 시간이나 사생활을) 침해하다, (장소 등을) 침범하다
- encroach on sth ~을 침해하다
- In my view, the death of Princess Diana was due to the press that **encroaches on** the privacy of celebrities.

▶ encroachment (명사) 침범(침해)

S trespass

0019 form
/fɔ́:rm/

1. 구성(형성)하다; 생기다(형성되다)
- Dental plaque is a yellow substance that forms on your teeth. It is the main cause of cavities.

2. 만들다
- form A into B: A를 B로 만들다
- **Form** the dough **into** medium-sized balls.

3. (단체나 조직 등을) 결성하다, 조직하다
- The band was formed in 1995.

S begin to exist, make up

0020 indicate
/índikèit/

(사실 임을) 보여 주다, 나타내다
- This evidence indicates that you are the criminal.

S suggest, show

0021 mediate
/mí:dièit/

중재하다
- He sent envoys in order to help mediate between Iran and Israel.

N
1. medicate (동사) 약을 투여하다
2. meditate (동사) 숙고하다, 명상하다

S arbitrate

0022 obliterate
/əblítərèit/
/어블리*터레이트/

파괴하다, 없애다
- When a fungus obliterated many potato fields, the Japanese farmers in the area began to grow other crops.

S remove, destroy

0023 prosper
/práspər/
/프라스퍼/

성공하다, 번영(번창)하다
- The country has prospered thanks to the export of its natural resources.

S flourish, thrive, succeed

0024 rebel
/ribél/

반항하다, 반란을 일으키다
- Teenagers often rebel against their parents.

▶
1. rebel (명사) 반역자, 저항 세력, 반항아
◇ rebel forces 반란군
2. rebellion (명사) 반역, 반란, 폭동

S disobey

S uprising

0025 reserve
/rizə́:rv/

1. 예약하다
- Can I reserve a table by the window for two?

2. 따로 두다, 남겨 두다, 저장하다
- This parking spot is reserved for people with disabilities.

3. (권리를) 보유하다
- All rights reserved 판권 소유

▶
1. reservation (명사) 예약; 인디언 보호 구역
2. reserve (명사)
1) 저장, 비축(물)
◇ fossil fuel reserves 화석 연료 비축물(매장량)
2) (동식물) 보호 구역
◇ wildlife reserve 야생 동물 보호 구역 / game reserve 수렵 보호 구역

S book

S set aside

0026 reveal
/rivíːl/

드러내다, 밝히다, 폭로하다
- ⓤ reveal that S주어 V동사 ~을 보여주다(드러내다)
- ◇ reveal secretes to sb ~에게 비밀을 폭로하다
- Gene studies have **revealed that** the Celtic population exceeded that of the invading Anglo-Saxons.
- After many hours of interrogation, he **revealed that** he had murdered his wife.

N
1. disclose (동사) (공개적으로) 밝히다
2. divulge (동사) (비밀 정보 등을) 누설하다

S disclose, show
A conceal 감추다

0027 spur
/spə́ːr/

(말(horse)에) 박차를 가하다, 가속화하다, 자극하다
- Some economists demand that trade barriers be removed in order to spur foreign investment.

▶ spur (명사) 박차, 자극

N on the spur of the moment 충동적으로
- On the spur of the moment, I decided to quit my job.

0028 store
/stɔ́ːr/

저장하다
- If you store vegetables and fruits improperly, they can become contaminated with bacteria.

▶ storage (명사) 저장, 보관

0029 trespass
/tréspəs/ or /tréspæs/

(재산, 토지 또는 가옥 등에 불법적으로) 침입(침해)하다
- You trespassed on my property.

0030 vanish
/vǽniʃ/

사라지다
- Many species are vanishing because of habitat loss.

S disappear

0031 wipe out
/waip aut/

(사람이나 동물을) 완전히 파괴하다, 없애다
- It's impossible to wipe out cockroaches.

N die out 사멸하다, 죽어 없어지다
- Following the introduction of the cane toad, some important species have died out. *following ~뒤에

S completely destroy, exterminate
S disappear

adjective 형용사

0032 abnormal
/æbnɔ́ːrml/

이상한, 비정상적인
- Abnormal levels of radiation were leaking out of the Chernobyl Nuclear Reactor.

S aberrant, deviant
A normal 정상적인

0033 analogous
/ənǽləgəs/
/어낼*러거스/

유사한, 비슷한
- ⓤ analogous to / with sth ~와 유사한, 비슷한
- In many ways, working in a zoo can be **analogous to** working in a kindergarten.

▶ analogy (명사) 유사(성), 비유

S similar
S similar to sth
S similarity
A dissimilarity 다름(차이)

0026 유전 연구는 켈트족의 인구가 쳐들어온 앵글로-색슨 민족의 인구보다 많았다는 것을 보여 줬다. / 여러 시간의 심문 후에 그는 그가 아내를 살해했다고 밝혔다. 0027 일부 경제학자들은 외국인 투자를 자극하기 위해 무역 장벽이 제거 되어야 한다고 요구한다. / 충동적으로, 나는 직장을 그만두기로 결심했다. 0028 만약 당신이 야채와 과일을 부적절하게 보관하면 그들은 박테리아에 오염될 수 있다. 0029 당신은 내 사유지에 불법 침입했다. 0030 많은 종들이 서식지 상실 때문에 사라지고 있다. 0031 바퀴벌레를 완전히 없애는 것은 불가능하다. / 사탕수수 두꺼비의 도입 뒤에 몇몇 중요한 종들이 죽어 없어졌다. 0032 체르노빌 원자로에서 비정상적 수준의 방사능이 새어 나오고 있었다. 0033 많은 점에서 동물원에서 일하는 것은 유치원에서 일하는 것과 비슷할 수 있다.

0034
asymmetric
/èisimétrik/
/에이시*메트릭/

비대칭의, 같지 않은
- Most human faces are asymmetric. For example, the right eye is bigger than the left eye.

A symmetric대칭의

0035
bare
/béər/
/베어/

1. 아무것도 걸치지 않은, 벌거벗은
- bare feet 맨발 / bare hands 맨손 / bare faces 맨얼굴
- bare mountain 민둥산 (나무나 식물 등이 없는 산)
- Don't walk around in your bare feet.
- His feet were bare.

S naked, exposed, uncovered

2. 비어 있는, (장식 같은 것이) 없는
- bare walls 장식이 아무것도 없는 벽
- The fridge was bare.

S empty, unfurnished

0036
common
/kámən/
/카먼/

1. 평범한, 흔한
- a common name 흔한 이름 / common knowledge 상식
- Two common types of trees are birch and oak.

S usual
A rare희귀한

2. 공동의, 공통의
- have sth in common 공통적으로 ~을 가지고 있다
- common interest 공통의 관심사 / common ground 공통점
- What charismatic people **have in common** is confidence in themselves.

▶ commonly (부사) 흔히
- the most commonly found disease in the elderly 노인들에게서 가장 흔히 발견되는 질병

0037
devoid
/divɔ́id/
/디보이드/

부족한, 없는
- be devoid of sth ~이 없다(부족하다)
- Diseases such as smallpox and even the flu, which can be treated nowadays, were fatal to native people **devoid of** immunity.
(=Diseases such as smallpox and even the flu, which can be treated nowadays, were fatal to native people lacking immunity.)

S void, lacking
S be void of sth, lack

0038
huge
/hjúːdʒ/

(크기나 양이) 엄청난
- A hydroelectric dam needs a reservoir that stores a huge amount of water, which causes the plants in the reservoir to be flooded.

S enormous, vast

0039
imperative
/impérətiv/
/임*페러티브/

필수의, 긴급한
- Since we live in the information age, improving Internet access is imperative.

S essential, vital, urgent긴급한

0040
legendary
/lédʒəndèri/
/레젼*데리/

1. 전설의, 전설상의
- a legendary character 전설상의 인물

S mythical, fabled

2. 전설적인
- The detective was legendary. He solved crimes that the police had failed to solve.

S famous, well-known

0041
martial
/máːrʃəl/

전쟁의, 군인의
- martial music 군가
- The martial regime was responsible for the slaughter of thousands of civilians in the province.

N martial arts 무술

S military

0034 대부분의 사람 얼굴은 비대칭이다. 예를 들면 오른쪽 눈이 왼쪽 눈보다 크다. 0035 맨발로 돌아다니지 마라. / 그는 맨발이다. / 냉장고가 비어 있었다. 0036 나무의 흔한 두 가지 종류는 자작나무와 참나무이다. / 카리스마가 있는 사람들이 공통적으로 가지고 있는 것은 그들 자신에 대한 자신감이다. 0037 오늘날 치료될 수 있는 천연두나 심지어 독감 같은 질병들도 면역력이 없는 원주민들에게 치명적이었다. 0038 수력 발전 댐은 엄청난 양의 물을 저장하는 저장소를 필요로 하는데, (이것이) 그 저장소에 있는 식물들이 물에 잠기게 만든다. 0039 우리는 정보 시대에 살기 때문에 인터넷 접속을 향상시키는 것은 필수적이다. 0040 그 형사는 전설적이었다. 그는 경찰이 해결하지 못했던 범죄들을 해결했다. 0041 그 군사 정권은 그 지방에서 수천 명의 민간인 학살에 책임이 있었다.

0042 obscure
/əbskjúər/
/업*스큐어/

알려지지 않은, 무명의
- The TV program travels to many cities in Korea and provides an opportunity for obscure singers to sing on television.

S unknown
A celebrated 유명한

0043 plausible
/plɔ́:zəbl/
/플로*저블/

그럴듯한, 사실인 것 같은
- The theory that sturgeons jump out of the water to eat flying insects seems plausible at first but is highly unlikely.

S likely to be true, reasonable
A implausible 믿기 힘든

0044 reasonable
/rí:zənəbl/
/리저너블/

1. 합리적인, 타당한
◇ a reasonable doubt 합리적 의심 / reasonable grounds 합리적 근거
- I have reasonable grounds for believing that the poor cannot access some of the important information online.

2. 합리적인 (가격 등이 비싸지 않은)
- The price of potatoes sold in the market these days is not reasonable.

S sensible

0045 sedentary
/sédntèri/
/세든*테리/

앉아서 지내는(하는), (몸을 많이) 움직이지 않는
◇ a sedentary job 앉아서 하는 직업
- Every time he weighs himself on the bathroom scale, he feels like he is gaining weight too easily. He thinks it is because of his sedentary lifestyle.

S inactive

adverb 부사

0046 approximately
/əpráksimətli/

대략, 약
- As of 2019, approximately 1.5 million people in the U.S. alone have been infected with the coronavirus. *as of '기간': '기간' 현재 (기간 기준으로)

S about, around, roughly

0047 clockwise
/klákwaiz/

시계 방향으로
- Ocean currents consist of two currents: surface currents and deep ocean currents. Water currents in the northern Pacific Ocean move in a circular motion, clockwise. *ocean current 해류

A counterclockwise 시계 반대 방향으로

0048 slightly
/sláitli/

약간
- I sold my house at a slightly higher price, hoping to buy another home later at a lower price.

S a little

0049 strangely enough
/streindʒli inʌf/

정말 신기하게도
- Strangely enough, I gained 10 pounds in a week after eating like Warren Buffett.

N interestingly enough 아주 흥미롭게도

S weirdly / oddly / curiously enough

0042 그 티브이 프로그램은 한국의 많은 도시들을 돌아다니며 무명 가수들이 텔레비전에서 노래할 수 있는 기회를 제공한다. 0043 철갑상어가 날아다니는 벌레들을 먹기 위해 물 밖으로 뛰어오른다는 이론은 언뜻 보기에 그럴듯한 것 같지만 가능성이 매우 낮다. 0044 나는 가난한 사람들이 온라인에서 몇몇 중요한 정보에 접근할 수 없다고 믿을 만한 타당한 근거를 가지고 있다. / 요즘 시장에서 팔리는 고구마 가격은 합리적이지 않다. 0045 욕실 저울에 체중을 잴 때마다 그는 그가 너무 쉽게 살이 찌는 것 같다고 느낀다. 그는 그것이 그의 앉아서 지내는 생활 방식 때문이라고 생각한다. 0046 2019년 현재 미국에서만 약 150만 명의 사람들이 코로나바이러스에 감염되었다. 0047 해류는 두 개의 흐름으로 구성된다: 표면 해류와 심해류. 북태평양의 해류는 원형으로, 시계 방향으로 움직인다. 0048 나는 나중에 또 다른 집을 더 낮은 가격에 살 바라며 약간 더 높은 가격에 집을 팔았다. 0049 정말 신기하게도 워렌 버핏처럼 먹은 후 일주일 만에 체중이 10파운드 늘었다.

DAY 02

ANGRY ENGLISH
ACADEMIC VOCABULARY

noun 명사
- ☐ consequence
- ☐ dwelling
- ☐ fraction
- ☐ ingredient
- ☐ nuance
- ☐ order
- ☐ preoccupation
- ☐ repercussion
- ☐ security
- ☐ swirl
- ☐ texture
- ☐ utility
- ☐ vanity

verb 동사
- ☐ abort
- ☐ assemble
- ☐ burden
- ☐ compel
- ☐ construe
- ☐ contact
- ☐ daub
- ☐ determine
- ☐ ease
- ☐ face
- ☐ identify
- ☐ palliate
- ☐ range
- ☐ sacrifice
- ☐ startle
- ☐ treat
- ☐ uncover
- ☐ unleash

adjective 형용사
- ☐ abiding
- ☐ balanced
- ☐ capable
- ☐ due
- ☐ futile
- ☐ grand
- ☐ idle
- ☐ innate
- ☐ judicious
- ☐ overriding
- ☐ packed
- ☐ prodigious
- ☐ relentless
- ☐ secondary

adverb 부사
- ☐ abroad
- ☐ hence
- ☐ seldom
- ☐ in search of

 MP3 파일 다운

noun 명사

0050 consequence
/kánsikwəns/

결과
- ⓤ have serious / far-reaching consequences for sth ~에 심각한/엄청난 결과를 가져오다
- As many people lost their jobs, their spending was greatly reduced, which in turn **had** negative **consequences for** the local economy.

S result, outcome, repercussion
S have repercussions for sth

0051 dwelling
/dwélin/

주거(지), 주택
- Native American dwellings, called tee-pees, are emblematic of their culture. *be emblematic of sth ~을 상징한다

▶ dweller (명사) 거주자(주민)
◇ cave dwellers 동굴 거주자

S home, house, residence

0052 fraction
/frǽkʃən/

일부, 소량
- ⓤ (only) a fraction of sth (극히) 일부의
- Only **a fraction of** people are allergic to nuts.

0053 ingredient
/ingríːdiənt/

1. (요리 등의) 재료
◇ the remaining ingredients 남은 재료
- Garlic is a basic ingredient in Korean cuisine.

2. 구성, 요소
- He has all the ingredients required to be a great golf player.

S part, component, element

0054 nuance
/núːɑːns/
/누안스/

미묘한 차이, 뉘앙스 미묘한 차이에서 오는 느낌이나 인상
- Her performance in the movie was fantastic. The subtle nuances of her characterization were perfect. *characterization (등장인물의) 성격 묘사

S a slight difference, variation

0055 order
/ɔ́ːrdər/

1. 순서, 순위
- ⓤ put / arrange sth in alphabetical / chronological order 알파벳 / 연대기 순서로 ~을 놓다/배열하다
- When historical events **are arranged in chronological order**, it is easy to find them.

2. 질서
- The army was brought in to restore order.

A disorder무질서, chaos혼란

3. 명령
◇ obey / follow an order 명령을 따르다 / give an order 명령을 내리다
- The chief commander gave an order to fire at innocent civilians.

4. (음료) 주문, (상품) 주문
- ⓤ take an order 주문 받다 / place an order 주문 하다

0056 preoccupation
/priákjupeiʃən/

몰두
- My main preoccupation these days is backpacking.

▶ preoccupied (형용사) 사로잡힌, 몰두하고 있는
ⓤ preoccupied with sth ~에 사로잡힌

S obsession

0057 repercussion
/ríːpərkʌʃən/

영향
- ⓤ have repercussions for sth ~에 결과를 가져오다(~에 영향을 미치다)
- The government's proposal would **have** serious **repercussions for** the local economy.

S consequence

0050 많은 사람들이 직업을 잃게 되어서 그들의 소비는 크게 줄었고, (이것은) 결과적으로 지역 경제에 부정적인 결과들을 가져왔다. 0051 티피라고 불리는 미국 원주민 주택들은 그들의 문화를 상징한다. 0052 극히 일부 사람들만 견과류에 알레르기가 있다. 0053 마늘은 한국 요리의 기본 재료이다. / 그는 위대한 골프 선수가 되기 위해 필요로 하는 모든 요소들을 다 가지고 있다. 0054 그 영화에서 그녀의 연기는 환상적이었다. 그녀가 맡은 인물의 성격 묘사의 미묘한 뉘앙스는 완벽했다. 0055 역사적 사건들이 알파벳 순서로 배열될 때, 그들을 찾는 것은 쉽다. / 군대는 질서를 회복하기 위해 투입되었다. / 최고 사령관이 무고한 민간인들에게 사격하라는 명령을 내렸다. 0056 요즘 내가 주로 몰두하고 있는 것은 백패킹이다. 0057 정부의 계획은 지역 경제에 심각한 결과를 가져올 것이다.

0058
security
/sikjúrəti/
/시큐*러티/

1. 보안, 안보, 보장
   - National security could be threatened by a series of nuclear experiments.

2. 담보
   - He has a plan to use his apartment as security for the loan he's going to take out.

0059
swirl
/swə́ːrl/
/스월/

소용돌이
- The street was empty at 4 a.m. except for a swirl of dust.

▶ swirl (동사) 소용돌이치다
- Rumors that the bitcoin bubble will soon burst swirled around Wall Street.

0060
texture
/tékstʃər/

1. (직물의) 감촉(질감)
   - When you touch the textile, you can feel how silky the texture is.

2. (음식의) 질감
   - Only fry the chicken long enough to achieve a crispy texture.

0061
utility
/juːtíləti/

1. 유용(쓸모 있는 것), 실용, 효용 — **S** usefulness
   - For the utility of education, the chairman demanded that practical skills like rice cultivation be taught at schools.

2. (전기, 가스, 수도 등의) 공공시설, 공공요금 utilities
   - Utilities are included in the rent.

▶
1. utility (형용사) 다용도의, 다목적의
   ◇ a utility camping knife 다목적 캠핑용 칼
2. utilitarian (형용사) 실용적인 — **S** functional, useful, practical

0062
vanity
/vǽnəti/

(자신의 성취감이나 외모에 대한 지나친) 자부심, 허영(심) — **A** modesty 겸손
- He is a vassal who has only vanity and is in debt to his master.
*vassal (중세 시대의) 가신

N words related to character traits
1. arrogance 오만, 거만
2. hypocrisy 위선 ◇ the hypocrisy of politicians 정치인들의 위선
3. deceit 기만, 속임수
4. conceit 자만

verb 동사

0063
abort
/əbɔ́ːrt/

중단하다 — **S** stop, end
- For some reason, a military operation to rescue 50 hostages held by a group of terrorists was aborted.

0064
assemble
/əsémbl/

1. 모으다; 모이다 — **S** collect, gather
   ◇ assemble data / evidence 데이터/증거를 모으다
   - All the students who had signed up for the quiz contest assembled in the library.

2. 조립하다 — **A** disassemble, take apart 분해하다
   - Even when assembling a car, they do not need to work with others because those who specialize in assembling the car do the work without any help or cooperation. *specialize in sth ~을 전문으로 하다

0058 국가 안보는 일련의 핵 실험으로 위협받을 수도 있다. / 그는 그가 받으려고 하는 대출의 담보로 그의 아파트를 사용할 계획을 가지고 있다. 0059 새벽 4시에는 소용돌이치는 먼지를 제외하고 거리는 텅 비어 있었다. / 비트코인 거품이 곧 터질 것이라는 소문이 월가 주위에 소용돌이쳤다. 0060 당신이 그 직물을 만졌을 때, 당신은 그 질감이 얼마나 부드러운지 느낄 수 있다. / 바삭한 질감을 얻을 수 있을 만큼만 오래 닭고기를 튀겨라. 0061 교육의 효용을 위해서 벼농사와 같은 실용적인 기술이 학교에서 가르쳐져야 한다고 의장은 요구했다. / 전기, 가스, 수도료는 집세에 포함되어 있다. 0062 그는 단지 허영심만 있고 그의 주인에게 빚을 지고 있는 가신이다. 0063 어떤 이유에서인지 한 테러리스트 집단에 억류된 50명의 인질들을 구출하기 위한 군사 작전이 중단되었다. 0064 퀴즈 대회에 참가 신청을 한 모든 학생들이 도서관에 모였다. / 심지어 자동차 한 대를 조립할 때도 그들은 다른 사람들과 일을 할 필요가 없는데 왜냐하면 자동차 조립을 전문으로 하는 사람들이 어떤 도움이나 협력도 없이 그 일을 한다.

0065
burden /bə́:rdn/

힘들게 하다, 어렵게 하다
- ⓤ be burdened with / by sth ~로 힘들어하다
- ○ In 2021, there were a million households **burdened with** mortgage loans. *mortgage 주택 담보 대출

[s] encumber
[s] be encumbered with sth

0066
compel /kəmpél/ /컴*펠/

강요하다
- ⓤ compel sb to do sth ~에게 ~을 강요하다
- ○ Her health, which got worse and worse, **compelled** her **to** stop writing novels.

▶ compelling (형용사) 설득력 있는, 강력한

[s] force, coerce
[s] force sb to do sth

[s] strong, persuasive

0067
construe /kənstrú:/

이해(해석)하다
- ⓤ construe A as B: A를 B로 해석하다
- ○ His comments could **be construed as** sexual harassment.

[s] interpret

0068
contact /kántækt/

연락하다
- ○ Jonathan contacted her previous psychiatrist.

▶ contact (명사) 연락, 접촉
Ⓝ contract (명사, 동사) 계약, 계약을 맺다

[s] get in touch with

0069
daub /dɔ́:b/

(페인트 등으로) 바르다, 칠하다
- ⓤ daub A with B: B로 A를 바르다 / daub A over B: B위에 A를 바르다
- ○ He **daubed** his face **with** charcoal to disguise himself.

[s] smear

0070
determine /ditə́:rmin/

1. 찾아내다, 밝혀내다
- ○ Medical advances have allowed scientists and doctors to determine what causes cancer.

2. 영향을 미치다, 결정하다
- ⓤ be determined by sth ~에 의해 영향을 받다, ~에 의해 결정되다
- ○ The religious and political orientation each individual has **is** usually **determined by** their socio-economic status.

3. (공식적으로) 결정하다
- ○ The final game determines the winner.

4. 결심하다
- ⓤ determine to do sth ~하기로 결심하다
- ○ He **determined to** succeed to the throne. *succeed to the throne 왕위를 계승하다

▶ determined (형용사) 결심한, 단호한
- ⓤ be determined to do sth ~하기로 결심하다

[s] discover, establish 밝혀내다

[s] make a firm decision

0071
ease /í:z/

완화하다, 덜어 주다
- ○ Tylenol is a painkiller that is used for easing pain, such as headaches and toothaches, as well as menstrual pain.

[s] relieve, alleviate

0072
face /féis/

1. 마주 보다
- ○ My apartment faces the Han River.

2. (문제 등을) 직면하다
- ○ Rising temperatures are the greatest hazard that American pikas with thick fur face.

3. (사실 등을) 받아들이다
- ⓤ face the fact that S주어 V동사 ~라는 사실을 받아들이다
- ○ It seems hard for the government to **face the fact that** so many people still refuse to get vaccinated.

[s] overlook

0065 2021년에 주택 담보 대출 이자로 힘들어하는 백만 가구들이 있었다. 0066 점점 더 나빠지는 그녀의 건강은 그녀에게 소설을 쓰는 것을 멈추도록 강요했다. 0067 그의 발언은 성희롱으로 해석될 수도 있다. 0068 조나단은 그녀의 이전 정신과 의사에게 연락했다. 0069 그는 자신을 변장하기 위해 숯으로 그의 얼굴을 칠했다. 0070 의학적 발전이 과학자들과 의사들이 무엇이 암을 유발하는지를 찾아내는 것을 가능하게 했다. / 각 개인이 가지고 있는 종교적이고 정치적인 성향은 대개 그들의 사회-경제적 지위에 의해 결정된다. / 결승전이 승자를 결정짓는다. / 그는 왕위를 계승하기로 결심했다. 0071 타이레놀은 생리통뿐만 아니라 두통과 치통 같은 통증을 완화하는 데 사용되는 진통제이다. 0072 우리 아파트는 한강을 마주보고 있다. / 상승하는 온도가 두꺼운 털을 가지고 있는 아메리칸 피카가 직면한 가장 큰 위험이다. / 아주 많은 사람들이 여전히 예방 접종을 받는 것을 거부한다는 사실을 정부가 받아들이는 것은 어려운 것 같다.

0073 identify
/aidéntifài/

1. 알아보다, 식별(분간)하다
   - John had changed so much that I couldn't identify him at first. *at first 처음에

2. 찾다, 발견하다
   - An archaeologist identified an enormous mound by a house called Pueblo Alto.

S recognize

0074 palliate
/pǽlièit/
/팰리*에이트/

(통증이나 심각성 등을) 줄이다, 완화시키다
- Folk medicine can temporarily palliate the pain that a disease causes, but it cannot cure the disease fundamentally.

S reduce, alleviate, mitigate

0075 range
/réindʒ/

(범위 등이) 이르다(걸치다)
- range from A to B: (범위가) A에서 B에 이르다
- He was supposed to give a lecture on the benefits of genetically modified crops to an audience **ranging from** children **to** elderly citizens.

0076 sacrifice
/sǽkrifàis/

희생하다
- sacrifice A for B: B를 위해 A를 희생하다
- Women often **sacrifice** their leisure time **for** their families.

0077 startle
/stá:rtl/
/스타틀/

(깜짝) 놀라게 하다
- For some reason, the competition horse assigned to her in the individual jumping event was startled, so she couldn't take part in the race.

S surprise, astonish, amaze

0078 treat
/trí:t/

1. (사람 등을) 대우하다, 대하다
   - treat sb/sth badly / cruelly / unfairly ~을 나쁘게/잔인하게/부당하게 대하다
   - At that time, factory owners often **treated** their workers **unfairly**.

2. (문제나 주제 등을) 다루다, 여기다
   - treat sth seriously / carefully ~을 심각하게/신중하게 다루다(여기다)
   - Tax issues must **be treated carefully**.

   S deal with, consider

3. 치료하다
   - be treated for sth ~ 치료를 받다
   - She **was treated for** breast cancer.

▶ treatment (명사) 치료

S therapy

0079 uncover
/ʌ́nkʌvəʳ/

1. (비밀 등을) 찾아내다, 발견하다
   - A recent study has uncovered a link between obesity and diabetes.

   S discover, reveal, find out

2. (땅 속에 묻힌 것을) 발굴(발견)하다
   - It is hard to uncover archaeologically important fossils.

   S excavate, unearth

0080 unleash
/ʌ́nli:ʃ/

1. 촉발시키다, 불러일으키다
   - The government's proposal to curb housing prices unleashed a wave of protest.

   S suddenly release

2. 놓아주다
   - unleash a dog 개를 풀어놓다
   - It is unclear if the accident happened as a result of him unleashing his dog.

adjective 형용사

0081 abiding
/əbáidiŋ/
/어바이딩/

오래 지속되는, 불변의, 지속적인
◇ abiding memory 오랫동안 있는 기억
○ I have an abiding respect for people like Gandhi, who always advocated for non-violent protests.

[S] lasting

0082 balanced
/bǽlənst/

균형 잡힌
○ It is important to have a balanced diet if you want to stay healthy.

[S] equalized

0083 capable
/kéipəbl/

할 수 있는
ⓤ be capable of Ving 동명사 ~을 할 수 있다
○ They **are capable of** preying on animals bigger than themselves.
*prey on ~을 잡아먹다

▶ capability (명사) 능력, 가능성

[A] incapable 할 수 없는
[S] be able to do sth

0084 due
/dúː/

1. ~할 예정인, (언제) ~까지 인, ~하기로 되어 있는
ⓤ be due to do sth ~하기로 되어 있다, ~할 예정이다
○ His fourth film **is due to** be released next year.
○ This assignment is due tomorrow.
○ The doctor told her when her baby was due.

2. (빌린 돈 등이) 만기인
◇ due date 만기일

[S] scheduled, expected

0085 futile
/fjúːtl/ or /fjúːtail/

쓸데없는, 헛된(무의미한), 소용없는
ⓤ in the futile hope that S 주어 V 동사 ~라는 헛된 희망에 / prove futile 헛된 것으로 판명되다
○ Learning about the past to deal with environmental problems today is futile because these issues did not even exist in the past.

▶ futilely (부사) 헛되이

[S] pointless, vain, fruitless
[A] worthwhile 가치 있는

[S] in vain, vainly, fruitlessly

0086 grand
/grǽnd/

원대한, (크기 등이) 웅장한
○ The airline's grand ambition is to operate flights to Eastern Europe by 2024.

[A] humble 초라한

0087 idle
/áidl/

1. (공장이나 기계 등이) 가동되지 않은, 휴직의, (사람 등이) 게으른
ⓤ stand / lie / remain idle 가동되지 않고 있다
○ It costs money to maintain airplanes that just sit idle.

2. 심각하지 않은, 뚜렷한 목적(의도)이 없는
○ I like learning about music, but it is just an idle curiosity. I have never taken any classes.

[S] unemployed 휴직의

0088 innate
/inéit/

타고난, 천성의, 선천적인
◇ innate ability / quality 천부적 재능/타고난 자질
○ Some behaviors that animals have, such as mating, are innate. Others, like hunting, are learned.

▶ innately (부사) 선천적으로

[S] inherent, built-in, inborn

0081 나는 항상 비폭력 시위를 옹호했던 간디 같은 사람들에 대한 지속적인 존경심을 가지고 있다. 0082 당신이 건강을 유지하고 싶다면 균형 잡힌 식단을 갖는 것은 중요하다. 0083 그들은 그들 자신보다 더 큰 동물들을 잡아먹을 수 있다. 0084 그의 4번째 영화가 내년에 개봉 예정이다. / 이 과제는 내일까지이다. / 의사는 그녀에게 출산 예정이 언제인지를 말했다. 0085 오늘날 환경 문제를 해결하기 위해 과거에 대해 배우는 것은 헛된 것인데 왜냐하면 이 문제들은 심지어 과거에 존재하지도 않았기 때문이다. 0086 그 항공사의 원대한 포부는 2024년까지 동유럽행 항공편을 운영하는 것이다. 0087 가동되지 않고 그냥 앉아 있는 비행기들을 유지하는 데는 돈이 든다. / 나는 음악에 대해 배우는 것을 좋아하지만 그것은 뚜렷한 목적이 없는 호기심일 뿐이다. 나는 어떤 수업도 들은 적이 없다. 0088 교배처럼 동물들이 가지고 있는 몇몇 행동들은 선천적이다. 사냥과 같은 다른 것은 학습된 것이다.

0089 judicious
/dʒuːdíʃəs/

현명한, 신중한
- It is essential to ensure the judicious use of nuclear reactors to produce electricity.

▶ judiciously (부사) 신중하게, 현명하게
- Even boring lectures can become more interesting if visual aids are used judiciously in class.

S wise, sensible, reasonable

0090 overriding
/óuvəraidiŋ/

가장 중요한
- My overriding concern is to find someone that I can leave my kid with while I'm at work.

S prime

0091 packed
/pækt/
/팩트/

1. 가득한
- packed with sth ~로 가득한
- The train was **packed with** people going to work.
- The small booklet is packed full of advice for healthy meals.

▶ pack (동사) (장소 등을) 가득 채우다

S full
S packed full of sth

0092 prodigious
/prədídʒəs/
/프러*디줘스/

(능력이나 양이) 엄청난, 거대한
- a prodigious number / amount of sth 엄청난 수/양의
- Boracay and Cebu had to close their beaches for a year because of the **prodigious amounts of** trash covering them.

S colossal, enormous

0093 relentless
/riléntləs/
/리렌트*러스/

1. 계속되는(끊임없는), 수그러들지 않는
- Relentless wildfires in California caused a lot of causalities.

2. 포기하지 않는, 단호한, 끈질긴
- He made relentless efforts to break the world record.

▶ relentlessly (부사) 끈질기게

S unrelenting
S determined 단호한

0094 secondary
/sékəndèri/

1. 부차적인, 별로 중요하지 않은
- be of secondary importance 별로 중요하지 않다
- A college degree **is of secondary importance** to the company. Creativity is what matters most to them.

2. 이차의
◇ a secondary infection 이차 감염
- Cancer cells that are separated from the primary cancer can move to other organs, settle there, and grow into a new cancer called secondary cancer. *primary cancer 원발암

3. 중등교육의
◇ secondary school 중고등학교

0089 전기를 생산하기 위해 원자로의 현명한 사용을 보장하는 것은 필수적이다. / 재미없는 강의라도 시각적인 보조 도구가 수업 시간에 현명하게 활용된다면 더욱 흥미로울 수 있다. 0090 나한테 가장 중요한 걱정은 내가 직장에 있는 동안 내가 내 아이를 맡길 수 있는 누군가를 찾는 것이다. 0091 기차는 출근하는 사람들로 가득했다. / 그 소책자는 건강한 식사를 위한 조언으로 가득하다. 0092 보라카이와 세부는 1년 동안 해변을 폐쇄해야만 했는데 왜냐하면 해변을 덮고 있는 엄청난 양의 쓰레기 때문이었다. 0093 켈리포니아에 수그러들지 않는 산불이 많은 사상자를 냈다. / 그는 세계 기록을 깨기 위한 끈질긴 노력을 하였다. 0094 대학 학위는 그 회사에게는 별로 중요하지 않다. 그들에게 가장 중요한 것은 창의성이다. / 원발암에서 분리된 암세포는 다른 장기로 이동하여 그곳에 정착하여 이차 암으로 불리는 새로운 암으로 자랄 수 있다.

adverb 부사

0095 abroad /əbrɔ́ːd/ /어*브로드/

해외에(서)
- travel abroad 해외여행을 하다
- The experience of studying abroad easily guarantees students success in the future.

N aboard (부사) 탑승한
- All the passengers aboard wore safety belts.

S overseas

0096 hence /héns/

그러므로
- Health problems can be caused by lack of access to health care. Hence, it is important to provide good health care services. *health care 사람들의 건강을 돌보는 행위 (건강 관리)

S for this reason, therefore

0097 seldom /séldəm/

좀처럼 ~않는
- My father seldom catches a cold.

S rarely

0098 in search of /in sɜːtʃ əv/

~을 찾아서
- People came to the state in search of gold.

0095 유학한 경험은 쉽게 학생들에게 미래에 성공을 보장한다. / 탑승한 모든 승객들이 안전벨트를 착용했다. 0096 건강 문제는 건강 관리에 대한 접근의 부족으로 야기될 수 있다. 그러므로, 좋은 건강 관리 서비스를 제공하는 것이 중요하다. 0097 우리 아버지는 좀처럼 감기에 걸리지 않는다. 0098 사람들은 금을 찾아 그 주에 왔다.

DAY 03

ANGRY ENGLISH
ACADEMIC VOCABULARY

noun 명사

- ☐ anomaly
- ☐ basis
- ☐ concern
- ☐ contact
- ☐ dye
- ☐ iceberg
- ☐ niche
- ☐ pastime
- ☐ reflection
- ☐ series
- ☐ support
- ☐ term
- ☐ variation

verb 동사

- ☐ abound
- ☐ assault
- ☐ bridle
- ☐ clarify
- ☐ compare
- ☐ contend
- ☐ damage
- ☐ detest
- ☐ echo
- ☐ freak
- ☐ gain
- ☐ ignite
- ☐ overlap
- ☐ pare
- ☐ rank
- ☐ sap
- ☐ stick
- ☐ trace

adjective 형용사

- ☐ absurd
- ☐ brisk
- ☐ conscientious
- ☐ deceptive
- ☐ gradual
- ☐ haphazard
- ☐ imminent
- ☐ inordinate
- ☐ logical
- ☐ overall
- ☐ paramount
- ☐ repellent
- ☐ selective
- ☐ tedious

adverb 부사

- ☐ ahead
- ☐ inevitably
- ☐ shortly
- ☐ instead of

MP3 파일 다운

noun
명사

0099
anomaly
/ənάməli/

이상한 것(사람) 이례적인 것, 변칙 예상했던 것과 다른 것
- anomalies in sth ~에서 이상한 점들
- They detected many **anomalies in** desert regions.

S irregularity

0100
basis
/béisis/

1. 기초, 근거
- on the basis of sth ~의 근거해서, ~때문에
- The Supreme Court ruled that segregating Black students from White students in public schools **on the basis of** race was unconstitutional. *rule 판결을 내리다 / unconstitutional 위헌의

2. 기준
- on a regular / monthly / weekly basis 정기적으로/월 단위로/주 단위로
- In a recent survey, one doctor suggested that the super foods listed below that help blood circulate be consumed on a daily basis.

0101
concern
/kənsə́:rn/

1. 우려
- concern that S주어 V동사 ~라는 우려
- There is (a) growing concern about the recent rise in new cases of COVID-19.
- There is **concern that** some people are not wearing a mask in public places.

2. 걱정거리 (가산)
- One of the major concerns that teens have is physical appearance.

3. 중요한 것, 관심사
- N명사 of concern to sb ~에게 중요한 명사
- topics of concern to young people 젊은 사람들에게 중요한 화제
- I don't have anyone who I can talk to about the issues that are **of** great **concern to** me.

0102
contact
/kάntækt/ or /kɔ́ntækt/

접촉, 연락
- come into contact with sb/sth ~와 접촉하다 / stay / keep in contact with sb/sth ~와 연락하고 지내다
- They had not **come into** direct **contact with** the world outside of their community.
- Under the terms of the contract, you must **stay in contact with** the agency by email on a monthly basis.

N contract (명사) 계약

0103
dye
/dái/

염료
- The plants were used for dyes by the ancient Celts of Britain. They used the dye to paint their bodies before a battle.

▶ dye (동사) 염색하다

0104
iceberg
/áisbə:rg/

빙산
- This attack is only the tip of the iceberg. Many more are expected to come.

N
1. glacier (명사) 빙하
2. glacial (형용사) 빙하의

0105 niche
/nítʃ/ or /ní:ʃ/

틈새
- It takes too long for other species to naturally fill niches left vacant by an extinct species.

0106 pastime
/pǽstàim/

여가, 취미
- One of my favorite pastimes is golf.

[S] hobby

0107 reflection
/riflékʃən/

1. 반영
- a reflection of sth ~의 반영
- I don't believe the survey results are **a reflection of** what the public really thinks.

2. (거울이나 물에 비친) 모습, 아주 비슷한 사람(것)
- One day, I happened to see a reflection of myself in a shop window, and I realized that I already look like I'm 50.
- I am a reflection of my father. I look like him and my personality is like his too.

3. 심사숙고
- on reflection 잘 생각해 보니
- **On reflection**, I think that I was wrong.

[S] sign, result

0108 series
/síri:z/

1. 일련, 연속
- a series of sth 일련의, 연속적으로 일어나는
- **A series of** murders took place across the city, causing great panic.

2. 시리즈, 연속물
- young Korean university students who enjoy watching American television series 미국 텔레비전 시리즈를 즐겨 보는 젊은 한국 대학생들

[S] sequence, string
[S] a string of sth

0109 support
/səpɔ́:rt/

지지, 지원
- be in support of sth ~을 지지하다
- government support 정부 지원
- She **was in support of** women's participation in politics.

[S] aid, help

0110 term
/tə́:rm/

1. 용어
- There is a large lexicon of legal terms to master. *lexicon 특정어휘

2. 기간, 임기
- in the long / short term 장기/단기적으로
- a short-term study visa 단기 학생 비자
- He was assassinated at the end of his second term in office.
- But **in the long term**, it will not affect the overall economy.

[N] in terms of N ~(측)면에서, (특정 분야의) 관점에서
- in terms of cost 비용 측면에서 / in geological terms 지질학적인 관점에서
- In terms of social organization, a chiefdom was more complex than a tribe or a band and less complex than a state.

0111 variation
/vèriéiʃən/

1. 변화, 차이
- temperature variations 온도 변화
- Anyway, the variation between the two editions of the book is marginal. *marginal 미미한

2. 변형
- a variation on sth ~의 변형
- This new noodle brand is **a** very spicy **variation on** the mild flavor of the original.

[S] change, difference

[S] modification, variant 변종

verb 동사

0112 abound
/əbáund/

풍부하다
- ⓤ abound in sth ~가 풍부하다(많다)
- ○ The city **abounds in** good restaurants and hotels.

ⓢ teem
ⓢ teem with sth

0113 assault
/əsɔ́:lt/

폭행하다, 공격하다
- ○ He was put on trial for sexually assaulting his peer.

▶ assault (명사) 공격
- ⓤ make an assault on sb ~을 공격하다

ⓢ attack, assail

ⓢ attack
ⓢ make an attack on sb

0114 bridle
/bráidl/

(말이나 동물에) 굴레를 씌우다
- ○ He went to a ranch last weekend, chose a horse on the ranch, saddled and bridled it, and took a selfie riding on it.

▶ bridle (명사) 굴레

0115 clarify
/klǽrifài/

명확하게 하다, 분명히 하다, 이해하기 쉽게 하다
- ○ A few points in the proposal, such as how to raise money for the program, need to be clarified in detail.

▶ clarification (명사) 설명

ⓢ explain, elucidate 상세히 설명하다

0116 compare
/kəmpéər/

1. 비교하다; 비교가 되다
- ○ You can compare prices on price comparison websites.
- ⓤ
- ① compare A with / to B: A를 B와 비교하다
- ② compared to / with sb/sth ~와 비교했을 때
- ○ The point I'm trying to make is that **compared with** cars powered by petroleum, cars running on hydrogen require less fuel when traveling the same distance.
- ③ compare with / to sb/sth ~와 비교가 되다
- ○ Simple events that arose in the past do not **compare with** the complicated issues we face today.

2. 비유하다
- ⓤ compare A to B: A를 B에 비유하다
- ○ The fat boy **compared** the smoke signal **to** something like a rope that someone throws to a person who is drowning.

ⓢ liken
ⓢ liken A to B

0117 contend
/kənténd/
/컨텐드/

1. 경쟁하다, 겨루다
- ⓤ
- ① contend against sb ~와 경쟁하다
- ○ Domestic automakers had to **contend against** other superior foreign car manufacturers.
- ② contend for sth ~을 놓고 경쟁을 벌이다

2. 주장하다
- ○ He contends that even before 1990, mobile phones were available in North Korea.

3. (어려운 것 등을) 다루다
- ⓤ contend with sth ~을 다루다
- ○ Seoul City has a lot of issues to **contend with**.

ⓢ compete

ⓢ compete against sb

ⓢ compete for sth

ⓢ insist, claim, maintain

ⓢ deal with sth, cope with sth

0112 그 도시에는 좋은 레스토랑과 호텔들이 많다. 0113 그는 그의 동료를 성폭행한 것 때문에 재판에 회부되었다. 0114 그는 지난 주말에 목장에 가서 목장에 있는 말을 골라 안장을 얹고 굴레를 씌우고 말 위에 올라탄 채 셀카를 찍었다. 0115 그 프로그램을 위해 돈을 모으는 방법과 같은 그 제안서의 몇 가지 요점들은 세부적으로 분명히 할 필요가 있다. 0116 당신은 가격 비교 사이트에서 가격을 비교할 수 있다. / 내가 말하고자 하는 요점은 휘발유로 움직이는 자동차와 비교했을 때, 같은 거리를 이동할 때 수소로 가는 자동차가 더 적은 연료를 필요로 한다는 것이다. / 과거에 일어났던 단순한 사건들은 오늘날 우리가 직면하고 있는 복잡한 문제들과 비교되지 않는다. / 그 뚱뚱한 소년은 그 연기 신호를 물에 빠진 사람에게 누군가가 던져 주는 밧줄 같은 것으로 비유했다. 0117 국내 자동차 회사들은 다른 우수한 외국 자동차 제조업체들과 경쟁해야 했다. / 그는 심지어 1990년 이전에도 북한에서 휴대 전화를 이용할 수 있었다고 주장한다. / 서울시는 다루어야 할 많은 문제들을 가지고 있다.

0118
damage
/dǽmidʒ/
/대미쥐/

피해를 입히다, 손상하다, 훼손하다, 해치다
◇ damage a building / the environment 건물/환경을 훼손하다
• Removing dead trees damaged by storms or forest fires helps damaged forests recover by making room for new trees to grow.
• The release of radioactive wastewater from the destroyed Fukushima nuclear power plant into the sea might damage the health of fishermen in the area.

[s] harm, cause damage to

0119
detest
/ditést/

정말(매우) 싫어하다
ⓥ detest doing sth ~하는 것을 정말 싫어하다
• Most employees detest having to go to work on legal holidays.

[s] hate, loathe, abhor

0120
echo
/ékou/

메아리 치다, 울려 퍼지다
ⓥ echo through / round sth ~에 울려 퍼지다
• His laughter echoed through the hall.

[s] reverberate, resonate

0121
freak
/frí:k/

(매우) 놀라게 하다; (매우) 놀라다
ⓥ
① freak sb out ~을 (매우) 놀라게 하다
• On the first day he went to the school, his face freaked his classmates out.
② freak out 깜짝 놀라다(기겁하다)
• If I tell my father I'm going to travel to France with my friend for my vacation, he'll freak out.

0122
gain
/géin/

얻다
◇ gain the support of sb ~의 지지를 얻다
• The movies he produced and directed in his later years were no longer popular with the general public. The popularity he had gained started to decline. *in one's later years 말년에

[s] obtain, attain

0123
ignite
/ignáit/
/이그나이트/

불을 붙이다; 불이 붙다, (논쟁이나 관심 등을) 일으키다
• The shot that a young Serbian patriot fired at Archduke Franz Ferdinand, the heir to the Austro-Hungarian Empire, ignited World War I.

[s] set fire to, light, provoke 일으키다

0124
overlap
/óuvərlæp/

겹치다(포개다), 중복되다
• The warehouse was full of overlapping cardboard boxes.
• The newest edition overlaps substantially with the second edition.

0125
pare
/péər/

1. (얇은 껍질 등을) 벗기다
ⓥ pare A from B: B에서 A를 벗기다
• The meatpacking workers pared the skin from the sliced meat with their knives.

2. 줄이다, 감축하다
• Congress decided to pare its defense budget to a minimum.

[s] reduce

0126
rank
/rǽŋk/

(등급이나 순위를) 매기다(정하다), (순위를) 차지하다
ⓥ rank / be ranked first among / in sb/sth ~에서 1위를 차지하다
• Fifty-seven percent of the respondents ranked healthcare as a top issue for the government to solve.

0127 sap
/sǽp/

(에너지 등을) 서서히 빼앗다, 약화시키다
ⓤ
① sap one's energy / strength / confidence ~의 에너지/힘/자신감을 약화시키다
- Suppressing anger **saps** your **energy**, thus making you tired.
② sap A of B: A에게서 B를 빼앗다
- His subsequent failure **sapped** him **of** confidence.

▶ sap (명사) 수액

[S] weaken

0128 stick
/stík/
*stick-stuck-stuck

1. 붙이다; 붙다(들러붙다)
- Stick the pieces together with glue.

2. (차량 등을) 갇히게 하다
ⓤ be / get stuck in a traffic jam / traffic 교통 체증으로 움직이지 못하다
- I better go now before I **get stuck in traffic**.

0129 trace
/tréis/

1. 추적하다, (추적하여) 찾아내다
- Eventually, they traced him to an apartment in New York.
(=Eventually, they tracked him down to an apartment in New York.)

2. (기원, 원인 등을) 추적하다; 거슬러 올라가다
ⓤ be traced (back) to / trace (back) to sth ~로 거슬러 올라가다
- Modern English can **be** clearly **traced back to** Germanic languages and not those of the Celts.

[S] track down

adjective
형용사

0130 absurd
/əbsə́:rd/

완전히 바보 같은, 터무니없는
- For cities that already have a working recycling system, it is absurd to switch to a single-stream recycling solution.

[S] ridiculous, ludicrous

0131 brisk
/brísk/

빠른, 활기찬
- I go for a brisk, early morning walk everyday. That is what keeps me healthy.

[S] energetic, lively, vigorous
[A] sluggish느린, lethargic활발하지 못한

0132 conscientious
/kánʃiénʃəs/
/칸쉬*엔셔스/

성실한, 양심적인
- He is a conscientious student who always hands in school assignments on time and earns good grades on tests.

▶ conscientiously (부사) 성실하게

[S] painstaking, diligent

0133 deceptive
/diséptiv/
/디셉*티브/

(남을) 속이는, 호도하는, 기만적인
- If you get a face-to-face interview with her, you may find that her appearance is deceptive.

▶ deception (명사) 속임수, 사기

[S] misleading, deceitful사기의

[S] deceit

0134 gradual
/grǽdʒuəl/

점진적인, 조금씩의
- The professor provided an acceptable solution for dealing with the gradual increase in Earth's temperature.

▶ gradually (부사) 조금씩, 천천히

[A] sudden갑작스러운

[S] slowly, steadily

0127 분노를 억제하는 것은 당신의 에너지를 약화시켜 결국 당신을 피곤하게 만든다. / 그의 계속되는 실패는 그에게서 자신감을 빼앗았다. 0128 풀로 그 조각들을 붙여라. / 내가 교통 체증으로 움직이지 못하기 전에 지금 가는 게 좋겠어. 0129 결국 그들은 그를 추적하여 뉴욕의 한 아파트에서 찾아냈다. / 현대 영어는 켈트족의 언어가 아니라 명백하게 게르만어로 거슬러 올라갈 수 있다. 0130 이미 작동하고 있는 재활용 시스템을 가지고 있는 도시는 단일 스트림 재활용 방안으로 전환하는 것은 터무니없는 짓이다. 0131 나는 매일 활기차고 이른 아침 산책을 한다. 그것이 나를 건강하게 유지해 주는 것이다. 0132 그는 언제나 학교 과제를 제때 제출하고 시험에서 좋은 성적을 받는 성실한 학생이다. 0133 만약 그녀와 서로 얼굴을 마주보고 하는 인터뷰를 한다면 너는 그녀의 외모가 기만적이라는 것을 알게 될지도 모른다. 0134 그 교수는 지구의 온도의 점진적인 상승을 다루는 데에 만족스러운 해결책을 제공했다.

0135 haphazard
/hǽphæzərd/
/햅*해저드/

무계획적인, 되는대로의
- ⓤ in a haphazard manner / fashion 마구잡이로
- The slums in the big cities were built **in a haphazard manner**.

▶ haphazardly (부사) 되는대로, 마구잡이로

S unsystematic, disorganized, disorderly
A planned, organized 계획된
S arbitrarily

0136 imminent
/íminənt/
/이미*넌트/

(뭔가 안 좋은 일이) 임박한, 긴박한
- Passengers at Kabul Airport were swiftly evacuated due to threats of an imminent terrorist attack. *evacuate 피난(대피)시키다

S impending

0137 inordinate
/inɔ́:rdinət/

지나친, 보통 때보다 많은
- There were inordinate flight delays.

▶ inordinately (부사) 지나치게
◇ an inordinately large number of sth 지나치게 많은

S excessive

0138 logical
/ládʒikl/

1. 타당한
- Taking a leave of absence is the only logical thing for me to do right now.

2. 논리적인
- The arguments provided in your reading passage do seem logical at first.

S reasonable, sensible
A illogical 비논리적인

0139 overall
/óuvərɔ:l/

전반적인 모든 것을 고려한(포함한), 전체의
◇ the overall situation 전반적인 상황
- This argument also has problems. Since humans only hunted otters in limited areas, the overall otter population was not seriously affected.

▶ overall (부사) 전반적으로, 모든 것을 다 고려했을 때

S general, total, gross, whole
S on the whole

0140 paramount
/pǽrəmàunt/
/패러*마운트/

가장 중요한, 최고의
- ⓤ sth be of paramount importance 가장 중요하다
- The monarch believed that the interests of the state must come first. To him, they **were of paramount importance**.

S principal, chief

0141 repellent
/ripélənt/
/리펠*런트/

역겨운, 혐오감을 주는
- Seeing people smoke is truly repellent to me.

▶ repellent (명사) 방충제

S repulsive, disgusting

0142 selective
/səléktiv/
/설렉티브/

1. 선택적인, 선택(선별)된 여러 사람 또는 물건 중에서 고른
◇ selective 6 NBA's best players in the 2020-21 season 2020-2021년 시즌에 선택된 6인의 NBA 최고 선수들
- Selective breeding with animals, such as dogs, has caused grotesque genetic mutations. *grotesque 기괴한

2. 조심해서 고르는
- Teenagers should be also selective when making friends.

▶ select (동사) 선발(선택)하다

S choose, pick

0143 tedious
/tí:diəs/

지루한
- Working in a factory can be really tedious. You must repeat the same action over and over.

▶ tediously (부사) 지루하게, 따분하게

S boring, dreary

0135 대도시의 빈민가들은 마구잡이로 지어졌다. 0136 카불 공항의 승객들은 임박한 테러리스트 공격의 위협 때문에 신속하게 대피했다. 0137 보통 때보다 많은 비행기 연착이 있었다. 0138 휴학하는 것이 지금 당장 내가 해야 할 유일한 타당한 일이다. / 지문에서 제시된 주장은 처음에는 논리적으로 보인다. 0139 이 주장 역시 문제를 가지고 있다. 인간은 한정된 지역에서만 수달을 사냥했기 때문에 전체 수달 인구는 심각할 영향을 받지는 않았다. 0140 그 군주는 나라의 이익이 최우선이 되어야 한다고 믿었다. 그에게 있어 그들은 가장 중요했다. 0141 사람들이 담배를 피우는 것을 보는 것은 나에게 정말 혐오감을 준다. 0142 개와 같은 동물과의 선택적 번식은 기괴한 유전적 돌연변이를 일으켰다. / 청소년들은 친구를 사귈 때 조심해서 골라야 한다. 0143 공장에서 일하는 것은 정말 지루할 수 있다. 너는 같은 동작을 계속해서 반복해야 한다.

adverb 부사

0144 ahead
/əhéd/

1. (시간이나 공간) 앞에
- The road ahead was completely obstructed by an overturned truck.

2. (시합이나 선거에서) 앞서 있는
- be (way / far) ahead (of sb) (~보다) (훨씬) 앞서 있다
- Hong **was** (way) **ahead of** Chung in a recent poll.

S in front 앞에, in advance 미리
A behind 뒤에

0145 inevitably
/inévitəbli/
/인*에비*터블리/

반드시, 불가피하게
- Internet banking services will inevitably cause problems for some users.

S unavoidably, ineluctably

0146 shortly
/ʃɔ́:rtli/

곧, 바로

① shortly after ~하자마자 바로 / shortly before ~하기 바로 전에
- **Shortly after** arriving in Korea, I got a job at an English academy.
② shortly thereafter 그 후에 바로
- "Are you ok now?" James asked. "I'm fine, don't worry about me," Joseph responded. **Shortly thereafter**, James went home.

S soon

0147 instead of
/instéd əv/

대신에
- Most Korean working parents spend all day working. In this circumstance, only an older brother or sister in a family can play with, dress, and feed his or her younger brothers and sisters instead of his or her parents.

S rather than

0144 앞 도로는 전복된 트럭에 의해 완전히 막혔다. / 홍은 정보다 최근 여론 조사에서 (훨씬) 앞서 있었다.　0145 인터넷 뱅킹 서비스는 불가피하게 일부 사용자들에게 문제를 일으킬 것이다.　0146 한국에 도착하자마자 바로, 나는 한 영어 학원에 취직했다. / "이제 괜찮아?" 제임스가 물었다. "난 괜찮아, 내 걱정은 하지 마." 조셉이 응답했다. 그 후에 바로 제임스는 집에 갔다.　0147 대부분의 한국의 직장인 부모들은 하루 종일 일을 한다. 이러한 상황에서 가족 중에 형이나 누나만이 부모 대신 어린 남동생과 여동생들에게 옷을 입히고 밥을 먹이고 그들과 놀아줄 수 있다.

DAY 04

ANGRY ENGLISH
ACADEMIC VOCABULARY

noun 명사

- [ ] amenity
- [ ] care
- [ ] drudgery
- [ ] flexibility
- [ ] joint
- [ ] mystery
- [ ] odds
- [ ] premise
- [ ] reed
- [ ] session
- [ ] tenacity
- [ ] urge
- [ ] variety

verb 동사

- [ ] abide
- [ ] array
- [ ] bulge
- [ ] camouflage
- [ ] commit
- [ ] contemplate
- [ ] deduce
- [ ] devote
- [ ] efface
- [ ] fade
- [ ] hustle
- [ ] immerse
- [ ] overlook
- [ ] pass
- [ ] reason
- [ ] seal
- [ ] stimulate
- [ ] toil

adjective 형용사

- [ ] accurate
- [ ] cardinal
- [ ] conducive
- [ ] eager
- [ ] fundamental
- [ ] impervious
- [ ] instantaneous
- [ ] oval
- [ ] painstaking
- [ ] proficient
- [ ] repetitive
- [ ] seminal
- [ ] sustainable
- [ ] telltale

adverb 부사

- [ ] alike
- [ ] invariably
- [ ] somewhat
- [ ] on the contrary

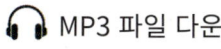 MP3 파일 다운

noun
명사

0148
amenity
/əménəti/
/어메*너티/

(마을이나 호텔 안에 수영장, 운동시설, 또는 쇼핑센터 같은) 생활 편의 시설 **amenities**
- Due to the civil war, the people lost access to basic amenities.

0149
care
/kéər/

1. 돌봄, 보살핌
ⓤ
① take care of sb ~을 돌보다
- She has more experience **taking care of** little kids.

② take care of sth ~을 신경쓰다
- People today are often judged by their physical appearance, so they **take** excessive **care of** the way they look.

③ take care of sth ~을 처리하다

2. 주의, 조심
ⓤ take care not to do sth ~하지 않도록 조심하다 / with (great) care (아주) 조심해서
- **Take care not to** make mistakes on the exam.
- You need to clean wine glasses **with** great **care**.

3. 염려, 근심, 걱정 cares
- He looks like a man with the cares of the world on his shoulders. We should cheer him up.

ⓢ care for sb, look after sb
ⓢ deal with sth
ⓢ attention
ⓢ concern, solicitude, anxiety

0150
drudgery
/drʌ́dʒəri/
/드러*줘리/

(공부 같이) 힘들고 지루한 일
- Many housewives complain about the drudgery of washing clothes.

ⓢ grind

0151
flexibility
/flèksəbíləti/
/플렉서빌*러티/

적응성, 융통성, 유연성
- The potato is a wonderful foodstuff because it allows a great degree of flexibility in how it can be cooked.

ⓢ adaptability

0152
joint
/dʒɔ́int/

(두 개가 만나는) 접합(연결) 부분, 관절
◇ wood joints 나무 접합 / a knee joint 무릎 관절
- Just as your joints get stiffer with age, so do your muscles.

▶
1. joint (동사) 결합하다
2. joint (형용사) 공동의, 합작의
◇ a joint venture 합작 사업 / joint names 공동 명의

ⓢ combine

0153
mystery
/místəri/
/미스터리/

신비함
ⓤ
① it's a mystery to sb why S주어 V동사 왜 ~하는지는 ~에게 신비로운 일이다
- **It's a mystery to** me **why** people vote for that man! He is so vile!
*vile 비열한

② be veiled / shrouded in mystery 신비에 싸여 있다
- How the buildings were used has **been veiled in mystery** for centuries.

0148 내전 때문에 사람들은 기본적인 편의 시설들을 접할 수 없었다. 0149 그녀는 어린 아이들을 돌본 더 많은 경험을 가지고 있다. / 오늘날 사람들은 종종 외모로 판단되어서 그들은 외모에 지나치게 신경을 쓴다. / 시험에서 실수하지 않도록 조심해라. / 당신은 와인 잔을 아주 조심해서 닦을 필요가 있다. / 그는 그의 어깨에 세상의 근심을 진 사람처럼 보인다. 우리가 그를 격려해야 한다. 0150 많은 주부들은 빨래하는 힘들고 지루한 일에 대해 불평한다. 0151 감자는 그것이 요리될 수 있는 방법에 있어서 상당한 정도의 적응성을 허용하기 때문에 훌륭한 식품이다. 0152 나이가 들수록 관절이 점점 더 뻣뻣해지는 것처럼 근육도 뻣뻣해진다. 0153 왜 사람들이 그 남자에게 투표하는지는 나에게는 신비로운 일이다. 그는 정말 비열하다. / 그 건물이 어떻게 사용되었는지는 수세기 동안 신비에 싸여져 왔다.

0154 odds
/ádz/

1. 가능성, 확률
- ① (the) odds are that S주어 V동사 ~할 가능성이 있다 (=(the) chances are that S주어 V동사) / (the) odds are good that S주어 V동사 ~할 가능성이 높다 (=(the) chances are good that S주어 V동사)
  - The **odds are that** private collectors who discover a lot of fossils will donate them to libraries and schools.
- ② (the) odds of (N명사) Ving동사 (명사가) ~할 가능성
  - The **odds of** Mickelson winn**ing** the PGA championship are 6-1.

2. 역경, 곤란
- ① against all (the) odds 모든 역경에 맞서(모든 역경에도 불구하고)
  - He succeeded in inventing the light bulb, **against all odds**.

S probability, likelihood, chance

0155 premise
/prémis/

전제
- ① be based on the premise that S주어 V동사 ~의 전제에 근거하다
- ② on a misguided / false premise 잘못된 전제 아래
  - The government's promise to the people was built **on a false premise**, which is why it failed.

S assumption

0156 reed
/ríːd/

갈대
- Reed boats were made out of papyrus reeds.

0157 session
/séʃən/

1. 회의, (의회의) 회기 개회하여 폐회 하기까지의 기간
- ◇ regular parliamentary session 정기 국회 회기
  - Shortly after Russia started invading Ukraine, the UN Security Council held an emergency session on Russia's military operations in Ukraine.

2. (특정 활동) 시간(기간)
- ◇ a tutoring session 교습 시간 / a practice session 연습 시간
  - The session with both children will be $40 and I may bring an activity for them to try.

S meeting

0158 tenacity
/tənǽsəti/

고집, 끈기
- I managed to finish the marathon with great tenacity.

S persistence

0159 urge
/ə́ːrdʒ/
/어쥐/

충동, 욕구
- ① have the urge to do sth ~하려는 충동(욕구)을 가지고 있다
- ① sexual urges 성욕
  - I **had** an overwhelming **urge to** punch him in the mouth.

S impulse, desire, appetite

0160 variety
/vəráiəti/

1. 다양성 (불가산)
- ① the variety of sth ~의 다양성
  - **The variety of** ice cream flavors at Baskin Robbins is incredible. In fact there are 31!

2. 여러 가지
- ① a variety of sth 다양한
  - In order for a restaurant to succeed, it should first develop **a variety of** menu items that will please its customers.

S diversity
A sameness 단조로움(동일)

verb 동사

0161 abide
/əbáid/

살다, 머무르다
- ⓥ abide in sth ~에 살다
  - Many tribes **abided in** the Great Plains.

Ⓝ
1. can't abide sb/sth ~을 몹시 싫어하다
   - I can't abide people who eat in the library.
2. abide by sth (규칙 등을) 따르다
   - ◇ abide by a rule / decision / agreement 규칙/결정/합의를 따르다
   - He would not abide by his team's decision.

ⓢ obey, accept

0162 array
/əréi/

배열(배치)하다, 진열하다
- They had all the products arrayed in the front window.

ⓢ arrange, display, lay out 배치하다

0163 bulge
/bʌ́ldʒ/
/벌쥐/

1. 부풀어 오르다, 불룩 나오다
- ⓥ bulge with sth ~로 불룩하다
  - The boy arrived home with his pockets **bulging with** marbles.

2. (눈이나 혈관 등이) 튀어나오다
  - His eyes bulge.

0164 camouflage
/kǽməflɑːʒ/
/캐머*플라쥐/

위장하다, (감정이나 상황 등을) 숨기다
- He camouflaged himself by wearing a mask with a bird-like beak.

ⓢ disguise, veil, conceal

0165 commit
/kəmít/

1. 저지르다, 범하다
- ◇ commit crimes 범죄를 저지르다 / commit murder 살해하다
  - With 5 minutes left in the final championship game, Michael Jordan committed a foul against Phil Jackson, so Jackson was given two free throws.
  - He committed suicide one morning in May.

ⓢ do, perform, carry out

2. (반드시 하겠다고) 약속(다짐)하다
- ⓥ commit to doing sth ~하겠다고 약속(다짐)하다
  - The president **committed to** lower**ing** the growing housing prices.

ⓢ promise

3. (돈이나 시간 등을) 쓰다
- ⓥ commit money / time to doing sth 시간/돈을 ~하는 데 쓰다
  - As a result, African governments have been **committing** a lot of **money to** reversing the damage that these non-native species have caused to their native species.

0166 contemplate
/kántəmpleit/
/칸텀*플레이트/

1. 심사숙고하다, 고려하다
- ⓥ contemplate Ving 동명사
  - She is **contemplating** immigrat**ing** to Canada to educate her kids.

ⓢ think of / about, meditate on
ⓢ consider Ving 동명사

2. 바라보다, 응시하다
- He waited for his name to be called, contemplating his hands.

0167 deduce
/didúːs/

추론하다
- ⓥ deduce (from sth) that S 주어 V 동사 (~에서) ~을 추론하다
  - You can **deduce** from this **that** farming was their main livelihood.
  *livelihood 생계 (수단)

ⓢ infer

0161 많은 부족들이 대평원에 살았다. / 난 도서관에서 먹는 사람들을 몹시 싫어한다. / 그는 팀의 결정을 따르지 않았다. 0162 그들은 모든 제품들을 앞 진열창에 진열되게 했다. 0163 그 소년은 주머니가 구슬로 불룩한 채 집에 도착했다. / 그의 눈은 튀어나왔다. 0164 그는 새처럼 생긴 부리를 가진 마스크를 써서 그 자신을 위장했다. 0165 마지막 챔피언 결정전에서 5분을 남겨둔 채, 마이클 조던은 필 잭슨을 상대로 파울을 범해서 잭슨은 두 개의 자유투를 얻었다. / 그는 5월 어느 날 아침 자살을 했다. / 대통령이 치솟는 집값을 낮추겠다고 약속했다. / 결과적으로, 아프리카 정부들은 이러한 외래종이 그들의 토착종에게 가한 피해를 되돌리는 데 많은 돈을 써 왔다. 0166 그녀는 아이들을 교육시키기 위해 캐나다로 이민 가는 것을 고려하고 있다. / 그는 손을 바라보면서 자신의 이름이 호명되기를 기다렸다. 0167 너는 이것으로부터 농업이 그들의 주된 생계 수단이었다는 것을 추론할 수 있다.

0168
devote
/divóut/

(시간이나 에너지를) 바치다, 쏟다, 전념하다
- ⓤ devote one's time / energy / life / oneself to (doing) sth 시간/에너지/생애/자기자신을 ~에 전념하다(쏟다)
- After the War of Independence, Congress would not give pensions to the soldiers who had **devoted** their **lives to** secur**ing** their country's independence.

S dedicate
S put one's time / energy / effort into sth

0169
efface
/iféis/

지우다, 없애다
- ⓤ efface A from B: B에서 A를 지우다
- Last night, I had a nightmare about serving in the military again, and I can't **efface** it **from** my mind.

S remove, erase

0170
fade
/féid/

(차츰) 사라지다, 약해지다
- My hair has been fading away for a couple of years. Now I am bald.

S fade away, wane, decrease

0171
hustle
/hʌ́sl/

(거칠게 사람을) 떠밀다, 밀고 나아가다
- Two policemen hustled a suspect into the police station.

S push, jostle

0172
immerse
/imə́ːrs/

1. 몰입시키다, 몰두하게 하다
- ⓤ immerse oneself in (doing) sth 자기자신을 ~(하는 데)에 몰입시키다 / be immersed in sth ~에 몰두하다, ~에 빠져 있다
- He **was immersed in** learn**ing** to play golf.

S engross

2. 담그다
- ⓤ immerse A in B: A를 B에 담그다
- When making boiled potatoes, first peel and cut the potatoes into small cubes. Then, **immerse** the cubed potatoes **in** boiling water.

0173
overlook
/óuvərlùk/

1. (건물 등이) 바라보다
- The hotel overlooks the beach.

2. 간과하다, (나쁜 행동을) 눈감아 주다, 용서하다
- The Internet does not necessarily offer only benefits; in fact, it sometimes causes problems we might overlook.
- Still, terrorism is way too important a global threat to be overlooked.

S miss, lose sight of 놓치다, turn a blind eye 눈감아 주다

0174
pass
/pǽs/

1. (시간 등이) 지나가다
- But as time passes, you will definitely become bored with the monotonous routine of life in the countryside.

S elapse

2. (정보나 지식 등을) 전하다
- ⓤ
- ① pass down A to B: A를 B에게 전하다
- Traditions **are passed down** orally from one generation **to** the next.
- ② pass on A to B: A(받은 것)를 B에게 건네주다

3. 전달하다, 건네주다, (소유권이나 재산 등을) 넘기다
- ⓤ pass sb sth / pass sth to sb ~에게 ~을 전달하다
- ◇ pass me the salt 소금 좀 줘
- Certain physical traits such as skin color are passed from parents to children.

0168 독립 전쟁 이후 의회는 조국의 독립을 지키는 데 일생을 바친 병사들에게 연금을 주는 것을 거부했다. 0169 어젯밤에 나는 다시 군대에 가는 악몽을 꿨는데, 머릿속에서 그것을 지울 수가 없다. 0170 2~3년 동안 머리가 차츰 없어지고 있다. 나는 지금은 대머리. 0171 두 명의 경찰관이 한 용의자를 경찰서 안으로 거칠게 떠밀었다. 0172 그는 골프를 배우는 데 몰두해 있었다. / 삶은 감자를 만들 때 먼저 껍질을 벗기고 감자를 작은 정육면체 모양으로 자른다. 그런 다음 그 정육면체 모양의 감자를 끓는 물에 담근다. 0173 그 호텔은 해변을 바라보고 있다. / 인터넷이 반드시 장점만을 제공하는 것은 아니다; 사실, 그것은 때때로 우리가 간과할 수도 있는 문제를 야기한다. / 그럼에도 불구하고, 테러는 너무 중요한 세계적 위협이어서 간과될 수 없다. 0174 하지만 시간이 지나가면서 당신은 시골 생활의 단조로운 일상에 분명히 싫증이 날 것이다. / 전통은 한 세대에서 다음 세대로 구두로 전해진다. / 피부색과 같은 어떤 신체적 특징은 부모에게서 자녀들에게로 전달된다.

0175
reason
/ríːzn/

판단하다
- ⓥ reason that S주어 V동사 ~라고 판단하다
- He **reasoned that** if we worked in conjunction with the other team, we could finish the project on time. *in conjunction with ~과 공동으로

0176
seal
/síːl/

(봉투 등을) 봉하다(봉인하다), (병 등을) 밀봉하다
- He tore open an envelope sealed with red wax.

▶ seal (명사) 1) 도장 2) 물개

0177
stimulate
/stímjulèit/
/스티*뮬레이트/

자극하다, 활발하게 하다
◇ stimulate one's imagination 상상력을 자극하다 / stimulate the economy / investment 경제/투자를 활발하게 하다
- Government spending can stimulate the economy. But on the negative side, it can inflate prices.

[S] encourage
[A] suppress 억누르다

0178
toil
/tɔ́il/
/토일/

열심히 일하다, (오랫동안) 열심히 하다
- They toiled in the field day and night to feed their families.

[S] work hard, labor

adjective 형용사

0179
accurate
/ǽkjurət/
/애큐럿/

정확한
- When writing your thesis, you must be very accurate when quoting your sources.

▶
1. accuracy (명사) 정확함
2. accurately (부사) 정확히

[S] exact, precise, pinpoint
[A] inaccurate 정확하지 않은

0180
cardinal
/káːrdinl/
/카디늘/

(매우) 중요한, 주요한
- Cleanliness played a cardinal role in reducing bubonic plague mortality rates in the 14th century when this disease killed two-thirds of the people living in Europe. *bubonic plague 선페스트 (흔히 흑사병으로 알려짐)

▶ cardinal (명사) 추기경
- South Korean Cardinal Kim has passed away.

[S] main, fundamental, principal

0181
conducive
/kəndjúːsiv/
/컨듀*시브/

도움이 되는
- ⓥ conducive to sth ~에 도움이 되는
- One of the best ways to create an environment that is **conducive to** learning is to help students achieve their academic goals.

[S] favorable, helpful

0182
eager
/íːgər/

갈망(열망)하는, ~하고 싶어하는, 열렬한
- ⓥ eager to do sth ~을 열망(갈망)하는
- I'm **eager to** learn new things.

Ⓝ
1. aspire to sth ~을 갈망(열망)하다
2. aspire to do sth ~하기를 갈망(열망)하다

[S] keen, anxious, enthusiastic

0183 fundamental
/fʌndəméntl/

1. 기본적인, 근본적인
◇ fundamental changes / differences 근본적인 변화/차이
○ Gravity is one of the fundamental forces of nature.

[S] basic, foundational

2. 필수적인, 중요한
ⓤ fundamental to (doing) sth ~에 필수적인
○ Given that it is the fundamental duty of any university to give more students benefits, universities should spend more money on computer facilities.

[S] essential, central
[S] essential to (doing) sth

0184 impervious
/impə́ːrviəs/
/임퍼*비어스/

1. 영향을 받지 않는
ⓤ impervious to sth ~에 영향을 받지 않는
○ Obama said, "I'm not saying I'm **impervious to** criticism."

[S] unaffected

2. (액체나 열 등을) 통과시키지 않는
ⓤ impervious to sth ~을 통과시키지 않는
○ All the camping gear I have is **impervious to** rain.

[S] resistant, impenetrable, impermeable
[A] permeable 스며들 수 있는

0185 instantaneous
/ìnstəntéiniəs/
/인스턴*테이니어스/

즉각적인
◇ an instantaneous reply / response 즉각적 답변/대응
○ Receiving an instantaneous reply from a teacher can help stimulate the intellectual curiosity of a student.

▶ instantaneously (부사) 즉각, 즉석에서

[S] immediate, prompt, instant

[S] immediately, on the spot

0186 oval
/óuvl/
/오우블/

계란형의
○ Carolina bays are oval in shape.

N words related to geometry
- irregular 고르지 못한 ◇ irregular teeth 고르지 못한 치아
- symmetrical 대칭의
- elliptical 타원형의
- spheroidal 공 모양의(구형의)
- square 정사각형의
- round 둥근
- oblong 직사각형의, 길쭉한 ◇ oblong face 길쭉한 얼굴
- spiral 나사모양의
- straight 일직선의 ◇ straight lines 직선
- conical 원뿔형의 ◇ conical houses 원뿔형의 집
- rectangular 직사각형의

[S] spherical

[S] cone-shaped

0187 painstaking
/péinsteikiŋ/

철저한, 공들인
○ The police are planning to launch a painstaking investigation into the wreck of the ship.

▶ painstakingly (부사) 공들여

[S] thorough, careful, meticulous

0188 proficient
/prəfíʃənt/
/프러*피션트/

능숙한
ⓤ proficient in sth (분야) ~에서 능숙한 / proficient at doing sth ~하는 데 능숙한
○ After years of studying, I am finally **proficient at** speak**ing** English.

[S] skilled, adept, experienced
[A] inept 서투른

0189 repetitive
/ripétətiv/
/리페*터티브/

반복적인, 되풀이 되는
- Women do repetitive household tasks that they don't get paid for.

S monotonous, boring, dull

0190 seminal
/séminl/
/세미늘/

중대한, 영향력이 큰
- The works of Alfred Stieglitz, an American photographer, played a seminal role in the development of American modernism.

S influential

0191 sustainable
/səstéinəbl/
/서스*테이너블/

지속 가능한
- We should find sustainable energy sources.

A unsustainable 유지할 수 없는

0192 telltale
/télteil/
/텔*테일/

숨길 수 없는, 명백하게 보여주는
- A sudden and deep drop in consumer spending is a telltale sign that an economic recession has started.

▶ telltale (명사) 고자질쟁이 (=tattletale)

adverb 부사

0193 alike
/əláik/

모두, 둘 다
- A four-day workweek would benefit employers and employees alike. *four-day workweek 주 4일 근무제

▶ alike (형용사) 비슷한
- Strangely enough, Toddy and his stepbrother look alike.

S similar

0194 invariably
/invériəbli/

변함없이, 언제나
- It is invariably true that tourism is good for the economy.

▶ invariable (형용사) 불변의

S always

S unchanging

0195 somewhat
/sʌ́mwat/

다소, 약간
- It seems expensive. It's somewhat expensive.

N somewhat of sth 다소 ~인
⊙ be / remain somewhat of sth 다소 ~이다 / 다소 ~로 남아있다
- He is an important figure historically, but he *is* also *somewhat of* a controversial figure.

S to some degree

0196 on the contrary
/a:n ðə ka:ntreri/

이와 반대로
- The passage states that deer antlers are used as weapons. On the contrary, the lecturer argues that the antlers cannot be used as weapons.

0189 여성들은 그들이 보수를 받지 못하는 반복적인 집안일을 한다. 0190 미국의 사진작가인 알프레드 스티글리츠는 미국 모더니즘의 발달에 중대한 역할을 하였다. 0191 우리는 지속 가능한 에너지원을 찾아야 한다. 0192 소비 지출의 갑작스럽고 심한 감소는 경기 침체가 시작되었다는 숨길 수 없는 신호이다. 0193 주 4일 근무제는 고용주와 직원 모두에게 이익이 될 것이다. / 기이하게도 토디와 그의 의붓동생은 닮았다. 0194 관광 산업이 경제에 좋다는 것은 변함없이 사실이다. 0195 비싼 것 같다. 약간 비싸다. / 그는 역사적으로 중요한 인물이지만 다소 논란의 여지가 있는 인물이기도 하다. 0196 지문은 사슴의 뿔이 무기로 사용된다고 말한다. 반대로, 강의자는 그 뿔은 무기로 사용될 수 없다고 주장한다.

DAY 05

ANGRY ENGLISH
ACADEMIC VOCABULARY

noun 명사
- ☐ access
- ☐ body
- ☐ condition
- ☐ dwarf
- ☐ experience
- ☐ fracture
- ☐ inroad
- ☐ overview
- ☐ precaution
- ☐ record
- ☐ service
- ☐ synthesis
- ☐ technique

verb 동사
- ☐ abuse
- ☐ arouse
- ☐ browse
- ☐ care
- ☐ commence
- ☐ contribute
- ☐ debilitate
- ☐ disapprove
- ☐ eject
- ☐ evade
- ☐ gaze
- ☐ impede
- ☐ outnumber
- ☐ precipitate
- ☐ reach
- ☐ rub
- ☐ search
- ☐ track

adjective 형용사
- ☐ acquainted
- ☐ brief
- ☐ casual
- ☐ disparate
- ☐ full
- ☐ hands-on
- ☐ implicit
- ☐ instrumental
- ☐ loose
- ☐ overt
- ☐ patient
- ☐ replete
- ☐ separate

adverb 부사
- ☐ allegedly
- ☐ mainly
- ☐ though
- ☐ more of

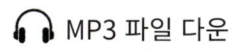 MP3 파일 다운

noun 명사

0197 access
/ǽkses/

접근
- have access to sth ~에 접근하다
- Researchers don't **have** the same **access to** a patient's medical records as doctors.

0198 body
/bádi/

1. 몸
- the human body / the body 신체
- He had severe injuries to **the body**.

2. 사체 (=dead body)
- Dead bodies were strewn on the streets.

3. 수역 물이 있는 넓은 지역
- There is a man in a boat floating on a body of water.

4. 많은 양
- a body of evidence / knowledge / information 많은 양의 증거/지식/정보
- There is **a vast body of** evidence for evolution.

0199 condition
/kəndíʃən/

1. 상태, 상황 — circumstance
- be in (형용사) condition ~(형용사)인 상태에 있다
- under these conditions 이러한 상황 아래서 / weather conditions 기상 상황
- The car **is in** pristine **condition**. *pristine 거의 새것 같은

2. (계약 상의) 조건 — terms
- Working conditions in factories during the Industrial Revolution were really awful.

▶ conditional (형용사) 조건부의
◇ conditional offer 조건부 입학

0200 dwarf
/dwɔ́ːrf/
/드워프/

난쟁이
- The Seven Dwarfs and Snow White is a story written from the perspective of the seven dwarfs.

0201 experience
/ikspíəriəns/
/익스*피어리언스/

경험
- Thanks to social media, people can easily share information, knowledge, and experience with millions of people all around the world.
- have experience (in) Ving 동명사 ~한 경험이 있다
- I **have** 16 years' **experience** teach**ing** students TOEFL.

0202 fracture
/frǽktʃər/

(갈라져 생긴) 금, 균열 — break, crack 깨진 틈
- Fractures in the building grew larger.

0203 inroad
/ínróud/

침투, 진출
- make inroads into / on sth (뭔가 긍정적인 것에) 영향을 미치기 시작하다, 침투(진출)하다
- The company has managed to **make** significant **inroads into** the European market.

0197 연구자들은 의사들처럼 환자의 진료 기록에 동일한 접근을 못한다. 0198 그는 몸에 심한 부상을 입었다. / 사체들이 거리에 흩어져 있었다. / 한 수역에 떠 있는 배 안에 한 남자가 있다. / 진화에 대한 엄청나게 많은 증거가 있다. 0199 그 차는 새것 같은 상태이다. / 산업 혁명 동안 공장의 노동 조건은 정말 끔찍했다. 0200 일곱 난쟁이와 백설 공주는 일곱 난쟁이의 관점에서 쓰여진 이야기이다. 0201 소셜 미디어 덕택에, 사람들은 쉽게 정보, 지식과 경험을 전 세계의 수백만 명들과 공유할 수 있다. / 나는 16년간의 학생들에게 토플을 가르친 경험을 가지고 있다. 0202 건물의 균열이 점점 커졌다. 0203 그 회사는 유럽 시장에 상당한 영향을 미치기 시작하는 데 성공했다.

0204 overview
/óuvərvjuː/

개관, 개요
- give a (brief) overview of sth ~에 대한 (간략한) 개관(개요)을 설명하다
- Before we start this meeting I will **give a** brief **overview of** how the project is going so far.

0205 precaution
/prikɔ́ːʃən/

예방 조치
- take precautions 예방 조치를 취하다
- They **took** various safety **precautions** to protect themselves from wild animals.

0206 record
/rékɔːd/
/레코드/

기록
- keep a record of sth ~을 기록하다
- I have the habit of **keeping a record of** everything I do.

on (the) record 공식적으로 집계된
- This summer was the hottest on record since 1957.

0207 service
/sə́ːrvis/

1. (공공기관이 제공하는) 서비스
- public services 공공 서비스 / the health service 의료 서비스 / goods and services 재화와 서비스
- Companies can charge higher prices by advertising the goods and services they produce.

2. (고객에게 주는) 서비스
- after-sales service 애프터서비스
- Domestic electronics companies provide better customer services than foreign ones.

3. 군대 the service
- the services 육군(the army), 해군(the navy), 공군(the air force)
- He spent 18 months in the service.

0208 synthesis
/sínθəsis/
/신써*시스/
syntheses 복수 /sinθəsiːz/

1. 종합, 통합, 합성 다른 두 개를 섞은 것 — combination, mixture / a mixture of A and B
- a synthesis of A and B: A와 B의 합성
- **A synthesis of** nationalism **and** racism was one of the causes of the Holocaust. *the Holocaust 유대인 대학살

2. (화학적 반응을 통한) 합성
- The synthesis of oxygen and carbon produces carbon dioxide.

▶
1. synthetic (형용사) 합성의, 인조의 — man-made
- synthetic fabrics 인조 섬유 / synthetic fertilizers 합성 비료
2. synthetically (부사) 합성적으로

0209 technique
/tekníːk/

1. 기술 — method
- techniques for doing sth ~하기 위한 기술들 / a technique of doing sth ~하는 방법(기술)
- a new technique of artificially growing cells 인위적으로 세포를 성장시키는 새로운 기술
- The department is in charge of teaching **techniques for** handl**ing** customer complaints.

2. (운동, 미술, 음악에서 훈련과 연습을 통해 얻은 미술적인 또는 스포츠적인) 기교, 솜씨
- the techniques of ballet 발레의 기교
- Lionel Messi's technique of playing football is unmatched by any other player.

verb 동사

0210 abuse
/əbjúːz/

1. 잘못 사용하다, 오용(남용)하다
- One of the main issues in the past was leaders abusing their power.

[S] misuse

2. 학대하다
- ◇ sexually / physically abuse sb ~을 성적으로/육체적으로 학대하다
- The charity was set up to help children who had **been sexually abused** to find adoptive parents.

[S] treat sb cruelly

0211 arouse
/əráuz/

자극하다, 불러일으키다
- ◇ arouse sb's interest / anger / curiosity / controversy ~의 관심/분노/호기심/논쟁을 자극하다(불러일으키다)
- It is celebrities themselves who arouse people's curiosity about their private lives.

[S] excite

0212 browse
/bráuz/

1. (풀 등을) (뜯어) 먹다
- ⓤ browse on sth ~을 먹다
- There are no leaves for deer to **browse on** throughout the winter.

[S] graze

2. 대강 훑어보다
- ◇ browse in a shop 상점에서 물건 등을 훑어보다 / browse (through) a book / a website 책/웹사이트를 대강 훑어보다

0213 care
/kéər/

신경을 쓰다, 관심을 갖다
- ⓤ care about sth ~에 대해 신경을 쓰다
- They do not care if others damage the environment.

[S] be concerned, be interested

0214 commence
/kəméns/
/커멘스/

시작하다
- Most important of all, summer school commences right after final exams are over.

[S] begin, start
[A] finish 끝내다(마치다)

0215 contribute
/kəntríbjuːt/

원인이 되다
- ⓤ contribute to sth ~의 원인이 되다
- Junk food **contributes to** obesity.

0216 debilitate
/dibílitèit/
/디빌리*테이트/

약화시키다, (쇠)약하게 하다
- The disease debilitates the body's immune system.

▶ debilitating (형용사) 쇠약하게 하는

[S] make sth weaker, weaken

0217 disapprove
/dìsəprúːv/
/디서*프루브/

반대하다
- ⓤ disapprove of sth ~을 반대하다
- Many people **disapprove of** animal experimentation.
  (=Many people don't agree with animal experimentation.)

[A] approve 찬성하다
[S] don't agree with sth

▶ disapproval (명사) 반대

[S] objection

0218 eject
/idʒékt/

1. 내쫓다
- ⓤ be ejected from sth for dong sth ~때문에 ~에서 쫓겨나다
- ○ Three fans of Chelsea **were ejected from** the stadium **for** hurling abuse at supporters of the opposing team. *hurl abuse at sb ~에게 욕설을 퍼붓다

2. (기계에서 무언가를) 나오게 하다
- ◇ eject the tape 테이프를 빼다

3. (조종사가 비행기에서) 탈출하다
- ○ The pilot had already been ejected from the plane before it crashed in a field.

0219 evade
/ivéid/

피하다, (법 등을) 빠져나가다
- ○ He succeeded in evading the police.
- ○ He was able to make a fortune because he knew how to evade the law.

[S] avoid, escape, bypass(장애물 등을) 우회하다

0220 gaze
/géiz/

응시하다
- ⓤ gaze at sb/sth ~을 응시하다
- ○ He **gazed at** a blurred photograph. *blurred 흐릿한

[N] gaze synonyms
- stare at (이상하거나 놀라서) 응시하다(쳐다보다)
- peer at (잘 보이지 않아서) 자세히 보다(응시하다)
- glare at 노려보다
- glimpse 흘끗 보다

0221 impede
/impíːd/

막다, 지연시키다, 방해하다
- ○ There are insects in Australia that impede the growth of paperbark trees by eating their leaves and flowers.

▶ impediment (명사) 방해, 장애

[S] hinder, hamper

0222 outnumber
/autnʌ́mbər/

~보다 수가 많다
- ○ In my country, apartments outnumber traditional stand-alone homes. *stand-alone home 단독 주택

0223 precipitate
/prisípitèit/
/프리*시피테이트/

촉발시키다, 재촉하다
- ○ The idea that e-cigarettes precipitate a reduced risk of lung cancer still remains a matter of debate.

[S] trigger, spark, bring on

0224 reach
/ríːtʃ/

1. 도착하다, 닿다
- ○ Columbus was the first explorer to reach the New World.

2. (어떤 상태나 단계에) 도달하다, 이르다
- ○ Today, the temperature will reach a daytime high of 35°C. *high (명사)정점, 최고 기록

[S] arrive

0225 rub
/rʌ́b/

문지르다, 닦다
- ○ They pounded the roots of plants, mixed them with vinegar and then rubbed the liquid on their bodies to keep insects and bees away.

[S] scrub, polish, shine

0218 세 명의 첼시의 팬들이 상대 팀의 팬들에게 욕설을 퍼부어서 경기장에서 쫓겨났다. / 조종사는 비행기가 들판에 추락하기 전에 이미 비행기에서 탈출했다. 0219 그는 경찰을 피하는 데 성공했다. / 그는 어떻게 법망을 빠져나가는지를 알았기 때문에 큰 돈을 벌 수 있었다. 0220 그는 흐릿한 사진을 응시했다. 0221 오스트레일리아에 페이퍼바크 나무의 잎과 꽃을 먹음으로써 그 나무의 성장을 막는 벌레들이 있다. 0222 우리나라에는 아파트가 전통적인 단독 주택보다 더 많다. 0223 전자 담배가 폐암의 위험 감소를 촉발시킨다는 생각은 여전히 논쟁거리로 남아 있다. 0224 콜럼버스는 신세계에 도착한 최초의 탐험가였다. / 오늘은 낮 최고 기온이 35도에 도달할 것이다. 0225 그들은 식물의 뿌리를 빻아서 그들을 식초와 섞은 다음 벌레와 벌들을 쫓아내기 위해 몸에 그 액체를 문질렀다.

0226 search
/sə́ːrtʃ/

1. 찾다
- ⓤ search for sb/sth ~을 찾다
- He **searched for** the coin in the grass.

[S] look for sb/sth

2. (장소나 가방 등을) 뒤지다, 수색하다
- ⓤ search sth/sb for sth ~을 찾기 위해 ~을 뒤지다(수색하다)
- The police started to **search** our house **for** drugs after showing us a warrant.

[S] scour 자세히 조사하다, comb

0227 track
/træk/

뒤쫓다, 추적하다
- We saw their footprints in the snow and continued to track them.

[S] chase, pursue, follow

▶ track (명사) (발)자국

[N] keep track of sth ~을 추적하다(계속 파악하고 있다) / lose track of sth ~을 놓치다

adjective 형용사

0228 acquainted
/əkwéintid/

1. 익숙한
- ⓤ acquainted with sth ~에 익숙한
- Firefighters must be **acquainted with** safety rules and regulations.

[S] familiar
[S] familiar with sth

2. 안면이 있는
- ⓤ acquainted with ~와 안면이 있는

0229 brief
/bríːf/

1. 짧은, 잠시(잠깐) 동안의
- She spent a brief spell as an environmental activist at Save Earth, an NGO established in India. *spell 한동안의 활동

[S] short, momentary 순간의, temporary

2. 간결한, 간단한
- You should write a brief summary of your research.

[S] concise, short

▶ briefly (부사) 1) 잠시 2) 간결하게

[S] concisely

0230 casual
/kǽʒuəl/

1. 아무렇지 않은, 무심한
- As time went by, people started to have a more casual attitude towards new surges of the virus.

[S] careless, indifferent

2. 형식적이지 않은, 격식을 차리지 않는
- ◇ casual clothes 캐주얼 복장(평상복)
- He dressed himself in casual clothes.

[S] informal

3. (관계 등이) 가벼운
- I don't want to be in a serious relationship. I just want a casual relationship.

[A] serious 진지한

[N] causal (형용사) 원인의, 인과 관계의
◇ a causal relationship 인과 관계 / make causal claims 인과 관계의 주장을 하다

0231 disparate
/díspərət/
/디스*퍼럿/

(모든 점에서 서로 전혀) 다른
- It is impossible for groups whose objectives are disparate to work together.

[S] different, contrasting, dissimilar

0232 full
/fúl/

1. 가득한
- full of sth ~로 가득한
- The old book he picked out of the bookcase was **full of** graphs that no one today would be interested in.

S filled, packed, crowded
A empty 비어 있는

2. 모든
- full story 전체 줄거리

S entire, complete

3. 완전한, 최고의
- full employment 완전 고용 / full speed 최고 속력
- She slammed a bottle with full force onto his head.

S maximum

N full of synonyms
packed with, packed full of, filled with, crowded with, rife with, fraught with, choked with (사람들로) 막힌
- The train was packed with people going to work.

0233 hands-on
/hǽndzɑːn/

직접 해 보는
- have hands-on experience doing sth 직접 ~해 본 경험을 가지고 있다
- In spite of her young age, she **has hands-on experience** liv**ing** in various countries.

0234 implicit
/implísit/
/임*플리싯/

1. 무언의, 암묵적인
- An implicit agreement was made between China and Russia.

S tacit

2. (은연 중에) 포함되어 있는, 잠재하는, 내포된
- implicit in sth ~에 포함되어 있는
- **Implicit in** her writing was a moral code.

S involved in sth

3. 절대적인
- implicit faith / belief 절대적 신앙/믿음
- His boss has implicit trust in him.

S absolute, unquestioning

0235 instrumental
/ínstrəméntl/
/인스트러*멘틀/

도움이 되는, 중요한
- be instrumental in doing sth ~하는 데 도움이 되다 / ~하는 데 중요하다
- His research **was instrumental in** explain**ing** the causes of the greenhouse effect.

S helpful, influential
S be important in doing sth

0236 loose
/lúːs/
/루스/

헐거워진, 풀린
- come loose 헐거워지다
- His shoelace **came loose** while he was running.

S unattached
S become loose / unattached

▶ loose (동사) (묶여 있던 것을) 풀다, 느슨하게 하다

0237 overt
/ouvə́ːt/
/오우*버트/

공개적인, 명백한
- overt support 공개적 지지
- He is an overt liar. It is so obvious that he is lying.

S open, obvious
A covert 비밀의

▶ overtly (부사) 공개적으로

0238 patient
/péiʃənt/

참을성(인내심)이 있는
- patient with sb/sth ~에 인내심(참을성)이 있는
- Parents should be **patient with** their kids.

A impatient 참을성 없는

▶ patience (명사) 참을성, 인내심

N patient (명사) 환자

0232 그가 책장에서 골라낸 그 옛날 책은 오늘날 아무도 관심을 갖지 않을 그래프로 가득했다. / 그녀는 그의 머리에 있는 힘껏 병을 내던졌다. / 기차는 출근하는 사람들로 가득했다. 0233 어린 나이에도 불구하고 그녀는 다양한 나라에서 직접 살아 본 경험을 가지고 있다. 0234 중국과 러시아 사이에 암묵적인 합의가 이루어졌다. / 도덕적 규준이 그녀의 글에 내포되어 있었다. / 그의 상사는 그에 대한 절대적 신뢰를 가지고 있다. 0235 그의 연구는 온실 효과의 원인을 설명하는 데 중요했다. 0236 그는 달리는 도중에 신발 끈이 풀렸다. 0237 그는 명백한 거짓말쟁이다. 그가 거짓말을 하고 있다는 것은 너무나 명백하다. 0238 부모들은 그들의 자녀들에 대해 인내심이 있어야 한다.

0239
replete
/riplíːt/

가득한
- replete with sb/sth ~로 가득한
- The museum is **replete with** interesting artworks by young architects.

S filled with sb/sth, full of sb/sth

0240
separate
/sépərət/
/세퍼럿/

(공간상으로) 분리된, 독립된, 다른
- Religion and politics should be separate.

S several, different

▶
1. separate (동사) 분리하다, 떼어놓다, 나누다
2. separable (형용사) 뗄 수 있는
- We are close friends. We are inseparable.

A inseparable 뗄 수 없는

N divided (형용사) 분단된

adverb 부사

0241
allegedly
/əlédʒidli/
/얼*레쥐들리/

1. 혐의로
- be arrested for allegedly doing sth ~했다는 혐의로 체포되다
- The actor **was arrested for allegedly** possess**ing** illegal drugs.

2. (사실로 밝혀진 것은 아니지만) ~라고 믿어지는, 전해지는 바에 따르면
- The photographs allegedly taken by him don't prove anything.

S supposedly

▶ alleged (형용사) 혐의의, 혐의를 받고 있는
◇ alleged fact 혐의 사실

0242
mainly
/méinli/

주로
- The rise in the death rate in 2020 and 2021 is mainly due to the pandemic.

S chiefly, primarily, principally

0243
though
/ðou/

비록 ~일 지라도
- Domestic products, though more expensive than foreign products, are convenient to use.

S although

0244
more of
/mɔːr əv/

(오히려) ~에 (더) 가까운
- be more of sth than sth ~라기 보다는 ~에 더 가깝다
- Gravity may be more of a factor in landslides than scientists think.

S be sth rather than sth

0239 그 박물관은 젊은 건축가들의 흥미로운 미술 작품으로 가득하다. 0240 종교와 정치는 분리되어야 한다. / 우리는 가까운 친구다. 우리는 뗄 수 없다. 0241 그 여배우는 불법 마약을 소지했다는 혐의로 체포되었다. / 그가 찍은 것으로 알려진 사진들은 아무것도 증명하지 못한다. 0242 2020년과 2021년의 사망률 증가는 주로 팬데믹 때문이다. 0243 국산품이, 비록 외국 제품보다 더 비싸지만, 사용하기 편리하다. 0244 중력은 과학자들이 생각하는 것보다 산사태의 더 가까운 요인일지 모른다.

DAY 06

ANGRY ENGLISH
ACADEMIC VOCABULARY

noun 명사
- [ ] admiration
- [ ] backbone
- [ ] cargo
- [ ] congestion
- [ ] credit
- [ ] defect
- [ ] drive
- [ ] foresight
- [ ] hope
- [ ] initiative
- [ ] patron
- [ ] reason
- [ ] severity
- [ ] threat

verb 동사
- [ ] access
- [ ] approach
- [ ] brace
- [ ] carry
- [ ] command
- [ ] contrive
- [ ] deem
- [ ] differ
- [ ] elevate
- [ ] etch
- [ ] feature
- [ ] implore
- [ ] optimize
- [ ] project
- [ ] recognize
- [ ] seize
- [ ] strain
- [ ] vow

adjective 형용사
- [ ] actual
- [ ] awful
- [ ] cautious
- [ ] efficient
- [ ] fractious
- [ ] imprecise
- [ ] improbable
- [ ] keen
- [ ] perceptible
- [ ] rigid
- [ ] sequential
- [ ] supposed
- [ ] tender
- [ ] wary

adverb 부사
- [ ] apart
- [ ] meanwhile
- [ ] thus
- [ ] none other than

 MP3 파일 다운

noun
명사

0245 admiration /ædməréiʃən/ /애드머*레이션/
존경
- I was deeply moved when my students expressed their profound admiration for my class.

[s] respect, tribute

0246 backbone /bǽkbòun/
근간
- The backbone of Korea's economy is the production and export of semiconductors.

0247 cargo /káːrgou/
화물
◇ a cargo plane 화물기
- A tanker with a cargo of oil sunk in the Caribbean Sea. *tanker 대형 선박, 유조선

[s] freight

0248 congestion /kəndʒéstʃən/ /컨*줴스천/
혼잡
◇ traffic congestion 교통 혼잡
- Congestion is a real problem in the center of the city.

▶ congested (형용사) 혼잡한

[s] overcrowding

[s] crowded, blocked

0249 credit /krédit/
칭찬, 인정, 공(로)
ⓤ
① get / take credit for (doing) sth ~(한 것)에 대한 인정을 받다
- Our boss **got** no **credit for** lead**ing** our company through this difficult time.
② deserve credit for (doing) sth ~(한 것)에 대한 인정(칭찬)받을 만하다
- I **deserve credit for** finish**ing** this project alone.
③ give sb credit for (doing) sth ~에게 ~(한 것)에 대한 공로를 인정하다
- They **gave Boxer** the **credit for** complet**ing** the windmill.

[s] praise, approval

0250 defect /díːfekt/
결함, 결점
- Let me enumerate the fatal defects in what the passage argues. *enumerate 열거하다

▶ defect (동사) (당이나 국가 등을 버리고 다른 편으로) 가다, 탈당하다
- He defected from the Democratic Party to the Republican Party.

[s] fault, flaw

0251 drive /dráiv/
1. 진입로, 개인 소유의 차도
- I had a car parked in my driveway removed.

2. 욕구
- Sexual drive is a natural urge that needs to be carefully controlled.

3. 적극적인 노력
- The government's drive to reduce traffic has also helped to reduce pollution in the city center.

[s] driveway

[s] desire

0252 foresight /fɔ́ːrsait/
선견지명
ⓤ have the foresight to do sth ~하는 선견지명을 가지고 있다
- He **had the foresight to** invest in the company early on. Now he is really rich. *early on 일찍부터

0245 나는 학생들이 내 수업에 대한 그들의 깊은 존경을 표현했을 때 크게 감동 받았다. 0246 한국 경제의 근간은 반도체의 수출과 생산이다. 0247 석유 화물을 실은 유조선이 카리브해에 침몰했다. 0248 혼잡은 도시 중심부의 진짜 문제이다. 0249 우리 사장님은 이 어려운 시기 내내 우리 회사를 이끈 공로를 인정받지 못했다. / 나는 이 프로젝트를 혼자서 끝낸 것에 대해 칭찬받을 만하다. / 그들은 복서에게 풍차를 완성한 것에 대한 공로를 인정했다. 0250 제가 지문이 주장하는 것의 치명적인 결함들을 열거해 보겠습니다. / 그는 민주당에서 탈당해서 공화당으로 옮겨갔다. 0251 나는 진입로에 주차된 차를 치웠다. / 성적 욕구는 신중하게 통제될 필요가 있는 자연스러운 충동이다. / 교통량을 줄이기 위한 정부의 적극적인 노력은 또한 도심지의 오염을 줄이는 것을 도와주었다. 0252 그는 일찍부터 그 회사에 투자를 하는 선견지명을 가지고 있었다. 지금 그는 정말 부자다.

0253 hope
/hóup/

희망, 기대
Ⓤ
① with (the) hope that S주어 V동사 ~라는 기대(희망)를 가지고
◦ People started to buy bonds **with** the **hope that** their value would later double.
② in the hope of / in hopes of ~의 희망(기대) 속에 / in hopes that S주어 V동사 ~라는 희망(기대) 속에
◦ Poor people in the countryside flocked to big cities **in hopes of** making money.
◦ People had hopes of their home prices increasing in the future.

0254 initiative
/iníʃətiv/
/이니*셔티브/

1. 결단(력)
◦ My daughter in middle school did her homework on her own initiative today. Usually, I have to force her to do it.

2. 주도(권) the initiative
Ⓤ
① have / take the initiative to do sth 주도적으로 ~하다(솔선수범하여 ~하다)
◦ My assistant **took the initiative to** visit the customers directly.
② seize / lose the initiative 주도권을 잡다/잃다

0255 patron
/péitrən/
/페이*트런/

1. 후원자   S supporter
◦ In the end, a wealthy patron showed up to finance their research.

2. (특정 상점, 식당, 호텔의) 고객   S customer
◦ What patrons don't know is that Costa's prices are as high as its competitors'.

0256 reason
/ríːzn/

1. 이유, 원인 (가산)   S cause
Ⓤ a (the) reason for the fire 그 화재의 원인 / a reason for doing sth ~을 한 이유
◦ One **reason for** this is that the companies that outsource to foreign countries can stay competitive by lowering labor costs and expanding their businesses. *outsource 외주 제작하다

2. (믿음에 대한) 근거 (불가산), **감정의 원인**
Ⓤ good / justified reason to do / for doing sth ~하는 타당한/정당한 근거
◦ There was **good reason for** execut**ing** the traitors.

Ⓝ
1. by reason of sth 때문에   S because of sth, due to sth
2. for reasons of economy / safety / security 경제상/안정상/보안상의 이유로

0257 severity
/sivérəti/
/시베*러티/

(문제, 질병, 부상 등의) 심각성, (날씨 등이) 심함, (처벌 등이) 가혹함   S seriousness, harshness 가혹함
◦ Many people are ignorant of the severity of climate change.
◦ The severity of the economic problem was exacerbated by the global pandemic. *exacerbate 악화시키다

▶ severe (형용사) 심각한(극심한), (처벌 등이) 가혹한

0258 threat
/θrét/

위협
Ⓤ pose a threat to sb/sth ~에 위협을 가하다 / a threat to sth ~에 위협
◦ Desertification is **a** serious **threat to** the area's wildlife.

verb 동사

0259 access /ǽkses/ /액세스/
접근하다
○ The Act allows a person to access any information that government organizations hold.

0260 approach /əpróutʃ/
1. 다가가다, 다가오다, 접근하다 — near, come up to
◇ footsteps approaching in the distance 멀리서 다가오는 발자국 소리
○ A woman approached me and introduced herself.
(=A woman came up to me and introduced herself.)

2. (문제 등을) 다루다 — deal with
◇ approach a problem / task / matter 문제를 다루다
○ The problems affecting the Everglades, a large area of wetlands, can be approached through simple efforts. There is still hope for the Everglades.

0261 brace /bréis/ /브레이스/
1. 떠받치다, 보강하다 — support
○ It costs a lot to brace the roof planted with shrubs and trees.

2. 대비를 하다 — prepare oneself for sth
ⓤ brace oneself for sth ~에 (스스로) 대비를 하다
○ We must **brace** ourselves **for** the winter. It will be colder than ever this year.

0262 carry /kǽri/
1. 나르다, 옮기다 — transport, convey
○ A fungus that insects carry can seriously affect trees. The fungus can cause a disease that can kill millions of them.

2. 휴대하다, 가지고 다니다
○ The state is unique in permitting people to legally carry a gun in public. *unique 유일한

0263 command /kəmǽnd/
1. 명령하다 — order
ⓤ
① command sb to do sth ~에게 ~하라고 명령하다 — order sb to do sth
② command that S주어 (should) V동사 ~해야 한다고 명령하다
○ The governor **commanded that** the dam be removed.

2. (존경, 관심, 애정, 지원 등을) 받다
ⓤ command respect 존경을 받다 / command affection 사랑받다
○ He is the only president who commands respect and affection from his citizens.

0264 contrive /kəntráiv/ /컨*트라이브/
1. (힘든 일을) 성공하다 — succeed / succeed in Ving동명사
ⓤ contrive to do sth ~하는 데 성공하다
○ After receiving advice from experts on YouTube on how to grow various types of flowers and plants, he **contrived to** run his own gardening store.

2. (계획이나 기계 등을) 만들다, 고안하다 — invent, make
○ A technique was contrived that uses sound to detect obstacles in the ocean.

0259 그 법령은 개인이 정부 기관이 보유하고 있는 모든 정보에 접근하는 것을 허용한다. 0260 한 여자가 나에게 다가와서 자신을 소개했다. / 대규모 습지대 지역인 에버글레이즈에 영향을 미치고 있는 문제점들은 단순한 노력들을 통해 다뤄질 수 있다. 에버글레이즈에는 아직 희망이 있다. 0261 관목과 나무가 심어진 지붕을 떠받치는 데는 많은 비용이 든다. / 우리는 겨울에 대비를 해야 한다. 올해는 그 어느 때보다 추울 것이다. 0262 곤충이 옮기는 곰팡이는 심각하게 나무에 영향을 줄 수 있다. 그 곰팡이는 수백만 그루의 나무를 죽일 수 있는 질병을 일으킬 수 있다. / 사람들이 공공장소에서 합법적으로 총기를 휴대하게 해 주는 주는 그 주가 유일하다. 0263 주지사는 그 댐이 제거되어야 한다고 명령했다. / 그는 시민들로부터 존경과 애정을 받는 유일한 대통령이다. 0264 유튜브에서 전문가들로부터 다양한 종류의 꽃과 식물을 키우는 방법에 대한 조언을 받은 후 그는 자신의 원예용품점을 운영하는 데 성공했다. / 바다에서 장애물을 탐지하기 위해 소리를 사용하는 기술이 고안되었다.

0265
deem
/díːm/

여기다, 생각하다
ⓥ
① deem it가목적어 형용사 to do진목적어 ~하는 것은 ~하다고 여기다
  ○ Many people **deem it** unsafe **to** travel to Ukraine.
② deem O목적어 to be 형용사/명사 ~을 ~라고 생각하다
  ○ Whales are often found dead or dying on beaches, and this **is deemed to be** a perfectly natural occurrence.

[S] consider, think

0266
differ
/dífər/

1. 다르다
ⓥ
① differ in sth ~점에서 다르다 / differ from sth ~과 다르다
  ○ Men's and women's brains **differ in** structure.
② A differ from B in that S주어 V동사 ~라는 점에서 A는 B와 다르다
  ○ Historically, chiefdoms **differed from** bands and tribes **in that** they were ruled by a single person called a chief who governed several villages including his own.

2. 생각이 다르다
ⓥ differ on / about / over sth ~에 관해 다르다
  ○ Accounts **differ about** what happened in the accident.

[S] disagree

0267
elevate
/éləvèit/

1. (들어) 올리다, 높이다
  ○ Stress can elevate your blood pressure.

2. 개선(향상)시키다
  ○ Women's suffrage resulted in elevating the status of women in society. *suffrage 참정권

▶ elevated (형용사)
1) 지위가 높은
2) (지대나 가격이) 높은

[S] raise, lift up

[S] improve

0268
etch
/étʃ/

새겨 넣다, 새기다
  ○ The names of her son and daughter are etched on her gravestone side by side with those of their families.

[S] carve

0269
feature
/fíːtʃər/

(중요한 점 등) ~의 특징을 이루다, 포함하다, 보여 주다
  ○ The hotel features rooms with ocean views and also has a hot spring.

▶ feature (명사) 특징

[S] include, show

0270
implore
/implɔ́ːr/

애원하다, 간청하다
ⓥ implore sb to do sth ~에게 ~하라고 간청(애원)하다
  ○ Sophie **implored** him **to** stay as long as possible.

[S] beg, plead

0271
optimize
/áptimaiz/
/압티*마이즈/

(기회나 상황 등을) 최대한 잘 활용하다, 최적화하다
  ○ The best way to optimize the use of limited resources is to let markets solve it.

0272
project
/prədʒékt/

1. 돌출되다
◇ projecting tooth 돌출된 치아

2. (이미지 등을) 보여 주다, (영상 등을) 비추다(투영하다)
  ○ He is seeking to project a modest image to local inhabitants.
  ○ In the ad, the company's logo is projected on the sky at night.

[S] protrude

0265 많은 사람들은 우크라이나로 여행가는 것은 안전하지 않다고 생각한다. / 고래들은 종종 해안에서 죽어 가고 있거나 죽은 채로 발견되는데 이것은 완전히 자연스러운 현상이라고 여겨진다. 0266 남자와 여자의 뇌는 구조 면에서 다르다. / 역사적으로, 족장 사회는 그들이 자신의 마을을 포함한 여러 마을을 통치하던 족장이라고 불리는 한 사람에 의해 통치되었다는 점에서 무리 사회와 부족 사회와 달랐다. / 그 사고에서 무슨 일이 일어났는지에 관해 설명이 다르다. 0267 스트레스는 혈압을 높일 수 있다. / 여성의 참정권은 사회에서 여성의 지위를 향상시키는 결과를 가져왔다. 0268 그녀의 아들과 딸의 이름이 그녀의 묘비에 그들의 가족의 이름과 나란히 새겨져 있다. 0269 그 호텔은 바다가 보이는 전망을 가지고 있는 객실을 포함하고 또한 온천을 가지고 있다. 0270 소피는 그에게 가능한 한 오래 머물러 줄 것을 간청했다. 0271 제한된 자원의 사용을 최적화하는 가장 좋은 방법은 시장이 그것을 해결하도록 내버려두는 것이다. 0272 그는 지역 주민들에게 겸손한 이미지를 보여 주려고 노력 중이다. / 그 광고에서 그 회사의 로고가 밤에 하늘에 투영되었다.

0273 recognize
/rékəgnàiz/

1. 알아보다
- I was able to recognize her because she always wears the same style of dress.

S identify

2. (사실이라고) 인정하다, (정식으로) 승인하다
- The U.S. didn't recognize the military government.

S acknowledge, approve

0274 seize
/síːz/

1. (갑자기 ~을) 잡다
- ⓤ seize sb by 신체 부위 ~의 ~을 잡다
- ◇ seize her by the waist 그녀의 허리를 잡다
- Initially he touched her softly on the arm, but later he **seized** her roughly **by** the arm.

S grab, snatch 잡아채다

2. 점령(장악)하다, 체포하다
- ⓤ seize A from B: B에게서 A를 장악하다
- Since the group has seized power in Afghanistan, concerns over renewed bomb threats are rising.

3. (기회 등을) 잡다
- ⓤ
- ① seize a chance / an opportunity to do sth ~할 수 있는 기회를 잡다
- ② seize the initiative 주도권을 잡다
- Ransom Olds was able to **seize the initiative** in the automobile market by introducing the assembly line.

0275 strain
/stréin/

1. (무리하게 사용하여 눈이나 몸을) 상하게 하다(버리다), (혹사하여 근육 등을) 다치다
- ◇ strain one's eyes 눈을 상하다 / strain a muscle 근육을 다치다
- Stress can strain the heart.

2. (세게) 잡아당기다
- ⓤ strain at sth ~을 잡아당기다
- He **strained at** the rope.

0276 vow
/váu/

맹세하다, 약속하다
- ⓤ vow that S주어 V동사 ~을 맹세하다 / vow to do sth ~하겠다고 다짐하다 (맹세하다)
- He **vowed** never **to** be late.

▶ vow (명사) 맹세

S promise, take / swear an oath 맹세하다

S oath

adjective 형용사

0277 actual
/ǽktʃuəl/

(기대하거나, 계획된 또는 보통 우리가 알고 있는 것과 다른) 실제의
- However, the author did not take into account the actual size of the Celtic population.

S real, true

▶ actually (부사) (사람들이 보통 생각하는 것과 달리) 실제로
- He is actually a very good father.

S really, in fact

0278 awful
/ɔ́ːfl/

끔직한
- During the Industrial Revolution, factory workers faced awful working conditions.

S terrible, dreadful

0279 cautious
/kɔ́ːʃəs/
/코*셔스/

(태도 등이) 신중한, 조심하는
- ⓤ cautious about sth ~에 대해 조심하는
- Parents should tell their children to be **cautious about** something dangerous like crossing a busy road.

S prudent, careful
A heedless 조심성 없는

0273 나는 그녀를 알아볼 수 있었는데 왜냐하면 그녀는 항상 같은 스타일의 옷을 입기 때문이다. / 미국은 그 군사 정부를 인정하지 않았다. 0274 처음에 그는 그녀의 팔을 부드럽게 만졌지만, 나중에 그는 그녀의 팔을 거칠게 잡았다. / 그 단체가 아프가니스탄에서 권력을 장악했기 때문에, 재개된 폭탄 위협에 대한 우려가 높아지고 있다. / 랜섬 올즈는 조립 라인을 도입함으로써 자동차 시장에서 주도권을 잡을 수 있었다. 0275 스트레스는 심장을 상하게 할 수 있다. / 그는 밧줄을 잡아당겼다. 0276 그는 절대로 늦지 않겠다고 맹세했다. 0277 그러나 저자는 켈트족의 인구의 실제 크기를 고려하지 않았다. / 그는 실제 매우 좋은 아버지이다. 0278 산업 혁명 동안 공장 노동자들은 끔찍한 노동 조건에 직면했다. 0279 부모들은 그들의 자녀들에게 혼잡한 도로를 건너는 것과 같은 뭔가 위험한 것에 대해 조심해야 한다고 말해야 한다.

0280 efficient
/ifíʃənt/

효율적인 시간, 돈, 또는 에너지를 낭비하지 않는, **유능한** 뭔가 일을 빨리 처리하는
◇ fuel-efficient cars 연료 효율이 높은 차들
○ He is highly efficient.
○ Free riding makes it more difficult for the group to produce efficient results.

A inefficient비효율적인

0281 fractious
/frǽkʃəs/
/프렉*셔스/

짜증을 잘 내는, 성을 잘 내는
○ Stressful situations can cause people to be more fractious than usual.

S irritable, easily annoyed

0282 imprecise
/imprisáis/
/임*프리사이스/

부정확한
○ All the data are imprecise.

S inaccurate, inexact, indefinite
A precise정확한

0283 improbable
/imprábəbl/
/임*프라버블/

~일 것 같지 않은, 개연성이 없는
○ It seems improbable that young people will hurt themselves when exercising.

S unlikely
A probable개연성이 있는, likely있을 법한

0284 keen
/kíːn/

1. 아주 ~하고 싶어하는
○ Many Korean students are keen to study abroad.

S eager, enthusiastic

2. 강한, 치열한
◇ keen competition 치열한 경쟁
○ Competition for jobs has become keener. So many people are now struggling to find a job.

S intense, fierce

3. 매우 좋아하는, 관심이 많은
ⓤ
① take a keen interest in sth ~에 강한 관심이 있다
② keen on sth ~에 관심이 많은
○ My dad is **keen on** playing golf.

▶ keenly (부사) 치열하게

0285 perceptible
/pərséptəbl/

지각할 수 있는, 감지(인지)할 수 있는
○ He has an accent but it is barely perceptible.

▶ perceptibly (부사) 알아차릴 정도로

S noticeable

S noticeably
A imperceptibly알아차릴 수 없게

0286 rigid
/rídʒid/
/리쥐드/

1. (규칙이나 방법 등이) 엄격한
◇ rigid discipline 엄격한 규율
○ In the past, strict social order and rigid social rules determined people's place in society.

S inflexible
A flexible유연한

2. 구부러지지 않는, 움직이지 않는, 경직된
○ He started to sob uncontrollably but he kept his body rigid.

S stiff
A flexible유연한

▶ rigidly (부사) 엄격하게

0287 sequential
/sikwénʃəl/
/시*퀜*셜/

순차적인 잇따라 일어나는
○ The project should be completed in a series of sequential steps.

▶ sequentially (부사) 순차적으로

0288 supposed
/səpóuzd/
/서*포우즈드/

1. ~하기로 되어 있는, ~해야 하는
ⓤ
① be supposed to do sth ~하기로 되어 있다, ~해야 한다
- I **was supposed to** come with my girlfriend, but she just hurt her back.
- I**'m supposed to** do all my homework before I go out to play.

② be not supposed to do sth ~해서는 안 된다
- Students **are not supposed to** be enrolled in more than one institution simultaneously.

2. 일반적으로 ~라고 믿어지는
ⓤ be supposed to do sth ~라고 한다, ~인 것으로 여겨진다
- The Galaxy Note 10 battery **is supposed to** last longer than any other battery made by Samsung.

S be expected to do sth
S be not allowed to do sth
S be said to do sth

0289 tender
/téndər/

1. 다정한, 친절한
◇ a tender smile 다정한 미소

2. (고기 등이) 부드러운
- The outside was so crispy, and the inside was so tender.

3. 어린
- He died at the tender age of 16.

S gentle, kind
A tough질긴

0290 wary
/wéri/
/웨리/

경계하는, 조심 하는
ⓤ wary of / about sth ~을 조심(경계)하는
- Although the idea that schools should teach children to be rude to strangers seems crazy at first, it is highly plausible because young children must learn to be **wary of** strangers.

S cautious, leery

adverb 부사

0291 apart
/əpáːrt/

1. 떨어져서
- I think young people who graduate from college should live apart from their parents.

2. 사이(간격)를 두고
- A big earthquake was followed by smaller earthquakes an hour apart.

N set sb/sth apart ~을 다르게(특별하게) 만들다
- A cheetah's ability to run so fast sets it apart from other animals.

A together같이, 함께

0292 meanwhile
/míːnwàil/

1. 그러는 동안에
- I was getting home from my nightshift. Meanwhile, my wife was going to work.

2. 한편
- It is winter in the northern hemisphere. Meanwhile, in the southern hemisphere it is summer.

S meantime, in the meantime

0293 thus
/ðʌs/

그러므로, 따라서
- Decaying wood leaves essential nutrients in the soil, thus resulting in new trees growing well.

S consequently

0294 none other than
/nʌn ʌðər ðən/

다름 아닌 바로 ~인 (사람이나 사물의 이름을 강조할 때 쓰임)
- The woman he is engaged to is none other than the movie star Kim.

S no other than

0288 내 여자친구와 같이 오려고 했는데 그녀가 좀 전에 허리를 다쳤다. / 나는 놀러 나가기 전에 모든 숙제를 해야 한다. / 학생들은 한 개 이상의 기관에 동시에 등록해서는 안 된다. / 갤럭시 노트 10의 베터리는 삼성이 만든 다른 어떤 배터리보다 더 오래간다고 한다. 0289 겉은 아주 바삭하고 안은 아주 부드러웠다. / 그는 16세의 어린 나이에 죽었다. 0290 비록 학교가 학생들에게 낯선 사람에게는 무례하도록 가르쳐야 한다는 생각이 처음엔 미친 것처럼 보이지만, 그것은 매우 그럴 듯 한데 어린 아이들은 낯선 사람들을 경계하는 법을 배워야 하기 때문이다. 0291 나는 대학을 졸업한 젊은 사람들은 부모님과 떨어져서 살아야 한다고 생각한다. / 큰 지진이 있고 나서 바로 한 시간 간격으로 더 작은 지진들이 일어났다. / 치타의 매우 빠르게 달릴 수 있는 능력은 치타를 다른 동물들과 다르게 만든다. 0292 나는 야간 근무를 마치고 귀가하고 있었다. 그러는 동안에 아내는 출근하고 있었다. / 북반부는 겨울이다. 한편 남반구는 여름이다. 0293 썩는 나무는 필수적인 영양분을 토양에 남기는데, (이것은) 따라서 새로운 나무들이 잘 자라는 결과를 가져온다. 0294 그가 약혼한 여자가 다름 아닌 바로 영화배우 김이다.

DAY 07

ANGRY ENGLISH
ACADEMIC VOCABULARY

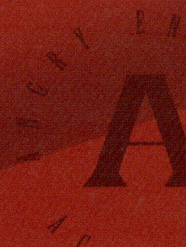

noun 명사

- ☐ advantage
- ☐ case
- ☐ dream
- ☐ extent
- ☐ force
- ☐ incidence
- ☐ malady
- ☐ parity
- ☐ reach
- ☐ span
- ☐ success
- ☐ tip
- ☐ velocity

verb 동사

- ☐ accommodate
- ☐ apply
- ☐ bother
- ☐ cause
- ☐ come across
- ☐ convey
- ☐ defer
- ☐ discard
- ☐ eliminate
- ☐ erase
- ☐ gear
- ☐ improve
- ☐ operate
- ☐ pledge
- ☐ redress
- ☐ risk
- ☐ serve
- ☐ tear

adjective 형용사

- ☐ acute
- ☐ ceaseless
- ☐ concerned
- ☐ consecutive
- ☐ discrete
- ☐ eminent
- ☐ fit
- ☐ improvised
- ☐ intent
- ☐ major
- ☐ perennial
- ☐ programmed
- ☐ robust
- ☐ severe
- ☐ superior

adverb 부사

- ☐ barely
- ☐ moreover
- ☐ usually
- ☐ nothing less than

MP3 파일 다운

noun 명사

0295 advantage
/ədvǽntidʒ/

장점, 이점
ⓤ
- have an advantage over sb/sth ~에 비해(보다) 장점을 가지고 있다 / take advantage of sb/sth ~을 이용하다
  - A four-day workweek **has** many **advantages over** a five-day workweek.

S benefit
A disadvantage 불리한 점, 약점

0296 case
/kéis/

경우, 상황
ⓤ
① in the case of sth ~의 경우
  - In my senior year in high school, I didn't study academic subjects except **in the case of** mathematics and English.

S situation, example

② sth be the case 사실이다(맞다)
  - By reading literature, adults can improve their vocabulary. But this **is** not **the case** for children. (=But this is not true for children.)
③ in case of emergency / fire 응급시 / 화재시
④ a case in point 좋은 예시
  - A friend of mine called J is **a case in point**.

S sth be true

S a good example

0297 dream
/drí:m/

1. (자면서 꾸는) 꿈
  - I had a dream about you last night.
  (=I dreamed about you last night.)

2. (장래의) 꿈
◇ fulfill a dream 꿈을 이루다
  - Being a homeowner is a staple of the American dream. *staple 주요소

▶ dream (형용사) 꿈의
  - Although he didn't do well in school, he still had hopes of getting into his dream university.

S realize a dream

0298 extent
/ikstént/

정도, 규모, 범위
◇ the extent of the damage 피해 규모
ⓤ
① to some extent 어느 정도까지 / to a large extent 상당한 정도까지(상당히)
  - I agree with you **to some extent**, but not completely.
② to such an extent that S주어 V동사 ~하는 정도까지(~할 정도로)
  - The U.S. has increased its spending on arms **to such an extent that** its military expenditure accounts for the lion's share of its annual budget. *the lion's share 가장 큰 비중
③ to the extent that S주어 V동사 ~하는 정도까지(~할 정도로)
  - **To the extent that** we can't buy any house at all, house prices in Seoul have increased.
④ to the extent of doing sth ~하는 정도까지
  - John dislikes his new school but not **to the extent of** mov**ing** to another school.
⑤ the extent to which S주어 V동사 ~하는 정도
  - Many studies show that **the extent to which** consumers can recognize a brand depends a lot on its simplicity. For example, everyone recognizes McDonalds through their famous M logo.
⑥ To what extent S주어 V동사 어느 정도까지
  - **To what extent** do you like your job?
⑦ to a lesser extent ~만큼은 크지 않지만 / to a greater extent ~보다 더 큰
  - The marine oil spill will affect Japan and, **to a lesser extent**, Korea.

S so much that S주어 V동사

0295 주 4일 근무가 주 5일 근무에 비해 많은 장점을 가지고 있다. 0296 고등학교 3학년 때, 나는 수학과 영어의 경우를 제외하곤 학과목들을 공부하지 않았다. / 문학 작품을 읽음으로써 성인들은 그들의 어휘력을 늘릴 수 있다. 하지만 이것은 아이들에게는 맞지 않는다. / J 라고 불리는 내 친구가 좋은 예시이다. 0297 나는 지난밤에 당신 꿈을 꾸었다. / 집 주인이 되는 것은 아메리칸드림의 주요소이다. / 비록 그가 학교에서 공부를 잘하지 못했지만 그는 여전히 그의 꿈의 대학에 들어가는 희망을 가지고 있었다. 0298 나는 어느 정도까지 당신에 동의하지만 완전히 동의하지는 않는다. / 미국은 연간 예산에서 국방비가 가장 큰 비중을 차지할 정도로 무기에 대한 지출을 늘렸다. / 우리가 어떠한 집도 살 수 없을 정도로 서울 집값이 올랐다. / 존은 새 학교를 싫어하지만 다른 학교로 옮길 정도는 아니다. / 여러 연구들이 소비자가 브랜드를 인지할 수 있는 정도는 단순함에 크게 좌우된다는 것을 보여 준다. 예를 들면, 모든 사람들은 맥도날드를 그들의 유명한 M로고를 통해 인지한다. / 당신은 어느 정도까지 당신의 직업을 좋아합니까? / 해양 기름 유출은 일본과 일본만큼은 크지 않지만 한국에 영향을 미칠 것이다.

0299 force
/fɔ́ːrs/

물리력, 폭력, 무력
- by force 폭력으로(힘으로), 무력으로, 강제로
- excessive force 과도한 무력 / the use of force 무력 사용
- The thief took my smartphone from me **by force**.
- In the end, the police decided to use force to stop the protests that had become violent.

0300 incidence
/ínsidəns/

(사건, 범죄, 질병 등의) 발생(률)
- a (high / low) incidence of sth (높은/낮은) 발생률의
- a low incidence of heart disease 낮은 심장병의 발생률
- Because of its violent content, the TV show caused the **incidence of crime** to increase.

S frequency, occurrence, rate

0301 malady
/mǽlədi/

1. 질병 (고어)

S illness, ailment

2. (사회의) 심각한 문제
- Even in China, income inequality is one of the maladies threatening social harmony.

S problem

0302 parity
/pǽrəti/

동등함
- parity with sb ~와 동등함
- The contract workers at IDEA are threatening to go on strike, demanding pay **parity with** the full-time workers.

S equality
A inequality 불평등

0303 reach
/ríːtʃ/

1. (손을 뻗어서 닿을 수 있는) 거리
- Keep laundry detergent out of the reach of children.

S limit 범위, range, scope

2. (영향력이나 능력의) 범위, 영향력
- This mine is beyond the reach of international law, which makes it hard to prevent reckless mining here.

0304 span
/spǽn/

1. 기간
- They have neither met nor talked over a span of five years.

S period, duration

2. 날개 길이, 폭(너비), 전장 끝에서 끝
- The bird has a large wing span.

0305 success
/səksés/

1. 성공
- success in (doing) sth ~에서의 성공
- Having a large investment of capital doesn't always guarantee a company's success.

A failure 실패

2. 성공한 것, 성공작, 성공한 사람
- a great success 대성공
- The operation to remove the cancer that he had in his jaw was a success.
(=The operation to remove the cancer that he had in his jaw was successful.)
- He thought that he was a failure as a scholar.

A failure 실패작(자)

0306 tip
/típ/

조언
- tips for / on sth ~에 대한 조언
- **Tips for** putting an end to compulsive spending include cutting up your credit cards and only buying things on your shopping list.

0307 velocity
/vəlásəti/
/벌라*서티/

속도
- wind velocity 풍속
- The wind is blowing at a velocity of 100 miles per hour.

S speed, pace

verb 동사

0308 accommodate
/əkámədeit/

(사람 등을) 수용하다, (다른 사람의 요구나 의견 등을) 받아들이다 (수용하다)
- The hotel accommodated dog owners.

S hold, house, accept

0309 apply
/əplái/

1. (법, 아이디어 등을) 적용하다
- ⓤ apply A to B: A를 B에 적용하다
- Game theory can **be applied to** many cases in real life.

2. 적용(해당)되다
- ⓤ apply to sth ~에 적용(해당)되다
- Rules about dress codes only **apply to** full-time workers during the week.

3. (페인트나 크림 등을) 바르다, 뿌리다
- They applied the liquid to their bodies to keep insects and bees away.

S rub

4. 지원(신청)하다
- ⓤ
- ① apply for a job / a scholarship 직업/장학금에 지원(신청)하다
- I'm going to **apply for** a patent on my invention to prevent someone from stealing my idea.
- ② apply to 장소 ~에 지원하다
- I **applied to** Harvard University.

N apply one's / the brakes 브레이크를 밟다

0310 bother
/báðər/

1. 신경 쓰이게 하다, 괴롭히다
- The thing that bothers me most is my son's test scores.

S worry, upset

2. 귀찮게 하다, 방해하다
- Jun, don't bother your brother while he's working with the tutor.
- Sorry to bother you.

S annoy, irritate, interrupt

3. 일부러 ~하다, 애쓰다 (주로 부정문과 의문문에서 사용)
- ⓤ don't bother to do or Ving동사 일부러 ~하지 않는다, 애써(굳이)~하지 않다
- Why bother learning to cook if you don't dream of becoming a chef?
- He **didn't** even **bother to** hide his face.

0311 cause
/kɔ́:z/

야기하다, 일으키다, 초래하다
- Scientists have long wondered what caused the Industrial Revolution in England.

S give rise to

0312 come across
/kʌm əkrɑ́:s/

1. 우연히 발견하다, 우연히 만나다
- He hurried to crumple up a photo of his ex when he came across it in a book.

S encounter

2. 이해되다
- His explanation of why the nuclear arms race should be stopped came across loud and clear. *loud and clear 명료하고 쉽게

0308 그 호텔은 개 주인들을 수용했다. 0309 게임 이론은 실생활의 많은 경우에 적용될 수 있다. / 복장 규정에 관한 규칙은 주중에 정규직 근로자에게만 적용된다. / 그들은 벌레와 벌들을 쫓아내기 위해 그 액체를 그들의 몸에 발랐다. / 나는 누군가가 내 아이디어를 훔치는 것을 막기 위해 내 발명품에 특허를 신청할 것이다. / 나는 하버드 대학에 지원했다. 0310 나를 가장 괴롭히는 것은 내 아들의 시험 성적이다. / 준, 형 과외 선생님이랑 공부하는 동안 귀찮게 하지 마라. / 방해해서 미안합니다. / 주방장이 될 꿈이 없다면 왜 굳이 요리하는 것을 배우는가? / 그는 심지어 애써 얼굴을 숨기진 않았다. 0311 과학자들은 무엇이 영국에서 산업 혁명을 일으켰는지 오랫동안 궁금해했다. 0312 그는 책에서 우연히 옛 애인의 사진을 발견했을 때 서둘러 그것을 구겨 버렸다. / 왜 핵무기 경쟁이 중단되어야 하는지에 대한 그의 설명은 명료하고 쉽게 이해되었다.

0313
convey
/kənvéi/

1. (생각이나 감정 등) 전달하다
   - Pictures help explain information to readers that is too complicated to convey in written form.

   S communicate, impart

2. 나르다, 운반하다
   - convey sth from A to B: ~을 A에서 B로 가져가다
   - They will **convey** your luggage **from** the hotel **to** the airport.

   S transport, carry

0314
defer
/difə́:r/

연기하다
- While young men whose parents were rich deferred military enlistment, poor young people were drafted into the army. *military enlistment 군(대) 입대 / be drafted into the army 군대에 징집되다

S postpone, procrastinate, put off

0315
discard
/diskɑ́:rd/

버리다
- Discarded waste is buried deep underground. *deep underground 땅속 깊이

S abandon, throw away

0316
eliminate
/ilímineìt/
/일리미*네이트/

제거하다
- It is important to develop ways to eliminate corn rootworms that are resistant to pesticides.

S remove, stamp out, weed out

0317
erase
/iréis/

(생각, 감정, 또는 기록된 것 등을) 지우다
- His intervention in the case gave the suspect a golden opportunity to erase all the decisive evidence on his computer and phone.

S delete, wipe out, remove

0318
gear
/gíər/

1. 맞게 조정하다(맞추다), 적응시키다, 적합하게 하다
   - gear A to B: A를 B에 맞추다 / A be geared to B: A는 B에 맞게 조정되다
   - They **geared** the course **to** children preparing for the SAT.
   (=The course **is geared to** children preparing for the SAT.)

0319
improve
/imprú:v/

향상시키다; 개선되다, 나아지다
- Ireland's economy improved while he was president.

S enhance

0320
operate
/ɑ́pəreit/
/아퍼*레이트/

1. (사업이나 기관 등을) 운영하다
   - In England before the Industrial Revolution in the late 18th century, goods such as cloth and thread had been produced manually by small-scale cottage industries, which operated mainly out of homes and small workshops.

2. 작동시키다; 작동하다, 움직이다
   ◇ a remotely operated vehicle 원격 조정 차량 / a remotely operated rifle 수동으로 작동되는 소총
   - The cost of operating a hydroelectric dam is very low, compared to the cost of operating traditional power plants that have to burn fossil fuels.

   S function, work

0321
pledge
/pléʤ/
/플레쥐/

맹세하다, 약속하다
① pledge A to B: A를 B에게 (주겠다고) 약속하다
   - She **pledged** her entire estate **to** the university.
② pledge to do sth ~하겠다고 약속하다
   - The candidate **pledged to** give the support fund to all citizens.

S promise, vow

▶ pledge (명사) 약속, 맹세, 서약
   make / take a pledge to do sth ~을 하겠다고 약속(맹세)하다

S promise, oath, vow

0322
redress
/rídres/

(잘못 된 것을) 바로잡다, 시정하다, 교정하다
- However, since the problems are a result of human activity, they are not difficult to redress.

S correct, compensate

0323
risk
/rísk/

~의 위험을 무릅쓰다
ⓥ risk doing sth ~하는 위험을 무릅쓰다
- If you want to make money in the stock market you should be willing to **risk** los**ing** money.

S venture

0324
serve
/sə́:rv/

1. 쓸모 있다, 도움이 되다, 기여(공헌)하다, 제공하다
ⓥ
① serve as sth ~로 쓸 수 있다
- This sofa can **serve as** a bed.
② serve a purpose / function 목적/기능을 제공하다
- This jacket **serves a** dual **purpose**.
(=This jacket serves two purposes.)
③ serve to do sth ~하는 데 도움이 되다, ~에 공헌(기여)하다
- His endeavor **served to** popularize reggae music. *popularize 대중화하다

2. 복역하다, 복무하다
- The executive director was sentenced to serve three years in prison for stealing money from the company.
- James Cho served as a sergeant in the Korean army for 5 years.

3. (음식이나 음료 등을) 제공하다
- Fish and chips are a traditional English dish served with drinks.

0325
tear
/téər/
/테어/
*tear-tore-torn

1. 찢다
ⓥ
① tear open sth 찢어서 열다 / tear off sth 찢어서 떼어 내다
- He **tore open** a corner of the coffee packet.
② tear sth apart (1) 갈기갈기 찢다 (2) (나라 또는 가족 등을) 분열시키다
- A pack of wolves **tore** a zebra **apart** violently.
- More than 60,000 families **were torn apart** by the Korean War.
③ be torn between A and B ~사이에서 망설이다
- I'**m torn between** the red one **and** the blue one.

2. 구멍을 내다
- If a hole is torn in the tent, use the repair kit to fix it.

▶ tear (명사) 눈물
◇ burst into tears 갑자기 울음을 터뜨리다
- I saw tears in Mom's eyes.

S rip

adjective 형용사

0326
acute
/əkjúːt/

1. (상황이나 문제 등이) 심각한
- One acute issue for the Everglades, a large area of wetlands, is invasive species: plants and animals introduced from other parts of the world.

S severe, serious

2. 예민한, 날카로운, 예리한
- Dogs have an acute sense of smell.
- His argument is just hypothetical, but his academic paper containing it presents an acute analysis of the economic situation.

S keen

0327 ceaseless
/síːsləs/

끊임없는
◇ ceaseless outbreaks of war 끊임없는 전쟁 발발
○ I had to call the police on my neighbor because of his ceaseless troublemaking. *call the police on sb ~을 경찰에 신고하다

▶ ceaselessly (부사) 끊임없이
○ She talks ceaselessly.

S incessant, constant

0328 concerned
/kənsə́ːrnd/
/컨선드/

1. 걱정하는
ⓤ
① concerned about sth ~에 대해 걱정하는
② be concerned that S주어 V동사 ~을 걱정하다
○ People **are concerned that** the gap between the rich and the poor is widening.

2. 관련된
ⓤ concerned with / in sth ~와 관련이 있는
○ Cultural anthropology is **concerned with** the study of different cultures around the world.

3. 관심을 가진
ⓤ concerned with sth ~에 관심을 가진
○ Young voters are increasingly **concerned with** the global economy.

N
1. as far as I'm concerned 내가 보기에는
2. as far as sth be concerned ~과 관련해서는, ~에 관한 한
○ As far as other costs spent on hydroelectric dams are concerned, the dams are not cost-effective.

S worried
S worried about sth
S be worried that S주어 V동사

S interested in sth

0329 consecutive
/kənsékjutiv/

(숫자 등이) 연이은, 잇따른
◇ consecutive holidays 연휴 / successive defeat / victory 연이은 패배/승리
○ The team suffered four consecutive defeats.
○ The economy has been growing for three successive years.

N serial (형용사) 연쇄적인, 연재되는
◇ serial killings 연쇄 살인 / a serial novel 연재소설

S successive

0330 discrete
/diskríːt/

분리된, 별개의, 독립된
○ After the company collapsed it was divided into discrete units and sold off piece by piece.

S separate, independent

0331 eminent
/émɪnənt/

저명한
○ Jeremy Irons, an eminent scientist and professor, allocates most of his time to meetings with his students which take place twice a week.

S prominent

0332 fit
/fít/

적합한
ⓤ be fit for sth ~에 적합하다 / be fit to do sth ~하기에 적합하다
◇ organisms less fit to survive 생존에 덜 적합한 생물
○ The patient **is** not **fit to** drive.

S suitable
A unfit 부적합한

0333 improvised
/ímprəvàizd/

임시방편의, (연주나 연설 등의) 즉흥의
◇ an improvised speech 즉흥 연설
○ Today, I'll be teaching you how to build improvised shelters out of natural resources like bamboo.

0334
intent
/intént/

몰두(열중)하고 있는, 단호한
- intent on / upon sth ~하기로 결심한
- The president is **intent on** curbing soaring housing prices.

▶ intently (부사) 집중하여, 열심히
- He listened intently to what I said.

[S] determined to do sth

0335
major
/méidʒər/

중요한
- One of the major concerns that teens have is physical appearance.

[S] significant, vital, principal
[A] minor 사소한

0336
perennial
/pəréniəl/

(오랫동안) 지속되는, (계속) 반복되는
- Infectious diseases are a perennial threat to humans.

[S] continuing, recurrent

0337
programmed
/próugræmd/

계획된
- programmed for sth ~을 위해 계획된
- My computer is **programmed for** my work only.

[S] planned

0338
robust
/roubʌ́st/
/로우*버스트/

강한, (체제나 조직이) 튼튼한
◇ a robust economy 튼튼한 경제
- The president dipped himself in the icy waters to create an image of himself as a robust man, but he later died of a heart attack.

▶ robustly (부사) 튼튼하게

[S] sturdy

0339
severe
/sivíər/
/시비어/

1. 심각한, 심한
◇ severe damage 심각한 피해 / severe drought 심한 가뭄
- His injury was not very severe.
- Severe drought is not the only possible explanation for the fall of the Akkadian Empire.

2. (처벌이나 비평 등이) 가혹한, 혹독한
◇ severe punishment 가혹한 처벌 / severe criticism 혹독한 비평
- Last year, the government of Seoul, the capital city of my country, imposed a severe penalty on the electronics company SamG, for disposing of toxic chemicals into the river.

3. 엄한, 엄격한
◇ a severe look 엄한 표정 / in a severe voice 엄한 목소리로

▶ severity (명사) 가혹함, 심함

[S] extreme, serious

[S] harsh

[S] harshness

0340
superior
/supíəriər/
/수피*리어/

1. 우수한, 우월한, 더 나은
- superior to sth ~보다 더 나은
- The company is **superior to** its competitors in the same industry.

2. (지위가) 높은, 상급의
◇ superior officer 상관

▶ superiority (명사) 우월함

[S] better
[A] inferior 열등한, 열악한

[S] higher in rank, senior

adverb 부사

0341 barely
/bέəli/
/베얼리/

1. 겨우, 간신히, 가까스로
- could barely V동사 간신히 ~할 수 있었다
- He was barely 16 when his mother remarried.
- I **could barely** understand what she said.

[S] only just 겨우

2. 거의 ~않다
- barely audible / perceptible / visible 거의 들리지 않는/거의 인지할 수 없는/거의 보이지 않는
- He has an accent but it is **barely perceptible**.

[S] hardly

0342 moreover
/mɔːróuvər/

게다가
- Moreover, it is better to have a dress code because wearing the same clothes makes people look professional.

[S] in addition, what's more

0343 usually
/júːʒuəli/

대개, 보통
- I usually go to bed at midnight.

[S] more often than not

0344 nothing less than
/nʌθiŋ les ðən/

(다름 아닌) 바로, 그야말로 (내용을 강조할 때 사용)
- His election as president was nothing less than a disaster for the country.

0341 그의 어머니가 재혼을 하였을 때 그는 겨우 16살이었다. / 나는 그녀가 말한 것을 간신히 이해할 수 있었다. / 그는 억양이 있지만 그것은 거의 인지할 수 없을 정도이다. 0342 게다가, 같은 옷을 입는 것은 사람들을 전문적으로 보이기 만들기 때문에 복장 규정을 두는 것이 좋다. 0343 나는 보통 자정에 잔다. 0344 대통령으로서 그의 당선은 그야말로 그 나라의 재앙이었다.

DAY 08
ANGRY ENGLISH
ACADEMIC VOCABULARY

noun 명사
- [ ] apex
- [ ] bulb
- [ ] complex
- [ ] domain
- [ ] flake
- [ ] impact
- [ ] occasion
- [ ] practice
- [ ] realm
- [ ] rye
- [ ] solution
- [ ] trace
- [ ] vessel

verb 동사
- [ ] acknowledge
- [ ] assert
- [ ] bolster
- [ ] caution
- [ ] combine
- [ ] convince
- [ ] define
- [ ] discharge
- [ ] elongate
- [ ] equip
- [ ] feed
- [ ] incorporate
- [ ] occur
- [ ] precede
- [ ] reduce
- [ ] shatter
- [ ] stress
- [ ] vent

adjective 형용사
- [ ] aggressive
- [ ] bountiful
- [ ] central
- [ ] fiery
- [ ] gratifying
- [ ] inactive
- [ ] intolerable
- [ ] magnificent
- [ ] periodic
- [ ] routine
- [ ] sheer
- [ ] superficial
- [ ] tentative
- [ ] weak

adverb 부사
- [ ] candidly
- [ ] normally
- [ ] wholly
- [ ] nothing more than

MP3 파일 다운

noun
명사

0345 apex /éipeks/
꼭대기, 정상, 정점
- Each weekend, my aunt and uncle like to climb to the apex of a mountain.

S peak, culmination, height

0346 bulb /bʌ́lb/
1. 전구
- Edison is said to have failed 10,000 times before inventing the light bulb.

2. 구근 양파같이 생긴 꽃과 식물의 뿌리
- Feeling that tulip bulbs were a good investment, many people began to speculate in these flowers.

0347 complex /kámpleks/ /캄*플렉스/
(대형) 단지 비슷한 모양을 가지고 있는 집이나 건물들이 모여 있는 곳
◇ a housing complex 주택 단지 / an apartment complex 아파트 단지
- A new government office complex will be built on this site next year.

▶ complex (형용사) 복잡한

0348 domain /douméin/
영역, 분야
ⓒ within / outside the domain of sth ~의 영역 안에/밖에
- Many people say that medicine should be kept **outside the domain of** religion.

0349 flake /fléik/
(얇은) 조각
◇ flakes of snow 눈송이 / cornflakes 콘플레이크
- You can also put dried onion flakes in soups instead of fresh onions.

S chip, bit

0350 impact /ímpækt/
1. 충격, 충돌
- The crater was made by the impact of a meteorite.
- The bumper absorbs the impact of a car crash.

S collision

2. (강력한) 영향
ⓒ have an impact on sb/sth ~에 영향을 미치다
- It is incorrect to say that new species **have** little or no **impact on** native species in many regions of the world where they have been introduced.

S effect, influence

0351 occasion /əkéiʒən/
1. 경우, 때(시간)
ⓒ on this / that occasion 이/그 경우 / on several occasions 여러 번 / an occasion when S주어 V동사 ~한 경우
- On one occasion, I didn't get paid.

2. 중요 행사
◇ special occasions 특별 행사
- The hotel is notorious for catering at various occasions such as weddings; they sometimes serve live insects.

S event

▶
1. occasional (형용사) 가끔의
2. occasionally (부사) 가끔

0345 매주 우리 숙모와 삼촌은 산의 정상에 오르는 것을 좋아한다. 0346 에디슨은 전구를 발명하기 전에 만 번이나 실패했다고 한다. / 튤립 구근이 좋은 투자재라고 느끼면서 많은 사람들이 이 꽃에 투기하기 시작했다. 0347 신규 정부 사무실 단지가 내년에 이 지역에 건설될 것이다. 0348 많은 사람들은 의학은 종교의 영역 밖에 있어야 한다고 말한다. 0349 당신은 역시 신선한 양파 대신 수프에 마른 양파 조각도 넣을 수 있다. 0350 그 분화구는 한 운석의 충돌에 의해 만들어졌다. / 그 범퍼는 자동차 사고의 충격을 흡수한다. / 신종이 그들이 도입된 세계의 많은 지역에 있는 토착종에 영향을 미치지 않는다거나 거의 영향을 미치지 않는다고 말하는 것은 틀리다. 0351 한 번은 월급을 못 받았다. / 그 호텔은 결혼식 같은 다양한 행사에서 음식을 제공하는 것으로 악명 높다; 그들은 가끔 살아 있는 곤충을 제공한다.

0352
practice
/prǽktis/

1. 연습 [S] exercise, drill 연습, 훈련
- ◇ hockey practices 하키 연습들
- ○ I need to get some practice.
- ○ It takes a lot of practice to play ice hockey well.

2. 실행
- ⓤ put sth into practice ~을 실행에 옮기다
- ○ You are good at giving advice to other people, but you don't **put** that advice **into practice** yourself.

3. 습관, 관습(관행)
- ⓤ the practice of doing sth ~하는 습관(관행) / it's common practice to do sth ~하는 것은 관행이다
- ○ **It's common practice to** give a favorable judgment to defense lawyers who have recently resigned from the prosecution.

0353
realm
/rélm/
/렐엄/

1. 관심 분야, 활동 분야, 영역 [S] field
- ⓤ in the realm of sth ~의 분야(영역)에서
- ○ This book is **in the realm of** science fiction.

2. 왕국 [S] kingdom

0354
rye
/rái/

호밀
- ○ The Catcher in the Rye is a semi-autobiographical novel by J.D. Salinger.

- Ⓝ types of grains
- ▪ oats 귀리 / barley 보리 / maize 옥수수 (=corn) / wheat 밀 / turnip 순무 / beet 비트

0355
solution
/səlúːʃən/
/설루션/

1. 해결책
- ⓤ a solution to / for sth ~에 대한 해결책
- ○ Genetically modified trees could be **a solution for** meeting the increasing demand for timber.

2. (문제의) 정답
- ⓤ the solution to a problem 질문의 답
- ◇ the solution to last week's quiz 지난주 퀴즈 정답

3. 용액 두 종류 이상의 물질이 고르게 섞인 혼합물 [S] mixture
- ◇ nutrient solutions 영양액(배양액)
- ○ Nutrient solutions for plant growth are categorized as synthetic and organic.

0356
trace
/tréis/

흔적, 자취 [S] mark, sign
- ⓤ traces of sth ~의 흔적, 자취 / disappear without (a) trace 흔적없이 사라지다
- ○ The stone buildings called the great houses contain no **traces of** maize or maize containers.

0357
vessel
/vésl/
/베슬/

1. 큰 배, 선박
- ◇ a cargo vessel 화물선 / a fishing vessel 어선
- ○ Sonar equipment is used by naval vessels.

2. (물 담는) 그릇
- ◇ earthenware vessels 항아리
- ○ Native Americans molded vessels and other objects out of clay.

3. 혈관
- ◇ blood vessels 혈관

- Ⓝ vassal (명사) (중세의) 가신

verb 동사

0358 acknowledge
/əknálidʒ/ or /æknálidʒ/
/액날리지/

1. (사실로) 인정하다
  ◦ Even though the lecturer acknowledges that menhaden are an important source of protein for livestock, he argues that there is another important source of protein, soybeans.

2. (권위나 자격 등을) 인정하다
  ⓤ be (widely) acknowledged as / to be ~인 것으로 (널리) 인정받다
  ◦ He **is** widely **acknowledged as** the best hockey player ever.

[S] admit, recognize, accept

[S] recognize

0359 assert
/əsə́ːrt/

주장(단언)하다
  ⓤ assert that S주어 V동사 ~을 주장하다
  ◦ He **asserts that** a group of terrorists put bombs in a bar.

▶ assertion (명사) 주장

[S] affirm, predicate, declare선언하다

0360 bolster
/bóulstər/
/보울*스터/

강화하다, 개선하다
  ◦ The government bolstered the car industry with tax policies.

[S] boost, support, improve

0361 caution
/kɔ́ːʃən/

경고하다
  ⓤ
  ① caution A against / about B: A에게 B에 대해 경고하다
  ② caution sb to do sth ~에게 ~하라고 경고하다
  ◦ Pizarro demanded that a room be filled with gold in exchange for Atahualpa's release. No one had **cautioned** Atahualpa **against** the Spaniards.

[S] warn, alert

[S] warn A of B, alert A to B

0362 combine
/kəmbáin/

결합시키다; 결합되다
  ◦ When combined physically with other substances, aluminum becomes stronger.
  ◦ Uranium combines vigorously with oxygen.

[N] combined with sth ~과 결합된

[S] mix, alloy, joint

[S] coupled with sth

0363 convince
/kənvíns/

설득하다, 납득시키다
  ⓤ convince A of B: A에게 B를 납득시키다 / convince sb that S주어 V동사 ~에게 ~을 설득시키다 / convince sb to do sth ~에게 ~하도록 납득시키다
  ◦ It's difficult to **convince** him **to** change his mind.

[S] persuade

0364 define
/difáin/

1. 규정하다, 밝히다
  ◦ It's hard to define the duties of the government.

2. (단어 뜻을) 정의하다
  ⓤ define A as B: A를 B로 정의하다
  ◦ The term "debris flow" is hard to define.
  ◦ The term "debris flow" **is defined as** a fast-moving landslide.

▶ definition (명사) 정의

0365
discharge
/dístʃá:rdʒ/

1. 퇴원시키다, 제대시키다, 석방하다
   - ⓥ discharge sb from sth ~에서 ~을 퇴원(제대)시키다/석방하다
   - He pretended to be sick to **be discharged from** the army.

2. (기체나 액체 등을) 방출하다
   - The drinking water is contaminated by toxic substances that factories discharge illegally into the river.

[s] send out

0366
elongate
/iló:ŋgeit/
/일롱*게이트/

길게 하다; 길어지다(길게 되다)
- Trees store food in their elongated roots.

▶ elongated (형용사) 가늘고 긴, 길쭉한
- Baguettes are elongated sticks of bread.

[s] become longer, lengthen

0367
equip
/ikwíp/

(장비 등을) 제공하다
- ⓥ be equipped with sth (장비 등을) 갖추고 있다
- The aircraft carrier **is equipped with** a system to defend against enemy planes and missiles.

[s] supply, provide

0368
feed
/fí:d/

1. 먹이를 주다
   - ⓥ feed A B / feed B to A : A에게 B를 먹이다
   - Farmers **feed** menhaden **to** livestock.
   - Feed the kids first.

2. (동물들이 먹이를) 먹다
   - Bats feed at night.

3. 먹여 살리다
   - I have 5 people to feed on my own.

0369
incorporate
/inkó:rpərèit/
/인코퍼*레이트/

1. 포함시키다
   - ⓥ incorporate A in / into B: A를 B에 포함시키다
   - The surrounding towns **were incorporated into** the city.

2. 법인으로 만들다
   - In an attempt to evade taxes, the company was incorporated in 1988.

▶ incorporated (형용사) 일부분이 된, 법인의
◇ Mastercard Incorporated (=Mastercard Inc.) 마스터카드 (법인) 주식회사

[s] include

0370
occur
/əkó:r/
/어커/

발생하다
- Economic bubbles often occur, so many countries try hard to prevent this type of economic crisis.

[s] happen, transpire, break out
((전쟁 또는 질병 등이) 발발(발생)하다)

0371
precede
/prisí:d/
/프리*시드/

앞서다, 선행하다, ~보다 먼저(전에) 일어나다
- ⓥ A be preceded by B: A전에 (바로) B가 있다
- ◇ the musicians who preceded him 그 보다 앞서 간 (선배) 음악가들
- His speech (11:00 a.m.) will precede lunch (12:00 p.m.).
- Lunch (12:00 p.m.) will **be preceded by** his speech (11:00 a.m.).
- Lunch (12:00 p.m.) will follow his speech (11:00 a.m.).
- His speech (11:00 a.m.) will be followed by lunch (12:00 p.m.).

[N] proceed (동사) 계속해서 ~하다
- ⓥ proceed to do sth 계속해서 ~하다

[s] happen before
[A] follow~후에 일어나다

[s] go on
[s] go on to do sth

0372 reduce
/ridúːs/

줄이다
- The Virginian government has decided to reduce the menhaden catch limit.

S cut

0373 shatter
/ʃǽtər/
/쉐터/

박살을 내다; 박살나다(산산이 부서지다)
- He suffered severe leg injuries in a car crash. The damaged bone shattered into many pieces.
- I fell as I was carrying a glass of wine, and the glass shattered into tiny pieces.

S break into small pieces

0374 stress
/strés/

강조하다
- **U** stress that S주어 V동사 ~을 강조하다 / stress the importance of sth ~의 중요성을 강조하다
- The professor **stressed that** the government should implement the policies necessary to sustain economic growth.

- **N** cannot stress too much sth ~은(는) 아무리 강조해도 지나치지 않는다
- I can't stress too much how important having a healthy diet is.

S emphasize, underline, accentuate

0375 vent
/vént/

(액체, 기체 또는 감정 등을) 분출하다
- **U** vent A on B: A를 B에 분출하다
- Most of the high school seniors in my country are stressed about the college entrance exam. They **vent** their anger **on** their parents.

▶ vent (명사) 분출구, 배출구
◇ an outlet for sexual instincts 성적 본능의 배출구

S express, release

S outlet

adjective 형용사

0376 aggressive
/əgrésiv/

공격적인
- People like Jeff Bezos and Elon Musk were able to achieve wealth and status because of their aggressive approach to business.

S hostile, militant 호전적인
A submissive 순종(복종)하는

0377 bountiful
/báuntifl/

많은, 풍부한
- In modern times, food is bountiful. In most advanced countries, there have been no food shortages for around a century.

S plentiful, abundant, ample

0378 central
/séntrəl/

1. 중앙(중심)의
◇ Central Asia 중앙아시아
- There are many microbes that can infect the central nervous system of whales. This type of infection causes disorientation and unusual behavior.

2. (가장) 중요한, 핵심(중심)적인
- **U** central to sth ~에 중요한 / play a central role in sth ~에서 중요한 역할을 하다 / be of central importance 매우 중요하다
- I know money is **central to** our lives, but it **is** not **of central importance** in making us happy.

0379 fiery
/fáiəri/
/파이어리/

불의(불타는 듯한), (성격 등이) 불같은, 격렬한
◇ fiery temper 불같은 성격
○ When the sun set, the sky turned fiery red.
○ He participated in a fiery debate over whether humanitarian aid should be continuously sent to North Korea.

S passionate

0380 gratifying
/grǽtifàiiŋ/

기쁜, 만족스러운
○ It's gratifying to meet an old friend who you've not seen in many years.

▶ gratify (동사) 만족시키다

S pleasing, satisfying

0381 inactive
/inǽktiv/

1. 움직이지 않는, 활동하지 않는
○ It is really unhealthy for people, especially old people, to be physically inactive.

2. 사용되지 않는
◇ inactive oil wells and abandoned gas wells 사용되고 있지 않는 유정과 버려진 가스정

S motionless, still, inert
A active 활동적인

0382 intolerable
/intálərəbl/
/인*탈러*러블/

참을 수 없는, 견딜 수 없는
○ God gives humans bearable pains they can overcome. He doesn't give us intolerable ones.

▶ intolerably (부사) 참을 수 없을 정도로
◇ ache intolerably 참을 수 없을 정도로 아프다

S unbearable, unendurable

S unbearably

0383 magnificent
/mægnífisnt/
/메그*니피슨트/

매우 아름다운, 인상적인, 웅장한
○ The Grand Canyon is one of the world's most magnificent canyons.

S splendid, majestic, striking

0384 periodic
/pìriádik/
/피리*아딕/

주기적인, 반복되는
○ In the process of burning forests on a periodic basis, many animals are killed.

▶ periodically (부사) 주기적으로

S at regular intervals, repeated

0385 routine
/ru:tí:n/

정기적인
◇ a routine blood test 정기 혈액 검사
○ A routine blood test is done to check your general state of health, and a week later you'll get the test results.

▶ routinely (부사) 일상적으로, 정기적으로

S usual, standard, normal

S regularly

0386 sheer
/ʃíər/
/쉬어/

1. (크기, 양, 정도 등을 강조하여) 오로지 ~만으로
ⓤ the sheer number of sth 오로지(순전히) ~의 숫자만으로
○ The region can subsist on **the sheer number of** tourists who come to camp and enjoy water sports at the lake. *subsist 먹고 살다

2. (다른 것과 섞이지 않고 그것만을 가진) 순전한, 완전한
○ The point in the passage about trapping animals is sheer nonsense.

▶ sheer (부사) 완전히

S complete, utter

0379 해가 질 때, 하늘은 불타는 듯한 붉은색으로 변했다. / 그는 북한에 인도적 지원을 계속 보내야 하는지에 대한 격렬한 논쟁에 참여했다. 0380 수년간 당신이 보지 못했던 오랜 친구를 만나는 것은 기쁜 일이다. 0381 사람들, 특히 노인들이 신체적으로 활동하지 않는 것은 정말 건강에 좋지 않다. 0382 신은 인간에게 그들이 극복할 수 있는 견딜 수 있는 고통을 준다. 그는 우리에게 견딜 수 없는 고통은 주지 않으신다. 0383 그랜드 캐니언은 세계에서 가장 웅장한 협곡들 중에 하나이다. 0384 주기적으로 숲을 태우는 과정에서 많은 동물들이 죽는다. 0385 당신의 전반적인 건강 상태를 체크하기 위해 정기 혈액 검사를 하고 일주일 후에 당신은 검사 결과를 받을 것이다. 0386 그 지역은 오로지 그 호수에서 캠핑하고 수상 스포츠를 즐기러 오는 관광객의 숫자만으로도 먹고 살 수 있다. / 동물들을 가두는 것에 관한 지문에서의 주장은 완전한 난센스이다.

0387 superficial
/sùːpərfíʃəl/
/수퍼*피셜/

외관상의, 피상적인 주의 깊게 보지 않고 눈에 띄는 것만 보는
- Although there are superficial similarities between the two genres, they are fundamentally different.

▶ superficially (부사) 피상적으로 깊이 생각하지 않고
- He answered the question superficially.

0388 tentative
/téntətiv/
/텐터*티브/

잠정적인, 임시의, 시험적인
◇ tentative plans 잠정 계획
- Two tentative conclusions were drawn from the communication between management and employees.

▶ tentatively (부사) 잠정적으로, 시험 삼아
◇ ask tentatively 시험 삼아 물어보다

[S] provisional, unconfirmed, indefinite
[A] definite 확정된

0389 weak
/wíːk/

1. 약한
- For instance, a lion simply follows a flock of zebras until a weak zebra falls behind the flock, and then catches it.

2. 약한 능숙하지 못한
- She's weak in mathematics.

[S] fragile

adverb 부사

0390 candidly
/kǽndidli/

솔직히
- He candidly acknowledged that he had lied about his age.

▶ candid (형용사) 솔직한
ⓒ candid about sth ~에 대해 솔직한 / candid with sb ~에게 솔직한

[S] honestly, frankly
[S] frank, honest

0391 normally
/nɔ́ːrməli/

1. 보통, 대개
- Normally, Korean students prepare for the tests in the library.

2. 정상적으로
- The elevator works normally now.

▶ normalization (명사) 정상화
◇ a normalization of relations between the two countries 양국 사이의 관계 정상화

[S] usually, for the most part
[A] abnormally 비정상적으로

0392 wholly
/hóulli/

완전히
- Multiple important fossils have been wholly destroyed by weathering processes.

[S] completely, totally, entirely

0393 nothing more than
/nʌ́θiŋ mɔːr ðən/

~에 지나지 않는, ~에 불과한
- We're nothing more than friends.

[N] nothing less than 바로 ~인 (내용을 강조할 때 사용)
- Its mission is nothing less than to provide impartial information.

[S] only

DAY 09

ANGRY ENGLISH ACADEMIC VOCABULARY

noun 명사
- ☐ advice
- ☐ complaint
- ☐ diversion
- ☐ fun
- ☐ instrument
- ☐ intent
- ☐ lifespan
- ☐ news
- ☐ origin
- ☐ patch
- ☐ pursuit
- ☐ ramification
- ☐ scoop
- ☐ vestige

verb 동사
- ☐ act
- ☐ assign
- ☐ cast
- ☐ collide
- ☐ consent
- ☐ defy
- ☐ discount
- ☐ drive
- ☐ elude
- ☐ epitomize
- ☐ grasp
- ☐ incur
- ☐ occupy
- ☐ predominate
- ☐ refer to
- ☐ stem from
- ☐ switch
- ☐ view

adjective 형용사
- ☐ agile
- ☐ aware
- ☐ certain
- ☐ diligent
- ☐ energetic
- ☐ inadvertent
- ☐ isolated
- ☐ natural
- ☐ permanent
- ☐ prime
- ☐ seamless
- ☐ superb
- ☐ swift
- ☐ tolerant

adverb 부사
- ☐ consistently
- ☐ otherwise
- ☐ in unison
- ☐ now that

MP3 파일 다운

noun
명사

0394 advice
/ədváis/ or /ædváis/

충고 (불가산)
- Getting advice from friends who are older than you is better than getting advice from friends who are the same age.

▶
1. advisability (명사) 타당함
2. adviser (=advisor) (명사) 조언자, 고문

S tip, pointer

S consultant

0395 complaint
/kəmpléint/

1. 불평, 불만, 고소
ⓤ make a complaint to sb about sth ~에게 ~에 대해 불평하다(불만을 얘기하다) / complaints from sb ~에게서 나온 불만
◇ complaints from residents 주민들에게서 나온 불만
- I had to **make a complaint to** the police **about** my neighbors. They were making so much noise every night.

2. 질환
- I have a heart complaint, so I need to get surgery.

0396 diversion
/divə́ːrʒən/

(방향이나 사용되는 것의) 전환, 유용
- The diversion of the river Nile happens at Khartoum in Sudan.

0397 fun
/fʌ́n/

재미, 즐거움
ⓤ have fun doing sth ~하며 즐거워하다(~하면서 놀다)
- I watched a girl **have fun** play**ing** in a fountain.

▶ fun (형용사) 재미있는, 즐거운
◇ fun things 재미있는 것들 / fun activities 재미있는 활동 / have a fun time 재미있는 시간을 가지다
- For kids, it would be fun eating in the dark.

Ⓝ funny (형용사) 웃기는

S enjoyable

0398 instrument
/ínstrəmənt/

1. (과학적 또는 전문가의) 도구
◇ surgical / scientific instruments 수술/과학적 도구
- He can play different musical instruments.

2. 수단, 방법
- The central bank can use interest rates as an instrument for dealing with inflation.

S method

0399 intent
/intént/

의도
ⓤ with intent to do sth ~하려는 의도로
- She started a nonprofit organization **with** good **intent to** help the homeless.

S intention, purpose

0400 lifespan
/láifspæn/

수명
◇ the average human lifespan 인간의 평균 수명
- The lifespan of running shoes is shorter than that of walking shoes.
- Compared with walking shoes, running shoes have a limited lifespan.

S lifetime

0394 당신보다 나이가 많은 친구들에게 조언을 얻는 것이 같은 나이의 친구들에게서 조언을 얻는 것보다 더 낫다. 0395 나는 경찰에 내 이웃에 대해 불만을 얘기해야 했다. 그들은 매일 밤 너무 시끄럽게 했다. / 나는 심장 질환이 있어서 수술을 받을 필요가 있다. 0396 나일강의 전환은 수단의 카르툼에서 일어난다. 0397 나는 한 여자아이가 분수대 안에서 뛰놀며 즐거워하는 것을 바라보았다. / 아이들에게는 어두운 곳에서 먹는 것이 재미있을 것이다. 0398 그는 다양한 악기를 연주할 수 있다. / 중앙은행은 인플레이션을 다루기 위한 수단으로 이자율을 사용할 수 있다. 0399 그녀는 노숙자들을 돕기 위한 좋은 의도로 비영리 단체를 차렸다. 0400 러닝화의 수명은 워킹화의 수명보다 더 짧다. / 워킹화와 비교해서 러닝화는 제한된 수명을 가지고 있다.

0401
news
/njúːz/

소식, 뉴스
- ⓤ the news about sth ~에 관한 소식 / the news that S주어 V동사 ~라는 소식
  - Have you heard **the news about** Kevin? He's got cancer.
  - I heard about the U.S. invasion of Iraq on the news.

0402
origin
/ɔ́ːridʒin/

기원, 원인 — [s] beginning, cause
- ⓤ the origin of sth ~의 기원(원인)
- ◇ the origin(s) of the universe 우주의 기원 / the origins of the Korean War 한국전의 기원
  - They still haven't found any conclusive evidence of **the origin of** the virus.

0403
patch
/pǽtʃ/

1. (주변과 모양이 다른) 작은 부분 — [s] a small piece
- ◇ a black cat with a white patch on its chest 가슴에 흰 반점이 있는 검은 고양이

2. 작은 땅, 작은 밭
- ◇ a cabbage patch 배추밭
  - There is a small patch of grass behind my apartment building where I like to go and sit on warm, sunny days.

3. (구멍 난 곳을 메우기 위한) 헝겊 조각
- I asked a tailor to sew patches on the elbows of my black suit.

0404
pursuit
/pərsúːt/

1. 추구, 추격 — [s] chasing after
- ⓤ in pursuit of sth ~을 쫓아서
  - Many people immigrate to the USA **in pursuit of** money.
  - The government protects the right to the pursuit of happiness for everyone.

2. 취미 활동 pursuits
- ◇ leisure pursuits 여가 활동 / outdoor pursuits 야외 활동

0405
ramification
/ræmifikéiʃən/
/래미피*케이션/

파문, 영향 ramifications — [s] complication
- ⓤ have (significant) ramifications for sth ~에 (상당한) 파문(영향)을 일으키다(몰고 오다)
  - The new tax reform may **have ramifications for** the aggregate changes in the economy.

0406
scoop
/skúːp/

(아이스크림 등을 푸는) 큰 숟가락 — [s] spoonful
- ⓤ one / two scoops of sth ~의 한/두 숟가락
  - He put **two scoops of** ice cream on his plate, placed it on the counter, and paid for it.

▶ scoop (동사) 푸다

0407
vestige
/véstidʒ/
/베스*티쥐/

흔적, 자취 — [s] trace
- ◇ a vestige of blood 핏자국
  - The president lost all vestige of respectability when the scandal was exposed.

0401 케빈에 관한 소식 들었어요? 그가 암에 걸렸대요. / 나는 뉴스에서 미국의 이라크 침공에 관해서 들었다. 0402 그들은 여전히 그 바이러스의 원인에 대한 어떠한 결정적인 증거도 찾지 못했다. 0403 따듯하고 화창한 날에 내가 가서 앉기를 좋아하는 우리 아파트 건물 뒤에 작은 풀밭이 있다. / 나는 재단사에게 내 검은색 정장 팔꿈치에 헝겊 조각을 꿰매 달라고 부탁했다. 0404 많은 사람들이 돈을 쫓아서 미국으로 이민을 간다. / 정부는 모든 사람의 행복 추구권을 보호한다. 0405 그 새로운 세제 개혁은 경제의 총체적인 변화에 파문을 일으킬지 모른다. 0406 그는 아이스크림 두 숟가락을 접시에 담아 카운터에 놓고 계산을 했다. 0407 그 스캔들이 드러났을 때 대통령은 존경할 만한 점의 모든 자취를 잃었다.

verb 동사

0408 act
/ækt/

1. 행동하다, 굴다
◇ act strangely / suspiciously / childishly 이상하게/수상하게/유치하게 행동하다(굴다)
○ Call the police if you see someone act suspiciously.
○ At the age of 18, young people become adults. They should act more like adults when they reach this age.

2. 대응하다
ⓤ act 부사 to do sth ~하기 위해 ~하게 대응하다
○ The government must **act** quickly **to** curb skyrocketing home prices.

3. 역할하다
ⓤ act as sth ~로 역할하다
○ Living roofs **act as** insulators.

[S] behave

[S] serve as sth, play a role as sth

0409 assign
/əsáin/

(임무나 숙제 등을) 주다, 할당하다, 배정하다
ⓤ assign A B: A에게 B를 주다
○ I was assigned the task of sorting the old nails and screws in the box.
○ Your assigned reading provided some theories about the extinction of Steller's sea cow.
○ He assigns 10 minutes to a vocabulary test.

[S] give, allocate

0410 cast
/kǽst/
*cast-cast-cast

1. 캐스팅을 하다
○ He was cast as Julius Caesar.

2. 던지다
ⓤ
① cast a vote (for sb) in an election 선거에서 (~에게) 투표하다
○ They **cast a vote** for electors who then vote for the president.
② cast doubt / suspicion on sth ~에 의문을 제기하다
○ The lecturer **casts doubt on** the passage, which states that the method kills animals in the forest.
③ cast a light / shadow on / over sth ~에 빛/그림자를 드리우다
○ A tree **casts a shadow over** a grassy area.

[S] throw

0411 collide
/kəláid/
/컬*라이드/

충돌하다, 부딪히다
ⓤ collide with sth ~와 부딪히다
○ The crater was made by an asteroid **colliding with** Earth.
(=The crater was made by an asteroid crashing into Earth.)

▶ collision (명사) 충돌

[S] crash
[S] crash into sth

0412 consent
/kənsént/

동의하다, 허락하다
ⓤ consent to do sth / consent to sth ~(하는 것)에 동의하다
◇ consent to the proposal 그 제안에 동의하다
○ She **consented to** the use of her portrait as an illustration in the book.
○ She **consented to** let us use her portrait as an illustration in the book.

[A] refuse 거절하다
[S] agree to do sth

0413
defy
/difái/
/디*파이/

1. 반항하다, 거역하다
- A majority of small shops have been defying the ban on private gatherings of five or more people.

2. 부추기다
- ⓤ defy sb to do sth ~에게 한번 ~해 보라고 부추기다
- Actually, the shooting did happen. A citizen **defied** a British soldier **to** shoot him.

▶ defiant (형용사) 반항적인

[S] resist
[A] comply with 따르다

0414
discount
/dískaunt/

1. 무시하다
- We shouldn't discount the possibility that the interest rate may rise soon.

2. 할인하다
- The supermarket sells certain items at discounted prices at particular times of the day.

[S] dismiss

[S] cut, reduce, lower

0415
drive
/dráiv/

1. (어떤 상태에) 이르게 하다, 만들다
- ⓤ drive sb crazy 누구를 화나게 하다
- My mother has a talent for **driving** me **crazy**.

2. (강제로 ~한 상태로) 만들다
- ⓤ drive sb to do sth ~에게 ~을 (강제로)하게 하다
- The scandal **drove** him **to** resign.

3. (기계 등을) 작동시키다, 돌리다
- ◇ drive the turbines 터빈을 돌리다

4. (못 등을) 박다
- ◇ drive a nail into a fence 울타리에 못을 박다

[N] drive 운전하다 자신이 운전하는 경우 / ride 타다 타인이 운전하는 경우
- People who live in big cities normally ride subway trains to commute to school or work rather than drive their own cars.

[S] make

[S] force, compel

0416
elude
/ilú:d/

잘 피하다, 따돌리다, 도망치다
- He succeeded in eluding the police by disguising himself as a priest.

▶ elusive (형용사) 찾기 어려운, 정의하기 어려운, 달성하기 어려운
- No matter how hard he tried, success remained elusive for him.

[S] avoid, escape, evade

0417
epitomize
/ipítəmàiz/
/이피터*마이즈/

~의 완벽한 예시이다
- *Wall Street*, by Oliver Stone, epitomizes the archetypal portrayal of stockbrokers' greed for profit in the 1980s in the U.S. *archetypal 전형적인 / portrayal 묘사

0418
grasp
/græsp/
/그래스프/

1. (꽉) 쥐다, 붙잡다
- Jack grasped a snake by the tail.

2. (뭔가 어려운 것을) 이해(파악)하다
- The only way I could grasp the main points of what the professor was trying to stress was by reading the textbook.

[S] grip, clutch, hold

[S] apprehend, understand, digest

0419 incur
/inkə́:r/
/인커/

1. (손해 또는 비용 등을) 초래하다, 발생시키다, 입다
◇ incur debts 빚을 지다 / incur fines 벌금을 내다 / incur losses 손실을 입다 / incur expenses 비용을 초래하다
○ Students who plan to study abroad should think carefully about the expenses they may incur while living abroad in addition to tuition.

2. (뭔가 안 좋은 것을) 초래하다
ⓤ incur one's wrath / the wrath of sb ~의 분노(노여움)를 사다
○ I **incurred the wrath of** my mother by breaking her favorite vase.

0420 occupy
/άkjupai/

1. 차지하다
○ Several big companies occupy a large share of the market.
[S] take up

2. 점령(점거)하다
○ Germany was occupied by the four allies: the United States, Great Britain, the Soviet Union, and France.
[S] take over

0421 predominate
/pridάmineit/
/프리*다미네이트/

(수적으로) 우세하다, 가장 많다
○ When different breeds are crossbred, the best traits usually predominate.
[S] prevail

0422 refer to
/rifə́:r tu/

1. 언급하다
ⓤ refer to A as B: A를 B로 언급하다
○ The city **is** often **referred to as** a typical example of an industrial town.
[S] mention, talk about

2. 말한다
○ Bread shuttles refer to the helpless victims of bullies – called Iljins – at school.
[S] describe

3. 참고(참조)하다
◇ a script to refer to 참조해야 할 대본
○ Please refer to the user manual for more details about the product.

0423 stem from
/stem frəm/

(문제점 등이) ~에서 기인하다
○ The protests **stemmed from** the people feeling disenfranchised by the government. *disenfranchise 선거권을 박탈하다
[S] come from, spring from, develop from

0424 switch
/swítʃ/

1. 전환하다
ⓤ switch to sth ~로 전환하다
○ For cities that already have a working recycling system, it is absurd to **switch to** a single-stream recycling solution.

2. 바꾸다
◇ switch seats 좌석을 바꾸다
○ I forgot to switch my clothes from the washer to the dryer.

[N] switch sth on (불/전등)을 켜다 / switch sth off (불/전등)을 끄다
○ I told you to switch it off before you leave.

0425 view
/vjú:/

1. 보다, 간주하다
ⓤ view A as B: A를 B로 보다
○ He **is viewed as** an unsuitable candidate.
[S] see, consider, regard

2. 보다, 구경하다
○ A married couple who came to view the house has called and told me that they want to take a closer look at it.

0419 해외에서 공부하는 것을 계획하는 학생들은 학비 외에 외국에서 사는 동안 그들이 초래할 수 있는 비용에 대해서 신중하게 생각해야 한다. / 나는 어머니가 가장 좋아하는 꽃병을 깨뜨려 어머니의 노여움을 샀다. 0420 몇몇 대기업들이 시장의 큰 부분을 차지한다. / 독일은 미국, 영국, 소련 그리고 프랑스 등 4개국 연합군에 의해 점령되었다. 0421 다른 종들이 교배가 되었을 때, 가장 좋은 특성들이 대개 우세하다. 0422 그 도시는 산업 도시의 전형적인 예로 자주 언급된다. / 빵 셔틀은 학교에서 일진이라고 불리는 불량배들의 무력한 피해자들을 말한다. / 제품에 대한 더 자세한 사항은 사용 설명서를 참조하시오. 0423 그 시위들은 국민들이 정부로부터 선거권을 박탈당했다고 느끼는 데서 기인했다. 0424 이미 작동하고 있는 재활용 시스템을 가지고 있는 도시들이 싱글 스트림 재활용 방안으로 전환하는 것은 바보 같은 짓이다. / 나는 세탁에서 건조로 옷을 바꾸는 것을 잊었다. / 떠나기 전에 불을 끄라고 내가 말했지. 0425 그는 적합하지 않은 후보로 간주된다. / 집을 보러 온 결혼한 부부가 전화를 걸어 그들이 더 자세히 살펴보고 싶다고 나에게 말했다.

adjective 형용사

0426 agile
/ǽdʒəl/ or /ǽdʒail/

(행동이) 민첩한, 날렵한
- Cats are much more agile than dogs, which is why they are so quiet when walking around.

▶ agilely (부사) 민첩하게
◇ move agilely 민첩하게 움직이다

S nimble

0427 aware
/əwéər/

알고 있는, 의식하는
- aware of sth / aware that S주어 V동사 ~을 알고 있는
- He set up an organization called 'Save Our Planet' to make people *aware of* environmental issues.

S conscious
A oblivious, unaware 모르는

0428 certain
/sə́:rtn/

1. 확실한
- be certain about / of sth ~에 대해 확실하다 / be certain that S주어 V동사 ~을 확신하다
- The legitimacy of the claim is not certain, so we need to investigate further.

2. 어떤, 특정한
- For certain personal reasons, he dropped out of school.

S sure

0429 diligent
/dílidʒənt/

근면한, 성실한
- He is a diligent student who always hands in school assignments on time and earns good grades on tests.

▶ diligently (부사) 성실히

S hard-working, conscientious

0430 energetic
/ènərdʒétik/
/에너*제틱/

에너지가(열정이) 넘치는, 생동감 있는
- Husbands who are usually exhausted fall asleep while watching TV after dinner, whereas wives are always energetic. That's why they fight.

▶ energetically (부사) 활동적으로

S lively, vigorous

S vigorously

0431 inadvertent
/ìnədvə́:rtnt/
/이너드*버튼트/

우연한, 의도하지 않은
- You should wear outfits that cover your arms and legs in an effort to avoid inadvertent exposure to UV light. *in an effort to do sth ~하기 위한 노력으로

▶ inadvertently (부사) 우연히

S accidental, unintended, unintentional

S accidently
A deliberately 고의로, 의도적으로

0432 isolated
/áisəlèitid/

1. 고립된, 격리된, 단절된, 소외된
- feel isolated 소외감을 느끼다
- North Korea was deliberately isolated from western countries by the mid 1980s.
- Single moms often **feel isolated**.

2. 외딴
◇ an isolated island 외딴 섬
- He always spends his holidays reading books in an isolated house next to a placid lake. *placid 고요한

S feel alienated

S remote

0426 고양이는 개보다 훨씬 민첩해서 그것 때문에 걸어 다닐 때 그들은 매우 조용하다. 0427 그는 사람들이 환경 문제를 알게 하기 위해 '우리의 행성을 구하자'라고 불리는 한 단체를 세웠다. 0428 주장의 정당함은 확실치 않아서 우리는 더 조사할 필요가 있다. / 어떤 개인적 이유 때문에 그는 학교를 그만두었다. 0429 그는 언제나 학교 과제를 제때 제출하고 시험에서 좋은 성적을 받는 성실한 학생이다. 0430 대개 지쳐 있는 남편들은 저녁 식사 후에 티비이 보다가 자고 반면에 아내들은 늘 에너지가 넘쳐 있다. 그것 때문에 그들은 싸운다. 0431 너는 자외선에 의도하지 않은 노출을 피하기 위한 노력으로 팔과 다리를 가리는 옷을 입어야 한다. 0432 북한은 1980년 중반까지 일부러 서방 국가와 단절되어 있었다. / 미혼모들은 자주 소외감을 느낀다. / 그는 언제나 그의 휴가를 고요한 호수 옆에 있는 외딴집에서 책을 읽는 데 보낸다.

0433 natural
/nǽtʃərəl/

1. 자연의, 천연의
◇ natural resources 천연자원 / natural disasters 자연재해 / the natural environment 자연환경
○ Lightning is a leading natural cause of forest fires.

2. 자연스러운
○ Humans have the natural instinct to survive.

3. 당연한
○ Today, it is natural not to put infants to sleep on their stomachs.

[A] artificial 인공의

[A] unnatural 부자연스러운

0434 permanent
/pə́:rmənənt/ /퍼머넌트/

영구적인
◇ permanent job 정규직
○ The right of permanent residence means permission to reside and work in a country without restriction.

▶ permanently (부사) 영구적으로

[S] lasting
[A] temporary 일시적인

[A] temporarily 일시적으로

0435 prime
/práim/ /프라임/

1. 가장 중요한
ⓤ be of prime importance 가장 중요하다
○ The prime goal of the Marshall Plan was to prevent communism from spreading.

2. (질이) 최고의(최상의), 시청률이 최고 높은
◇ prime beef 최고급 소고기
○ TV ads that run between shows aired during prime time are expensive.

[S] main, chief, principal

0436 seamless
/sí:mləs/ /심러스/

솔기가 없는 이음매가 없는
○ Seamless tights are winning popularity with young women.

▶ seam (명사) 솔기 바느질 봉합 부분, 경계선

0437 superb
/supə́:rb/ /수퍼브/

훌륭한
○ The movie was superb.
○ The most superb movie of this year for me was *Minari*.

[S] excellent, outstanding, magnificent

0438 swift
/swíft/

1. 신속한, 재빠른
ⓤ be swift to do sth 빠르게 ~하다
◇ take swift action 신속한 조치를 취하다
◇ a swift decision / reply 빠른 결정/답변
○ She **was swift to** deny all the allegations

2. (움직임이) 빠른
◇ a swift current 급류

▶ swiftly (부사) 신속하게, 빠르게
○ Passengers at Kabul Airport were swiftly evacuated.

[S] quick, immediate

0439 tolerant
/tálərənt/

관대한, 너그러운
ⓤ tolerant of sth ~에 대해 관대한
○ A tolerant society is one in which we are ready to embrace opinions different from our own. *embrace 포용하다

[A] intolerant 너그럽지 못한

0433 번개는 산불의 주된 자연적 원인이다. / 인간은 살려는 자연스러운 본능을 가지고 있다. / 오늘날, 유아들을 엎드려 재우지 않는 것은 당연하다. 0434 영주권은 한 나라에서 제약 없이 거주하고 일할 수 있는 허가를 의미한다. 0435 마셜 플랜의 가장 중요한 목표는 공산주의가 퍼지는 것을 막는 것이었다. / 황금 시간대에 방영되는 쇼 사이에 상영되는 티브이 광고들은 비싸다. 0436 이음매가 없는 몸에 딱 붙는 바지가 젊은 여성들에게 인기를 얻고 있다. 0437 그 영화는 훌륭했다. / 나한테 올해의 가장 훌륭한 영화는 *미나리*이다. 0438 그녀는 빠르게 모든 혐의를 부인하였다. / 카불 공항의 승객들은 신속하게 대피했다. 0439 관대한 사회는 우리가 우리 자신과 다른 의견을 포용할 준비가 되어 있는 사회다.

adverb
부사

0440 consistently
/kənsístəntli/

변함없이, 일관되게
- The Green Party has consistently argued that global warming is happening.

S always the same

0441 otherwise
/ʌ́ðərwaiz/

1. 다르게, 다른 방법으로
- say / prove / suggest / think otherwise 다르게 말하다/증명하다/제안하다/생각하다
- Steller's sea cow, otherwise known as Hydrodamalis gigas, is a large marine mammal that is extinct now.

S differently, in another way

2. 그것만 아니었다면, (앞에서 언급 한 것이 아니었다면) ~했을; (앞에서 말한 것) (그것) 빼고는(제외하고)
- Old buildings bring life and color to their towns that would otherwise be dull and gloomy.
- The farmers cultivated crops low in protein like wheat, barley, and corn. Many otherwise edible plants were grown only by hand.
- It's cold, but otherwise it is nice to sit outside on a bench.
- The poor visual aids ruined an otherwise good presentation.

▶ otherwise (접속부사) '그렇지 않(았)다면', '그렇지 않는다면'
- S주어 V동사. Otherwise, S주어 V동사. (=S주어 V동사, otherwise S주어 V동사)
- I'd better go now. **Otherwise**, my mom will start to worry.
(=I'd better go now, **otherwise** my mom will start to worry.)

0442 in unison
/in junisn/

1. 동시에
- The kids gave the teacher the same answer in unison.

2. 함께
- work in unison 함께 일하다
- Two political parties decided to **work in unison** to overcome the current economic crisis.

S together
S work together

0443 now that
/nau ðæt/

(이제) ~니까
- Now that S주어 V동사, S주어 V동사. (이제) ~니까, ~이다
- **Now that** you know the truth, you have to keep it secret.

DAY 10

ANGRY ENGLISH
ACADEMIC VOCABULARY

noun 명사

- ☐ archive
- ☐ burrow
- ☐ coinage
- ☐ fire
- ☐ impression
- ☐ pattern
- ☐ ratio
- ☐ rust
- ☐ shed
- ☐ structure
- ☐ underpinning
- ☐ viability
- ☐ volume

verb 동사

- ☐ adapt
- ☐ appease
- ☐ bode
- ☐ cater
- ☐ collect
- ☐ correlate
- ☐ degrade
- ☐ discriminate
- ☐ embark on
- ☐ enumerate
- ☐ fill
- ☐ indulge
- ☐ observe
- ☐ present
- ☐ prohibit
- ☐ refine
- ☐ revert
- ☐ traverse

adjective 형용사

- ☐ alarming
- ☐ blind
- ☐ chief
- ☐ fervent
- ☐ hazardous
- ☐ incessant
- ☐ involved
- ☐ marvelous
- ☐ outstanding
- ☐ perpetual
- ☐ stable
- ☐ succeeding
- ☐ trivial
- ☐ willing

adverb 부사

- ☐ eminently
- ☐ particularly
- ☐ according to
- ☐ as opposed to

 MP3 파일 다운

noun
명사

0444
archive
/ˈɑːrkaiv/
/아카이브/

기록 보관소
- The archives of England are kept in the Parliament building.

0445
burrow
/ˈbɜːrou/
/버로우/

굴
- A meerkat came out of its burrow.

0446
coinage
/ˈkɔinidʒ/
/코이*니쥐/

조어 새로운 말을 만듦, 신조어
- An example of the coinage of a new word is "chillax." It combines "chill out" and "relax." *chill out 침착해지다

0447
fire
/fáiər/

1. 불
- put out / extinguish fire 불을 끄다 / set sth on fire ~에 불을 지르다 / set fire to 장소 ~에 불을 내다 / sth is on fire 불타는 중이다
- Humans made fire with simple tools like sticks.
- He **set** a kid's bike **on fire**.

2. 모닥불 (가산)
- The forest fire that broke out in Son-ja-rung, seen as a sacred place for camping by campers, was attributable to a careless camper who made a fire.

0448
impression
/impréʃən/

1. 생각, 인상
- have / get the impression that S주어 V동사 ~라는 인상을 가지다
- Be careful when sending a text message because it could give a false impression.
- Teenagers may **have** a false **impression that** violence is okay.

2. 감명, 감동, 인상
- make / leave a strong impression on sb ~에게 강한 감명(인상)을 남기다
- My travels in Canada with my family **made a strong impression on** me.

3. (표면을 눌렀을 때 생기는) 자국   **S** mark, imprint, depression
- make / bear / leave an impression on sth ~에 자국을 남기다 / dental impression 의치의 틀
- She **left an impression on** the concrete with her hands.

0449
pattern
/pǽtərn/

1. 무늬
- Indian tapestries tend to have many elaborate patterns and vibrant colors. *tapestry 태피스트리(무늬를 놓은 양탄자)

2. 양식
- behavior patterns 행동 양식
- **Behavior patterns** can be changed through reward and punishment.

0450
ratio
/réiʃiou/ or /réiʃiou/

비율   **S** proportion
- the ratio of A to B: A 대 B의 비율(AB 비율)
- **The ratio of** boys **to** girls in the class is 2:1.
- Modern flying birds have **the** appropriate **ratio of** wing **to** body.

0444 영국의 기록 보관소들은 의회 건물에 보관되어 있다. 0445 미어캣 한 마리가 굴에서 나왔다. 0446 새로운 단어의 조어의 한 예시는 'chillax'이다. 그것은 'chill out'과 'relax'를 결합한 것이다. 0447 인간은 막대기와 같은 간단한 도구로 불을 피웠다. / 그는 한 아이의 자전거에 불을 질렀다. / 캠퍼들에 의해 캠핑의 성지로 여겨지는 선자령에서 난 산불은 모닥불을 피운 한 부주의한 캠퍼 때문이었다. 0448 문자 메시지를 보낼 때는 주의해야 하는데 왜냐하면 그것이 잘못된 인상을 줄 수도 있다. / 십대들은 폭력이 괜찮다는 잘못된 인상을 가질 수 있다. / 나의 가족과 캐나다에서 여행은 나에게 강한 감명(인상)을 남겼다. / 그녀는 손으로 콘크리트에 자국을 남겼다. 0449 인도의 태피스트리는 많은 정교한 무늬와 선명한 색을 가지고 있는 경향이 있다. / 행동 양식은 보상과 처벌을 통해 바뀔 수 있다. 0450 그 반에서 남자아이 대 여자아이의 비율은 2:1이다. / 현대의 나는 새들은 날개 대 몸통의 적절한 비율을 가지고 있다.

0451 rust
/rʌ́st/

녹
- I removed the rust from my trailer and then had it painted.

▶ rusty (형용사) 녹슨
◇ a rusty trailer 녹슨 트레일러

0452 shed
/ʃéd/

창고
◇ a cow shed 축사
- There was also a small table on which we put food for the birds and a shed in which we kept garden tools. *keep 보관하다

0453 structure
/strʌ́ktʃər/

1. 구조
◇ political / economic / social structure 정치/경제/사회 구조
- Men's and women's brains differ in structure.

2. (큰) 건축물
- The structures stand three stories high.

[S] building

0454 underpinning
/ʌ́ndərpiniŋ/

기초, 토대
- His belief that there should not be an exception to the principle that all men are equal formed the underpinning of democracy.

[S] foundation, basis

0455 viability
/vàiəbíləti/
/바이어*빌러티/

(실행) 가능성
- The viability of humans colonizing Mars is very low.

▶ viable (형용사) 실행 가능한

[S] feasibility

0456 volume
/válju:m/

용량, 양
◇ the volume of traffic on the roads 도로의 교통량
- What is the volume of a gallon of milk?

verb 동사

0457 adapt
/ədǽpt/

바꾸다, 변경하다
ⓥ adapt sth for sb ~을 위해 ~을 바꾸다
- We had to adapt our plan in order to meet customers' needs.
- The teaching materials used by our instructors should **be adapted for** advanced students.

▶ adapted (형용사) 개조된
◇ a specially adapted car that enables disabled people to drive themselves 장애인들이 스스로 운전할 수 있도록 특별히 개조된 차

[S] modify, change

[S] modified

0458 appease
/əpíːz/

진정시키다, 달래다
- The emperor spent large sums of money on appeasing foreign mercenaries. *mercenary 용병

0459 bode
/bóud/

징조(조짐)이다
ⓥ bode well / ill for sth ~에 있어 좋은/나쁜 징조이다
- The country's excessive reliance on foreign capital **bodes ill for** its economic development.

0460
cater
/kéitər/
/케이터/

1. (음식이나 서비스 등을) 제공하다
◇ cater (for) an occasion such as a wedding or party 결혼식이나 파티 같은 행사에 음식을 제공하다
○ The hotel is notorious for catering at various occasions such as weddings; they sometimes serve live insects.

2. (특정 그룹에게 그들이 필요한 것이나 원하는 것을) 제공하다
ⓤ cater for / to sb/sth ~ (특정 그룹)에게 그들이 원하는 것을 제공하다
○ Merchants in colonial cities **catered to** their mayors.
○ At this time, parks **catered to** the wealthy.

0461
collect
/kəlékt/

모으다, (세금 등을) 징수하다
◇ collect data / evidence / information 데이터/증거/정보를 모으다
○ People in the past lived by hunting animals and collecting food. That is why they are called hunter-gathers.
○ Aristocrats collected taxes and harvests from farmers who farmed their lands.

[S] gather, assemble, compile(자료 등을) 수집하다

0462
correlate
/kɔ́:rəlèit/
/코럴*레이트/

서로 연관시키다; 서로 연관되어 있다
ⓤ correlate to sth ~와 연관이 있다 / correlate A with B: A와 B를 서로 연관시키다 / be correlated with ~와 연관(관련)되어 있다
○ Changes in agricultural crop prices **are correlated with** climate change.

0463
degrade
/digréid/

1. 비하하다
○ Many of the movies produced during the 1960s degraded women.

2. (가치나 아름다움을) 떨어뜨리다, 파괴하다, 망치다
○ Madagascar's habitat is being degraded by increased population growth.

[S] spoil, ruin, mar

0464
discriminate
/diskrímineit/

1. (차이점 등을) 구별하다
ⓤ discriminate A from B: A를 B와 구별하다
○ It can be hard for young children to **discriminate** fiction **from** reality.

2. 차별하다
ⓤ discriminate in favor of sth ~을 유리하게 차별하다 / discriminate against ~을 나쁘게 차별하다
○ The Act passed in Congress made it illegal to **discriminate against** women and minority groups.

▶ discriminatory (형용사) 차별적인
◇ discriminatory laws that limit the civil rights of African Americans 흑인들의 민권을 제한하는 차별적인 법률들

[S] differentiate, distinguish

0465
embark on
/imba:rk a:n/

~에 착수하다, 시작하다
○ He embarked on a new journey to find himself. But it ended in failure.
▶ embark (동사) 승선하다(배에 타다), (배에) 싣다

[N] set out on sth, set out to do sth ~을 착수(시작)하다
○ He set out to discover if Earth was flat or not.

[S] start, set out on, undertake

[A] disembark 내리다

0466
enumerate
/injú:mərèit/
/이뉴머*레이트/

열거하다
○ Let me enumerate the fatal defects in what the passage argues.

0460 그 호텔은 결혼식 같은 다양한 행사에서 음식을 제공하는 것으로 악명 높다; 그들은 가끔 살아 있는 곤충을 제공한다. / 식민지 도시의 상인들은 그들의 시장이 원하는 것을 제공하였다. / 이 시기에, 공원은 부자들에게 제공되었다. 0461 과거에 사람들은 동물들을 사냥하고 식량을 모으면서 살았다. 그것 때문에 그들은 수렵-채집민이라 불린다. / 귀족들은 자신들의 땅에서 농사를 지은 농부들로부터 세금과 수확물을 징수했다. 0462 농산물의 가격의 변화는 기후 변화와 관련되어 있다. 0463 1960년대 동안 제작된 많은 영화들은 여성들을 비하했다. / 마다가스카르의 서식지는 늘어난 인구 증가에 의해 파괴되고 있다. 0464 어린 아이들이 소설을 현실과 구별하는 것은 어려울 수 있다. / 의회에서 통과된 그 법령은 여성과 소수 집단을 차별하는 것을 불법화했다. 0465 그는 자신을 찾기 위해 새로운 여정을 시작했다. 그러나 그것은 실패로 끝났다. / 그는 지구가 평평한지 아닌지를 밝히는 일을 시작했다. 0466 제가 지문이 주장하는 것의 치명적인 결함들을 열거해 보겠습니다.

0467 fill
/fíl/

1. 채우다
ⓤ
① fill A with B: A를 B로 채우다
② filled with sth ~로 채워진, 가득한
- A medieval castle was fortified against attacks with a moat, a long, wide hole dug around the castle and **filled with** water. *fortify 요새화하다 / moat 해자 (성 주위로 땅을 파서 물을 채운 곳)

2. (빈 공간을) 메우다
- It takes too long for other species to fill the gap left by an extinct species.

0468 indulge
/indʌ́ldʒ/
/인덜쥐/

1. (뭔가 나쁜 것을) 실컷 즐기다
ⓤ indulge in sth ~에 빠지다/탐닉하다
- Because a large number of people **indulge in** too much drinking, the rates of liver cancer have greatly increased.

2. (뭔가 불법적인 일에) 가담하다
ⓤ indulge in sth ~에 가담하다
- The rumor circulated quickly that he had **indulged in** criminal activities.

▶ indulgence (명사) 탐닉

0469 observe
/əbzə́ːrv/

1. 보다, 목격하다, 관찰하다
ⓤ
① observe sb/sth V동사 / Ving동명사 ~가 ~한 것을/하고 있는 것을 목격하다
- The journalist had **observed** the politician **take** bribes many times.
② observe that S주어 V동사 ~을 보다, ~라는 것을 알다
- Scientists have **observed that** when mothers breast-feed their babies, the babies have strong immunity to infection.

2. (법률 등을) 지키다, 준수하다
- Knights were supposed to observe a strict set of rules enforced by their lords.

▶
1. observation (명사) 관찰
2. observance (명사) 준수

S see, notice, witness

0470 present
/prizént/
/프리젠트/

1. (공식적으로) 수여(증정)하다, 제공하다
ⓤ present A with B: A에게 B를 수여(제공)하다 / present B to A: A에게 B를 수여(제공)하다
- The researchers **presented** mice **with** equal portions of a weak sugar solution and regular food. *portion (음식의) 1인분

2. (공식적으로) 제출하다
- A Member of Parliament (MP) presented a petition to the House of Commons.

3. 보여 주다
- Data recorded during an experiment presents the accuracy of the experiment's results.

S show

4. 공연(방송)하다, 상연하다
- The Globe Theatre, an open-air theater built in 1599, presented most of William Shakespeare's plays.

0471 prohibit
/prouhíbit/

금지하다
ⓤ prohibit O목적어 from Ving동명사 목적어가 ~하는 것을 금지하다
- They **are prohibited from** eat**ing** pork.

S ban, forbid, outlaw
A license 허가하다

0467 중세의 성곽은 성 주위를 파서 물로 채워진 길고 넓은 구멍인 해자로 공격에 대비해서 요새화되었다. / 다른 종들이 멸종한 종이 남긴 간격을 메우는 데는 너무 많은 시간이 걸린다. 0468 많은 사람들이 지나친 음주에 빠지기 때문에 간암 비율이 크게 증가했다. / 그가 범죄 행위에 가담했다는 소문이 빠르게 퍼졌다. 0469 그 기자는 그 정치인이 뇌물을 받는 것을 여러 번 목격한 적이 있었다. / 과학자들은 엄마들이 아기에게 모유를 먹일 때, 아기가 감염에 강한 면역력을 가진다는 것을 보았다(알았다). / 기사들은 그들의 영주들에 의해 시행되는 엄격한 규칙들을 지키기로 되어 있었다. 0470 그 연구원들은 쥐들에게 약한 설탕 용액과 규칙적인 음식의 동일한 양을 제공했다. / 한 하원 의원이 하원에 청원서를 제출하였다. / 실험 중에 기록된 데이터는 그 실험의 결과의 정확성을 보여 준다. / 1599년에 지어진 야외극장인 Globe 극장은 윌리엄 셰익스피어의 희곡 대부분을 상연했다. 0471 그들은 돼지고기를 먹는 것이 금지되어 있다.

0472
refine
/rifáin/

1. 정제하다
◇ refine crude oil 원유를 정제하다
○ Refined crude oil is used for a wide range of petroleum products in our daily lives such as the gasoline we use to move vehicles and the kerosene that we use to heat buildings.

[S] make sth pure, purify

2. 개선하다
○ The medical technologies used to treat cancer are being refined.

[S] improve

▶
1. refinement (명사) 개선
2. refinery (명사) 정유(제)소

[S] improvement

0473
revert
/rivə́:rt/
/리버트/

(이전 상태로) 되돌아가다
ⓤ revert to normal 정상으로 되돌아가다
○ If you want things to **revert to normal**, don't panic.
(=If you want things to get back to normal, don't panic.)

[S] go back to, return to
[S] get back to normal

0474
traverse
/trǽvə:rs/ or /trəvə́:rs/

횡단하다, 넘다
○ He is the first Black American to traverse the African continent from Dakar to Cairo in a car.

[S] go across, cross

adjective 형용사

0475
alarming
/əlá:rmiŋ/
/얼라밍/

놀라운
◇ alarming news 놀라운 소식
○ The zebra mussel is a species that reproduces at an alarming speed.

[S] frightening, shocking

0476
blind
/bláind/

1. 장님의, 눈먼
ⓤ be born blind 장님으로 태어나다
○ The Teacher of the Year Award is given to Diana Muller, who has been blind since birth.

2. 깨닫지 못하는, 못 보는
ⓤ be blind to sth ~을 깨닫지 못하다 / be blind to the fact that S주어 V동사 ~의 사실을 깨닫지 못하다
○ People who find faults in others tend to **be blind to** their own faults.

[S] unaware

3. 맹목적인
◇ blind faith 맹목적 신앙

▶ blindly (부사) 맹목적으로

0472 정제된 원유가 우리가 차량을 이동하기 위해 사용하는 가솔린과 우리가 건물을 따뜻하게 하기 위해 사용하는 등유와 같은 일상생활에서 광범위한 석유 제품에 사용된다. / 암을 치료하기 위해 사용되는 의료 기술이 개선되고 있다. 0473 만약 당신이 일들이 정상으로 되돌아가기를 원한다면, 겁먹지 마라. 0474 그는 다카르에서 카이로까지 차를 타고 아프리카 대륙을 횡단한 최초의 아프리카계 미국인이다. 0475 얼룩무늬 홍합은 놀라운 속도로 번식하는 종이다. 0476 올해의 교사상은 태어나면서부터 맹인인 다이아나 뮬러에게 주어진다. / 다른 사람에게서 결함을 찾는 사람들은 그들 자신의 결함을 못 보는 경향이 있다.

0477 chief
/tʃiːf/

1. 가장 중요한, 주요한
   - Bison meat was the chief food of the tribes.

2. (계급이나 직급에서) 가장 높은, 최고의
   ◇ CEO (chief executive officer) 최고 경영자 / commander-in-chief 최고 사령관

   ▶ chiefly (부사) 주로
   - The Indian teepees were made chiefly of animal hides, especially buffalo ones, sewn together. *teepee 원뿔형 천막집

[s] highest in rank

0478 fervent
/fɜːrvənt/

(사람 등이) 열심인, 열렬한
- He is a fervent believer in free markets.

[s] enthusiastic, ardent

0479 hazardous
/hæzərdəs/

위험한
- hazardous to sb/sth ~에 위험한
- Sorting collected materials such as plastic, bottle or paper by hand is hazardous.

[s] dangerous

0480 incessant
/insésnt/
/인세*슨트/

끊이지 않는, 끊임없는
◇ incessant noise / complaints 끊이지 않는 소음/불만
- Firstly, the animal could have been eliminated through incessant hunting by groups of native Siberian people.

▶ incessantly (부사) 끊임없이

[s] constant, ceaseless

0481 involved
/inválvd/

1. 관련된
   - involved in sth ~와 관련된
   - Individual investors called 'ants' should be made aware of the risks **involved in** investing.

2. (사건 등에) 연루된, 참여한, 가담한
   - involved in sth ~에 연루된
   - He denies that he was **involved in** the conspiracy.

[s] connected

[s] embroiled (논쟁 등에) 휘말린

0482 marvelous
/máːrvələs/

끝내주는, 경이로운, 멋진, 놀라운
- I spent a marvelous time in London, studying and hanging out with friends from different countries.

▶
1. marvel (명사) 경이로움
   ◇ marvels of the world that people have never visited 사람들이 한 번도 가 본 적이 없는 세계의 경이로움
2. marvelously (부사) 훌륭하게, 멋지게

[N] marble (명사) 대리석, 구슬

[s] fantastic, splendid, excellent

[s] wonder

0483 outstanding
/áutstændiŋ/

1. 뛰어난
   - His performance is outstanding.

2. 두드러진, 중요한
   - The Stock Market Crash in the U.S. in 1929 is an outstanding example of an overheated economy.

[s] excellent

[s] prominent

0484 perpetual
/pərpétʃuəl/
/퍼페*츄얼/

영구적인, 계속되는, 끊임없는
◇ the perpetual noise from the construction site next door 옆집 공사 현장에서 나는 계속되는 소음
- I'm sick and tired of my mom's perpetual nagging.

▶ perpetually (부사) 계속해서

[s] continuous, continual

[s] continuously, continually

0477 들소 고기는 그 부족들의 가장 중요한 식량이었다. / 인디안의 원뿔형 천막집은 함께 이어져 꿰매어 붙여진 동물 가죽, 특히 버팔로 가죽으로 주로 만들어졌다. 0478 그는 열렬한 자유 시장의 신봉자이다. 0479 손으로 플라스틱, 병 또는 종이 같은 모아진 재료들을 분류하는 것은 위험하다. 0480 첫째로 그 동물은 시베리아 원주민 집단에 의한 끊임없는 사냥으로 제거되었을 수도 있었다. 0481 '개미'라고 불리는 개인 투자자들이 투자와 관련된 위험들을 인지하게 해야 한다. / 그는 그가 그 음모에 가담했다는 것을 부정한다. 0482 나는 다른 나라에서 온 친구들과 어울리고 공부하면서 런던에서 멋진 시간을 보냈다. 0483 그의 공연은 뛰어났다. / 1929년의 미국에서의 주식 폭락은 과열된 경제의 중요한 예이다. 0484 나는 우리 엄마의 끊임없는 잔소리가 지겹다.

0485 **stable** /stéibl/	안정된, 안정적인 ○ Still, the population was able to stay stable rather than rise dramatically. ▶ 1. stable (명사) 마구간, 외양간 2. stabilize (동사) 안정시키다; 안정되다 ◇ stabilize prices 물가를 안정시키다	**S** steady **A** unstable 불안정한
0486 **succeeding** /səksí:diŋ/	다음의 ◇ succeeding generations 다음 세대들 ○ Dead trees are important for succeeding generations of trees.	**S** following **A** preceding 앞의
0487 **trivial** /tríviəl/ /트리*비얼/	사소한, 대수롭지 않은 ○ In the past, sheer survival was the most important matter that humans had to deal with, but today that matter is trivial.	**S** trifling, unimportant, minor **A** weighty 중요한
0488 **willing** /wíliŋ/	기꺼이 ~하는, 꺼리지 않는 ⓤ willing to do sth 기꺼이 ~하는(~하는 것을 꺼리지 않는) ○ By all accounts, he earned a bad reputation as a cutthroat businessman **willing to** do anything to succeed. *by(from) all accounts 많은 사람들이 얘기하는 거에 따르면 / cutthroat 잔인한, (경쟁 등이) 치열한	**S** eager **A** reluctant, unwilling 꺼리는

adverb 부사

0489 **eminently** /émɪnəntli/	대단히, 매우 ○ I waited three hours to watch the movie, but it was eminently worth it.	**S** highly, very, extremely
0490 **particularly** /pərtíkjulərli/	특히 ○ This is particularly a problem for them in the winter when snow comes.	**S** especially
0491 **according to** /əkɔːrdiŋ tu/	1. ~에 따르면 ○ According to a report published by the U.S. Department of Labor, between 1997 and 2007, 67,000 computer programmers lost their jobs due to foreign outsourcing, but more than 117,000 workers found employment in the same field. *Department of Labor 노동부 2. ~에 따라, 비례하여 ○ Each individual can take out a loan according to his ability to pay. *take out a loan 대출하다	 **S** in proportion to
0492 **as opposed to** /æz əpouzd tu/	1. ~와 반대로, ~와는 대조적으로 ○ Thanks to the Internet, we can contact people on the other side of the world in a matter of seconds, as opposed to the many weeks or months it took in the past. *a matter of sth 단지 .... 만에 2. ~보다는 오히려 ○ The television program provides users with only interesting pieces of gossip as opposed to giving them more useful information.	**S** in contrast to / with **S** rather than, instead of

0485 그럼에도 불구하고 인구는 극적으로 증가하기보다는 안정을 유지할 수 있었다. 0486 죽은 나무들은 다음 세대의 나무들에게 중요하다. 0487 과거에는 오로지 살아남는 것만이 인간이 다뤄야 하는 가장 중요한 문제였지만 오늘날 그 문제는 대수롭지 않다. 0488 많은 사람들이 얘기하는 거에 따르면 그는 성공하기 위해 무엇이든 기꺼이 하는 잔인한 사업가로서 나쁜 명성을 얻었다. 0489 나는 그 영화를 보려고 3시간이나 기다렸지만 그것은 매우 그럴 만한(기다릴 만한) 가치가 있었다. 0490 이것은 특히 눈이 오는 겨울에 그들에게 문제가 된다. 0491 미국 노동부가 발표한 한 보고서에 따르면 1997년부터 2007년 사이에 6만 7천 명의 컴퓨터 프로그래머들이 해외 아웃소싱으로 일자리를 잃었지만, 같은 분야에서 11만 7천 명 이상의 근로자들이 일자리를 찾았다. / 각 개인은 지불 능력에 따라 대출할 수 있다. 0492 인터넷 덕분에 우리는 몇 주 또는 몇 달이 걸리던 과거와 반대로 단지 몇 초 만에 지구 반대편에 있는 사람들과 연락할 수 있다. / 그 티브이 프로그램은 사용자에게 더 유용한 정보를 제공하기보다는 단지 흥미로운 가십 기사만을 제공한다.

DAY 11

ANGRY ENGLISH
ACADEMIC VOCABULARY

noun 명사

- [ ] appearance
- [ ] burden
- [ ] chunk
- [ ] distinction
- [ ] furnace
- [ ] hindrance
- [ ] potential
- [ ] purpose
- [ ] roster
- [ ] routine
- [ ] shortcoming
- [ ] successor
- [ ] vigor

verb 동사

- [ ] address
- [ ] appear
- [ ] blot
- [ ] characterize
- [ ] coincide
- [ ] count
- [ ] decline
- [ ] delineate
- [ ] embed
- [ ] eventuate
- [ ] inflict
- [ ] name
- [ ] override
- [ ] prevent
- [ ] reflect
- [ ] secrete
- [ ] shred
- [ ] weigh

adjective 형용사

- [ ] ambitious
- [ ] close
- [ ] conscious
- [ ] destined
- [ ] doomed
- [ ] enthusiastic
- [ ] hesitant
- [ ] incidental
- [ ] mean
- [ ] original
- [ ] pervasive
- [ ] pronounced
- [ ] scrupulous
- [ ] troublesome
- [ ] wanton

adverb 부사

- [ ] especially
- [ ] perpetually
- [ ] as is the case with
- [ ] as well

noun
명사

0493 appearance /əpíərəns/

1. 출현, 출석
- ⓤ make an appearance at sth ~에 출현(참석)하다
- ◇ make a television appearance TV 출현하다
- ○ The mayor **made an appearance at** the opening of the new department store.

2. 외모 physical appearance
- ○ One of the major concerns that teens have is physical appearance.

3. 출현, 등장 — emergence, occurrence
- ⓤ the appearance of sth ~의 등장
- ○ **The appearance of** modern humans some 10 million years ago has changed the Earth more than any other life form.

0494 burden /bɜ́ːrdn/

부담, 짐
- ⓤ a burden to sb ~에게 부담 / put / place a burden on sb ~에게 부담을 주다
- ○ Increasing gas taxes can **put a** financial **burden on** people.
- ○ I don't want to be **a burden to** my sons.

0495 chunk /tʃʌ́ŋk/

1. 큰 덩어리 — piece
- ⓤ a chunk of sth ~의 한 덩어리
- ◇ a chunk of bread / cheese 빵/치즈 한 덩어리
- ○ Large **chunks of** cheese that look delicious are displayed for sale on the stand.

2. 상당한 양(부분)
- ◇ a chunk of revenue 상당한 수익

0496 distinction /distíŋkʃən/

1. 차이 — difference
- ⓤ a distinction between A and B: A와 B의 차이
- ○ There is no clear **distinction between** male and female test results.

2. 구별, 구분
- ⓤ draw a distinction 구분(구별)하다
- ○ I like to **draw a distinction** between my feelings and my thoughts.

3. 뛰어남, 탁월함 — excellence
- ◇ a writer / director of distinction 뛰어난 작가/감독
- ○ Bong Joonho has been given a lot of distinction by the American Academy of Film.

0497 furnace /fɜ́ːrnis/

용광로 (=blast furnace)
- ◇ iron made in blast furnaces 용광로에서 만들어지는 철
- ○ Industrial metals are made in blast furnaces.

0498 hindrance /híndrəns/

장애, 방해 — obstacle
- ⓤ sb/sth be more of a hindrance than a help 도움이 되기보다 방해가 되다
- ○ The team leader **was more of a hindrance than a help**.

0493 시장이 새 백화점 창립 행사에 참석했다. / 청소년들이 가지고 있는 중요한 걱정거리 중 하나는 외모이다. / 약 천만년 전에 현대 인간들의 등장은 어떠한 다른 생명체보다 더 지구를 바꾸어 놓았다. 0494 유류세를 인상하는 것은 사람들에게 경제적 부담을 줄 수 있다. / 나는 내 아들들에게 짐이 되고 싶지 않다. 0495 맛있어 보이는 치즈 덩어리들이 진열대 위에 팔려고 전시되어 있다. 0496 남성과 여성의 테스트 결과의 명백한 차이는 없다. / 나는 내 감정과 생각을 구분하는 것을 좋아한다. / 봉준호는 미국 아카데미로부터 탁월함을 인정받았다. 0497 공업용 금속은 용광로에서 만들어진다. 0498 팀 리더는 도움이 되기보다 방해가 되었다.

0499 potential
/pəténʃəl/

가능성, 잠재력
- ⓤ potential for sth ~에 대한 가능성 / have the potential to do sth ~할 수 있는 가능성(잠재력)을 가지고 있다
- The company **has the potential to** be listed on the New York Stock Exchange (NYSE).

S promise

0500 purpose
/pə́:rpəs/ /퍼*퍼스/

목적
- ⓤ on purpose 일부러, 의도적으로, 고의로
- Controlled burning, which means setting a wildfire **on purpose**, provides benefits which far outweigh the disadvantages.

S intentionally, purposely

0501 roster
/rástər/

명단, 명부
- ⓤ on a roster 명부(명단)에 / a roster of sth ~의 명부(명단)
- The team has **a roster of** 20 key players, and the owner has added my name to it.

S list

0502 routine
/ru:tí:n/

루틴, 일상적인 것
- Today, I want to share with you how you can make writing a short essay part of your daily routine.

0503 shortcoming
/ʃɔ́:rtkʌmiŋ/

단점, 결함
- As a teacher, he has a lot of shortcomings.

S defect

0504 successor
/səksésər/

후계자, 후임자, 후손
- They are still proud to be the successors of the Roman Empire.

S heir
A predecessor 전임자

0505 vigor
/vígər/ /비거/

힘, 활력, 열정
- You need to work with vigor if you want to be promoted.

S vitality, strength, enthusiasm

verb 동사

0506 address
/ədrés/

1. (단체, 집회 등에서) 연설하다
- Professor Yun-joon addressed an audience of 10,000 students on the benefits of genetically modified crops.

S give a speech

2. (문제점 등을) 다루다, 처리하다
- The government should take urgent action to address carbon dioxide emissions. *take action 조치를 취하다

S deal with

▶ address (명사) 주소, 연설

0507 appear
/əpíər/

1. 나타나다
- The symptoms don't appear immediately.

S emerge, arise, occur
A disappear, fade(차츰) 사라지다

2. (~인 것) 같다, (~같이) 보이다
- ⓤ
- ① appear 형용사/명사 ~인 것 같다, ~처럼 보이다
- His face that had previously **appeared** devoid of feeling turned lively after he met a girl. *lively 생기발랄한 / devoid 없는
- ② appear to do sth ~인 것 같다, ~처럼 보이다
- The new neighbor **appears to** be unfriendly.
- ③ it seems that S주어 V동사 ~인 것 같다 / it seems likely / unlikely that S 주어 V동사 가능성이 있어/없어 보인다
- **It seems likely that** the number of new cases of the virus will double in three days.

S look, seem

0508 blot
/blát/

(액체 등을) 닦아 내다
- ⓥ blot sth (up) ~을 닦아 내다
- ○ I've spilled my coffee. I need some paper towels to **blot** it **up** with.

Ⓝ blot out (빛 등을) 가리다
- ○ Smog is blotting out the sun.

0509 characterize
/kǽriktəràiz/
/캐릭터*라이즈/

1. ~의 전형이다 — Ⓢ be typical of
- ○ His technique of making the face appear in shadow characterizes his paintings.

2. 특징짓다, 묘사하다 — Ⓢ portray, describe
- ⓥ characterize A as B: A를 B로 묘사하다
- ○ Frederick Olmsted, who designed New York's Central Park, **characterized** public parks **as** being accessible to the public.

0510 coincide
/kòuinsáid/

일치하다, 동시에 일어나다 — Ⓢ synchronize
- ○ All that must be considered is to how to make the fire coincide with the time of the year when animals are not reproducing.

▶ coincidence (명사) (우연의) 일치, 동시 발생
- ○ It is just a coincidence that we live near each other.

0511 count
/káunt/

1. (수를) 세다, 포함시키다(셈에 넣다)
- ○ He counted the gold coins.

2. 중요하다 — Ⓢ matter
- ○ Health counts more than wealth, power, and fame.
(=Health is more important than wealth, power, and fame.)

3. 간주하다, 여기다; 여겨지다 — Ⓢ consider
- ⓥ count as sth / be counted as sth ~로 여겨지다 / count A as B: A를 B로 여기다
- ○ He **counts** himself **as** one of the leading figures in American literature.

Ⓝ
1. count on sb ~을 믿다 — Ⓢ depend on sb
- ○ You can count on me.
2. count for nothing 중요하지 않다, 아무런 영향을 미치지 못하다
- ○ TOEFL scores count for nothing if applicants got their diploma abroad.

0512 decline
/dikláin/

1. 감소하다, 줄어들다 — Ⓢ decrease
- ⓥ decline by -% -퍼센트까지 줄다
- ○ The company's profits have **declined by** 10% this year.

2. 거절하다 — Ⓢ refuse, turn down
- ○ The country requested to IMF that the repayment be postponed, but IMF declined to do so.

▶ decline (명사) 감소
- ⓥ be on the decline 감소하고 있다
- ○ The number of unemployed **is on the decline**.

0513 delineate
/dilínièit/
/딜리니*에이트/

(상세하게) 그리다, 설명하다, 묘사하다 — Ⓢ describe, outline
- ○ The law should delineate and prohibit behavior that is socially abhorrent. *abhorrent 혐오감을 일으키는

0514 embed
/imbéd/

박다, 끼워 넣다
- ⓤ embedded in sth ~에 박혀 있는
- ◦ The American soldier had an operation to remove a bullet **embedded in** his right leg.

Ⓢ fix

0515 eventuate
/ivéntʃuèit/
/이벤츄*에이트/

(결과로서) 일어나다
- ⓤ eventuate in (doing) sth 결국 ~이 되다
- ◦ The government's proposal to cut the welfare budget by half is likely to **eventuate in** many people los**ing** their jobs.

Ⓢ result
Ⓢ result in (doing) sth

0516 inflict
/inflíkt/
/인*플릭트/

(고통 등을) 가하다, 입히다
- ⓤ inflict harm / damage on sb/sth ~에 해/손상을 가하다
- ◇ inflict an injury 부상을 입히다
- ◦ Hydroelectric dams do not **inflict** serious **damage on** wildlife either, especially river wildlife.

0517 name
/néim/

명명하다
- ⓤ name A B: A를 B라고 이름 짓다
- ◦ A friend of mine **named** Kazya is a good example of this.

Ⓝ
1. call A B: A를 B라고 부르다
- ◦ You are called J? Right?
2. dub A B: A를 B라는 별명으로 부르다
- ◦ Her knowledge of vocabulary was so excellent that she was dubbed a "walking dictionary."

0518 override
/óuvərraid/
*override-overrode-overridden

1. ~보다 더 중요하다(우선하다)
- ◦ The needs of the country as a whole must override the needs of individuals. *as a whole 대체로

2. (자신의 권력을 이용하여) 바꾸다(뒤엎다), 기각하다(무효로 하다)
- ◦ My boss didn't like what my coworker was doing, so he overrode her decision.

Ⓢ outweigh

Ⓢ overrule, overturn, cancel 무효로 하다

0519 prevent
/privént/

1. 막다
- ⓤ prevent O목적어 from Ving동명사 목적어가 ~하는 것을 막다
- ◦ If I had not told Mom to hurry, the car accident could have been prevented.

2. 예방(방지)하다
- ◦ There should not be any exceptions to policies to prevent asset bubbles.

Ⓢ stop
Ⓢ stop O목적어 from Ving동명사

0520 reflect
/riflékt/

심사숙고하다
- ⓤ reflect on sth ~을 심사숙고하다
- ◦ The editor **reflected on** the changes to the book requested by the author.

Ⓢ consider, think of
Ⓢ meditate on sth

0521 secrete
/sikríːt/
/시크릿/

(작은 것 등을) 감추다
- ⓤ secrete A in B: A를 B에 감추다
- ◦ He **secreted** cottonseed **in** the hole of his writing brush.

0522 shred
/ʃréd/
/쉬레드/

(잘게) 자르다(썰다), 찢다
- ◦ Evenly scatter shredded cheese over the potatoes.

Ⓢ tear up, cut up

0514 그 미국인 병사는 그의 오른쪽 다리에 박힌 총알을 제거하는 수술을 받았다. 0515 복지 예산을 반으로 줄이려는 정부의 제안은 결국 많은 사람들이 그들의 일자리를 잃게 될 가능성이 있다. 0516 수력 발전 댐은 역시 야생 동물, 특히 강에 사는 야생 동물에게 심각한 손상을 가하지 않는다. 0517 카즈야란 이름의 내 친구는 이것의 좋은 예이다. / 당신 J라고 불리죠? 맞죠? / 그녀의 어휘에 대한 지식은 매우 뛰어나서 그녀는 "걸어 다니는 사전"이라고 불렸다. 0518 대체로 국가의 요구가 개인의 요구보다 우선해야 한다. / 내 상사는 내 동료가 하는 일이 마음에 들지 않아 그는 그녀의 결정을 바꿨다. 0519 내가 엄마에게 서두르라고 말하지 않았다면 그 교통사고는 막을 수 있었을 것이다. / 자산 거품을 방지하기 위한 정책에는 예외가 있어서는 안 된다. 0520 그 편집자는 저자에 의해 요구된 책의 변경 사항을 심사숙고했다. 0521 그는 목화씨를 그의 붓의 구멍에 감추었다. 0522 잘게 썬 치즈를 감자 위에 골고루 뿌려라.

0523
weigh
/wéi/

1. 무게를 달다(재다)
◇ weigh sth on a scale ~을 저울에 달다
○ Every time he weighs himself on the bathroom scale, he feels like he is gaining weight too easily.

2. 무게가 나가다
○ These are huge animals that we are talking about. They could be as much as 9 meters long and weigh up to 10 tons.

3. (신중히) 고려하다
○ He admitted his mistake of not weighing the possibility of construction companies facing bankruptcy.

S consider, examine, contemplate

adjective 형용사

0524
ambitious
/æmbíʃəs/

야심적인, (계획 등이) 야심 찬
○ Writing this book is a very ambitious project, but it can be done.

S demanding, hard

0525
close
/klóus/

1. (공간과 시간상) 가까운
ⓤ close to sth ~에 가까운
○ On the first day of our trip, we arrived at the lodge **close to** a lake called Lake Powell.

2. (관계 등이) 가까운
○ The president tends towards closer relations with the United States, rather than China. *tend (어떤 방향으로) 나아가다

3. ~할 것 같은
ⓤ close to doing sth ~할 것 같은
◇ close to death 죽을 것 같은 / close to tears 눈물을 흘릴 것 같은
○ He is **close to** sign**ing** a three-year contract with Leed.
○ She was close to tears as she practiced interviewing.

4. 막상막하인
○ She lost a close election.

N come close to doing sth ~할 뻔하다
○ A woman walked quietly into his office, shot him, and walked away. He **came close to** dying.

S near

S very likely

S almost do

0526
conscious
/kánʃəs/
/칸셔스/

의식(지각)하고 있는, 알고 있는
ⓤ conscious of sth ~을 알고 있는
○ Meanwhile, they will be **conscious of** the most suitable time to sell their cars with better gas mileage. *gas mileage 연비
○ IKEA is one of the world's most environmentally conscious companies.

N conscience (명사) 양심

S aware
A unconscious 무의식의

0527 destined
/déstind/
/데스*틴드/

1. ~할 운명에 있는
- ⓤ destined to do sth ~할 운명인
- Napoleon was **destined to** fail to invade Russia.

2. ~행인
- ⓤ destined for sth ~행인
- The train is **destined for** London.

0528 doomed
/dú:md/

(불운한) 운명에 처한
- ◇ doomed to failure / extinction / defeat 실패/멸종/패배할 운명에 처한
- The sea cow was doomed to be extinct.
  (=The sea cow was doomed to extinction.)

▶ doom (동사) (불운한) 운명에 처하게 하다

[S] ill-fated

0529 enthusiastic
/inθùːziǽstik/
/인쑤*지애스틱/

열렬한, 열광적인, 열중하는
- ⓤ enthusiastic about sth ~에 대해 열중해 있는
- He became an enthusiastic supporter of the reform of the country's educational system.

▶ enthusiasm (명사) 열정

[S] ardor, fervor, passion

0530 hesitant
/hézitənt/

망설이는, 주저하는
- ⓤ hesitant about sth ~에 대해 망설이는 / hesitant to do ~하는 것을 주저하는
- She is always **hesitant to** ask for help when she needs it.

▶
1. hesitate (동사) 망설이다
2. hesitantly (부사) 주저하며, 마지못해

[S] reluctant, uncertain
[A] willing 기꺼이 ~하는

[S] reluctantly

0531 incidental
/ìnsidéntl/
/인시*덴틀/

부수적인, 중요하지 않은
- I'm sorry but your love life is incidental to me. Please stop telling me about it.

[S] minor, secondary, subordinate
[A] basic 근본적인(필수적인)

0532 mean
/míːn/

비열한, 심술궂은, 불친절한(냉정한), 잔인한
- ⓤ mean to sb ~에게 못되게 구는
- The main character was depicted in the novel as being a mean merchant.
- It was mean of me to tell you that you look fat. I'm sorry.
- He is deliberately **mean to** her due to a grudge.

[S] cruel, unkind

0533 original
/ərídʒənl/

1. 최초의, 본래의(원래의)
- In the novel, the fireman's original plan was to read the books that he had taken out of houses that he had set on fire.

2. 원본의
- You should be faithful to the original text. *faithful to sth ~에 충실한

3. 독창적인
- There were several scenarios with original ideas.

[S] initial, first, early

[S] authentic, genuine

[S] new, fresh, novel

0534 pervasive
/pərvéisiv/

(뭔가 안 좋은 것이) 만연하는, 배어드는(스며드는)
- Sadly, negativity and hate are pervasive on social media.

[S] pervading, permeating, widespread

0535 pronounced
/prənáunst/
/프러*나운스트/

뚜렷한, 명백한(분명한)
- One of the most pronounced changes in society in recent years has been multiculturalism.

[S] noticeable, marked, definite

0527 나폴레옹은 러시아를 침공하는 데 실패할 운명이었다. / 그 기차는 런던행이다.　0528 바다소는 멸종할 운명에 처했다.　0529 그는 그 나라의 교육 제도 개혁의 열렬한 지지자가 되었다.　0530 그녀는 그녀가 도움이 필요할 때 언제나 도움을 청하는 것을 주저한다.　0531 미안하지만 당신의 애정 생활은 나에게는 중요하지 않습니다. 부탁인데 나에게 그것에 대해 말하는 것을 그만하세요.　0532 주인공은 소설에서 냉정한 상인으로 묘사되었다. / 내가 당신에게 당신이 뚱뚱해 보인다고 말한 것은 잔인했어요. 미안합니다. / 그는 원한 때문에 일부러 그녀에게 못되게 군다.　0533 그 소설에서 그 소방관의 원래 계획은 그가 불을 지른 집에서 그가 꺼낸 책을 읽는 것이었다. / 너는 원본에 충실해야 한다. / 독창적인 아이디어가 담긴 여러 시나리오가 있었다.　0534 안타깝게도 부정성과 증오는 소셜 미디어에 만연해 있다.　0535 최근 몇 년간 사회에서 가장 뚜렷한 변화 중 하나는 다문화주의이다.

0536 scrupulous
/skrúːpjuləs/
/스크루*플러스/

양심적인
- ⓥ scrupulous in sth ~에 있어서 양심적인
- ○ The company is very **scrupulous in** its dealings with customers. *dealings 거래

▶ scruple (명사) 양심의 가책
- ⓥ have no scruples about (doing) sth ~에 대해 양심의 가책을 느끼지 않다 / without scruple 양심의 가책 없이
- ○ He **has no scruples about** lying.

[A] unscrupulous 비양심적인

0537 troublesome
/trʌ́blsəm/

문제를 일으키는, 힘든, 말썽부리는
- ◇ a troublesome child 말썽꾸러기 아이
- ○ One of the most common troublesome complications of gastric bypass surgery is malnutrition. *gastric bypass operation 위장문합수술 / complication 합병증

0538 wanton
/wántən/
/완턴/

고의적인, 악의적인
- ◇ an wanton action 고의적인 행위
- ○ This wanton destruction of the ecosystem endangers people living today.

[S] willful, senseless, mindless

adverb 부사

0539 especially
/ispéʃəli/

특히
- ○ Adolescents can be self-centered, impulsive, and aggressive. This is especially true of adolescent boys.

[S] particularly, specially

0540 perpetually
/pərpétʃuəli/

1. 계속해서
- ○ My second son is perpetually asking me to buy him toys.

[S] continuously, continually

2. 영구히
- ◇ perpetually expelled from his political party 정당에서 영구 제명

[S] permanently

0541 as is the case with
/æz iz ði keis wið/

~과 마찬가지로
- ○ As is the case with salmon, strong species of fish can pass through dams safely.
- ○ In the same way that salmon can pass through dams safely, strong species of fish can do so, too.

[S] in the same way that S주어 V동사

0542 as well
/æz wel/

또한, 역시
- ○ His wife is busy as well. She attends an English academy to improve her English abilities so that she can have a better chance for a promotion at work.

[N] might (just) as well do sth (마땅히 다른 것이 없어서) ~하는 것이 낫다
- ○ I might (just) as well go home and rest.

[S] also, too, in addition

0536 그 회사는 소비자들과의 거래에 있어서 매우 양심적이다. / 그는 거짓말 하는 것에 대해 양심의 가책을 느끼지 않는다. 0537 위장문합수술의 가장 흔한 힘든 합병증 중 하나는 영양실조다. 0538 이러한 고의적인 생태계 파괴는 오늘날 살고 있는 사람들을 위험에 빠뜨린다. 0539 청소년들은 자기중심적이고 충동적이며 공격적일 수 있다. 이것은 특히 사춘기 소년들에게도 해당된다. 0540 우리 둘째 아들이 나에게 장난감을 사 달라고 계속 말한다. 0541 연어와 마찬가지로 강한 어종은 댐을 안전하게 통과할 수 있다. / 연어가 댐을 안전하게 통과할 수 있는 것과 마찬가지로 강한 어종은 역시 그렇게 할 수 있다. 0542 그의 아내 역시 바쁘다. 그녀는 직장에서 승진을 위한 더 나은 기회를 가질 수 있도록 영어 능력을 향상시키기 위해 영어 학원에 다닌다. / 집에 가서 쉬는 게 낫겠다.

DAY 12

ANGRY ENGLISH
ACADEMIC VOCABULARY

noun 명사
- [ ] application
- [ ] bounds
- [ ] calligraphy
- [ ] category
- [ ] conflict
- [ ] distance
- [ ] expedition
- [ ] figure
- [ ] ground
- [ ] magnitude
- [ ] pillar
- [ ] respect
- [ ] skeleton
- [ ] stress
- [ ] zone

verb 동사
- [ ] adhere
- [ ] analyze
- [ ] charge
- [ ] complement
- [ ] demand
- [ ] disgust
- [ ] distract
- [ ] embody
- [ ] fix
- [ ] inform
- [ ] mount
- [ ] narrow
- [ ] procure
- [ ] refrain
- [ ] reproduce
- [ ] result from
- [ ] snatch
- [ ] spot

adjective 형용사
- [ ] ambivalent
- [ ] available
- [ ] clumsy
- [ ] guarded
- [ ] high
- [ ] incipient
- [ ] mediocre
- [ ] ordinary
- [ ] petrified
- [ ] prosperous
- [ ] rival
- [ ] sizable
- [ ] tapered
- [ ] true
- [ ] voracious

adverb 부사
- [ ] everywhere
- [ ] practically
- [ ] as for
- [ ] as such

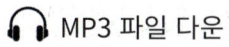

noun 명사

0543 application
/æplikéiʃən/

1. 지원, 신청
◇ a visa application 비자 신청 / one's application to the court for bail 보석 신청
○ I made an application to join Mensa.

2. 적용   [S] use, employment
◇ strict application of the law 법의 엄격한 적용

3. (연고나 페인트 등을) 바르기, 살포
◇ applications of pesticides 살충제 살포
○ The application of oil to the hinge will stop the door from squeaking.

▶ applicant (명사) 지원자

0544 bounds
/báundz/

한계, 한도   [S] limits
Ⓤ within / outside the bounds of sth ~의 한도(한계) 내의 / 밖의
◇ out of bounds (골프) 경기장을 벗어난
○ Don't go **outside the bounds of** my trust.

0545 calligraphy
/kəlígrəfi/

컬리그러피 글자를 아름답게 쓰는 기술, 서체
○ Steve Jobs decided to take a calligraphy class to learn how to produce beautiful handwriting.

0546 category
/kǽtəgɔ̀ːri/
/캐터고리/

범주, 부문, 분류   [S] class 부문, 종류, classification 분류
○ The sale of these three categories of drugs is strictly forbidden to people under the age of 18.
○ His songs that fit into the category of jazz vary widely.

▶ fall into a category ~의 범주에 들어가다

0547 conflict
/kánflikt/

갈등, 충돌, 분쟁   [S] clash, strife
Ⓤ a conflict between sth ~사이의 분쟁 / a conflict with sb over sth ~을 놓고 ~와의 갈등(분쟁)
◇ the clash of civilizations 문명의 충돌
○ **A** political **conflict between** two nations can lead to a war.

0548 distance
/dístəns/

거리
Ⓤ at a distance of sth ~거리에 있는 / in the distance 멀리서
○ I could see him kissing her **in the distance**.
○ The animal can see prey **at a distance of** half a kilometer.

Ⓝ travel / walk / run a distance 거리를 이동하다/걷다/뛰다
○ Back then, kids traveled long distances to get to school.

0549 expedition
/èkspədíʃən/
/엑스퍼디션/

탐험(원정)   [S] exploration
○ After he graduated from college, he planned an expedition to the North Pole.

0550 figure
/fígjər/

1. 인물
◇ a leading figure 중요 인물
○ He is an important figure historically.

2. 수치
◇ sales figures 매출 수치
○ The discrepancy between the real figures and the official figures is huge. *discrepancy 차이

3. 숫자
○ When the number of new cases of coronavirus became three figures, people started to take it more seriously.

4. (물건 등의) 모양, 동상
○ A bronze figure of a raging bull stands opposite the building.

0551 ground
/gráund/

1. 땅
◇ fall to the ground 땅에 떨어지다
○ When the soil is saturated, the rain is no longer absorbed into the ground. *saturate 흠뻑 적시다

2. 근거, 이유 grounds   **S** reason
ⓤ on (the) grounds of sth ~ 때문에 / on the grounds that S주어 V동사 ~라는 이유 때문에
◇ on grounds of religion / on religious grounds 종교적인 이유로
○ He got arrested **on** the **grounds of** robbery.

3. (특정 용도의) -장(소)
◇ spawning grounds 산란장

▶ groundless (형용사) 근거 없는

N common ground (당사자 간의) 공통된 입장(의견)

0552 magnitude
/mǽgnitùːd/

1. 크기, 규모
○ The magnitude of an earthquake is measured by a seismometer.

2 중요성
○ The government hasn't yet realized the magnitude of the problem.

0553 pillar
/pílər/
/필러/

1. 기둥, 기둥 모양
◇ a pillar of fire / cloud / smoke 불/구름/연기기둥
○ By day, the Lord went ahead of them in a pillar of cloud to guide them on their way, and by night in a pillar of fire to given them light, so that they could travel by day or night. (Exodus 13:21-22) *by day 낮에는 / by night 밤에는

2. 기둥 중요한 부분이나 사람
ⓤ a pillar of sth ~의 기둥
○ George is **a pillar of** this company. He has been here since the beginning and knows this business better than anyone else.

0554 respect
/rispékt/

1. (사람에 대한) 존경
ⓤ deserve respect 존경 받을 만하다 / earn / gain the respect of sb ~의 존경을 얻다
○ Tolerance is very important in **earning the respect of** your peers.

[s] deference

2. (권리나 지위에 대한) 존중
ⓤ with respect 존중해서 / show no respect for sth ~에 대해서 존중하지 않다
○ You should always treat your peers **with respect**.

3. 점, 관련
ⓤ in this respect 이런 점에서 / with respect to sth ~과 관련하여
○ **With respect to** your request, I regret to inform you that we don't have any new job vacancies at the moment. *vacancy 빈자리, 사람이 없음

[s] feature

▶
1. respectful (형용사) 존경(존중)하는, 공손한
2. respected (형용사) 존경받는

[s] admired

[N] awe and respect 경외심
○ He looked at Tiger Woods with awe and respect.

0555 skeleton
/skélətn/
/스켈*러튼/

1. 해골, 뼈(대)
○ A human skeleton was found 2 km away from the spot where the military aircraft crashed.

2. (건물의) 뼈대, (계획이나 이야기 등의) 골자, 뼈대
○ He fleshed out the skeleton of a proposal to curb property speculation. *flesh out sth ~에 살을 붙이다, ~을 구체화하다

[s] frame뼈대, outline골자

[N] skull (명사) 두개골

0556 stress
/strés/

1. 스트레스
○ Too much stress impedes physical growth. *impede 방해하다

2. 압박
ⓤ put (a great deal of) stress on sth ~에 (상당한) 압박을 준다
○ Being overweight can **put** a great deal of **stress on** your knees.

[s] force, pressure

3. 강조
ⓤ put / lay stress on sth ~을 강조하다
○ People today **put** too much **stress on** their appearance.

[s] emphasis

0557 zone
/zóun/

지역, 지대
◇ a danger zone 위험 지역 / a demilitarized zone 비무장 지대
○ The Rhineland, which borders Belgium, the Netherlands, and France, became a buffer zone established by the Treaty of Versailles.

[s] region, area

verb 동사

0558 adhere
/ædhíər/

들러붙다
- ⓥ adhere to sth ~에 들러붙다
- As parasites **adhere to** the surface of their bodies, sturgeons cannot remove them even though they hit the water with strong force as they jump out of it. *sturgeon 철갑상어

▶
1. adhesive (명사) 접착제
2. adhesion (명사) 부착

ⓢ stick to sth

0559 analyze
/ǽnəlàiz/
/애널*라이즈/

분석하다, 살펴보다
- You need to learn how to collect data and analyze it in detail.

▶
1. analysis (명사) 분석
2. analyst (명사) 분석가
3. analytic (형용사) 분석의, 분석적인

ⓢ study, examine

0560 charge
/tʃɑ́ːrdʒ/

1. (돈 등을) 청구하다, (세금 등을) 매기다
- ⓥ charge sb sth for sth ~에 대해서 ~에게 ~(얼마)를 청구하다 / charge taxes on sth ~에 세금을 매기다
- The restaurant **charged** us 200 dollars **for** a cheesy bottle of wine.

2. 고소(기소)하다, 고발하다
- ⓥ charge sb with doing sth ~을 ~한 것에 대해 기소하다
- The prosecution has **charged** the CEO **with** brib**ing** several politicians.

0561 complement
/kάmpliment/
/캄플리*멘트/

보완하다
- Red wine and steak complement each other perfectly.
- Red wine complements steak.
(=Red wine goes well with steak.)

▶ complement (명사) 보충, 보완(물)
- ⓥ a perfect complement to sth ~에 완벽한 보완물
- Red wine is **a perfect complement to** most steaks.

ⓝ compliment (동사) 칭찬하다

ⓢ go well with

ⓢ supplement

ⓢ praise, commend

0562 demand
/dimǽnd/

요구하다
- My dad demanded that I leave home.

ⓢ require

0563 disgust
/disgʌ́st/
/디스*거스트/

역겹게 만들다, 혐오감을 일으키다
- It disgusts many people that individuals who claim that they never do anything wrong, especially priests, do such terrible things.

▶ disgusting (형용사) 역겨운

ⓢ sicken, revolt, offend

ⓢ foul, vile

0564 distract
/distrǽkt/

산만하게 하다, 주의(관심)를 (딴 데로) 돌리다(빼앗다)
- ⓥ
- ① distract attention from sth ~로부터 주의(관심)를 돌리다
- Some animals release unpleasant odors to distract their enemies.
- ② distract sb from sb's studies ~의 공부를 방해하다
- My brother always **distracts** me **from** my **studies**.

ⓢ divert

0558 기생충이 몸 표면에 들러붙어 있기 때문에 철갑상어는 비록 그들이 물 밖으로 뛰어오르면서 강한 힘으로 물에 부딪혀도 그들을 제거할 수 없다. 0559 당신은 어떻게 데이터를 수집하고 어떻게 그것을 자세하게 분석하는지를 배울 필요가 있다. 0560 그 식당은 우리에게 싸구려 와인 한 병에 200달러를 청구했다. / 검찰은 그 최고 경영자가 여러 정치인들에게 뇌물을 준 것에 대해 기소했다. 0561 레드 와인과 스테이크는 서로를 완벽히 보완한다. / 레드 와인은 스테이크를 보완한다. / 레드 와인은 대부분의 스테이크에 완벽한 보완물이다. 0562 우리 아버지는 내가 독립할 것을 요구했다. 0563 자신은 어떤 잘못도 하지 않았다고 주장하는 사람들, 특히 성직자들이 그런 끔찍한 일을 하는 것은 많은 사람들에게 혐오감을 일으킨다. 0564 어떤 동물들은 적의 주의를 딴 데로 돌리기 위해 불쾌한 냄새를 방출한다. / 내 동생은 항상 나의 공부를 방해한다.

0565 embody
/imbádi/

1. 상징하다, 표현하다
   - The Statue of Liberty embodies liberty and democracy.

   [S] represent

2. 포함하다, 담다
   - Recently, some companies have succeeded in developing paints embodying special materials that protect buildings from acid rain.

   [S] include, contain

0566 fix
/fíks/

1. 고치다
   - The more skillful you are at dismantling a machine, the better able you will be to fix it. *dismantle (기계 등을) 분해하다

   [S] repair, mend, amend ((법 등을) 수정하다)

2. 고정시키다
   - fix A to / on B: A를 B에 고정시키다 / fix one's eyes on sth ~에 눈을 고정시키다
   - A solar panel **is fixed to** the outside of some homes.

   [S] attach, anchor

▶ fixed (형용사) 고정된, 수리된, 정해진
   - In Korea, notaries sign their name on a fixed paper form, not on individual forms that clients ask them to sign. *notary 공증인

0567 inform
/infɔ́:rm/

알리다, 통보하다
- inform A of / about B: A에게 B를 알리다 / inform sb that S주어 V동사 ~에게 ~을 알리다
- We regret to **inform** you **that** your application has been rejected.

[S] notify

0568 mount
/máunt/

1. 오르다
   - mount the throne 왕위에 오르다
   - In the end, he was able to **mount the throne** after purging his political opponents.

   [S] ascend, climb

2. 오르다, 증가하다
   - The number of deaths from COVID-19 continues to mount. *deaths 사망자

   [S] increase

3. (말 등에) 올라타다
   ◇ mount a horse 말에 올라타다

4. 탑재(설치)하다
   - mount A on / in B: A를 B위/안에 탑재하다
   - A real car **is mounted on** the wall of an exhibition room.

0569 narrow
/nǽrou/

좁아지다, 작아지다
- As the difference in prices narrows, brand recognition becomes more important.

[S] taper

0570 procure
/prəkjúər/
/프러*큐어/

획득(입수)하다, 조달하다
- Anti-government activists procured conventional weapons from China.

[S] obtain

▶ procurement (명사) 획득

[S] acquisition

0571 refrain
/rifréin/

그만두다, 멈추다, 삼가다(자제하다)
- refrain from doing sth ~하는 것을 삼가다(자제하다)
- Please **refrain from** hitt**ing** balls after 9 p.m.

[S] stop, desist, abstain

0572 reproduce
/riprədús/

1. (글 등을) 복제(복사)하다
   - Before the widespread use of the printing press, scribes reproduced manuscripts by hand. *scribe 필경사

2. 다시 만들어 내다, 재현하다
   - ◇ reproduce problems 문제를 재현하다
   - An archeologist was able to reproduce similar natural pigments using only natural substances that would have been used at that time.

[S] copy, duplicate

0573 result from
/rizʌlt frəm/

~에서 기인하다
- Desertification results from global warming.

[N] result in sth (결과적으로)~이 되다, ~을 일으키다(초래하다)
- Global warming results in desertification.

[S] occur as a result of

0574 snatch
/snætʃ/
/스내취/

1. 잡아채다, 낚아채다, 빼앗다
   - My bag was almost snatched from me.

2. (휴식이나 먹을 것 등을) (간신히) 얻다
   - I snatched 30 minutes of sleep in the subway on the way home.

[S] grab, seize, steal훔치다

0575 spot
/spát/

알아내다, 찾아내다, 발견하다
- Finally, I was able to spot the mistakes in my essay that I might have missed if I had not revised it and marked them with a highlighter.

[S] see, notice

adjective 형용사

0576 ambivalent
/æmbívələnt/
/앰비*벌런트/

상반하는 감정을 품은 긍정적·부정적 마음을 모두 가지고 있는
- ⓤ ambivalent about sb/sth ~에 대해 상반된 감정을 가진
- ◇ an ambivalent attitude 상반된 태도
- Many people in South Korea are **ambivalent about** the constant threats from North Korea.

[S] ambiguous, equivocal, uncertain

0577 available
/əvéiləbl/

1. 이용(사용)할 수 있는, 구할 수 있는(살 수 있는)
   - The iPad is available now.
   - Do you have any cars available now?
   - A well-developed public transportation system, including buses, subways, and trains, is available for people to use.

2. 시간이 있는
   - She is not available.

[S] accessible, obtainable

0578 clumsy
/klʌ́mzi/
/클럼지/

1. (행동 등이) 어설픈, 서투른
   - My son's clumsy stick handling made us decide to drop his ice hockey lessons.

2. (물건 등을) 다루기 힘든, 쓰기 불편한
   - It isn't easy to drive a truck because they are so clumsy to handle.

[S] (physically) awkward, inept

0572 인쇄기의 광범위한 사용 이전에 필경사들은 손으로 원고를 복사했다. / 한 고고학자가 그 당시에 사용되었을 천연 물질만을 사용해서 유사한 천연 색소들을 재현할 수 있었다. 0573 사막화는 지구 온난화에서 기인한다. / 지구 온난화는 사막화를 초래한다. 0574 내 가방이 거의 낚아채일 뻔했다. / 나는 집에 오는 길에 지하철에서 30분간 간신히 잤다. 0575 마침내 나는 만약 내가 에세이를 수정하지 않고 실수를 형광펜으로 표시하지 않았다면 놓쳤을지도 모르는 에세이에서의 실수들을 찾아낼 수 있었다. 0576 한국의 많은 사람들은 북한의 끊임없는 위협에 대해 상반된 감정을 가지고 있다. 0577 아이패드는 지금 구입할 수 있다. / 지금 쓸 수 있는 차 가지고 계신가요? / 버스, 지하철 그리고 기차를 포함한 잘 발달된 대중교통 체계는 사람들이 이용할 수 있다. / 그녀는 지금 시간이 없다. 0578 우리 아들의 어설픈 스틱 핸들링은 우리로 하여금 그의 아이스하키 수업을 그만두는 것을 결심하게 만들었다. / 트럭을 운전하는 것은 쉽지 않은데 왜냐하면 그들은 다루기 너무 힘들다.

0579 guarded
/gáːrdid/
/가디드/

조심스러운, 신중한
- South Korea issued a guarded response to a compromise agreement from the Japanese government. *compromise agreement 타협안 (절충안)

▶
1. guard (명사) 보초
◇ security guard 경비원
2. guardian (명사) 보호자
3. guard (동사) 보호하다

S cautious, careful

0580 high
/hái/

1. 높은
◇ high blood pressure 고혈압 / a high level of concentration 고도의 집중력
- Mount Everest is the world's highest mountain.
- Soybean is a source high in protein, which can be used for livestock and poultry farming.

2. (신분 등이) 높은
- The mounds were tombs for dead people with high status and much power, such as kings.

3. (바람 등이) 강한
- High winds hampered the rescue teams from getting to the top of the mountain. *hamper 방해하다

▶
1. high (명사)
1) 최고 기록(수준)
◇ an all-time high 사상 최고치
2) 행복감, 황홀감
2. high (부사) 높이, 위로
- The structures stand 3 stories high.

S peak
S ecstasy, rapture

0581 incipient
/insípiənt/
/인시피언트/

시작의, 초기의
- There are hopes of incipient economic recovery.

S (just) beginning, starting

0582 mediocre
/mìːdióukər/
/미디*오우커/

(지극히) 평범한
- The movie is pretty mediocre despite the fact that it was made by Bong who has a worldwide reputation as a renowned film director.

S average, ordinary

0583 ordinary
/ɔ́ːrdənèri/
/오더*네리/

1. 보통의
◇ ordinary people 보통 사람들
- His paintings are normally of ordinary people living in a big city.

2. 평범한
- They refused to live in traditional ways that were considered ordinary.

S common, normal, average

A unusual 평범하지 않은

0584 petrified
/pétrəfàid/
/페트러*파이드/

1. 무서운
ⓤ petrified of sth ~을 무서워하는
- I'm **petrified of** getting shots.

2. 석화된 나무 등이 오랜 시간에 걸쳐 돌 같은 것으로 변해 버린 것
◇ petrified tree 석화된 나무
- Petrified wood takes millions of years to be created.

▶ fossilized (형용사) 화석화된 화석의 형태로 보존된

S terrified

0585 prosperous
/práspərəs/
/프라스*퍼러스/

1. 부유한
- Prosperous nations in Africa are called "Lion Economies."

[S] well-off, wealthy, affluent
[A] poor 가난한

2. 번영하는, 성공한
◇ a prosperous country 번영의 나라 / a prosperous businessman 성공한 사업가

[S] flourishing, thriving

▶
1. prosperity (명사) 번영
2. prosper (동사) 잘 자라다, 번영하다

[S] thrive

0586 rival
/ráivl/

경쟁하는
◇ rival companies 경쟁사
- Al Capone ordered his men to eliminate the rival gang members.

[S] competing

0587 sizable
/sáizəbl/
/사이저블/

꽤 큰 (=sizeable)
- A man-made reservoir behind the dam called Lake Powell attracts a large number of tourists, generating income that accounts for a sizable proportion of the area's revenue.

[S] fairly large, considerable
[A] tiny 작은

0588 tapered
/téipəd/

끝으로 갈수록 좁아지는
- Tapered jeans are wider at the waist and narrower towards the bottom.

0589 true
/trú:/

사실의, 진짜의
- While it is true that the menhaden is an important source of protein for livestock and poultry, it is not the only available protein.
*menhaden (물고기) 청어

[S] sincere, genuine
[A] false 거짓의

▶ be true of / for sb/sth ~에 해당된다(~에게는 사실이다)
ⓤ
① this is (particularly / especially) true of / for sb/sth 이것은 (특히) ~에 해당된다
- By reading literature, adults can improve their vocabulary. But **this is** not **true for** children.
② the same is true of / for sb/sth ~에게도 마찬가지이다

[S] the same goes for sb/sth

0590 voracious
/vɔːréiʃəs/
/보레이*셔스/

1. (음식에 대해) 게걸스러운
◇ a voracious appetite 게걸스러운 식욕
- Charlie has an incredibly voracious appetite.

[S] greedy, insatiable 만족할 줄 모르는

2. (정보나 지식을) 열망하는, 열렬한
- You need a voracious appetite for knowledge rather than for food.

[S] avid

Ⓝ veracious (형용사) 진실한

[S] honest, trustful

0585 아프리카의 부유한 국가들은 "사자 경제"라고 불린다. 0586 알카포네는 그의 부하들에게 그의 경쟁 갱단들을 제거하라고 명령했다. 0587 그 댐 뒤에 파월호라고 불리는 인공 호수는 그 지역의 수입의 꽤 큰 부분을 차지하는 수입을 발생시키면서 많은 관광객을 끌어들인다. 0588 테이퍼드 바지는 허리가 넓고 아래쪽으로 내려가면서 좁아진다. 0589 청어가 가축과 가금류를 위한 중요한 단백질원인 것은 사실이지만, 그것이 유일하게 이용 가능한 단백질은 아니다. / 문학 작품을 읽음으로써, 어른들은 그들의 어휘력을 향상시킬 수 있다. 그러나 이것은 아이들에게는 해당되지 않는다(사실이 아니다). 0590 찰리는 엄청나게 게걸스러운 식욕을 가지고 있다. / 당신은 음식보다는 지식에 대한 열렬한 욕구를 필요로 한다.

adverb
부사

0591
everywhere
/évriwer/

여기저기, 도처에서, 모든 곳에서
- The young man was welcomed everywhere in Jerusalem.

0592
practically
/præktikəli:/

사실상, 실제로, 거의
- Practically all the schools in Korea were closed because of COVID-19. Only boarding schools stayed open.

[S] almost, virtually

0593
as for
/æz fər/

~에 관해서는
- As for safety measures, it is best to issue thick gloves to all workers.

[S] with regard to, concerning, regarding

0594
as such
/æz sʌtʃ/

1. 그런 이유로
- Businesses cannot send their marketing messages without their customers' consent, and as such, they require their customers to consent to receive the messages that they send via SMS.

2. 꼭, 정확히, 정확한 의미에서
- I'm not a moviegoer as such.

0591 그 젊은이는 예루살렘의 모든 곳에서 환영을 받았다. 0592 사실상 한국의 모든 학교가 코로나19 때문에 휴교했다. 기숙 학교만 문을 열었다. 0593 안전 대책에 관해서는 모든 노동자들에게 두꺼운 장갑을 나누어 주는 것이 최선이다. 0594 기업은 고객의 동의 없이 마케팅 메시지를 보낼 수 없는데 그런 이유로 그들은 그들의 고객에게 SMS를 통해 그들이 보내는 메시지를 수신하는 데 동의할 것을 요구한다. / 나는 정확한 의미에서 영화 보러 자주 가는 사람은 아니야.

DAY 13

ANGRY ENGLISH
ACADEMIC VOCABULARY

noun 명사

- ☐ affluence
- ☐ chamber
- ☐ direction
- ☐ feature
- ☐ hatred
- ☐ juncture
- ☐ level
- ☐ nuisance
- ☐ pose
- ☐ problem
- ☐ response
- ☐ sacrifice
- ☐ state
- ☐ view
- ☐ way

verb 동사

- ☐ adjoin
- ☐ attach
- ☐ choke
- ☐ cling
- ☐ coax
- ☐ deliver
- ☐ disintegrate
- ☐ emerge
- ☐ exacerbate
- ☐ hail
- ☐ halt
- ☐ inquire
- ☐ mock
- ☐ proceed
- ☐ relate
- ☐ sneak
- ☐ sting
- ☐ win

adjective 형용사

- ☐ amiable
- ☐ bold
- ☐ coincident
- ☐ dependable
- ☐ entire
- ☐ incisive
- ☐ mere
- ☐ obvious
- ☐ plain
- ☐ provisional
- ☐ selected
- ☐ silent
- ☐ strenuous
- ☐ typical
- ☐ vibrant

adverb 부사

- ☐ extensively
- ☐ pretty
- ☐ as of
- ☐ as with

 MP3 파일 다운

noun 명사

0595 affluence
/ǽfluəns/
/애플루*언스/

풍족함
- The author's advice is that poverty amid affluence in a capitalist society should not be considered normal.

▶
1. affluent (형용사) 돈 많은, 부유한
2. affluently (부사) 풍족하게

[S] wealth

[S] wealthy, opulent

0596 chamber
/tʃéimbər/

1. (생물체의) 실
◇ the four chambers of the heart 심장의 4심실
- The heart has four chambers through which blood flows.

2. (특정한 목적의) 방, 실
◇ a gas / torture chamber 가스/고문실
- Dozens of Jewish people including young boys were dying in the gas chamber, screaming in pain.

[S] room, hall

0597 direction
/dirékʃən/

방향
◇ in the direction of ~의 방향으로 / in all directions 사방으로 / in both directions 양방향으로 / in a clockwise 시계 방향으로 / anticlockwise direction 시계 반대 방향으로
- He looked in my direction.

0598 feature
/fíːtʃər/

1. 특징
- One of the distinguishing features of the new smartphone is its faster Internet speed.

2. (얼굴의) 이목구비
- My facial features are very similar to those of my mother, but my personality is like that of my father.

[S] characteristic, aspect, facet

0599 hatred
/héitrid/

증오, 혐오
ⓤ hatred of / for / towards sb/sth ~에 대한 증오
- The newspaper incited an extreme **hatred of** immigrants that was so intense that a crowd of people set fire to Korean stores in L.A.

[S] abhorrence
[A] love 사랑

0600 juncture
/dʒʌ́ŋktʃər/

(특별한) 단계, 시점
◇ at this juncture 이 시점에
- The scheme is at a critical juncture. It will either succeed or fail.

[S] occasion

0601 level
/lévl/
/레블/

1. 높이, 고도
◇ the water level of Stream Tan 탄천의 수위
- Melted glaciers lead to a rise in sea levels.

2. (양이나 질의) 수준(단계), 양
ⓤ a high level of sth 높은 수준(단계)의
◇ a high level of intelligence 높은 수준의 지능 / the lowest level 최저 수준 / the level of blood sugar 혈당량
- **High levels of** stress might cause people to get angry about tiny little things.
- Even on days when levels of fine dust are not that high, he still wears a mask while exercising.

3. (교육이나 스포츠에서 특정) 수준(단계), (특정) 지위
◇ a high-level meeting 고위급 회담 / advanced level students 상급반 학생들

[S] amount

0595 자본주의 사회에서 풍요 속의 빈곤은 정상적인 것으로 간주되어서는 안 된다는 것이 저자의 충고이다. 0596 심장은 피가 흐르는 네 개의 심실을 가지고 있다. / 어린 소년들을 포함한 수십 명의 유대인들이 고통 속에 비명을 지르며 가스실에서 죽어 가고 있었다. 0597 그는 내 쪽을 보았다. 0598 그 신형 스마트폰의 두드러진 특징 중 하나는 더 빨라진 인터넷 속도이다. / 얼굴의 이목구비는 어머니와 비슷하지만 성격은 아버지를 닮았다. 0599 그 신문은 이민자들에 대한 극도의 증오심을 자극하였는데 그 증오심은 아주 강렬하여 한 무리의 사람들이 L.A.에 있는 한인 가게에 불을 질렀다. 0600 그 계획은 중대한 시점에 있다. 그것은 성공하거나 실패할 것이다. 0601 녹은 빙하가 해수면 상승을 가져온다. / 높은 수준의 스트레스는 사람들로 하여금 아주 사소한 것들에 대해 화나게 만들 수 있다. / 미세 먼지 수준이 그다지 높지 않은 날에도 그는 운동을 하면서 여전히 마스크를 쓴다.

0602
nuisance
/njúːsns/
/뉴슨스/

짜증나게 하는 것, 문제를 일으키는 것, 골칫거리
- When completely drunk, my husband is a nuisance to me.

0603
pose
/póuz/

자세
◇ various poses 다양한 자세
- The murals depict people in various poses, standing, sitting, squatting, and kneeling.

[s] position

0604
problem
/prábləm/

문제
- There are some problems with this argument.
ⓤ have a problem with sb/sth
① ~에 동의하지 않는다(반대한다)
- Many scientists **have problems with** the arguments outlined in the passage.
② ~에/~와 문제가 있다
- I **have a problem with** my roommate.

0605
response
/rispáns/

1. 답장
- Thanks for your immediate response to my question.

2. 반응
- The smoking ban provoked an angry response from many smokers.

▶ in response to sth ~에 대응해서
- In response to the recent surge in oil prices, many car manufacturers are developing electric vehicles.

[s] reaction

0606
sacrifice
/sǽkrifàis/

1. 희생
ⓤ make sacrifices 희생하다
- Children today tend to take **sacrifices** their parents **make** for their success for granted. *take sth for granted ~을 당연시하다

2. 제물
◇ offer sacrifices to Gods 신들에게 제물을 바치다
- They put the sacrifices that they wanted to offer to the gods in a sacred place.

0607
state
/stéit/

1. 국가, (미국의) 주
- KEPCO is a state-owned company that provides electricity.

2. 상태
ⓤ in a state of sth ~의 상태에 있는
- When the ambulance arrived, she was already **in a state of** unconsciousness.

0608
view
/vjúː/

1. 견해
ⓤ a point of view about sth ~에 대한 견해(관점)
- The newspaper's point of view is highly partisan.

2. 전망
- The hotel features rooms with ocean views and also has a hot spring.

[s] perspective

[s] panorama 전경(넓은 곳의 전망)

0609 way
/wéi/

1. 방식
- the way S주어 V동사 ~하는 방식
- the way he's dressed 그가 옷 입는 방식
- I don't like **the way** people shout at me like that.

2. 방법
- find alternative ways to reduce packaging waste 포장 쓰레기를 줄이는 대안적인 방법을 찾다
- There are many ways in which four couples can be seated at a round table.

3. (특정한 행동) 방식, 태도
- The inhabitants behaved toward us in a hostile way.

[S] manner

verb 동사

0610 adjoin
/ədʒɔ́in/ /어조인/

~에 인접하다, 붙어 있다
- The house adjoins a historic monument.

▶ adjoining (형용사) 인접한, 가까운

[S] be next to

0611 attach
/ətǽtʃ/

1. 붙이다
- attach A to B: A를 B에 붙이다
- Lots of materials **are attached to** metals in the deposits, which makes it difficult to extract precious metals through this method.

2. (파일 등을) 첨부하다
- I've attached the file to this email.

[A] detach 떼어 내다

0612 choke
/tʃóuk/

1. 질식시키다
- choke (a person) to death 질식사하다
- A camper **choked to death** in his sleep.

2. 가득 채우다
- be choked with traffic 차량으로 꽉 막히다
- The roads **are choked with traffic**.

[S] suffocate

[S] clog, block

0613 cling
/klíŋ/

매달리다, 달라(들러)붙다
- cling to sth ~에 달라붙다
- Penguins cling together to stay warm in cold weather.

[S] stick

0614 coax
/kóuks/ /콕스/

달래다
- coax sb into doing sth 간신히 ~을 ~하게하다
- His parents **coaxed** Auggie **into** go**ing** to school.

0615 deliver
/dilívər/

1. 배달(전달)하다
- have sth delivered (to sth) (~로) 배달받다
- Restaurants are still closed but you can **have** food **delivered**.

2. (판결 등을) 내리다, (강의나 연설 등을) 하다
- deliver a speech 연설하다 / deliver a lecture 강의하다 / deliver a verdict 판결을 내리다
- Susan B. Anthony was famous for **delivering** passionate anti-slavery **speeches**.

3. (타격 등을) 가하다
- deliver a blow 타격을 가하다

0609 나는 사람들이 나에게 그렇게 소리치는 방식을 좋아하지 않는다. / 둥근 테이블에 4쌍의 커플이 앉을 수 있는 많은 방법이 있다. / 주민들은 우리에게 적대적인 태도로 행동했다. 0610 그 집은 역사적으로 중요한 기념물에 인접해 있다. 0611 많은 물질들이 퇴적물 속 금속에 붙어 있어서, (이것이) 이 방법을 통해 귀중한 금속을 추출하는 것을 어렵게 만든다. / 이 이메일에 파일을 첨부했습니다. 0612 한 야영객이 자다가 질식사했다. / 도로는 차량으로 꽉 막혀 있다. 0613 펭귄들은 추운 날씨에 따뜻하게 유지하기 위해 서로 달라붙어 있다. 0614 그의 부모님은 간신히 Auggie를 학교에 가게 했다. 0615 식당들은 여전히 문을 닫고 있지만 당신은 음식을 배달받을 수 있다. / 수잔 B. 앤서니는 열정적인 노예 제도 반대 연설을 한 것으로 유명했다.

0616
disintegrate
/disíntigrèit/

1. 해체(분해)되다
   - ⓥ disintegrate into sth ~로 분해되다
   - ○ The empire **disintegrated into** small city states.

2. 파괴되다, 산산조각이 나다
   - ○ The engines of the plane disintegrated as a flock of birds was sucked into them.

ⓢ break into small pieces, break up, fall apart

0617
emerge
/imə́:rdʒ/

1. 나타나다, 나오다
   - ⓥ emerge from sth ~에서 나오다
   - ○ The sun **emerged from** dark clouds.

ⓢ appear, come out
ⓢ come out of sth

2. (사실이나 증거 등이) 드러나다, 알려지다
   - ○ It emerged that he had had an affair with her.

ⓢ transpire

▶ emergence (명사) 출현

0618
exacerbate
/igzǽsərbèit/
/이그재서*베이트/

악화시키다
- ○ This lack of exercise, of course, exacerbates people's ill health.

ⓢ aggravate, worsen

0619
hail
/héil/

(높이) 평가하다
- ⓥ be hailed as sth ~로 (높이) 평가받고 있다
- ○ Draisaitl, an ice hockey player from Germany, has **been hailed as** one of the best athletes in the world.

0620
halt
/hɔ́:lt/

멈추다, 중단하다
- ○ Production has (been) halted because of a strike.

ⓢ stop

▶ halt (명사) 멈춤
- ⓥ bring sth to a halt ~을 멈추게 하다 / come to a halt 멈추다
- ○ The whole city **came to a halt** because of the pandemic.

0621
inquire
/inkwáiər/

1. 물어보다
   - ⓥ inquire about sth ~에 대해 물어보다
   - ○ I called the theater to **inquire about** the price of a ticket.

2. 조사하다
   - ⓥ inquire into sth ~을 조사하다
   - ○ The committee will **inquire into** the allegations of sexual harassment brought against the Managing Director Designate.

ⓢ investigate

0622
mock
/mák/

조롱하다, 비웃다, 흉내를 내며 놀리다
- ○ Among the politicians was the former minister who had been laughed at and mocked by comedians who copied the way he behaved and spoke.

ⓢ make fun of, ridicule, laugh at

▶ mock (형용사) 가짜의
◇ a mock interview 모의 인터뷰

0623
proceed
/prəsí:d/

1. 나아가다, 전진하다
   - ○ Preparations for the event have not proceeded according to plan.

ⓢ go ahead

2. 계속하다
   - ⓥ proceed to do sth 계속해서(이어서) ~을 하다
   - ○ She took off her mask and then **proceeded to** sit down on the floor at Cosco.
   - ○ The coach **proceeded to** tell him the news.

ⓢ go on

0616 그 제국은 작은 도시 국가들로 해체되었다. / 한 무리의 새떼들이 엔진으로 빨려 들어갔을 때 비행기 엔진이 산산조각이 났다. 0617 해가 검은 구름에서 나왔다. / 그가 그녀와 바람을 피웠다는 것이 드러났다. 0618 물론 이런 운동 부족은 사람들의 좋지 않은 건강을 악화시킨다. 0619 독일 출신의 아이스하키 선수인 Draisaitl은 세계 최고의 운동선수 중 한 명으로 높이 평가받고 있다. 0620 파업으로 생산이 중단되었다. / 도시 전체가 팬데믹 때문에 멈추었다. 0621 나는 극장에 입장권 값에 대해 물어보기 위해 전화했다. / 위원회는 상무 이사 지명자에 대해 제기된 성희롱 혐의를 조사할 것이다. 0622 정치인들 중에는 그가 행동하고 말하는 방식을 흉내 낸 코미디언들에 의해 비웃음과 조롱을 받았던 전임 장관도 있었다. 0623 행사 준비는 계획대로 나아가지 않았다. / 그녀는 마스크를 벗고 나서 이어서 코스코 바닥에 앉았다. / 코치는 계속해서 그에게 그 소식을 말했다.

0624
relate
/riléit/

1. 관련(결부)시키다 — connect
- relate A to B: A와 B를 결부시키다
- Linguistic evidence **relates** English **to** French.

2. ~을 이야기하다 — tell
- relate A to B: B에게 A를 이야기하다
- Initially, his colleagues **to** whom he **related** the story were as speechless as I was.

N relate to sb/sth ~와 관련이 있다 — have (something) to do with sb/sth
- Please be aware of the laws and regulations relating to students with disabilities.

0625
sneak
/sníːk/
*sneak-snuck-snuck

조용히 몰래 가다 — go secretly
- She snuck into her room so that she didn't wake her father up.

▶ sneak (형용사) 몰래 하는 — stealthy, furtive

0626
sting
/stíŋ/
*sting-stung-stung

(식물, 곤충, 동물 등이) 찌르다, 쏘다
- Be careful not to be stung by a bee.

0627
win
/wín/

1. 이기다
① win sb sth / win sth for sb ~에게 ~을 이기게 해 주다
- Three critical errors made by their opponents **won** the match **for** the Giants.
② win a race / an election / a game / a war / an argument / a case 시합/선거/게임/전쟁/논쟁/소송을 이기다
- The lawyer was able to **win** the **case** because of the forensic evidence. *forensic 법의학적인

2. (상을) 타다, (복권 등에) 당첨되다, (노력을 통해) 얻다 — gain
- He won the Nobel Prize in Literature in 1989.
- His life has changed radically since he won the lottery.
ⓤ win a victory over sb/sth ~을 상대로 승리를 거두다 / win a contract 계약을 따내다 / win support for sth ~에 대해 지지를 얻다 / win sb sth / win sth for sb ~에게 ~을 얻게 해 주다
- Joe Biden **won a** narrow **victory over** Donald Trump in the presidential election.
- This sea battle **won** him a great victory.
(=This sea battle **won** a great victory **for** him.)

0624 언어적 증거는 영어와 프랑스어를 결부시킨다. / 처음에 그가 그 스토리를 이야기한 그의 동료들은 나만큼 말문이 막혔다. / 장애 학생과 관련이 있는 규제와 법률을 알기 바란다. 0625 그녀는 그녀의 아버지를 깨우지 않기 위해 그녀의 방으로 몰래 들어갔다. 0626 벌에게 쏘이지 않도록 조심해라. 0627 상대편이 저지른 결정적인 실책 3개가 자이언츠에게 그 시합을 이기게 해 주었다. / 그 변호사는 법의학적 근거로 그 소송을 이길 수 있었다. / 그는 1989년에 노벨 문학상을 탔다. / 그가 복권에 당첨된 이래로 그의 인생은 빠르게 바뀌고 있다. / 조 바이든은 대통령 선거에서 도널드 트럼프를 상대로 아슬아슬한 승리를 거두었다. / 이 해전이 그에게 큰 승리를 얻게 해 주었다.

adjective 형용사

0628 amiable
/éimiəbl/ /에이미*어블/

상냥한, 친절한
- My neighbor, who lives on the 25th floor, is amiable and polite.

S friendly, pleasant, kind

0629 bold
/bóuld/

용감한, 대담한
- King Cnut was not only a great king, but he was also a bold soldier himself. He would fight side by side with his men.

▶ boldly (부사) 용감하게

S courageous, fearless, daring

0630 coincident
/kouínsidənt/ /코우인*시던트/

(사건이) 동시에 일어나는
- coincident with sth ~와 동시에 일어나는
- The extinction of the sea cow was **coincident with** the appearance of European fur traders who came to the islands to hunt them.

0631 dependable
/dipéndəbl/

믿을 수 있는, 신뢰할 만한
- The problem with using wind as an energy source is that sometimes it is very strong and sometimes it is totally absent. Basically, it is not dependable.

S reliable
A unreliable 믿을 수 없는

0632 entire
/intáiər/ /인*타이어/

전체의, 전부의
◇ the entire family 전(체) 가족 / an entire set of music 전곡
- Another reason to oppose this law is that the law is not reasonable because it applies a single standard to the entire country.

S whole, total, complete 모두의

0633 incisive
/insáisiv/ /인*사이시브/

예리한, 날카로운, 신랄한
◇ incisive criticism 신랄한 비판
- The new programs presented a brief but incisive analysis of the economic situation.

▶ incisively (부사) 신랄하게, 날카롭게

S sharp, keen, acute

0634 mere
/míər/

1. 겨우 ~의, (단지) ~에 불과한
- The tsunami struck mere minutes after the earthquake. *strike (재난 등이) 발생하다, 덮치다

2. 단순한, 단지 ~만의
- the mere fact / possibility / prospect / thought 단순한 사실/가능성/전망/생각
- **The mere thought** of losing my job scares me so much.

▶ merely (부사) 한낱, 그저, 단지

S just, only, simply

0635 obvious
/ábviəs/

분명한, 명백한
- One obvious reason is that the Celtic population vastly outnumbered the invading Anglo-Saxons. *outnumber ~보다 수가 많다 / vastly 매우

▶ obviously (부사) 분명히, 명백하게, 확실히
- The animal was obviously destined to become extinct.

S clear, apparent
A unclear 분명하지 않은

S evidently

0636 plain
/pléin/

1. 명백한, 분명한
◇ plain truth 명백한 사실
○ It is quite plain that children can't cheat when their parents sit next to them while they are doing their homework.

→ obvious

2. 평범한, 꾸미지 않은, (섞인 것이 없이) 순수한
◇ plain paper 선 없는 백지
○ You might as well eat plain yogurt. It is less fattening.

→ simple

N plain (명사) 평원
○ The deer species inhabits the marshy plain along the Colorado River.

0637 provisional
/prəvíʒənl/
/프러비*저늘/

임시의, 일시적인, 잠정적인
◇ a provisional ball (골프) 잠정구 결과를 확인하기 전에 잠정적으로 치는 볼
○ He continued to play the provisional ball even after he found his original ball that he had thought was out of bounds.

→ temporary

▶ provisionally (부사) 일시적으로
○ The rapid spread of the virus led to schools, public institutions like museums, and many restaurants closing provisionally.

0638 selected
/səléktid/
/설렉*티드/

선발된, 선택된
be / get selected for sb/sth ~로 선발되다 / be / get selected as sb/sth ~로서 선발되다
○ In the end, she **got selected for** the national team.
○ *Nineteen Eighty-Four (1984)* is one of the novels selected for you to read.

0639 silent
/sáilənt/

1. 침묵의, 고요한
○ He remained silent for a few minutes.

→ mute

2. 소리 없는
○ Please put your phone on silent mode.

0640 strenuous
/strénjuəs/
/스트레*뉴어스/

1. 힘든, 고된
○ Strenuous physical exercise in hot weather is bad for senior citizens.

→ arduous, hard, demanding

2. 적극적이고 단호한
make a strenuous effort to do sth ~하기 위한 적극적이고 단호한 노력을 하다
○ The government **made a strenuous effort to** end the pandemic.

→ active and determined

0641 typical
/típikl/

전형적인, 대표적인
◇ typical symptoms 전형적 증상 / a typical example of sth ~의 전형적인 예
○ Another typical example showing that children learn more from their parents is that children learn how to play sports from their parents. Parents are physically stronger than their children.

→ characteristic, archetypal, standard

0642 vibrant
/váibrənt/
/바이*브런트/

1. 활기찬
◇ a vibrant city 활기찬 도시 / one's vibrant personality 활기찬 성격
○ The Hopi Festival is recognized as one of the most vibrant festivals in India.

→ energetic, dynamic, lively

2. (색이) 밝고 강한
○ When corals bleach, their vibrant colors turn almost white. *bleach 희게 되다

→ brilliant

0636 부모들이 그들의 자녀들이 숙제를 하는 동안 그들 옆에 앉아 있을 때 아이들은 부정행위를 저지를 수 없다는 것은 아주 명백하다. / 차라리 플레인 요거트를 먹는 게 낫다. 그것은 덜 살찐다. 0637 심지어 경기장 밖으로 나갔다고 자신이 생각한 원래 공을 찾은 후에도 그는 잠정구로 계속 시합을 했다. / 그 바이러스의 빠른 확산은 학교, 박물관과 같은 공공 기관, 그리고 많은 식당들이 일시적으로 문을 닫게 만들었다. 0638 결국 그녀는 국가 대표로 선발되었다. / *1984*는 너희들이 읽어야 할 선정된 소설 중 하나이다. 0639 그는 몇 분 동안 침묵했다. / 핸드폰을 무음 모드로 해 주세요. 0640 더운 날씨에 힘든 육체적 운동은 노인들에게 안 좋다. / 정부는 팬데믹을 종식시키기 위한 적극적이고 단호한 노력을 하였다. 0641 아이들이 그들의 부모에게서 더 많이 배운다는 것을 보여 주는 또 다른 전형적인 예는 아이들이 그들의 부모에게서 운동하는 법을 배우는 경우이다. 부모들이 신체적으로 그들의 아이들 보다 더 강하다. 0642 호피 축제는 인도에서 가장 활기찬 축제 중 하나로 인정받고 있다. / 산호가 희게 되었을 때, 그들의 밝고 강한 색은 거의 하얗게 변한다.

adverb 부사

0643 extensively /iksténsivli/
광범위하게
- A man traveled extensively throughout Canada, hitchhiking.

0644 pretty /príti/
아주, 매우, 상당히
- And I'm pretty sure you will hear the same thing from him.

[S] fairly

0645 as of /æz əv/
1. 현재로, 현재의
- As of 2019, approximately 1.5 million people in the U.S. alone have been infected with the coronavirus.

2. ~로부터 시작하여
- As of today, all the nuclear power plants must not discharge radioactive waste water into the ocean.

[S] starting from

0646 as with /æz wið/
~와 마찬가지로
- as with A, B ~A와 마찬가지로 B는
- **As with** 'however', 'but' should be followed by a comma.

0643 한 남자가 히치하이킹을 하면서 캐나다 전역을 광범위하게 여행했다. 0644 그리고 당신도 그에게서 같은 말을 듣게 될 거라고 나는 매우 확신합니다. 0645 2019년 현재로 미국에서만 약 150만 명이 코로나바이러스에 감염되었다. / 오늘 부로 모든 원자력 발전소는 방사능 오염수를 바다로 배출해서는 안 된다. 0646 'however'와 마찬가지로 'but'뒤에는 쉼표가 와야 한다.

DAY 14

ANGRY ENGLISH
ACADEMIC VOCABULARY

noun 명사
- [ ] aftermath
- [ ] company
- [ ] discrepancy
- [ ] expansion
- [ ] incident
- [ ] loop
- [ ] maneuver
- [ ] odor
- [ ] platform
- [ ] punctuality
- [ ] relation
- [ ] responsibility
- [ ] sake
- [ ] stimulus
- [ ] temper

verb 동사
- [ ] adjust
- [ ] allow
- [ ] blame
- [ ] circulate
- [ ] comprehend
- [ ] credit
- [ ] dismantle
- [ ] enable
- [ ] exaggerate
- [ ] fling
- [ ] hamper
- [ ] inspire
- [ ] manipulate
- [ ] permit
- [ ] reject
- [ ] restrict
- [ ] soak
- [ ] strive

adjective 형용사
- [ ] animate
- [ ] comfortable
- [ ] consecutive
- [ ] genuine
- [ ] hostile
- [ ] inconclusive
- [ ] inconsequential
- [ ] meticulous
- [ ] obstinate
- [ ] pleasant
- [ ] puzzling
- [ ] slight
- [ ] strict
- [ ] varied

adverb 부사
- [ ] firmly
- [ ] previously
- [ ] properly
- [ ] at once

MP3 파일 다운

noun
명사

0647 aftermath
/ǽftərmæθ/

여파
- in the aftermath of sth ~의 여파로
- in the aftermath the war / the earthquake / the volcanic eruption 전쟁/지진/화산 분출의 여파로
- People began to stockpile food and supplies **in the aftermath of** the pandemic. *stockpile 비축하다

S effects, wake
S in the wake of sth

0648 company
/kʌ́mpəni/

1. 회사
- He sued the company for withholding payment.

2. 손님
- have company 손님이 있다

3. 교제, 친교
- the company of sb ~와의 교제 / enjoy the company of others 다른 사람들과 어울리는 것(친교)을 즐기다
- He hates **the company of** others.

0649 discrepancy
/diskrépənsi/
/디스*크레*펀시/

차이, 불일치
- the discrepancy between A and B: A와 B의 차이
- **The discrepancy between** the real figures **and** the official figures is huge.

S difference
A correspondece 일치(유사함)

0650 expansion
/ikspǽnʃən/

확장, 확대
- the expansion of sth ~의 확장
- **The** rapid **expansion of** cities in the 19th century exacerbated infectious diseases.

0651 incident
/ínsidənt/

(뭔가 안 좋은 또는 이상한) 사건, 사고
- historical incidents 역사적 사건
- Luckily, the election went on without incident.

S episode

0652 loop
/lùːp/

고리
- The man started to make a loop with a rope.

0653 maneuver
/mənúːvər/
/머누버/

1. 묘책, 책략
- Behind the success of the talks between North Korea and the U.S. are a series of diplomatic maneuvers by the Minister of Foreign Affairs of South Korea.

2. 능숙한 움직임, 조작
- The maneuvers that the pilot had performed in such an emergency situation saved all the passengers on board.

0654 odor
/óudər/

(불쾌한) 냄새
- When painting a room, you should avoid using cheap paint. The reason is simple. It is made of chemicals with a suffocating odor. *suffocate 질식사하다, 숨이 막히다

N fragrance (명사) 향기

S smell

S perfume

0647 사람들은 팬데믹의 여파로 식량과 물품을 비축하기 시작했다. 0648 그는 임금을 보류한 것에 대해 그 회사를 고소했다. / 그는 남들과 어울리는 것을 싫어한다. 0649 실제 수치와 공식적 수치 사이의 차이가 크다. 0650 19세기 도시의 급속한 확장은 전염병을 악화시켰다. 0651 다행히 선거는 사고 없이 치러졌다. 0652 그 남자는 밧줄을 가지고 고리를 만들기 시작했다. 0653 북미 회담의 성공 뒤에는 한국 외교부 장관의 일련의 외교적 책략이 있다. / 조종사가 그러한 비상 상황에서 한 조작은 탑승한 모든 승객을 구했다. 0654 방에 페인트칠을 할 때 너는 값싼 페인트를 사용하는 것을 피해야 한다. 이유는 간단하다. 그것은 숨이 막힐 정도의 냄새를 가진 화학 물질로 만들어지기 때문이다.

0655
platform /plǽtfɔːrm/

1. 승강장
◇ platform six 6번 승강장

2. 평평하고 땅 위에서 올라온 부분, 연단, 단상, 강단
○ In *Lord of the Flies*, a four-foot-high platform that looks like a raised jetty is the place where the boys gather to make significant decisions and discuss matters that concern them. *raised (주변 지대보다) 높은 / concern 영향을 미치다 (관련되다)

S stage, rostrum

3. 대 장비 등을 받치거나 올려놓게 만든 물건
◇ oil / gas platform (바다 위에) 석유/가스 굴착대 / viewing platform 전망대 / a launch platform 발사대

4. (정당의) 강령
○ He ran for president with the political platform that all men are created equal.

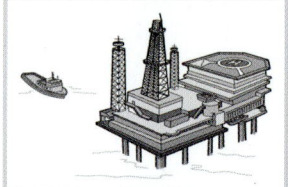

0656
punctuality /pʌ́ŋktʃuǽləti/

정확함
○ In her poems, we can find that she didn't take punctuality seriously.

▶ punctual (형용사) 정확한

S promptness

S prompt, on time

0657
relation /riléiʃən/

관계
Ⓤ relations between A and B: A와 B의 관계
◇ awkward relations with Japan 일본과의 어색한 관계
○ Several African countries severed diplomatic relations with Israel. *sever 단절하다

N relationship (명사) 관련, 연관성
◇ the relationship between squirrels and oak trees 다람쥐와 떡갈나무와의 연관성

0658
responsibility /rispánsibiləti/ /리스판*시빌러티/

1. 책임(감), 의무
Ⓤ it's sb's responsibility to do sth ~하는 것이 ~의 의무이다
○ It's my **responsibility to** deliver useful and valuable information.

S duty

2. (잘못된 일에 대한) 책임
Ⓤ take / accept (full) responsibility for sth ~에 대한 (모든) 책임을 지다
○ After World War I, the victorious Allies forced Germany to **take** full **responsibility for** the war.

S blame

3. (도덕적, 사회적) 책임감 (가산)
Ⓤ have a responsibility to sb ~에 대한 책임감을 가지고 있다 / have a responsibility to do sth ~해야 하는 책임감을 가지고 있다
○ Businesses also **have a responsibility to** protect the environment.

0659
sake /séik/

이익, 위함
Ⓤ for the sake of sb / for sb's sake ~을 (돕기) 위해
◇ for the sake of his children 그의 아이들을 위해
○ He quit his job **for the sake of** his health.

0660
stimulus
/stímjələs/
stimuli복수 /stímjəlai/

자극
- Plants grow in response to external stimuli, especially the amount of sunlight that they receive.

0661
temper
/témpər/

화, 성질(성미), 성격
- lose one's temper 화를 내다 / be in a temper 화가 나 있다
- His fiery temper often puts his family in a position that makes them uneasy.

N good-tempered (형용사) 착한 / bad-tempered (형용사) 욱하는 성격의

verb 동사

0662
adjust
/ədʒʌ́st/
/어저스트/

1. 조절(조정)하다
- Artists would have to adjust their projects to satisfy the political desires of the current government.

S change, tailor

2. 적응하다
- adjust to sth ~에 적응하다
- It took him a couple of minutes to **adjust to** the darkness in the room.

S adapt, change
S adapt to sth

3. (매무새 등을) 바로잡다, 단정히 하다
- Dad, adjusting his tie, told me not to spend the night at my friend's house. *spend the night at a friend's house 친구 집에서 자다

0663
allow
/əláu/

1. 허용하다
- allow O목적어 to do 목적어가 ~하는 것을 허용하다
- Scientifically important fossils are now being sold to private collectors who don't **allow** ordinary people **to** view their collections.

S permit, let

2. 가능하게 하다
- allow O목적어 to do 목적어가 ~하는 것을 가능하게 하다
- Government support **allows** students **to** get a higher-quality education.

S enable

N allow for sb/sth
1) 가능하게 하다
- The Hubble Telescope allowed for more discoveries about our solar system.
2) 고려하다
- The game doesn't allow for multiple players.

S consider

0664
blame
/bléim/

비난하다, 탓하다, 원인으로 보다
U
① blame A for B: A를 B한 것에 대해 비난하다
- Politicians often try to find a scapegoat to **blame for** things that go wrong. *scapegoat 희생양
② blame A for B / blame B on A: A를 B의 원인으로 보다
- Many scientists **blame** European fur traders **for** the extinction of sea cows.
(=Many scientists **blame** the extinction of sea cows **on** European fur traders.)
③ be to blame for sth ~의 원인이다
- Junk food **is to blame for** obesity.

S accuse, upbraid, reproach

S be the reason for sth, be responsible for sth

0660 식물은 외부 자극, 특히 그들이 받는 햇빛의 양에 반응하여 자란다. 0661 그의 불같은 성격은 종종 그의 가족을 불편하게 만드는 상황에 처하게 한다. 0662 예술가들은 현 정부의 정치적 욕구를 충족시키기 위해 그들의 프로젝트를 조정해야 할 것이다. / 그는 방안의 어두움에 적응하는 데 몇 분이 걸렸다. / 넥타이를 바로잡으면서 아빠는 나에게 친구 집에서 자지 말라고 말했다. 0663 과학적으로 중요한 화석들이 일반인들이 자신들의 수집품을 보는 것을 허용하지 않는 개인 수집가들에게 지금 팔리고 있는 중이다. / 정부 지원은 학생들이 더 높은 질의 고육을 받는 것을 가능하게 한다. / 허블 망원경은 우리의 태양계에 대한 더 많은 발견을 가능하게 했다. / 그 게임은 다수의 플레이어를 고려하지 않는다. 0664 정치인들은 자주 잘못되어 가는 일에 대해 비난할 희생양을 찾으려고 노력한다. / 많은 과학자들은 유럽 모피상들을 바다소의 멸종 원인으로 본다. / 정크 푸드가 비만의 원인이다.

0665 circulate
/sə́ːrkjulèit/
/서쿨*레이트/

1. (혈액 등이) 순환하다, 돌다
- The heart has four chambers through which blood flows, all of which need to function properly for blood to circulate well.

2. (소문, 뉴스 등이) 유포되다(퍼지다), (화폐 등이) 유통되다 [S] spread, get around, go around
- The news that President Trump had lost the election circulated quickly.
- Counterfeit money became a serious problem, as it circulated in a colony that is now Boston. *counterfeit 위조의, 가짜의

▶
1. circulation (명사) 유통
2. circulatory (형용사) (혈액 등이) 순환하는
◇ circulatory organs 순환기

0666 comprehend
/kɑ́mprihend/

이해하다 [S] understand, grasp, perceive
- Reading newspapers or magazines from a particular country does not always help you to understand that country very well.

0667 credit
/krédit/

믿다, 여기다, 인정하다 [S] believe, consider, admit
ⓤ credit A with B: A가 B(뭔가 좋은 것을)를 했다고 믿다(여기다)   [A] discredit 의심하다
- People **credit** Darwin **with** inventing the theory of evolution.
- Darwin **is credited with** inventing the theory of evolution.

0668 dismantle
/dismǽntl/
/디스*맨틀/

1. (기계 등을) 분해하다 [S] take apart
- The more skillful you are at dismantling a machine, the better able you will be to fix it.

2. (조직 등을) 해체하다 [S] abolish, end
- The have-nots started to dismantle the systems that enabled the haves to exploit them.

0669 enable
/inéibl/

가능하게 하다, 할 수 있게 하다 [S] allow
ⓤ enable O목적어 to do sth 목적어가 ~하는 것을 가능하게 하다   [S] allow O목적어 to do sth / make it possible for sb/sth to do sth
- Domestic animals that pulled plows used for turning over soil **enabled** people **to** move to the Great Plains to farm.
(=Domestic animals that pulled plows used for turning over soil made it possible for people to move to the Great Plains to farm.)

0670 exaggerate
/igzǽdʒərèit/
/이그재줘*레이트/

과장하다 [S] overstate, dramatize
- The argument that the introduction of new species disturbs the ecological balance seems to be quite exaggerated.

▶ exaggeration (명사) 과장

0671 fling
/flíŋ/
*fling-flung-flung

(거칠게) (내)던지다 [S] hurl, throw, chuck
- He was suspended for three months for flinging his bat at home plate.

0672 hamper
/hǽmpər/

방해하다 [S] hinder
ⓤ hamper O목적어 from doing sth 목적어가 ~하는 것을 방해하다
- High winds **hampered** the rescue teams **from** gett**ing** to the top of the mountain.

0665 심장은 피가 흐르는 네 개의 심실을 가지고 있는데, 이 심실 모두가 피가 잘 순환하기 위해 제대로 기능을 할 필요가 있다. / 트럼프 대통령이 졌다는 소식이 빠르게 퍼졌다. / 위조지폐는 지금의 보스톤인 식민지에서 유통되면서 심각한 문제가 되었다. 0666 특정 국가에서 온 신문이나 잡지를 읽는 것이 항상 당신이 그 나라를 잘 이해하도록 도와주는 것은 아니다. 0667 사람들은 다윈이 진화론을 창안했다고 믿는다. / 다윈이 진화론을 창안한 것으로 여겨지고 있다. 0668 당신이 한 기계를 분해하는 데 능숙할수록, 당신은 그것을 더 잘 고칠 수 있을 것이다. / 못 가진 자들이 가진 자들이 그들을 착취하는 것을 가능하게 만든 제도를 해체하기 시작했다. 0669 토양을 뒤집는 데 사용되는 쟁기를 끌던 가축들은 사람들로 하여금 농사를 짓기 위해 대평원으로 이동하는 것을 가능하게 했다. 0670 새로운 종의 도입이 생태적 균형을 교란시킨다는 주장은 상당히 과장된 것 같다. 0671 그는 홈 플레이트에 방망이를 내던진 것 때문에 3개월 동안 출전 정지를 당했다. 0672 강풍은 구조대가 산 정상에 이르는 것을 방해했다.

0673 inspire
/inspáiər/
/인스*파이어/

1. 고무(격려)하다
- ⓥ inspire sb to do ~에게 ~하도록 고무시키다
- In the 1960s, for example, the Korean government **inspired** its people **to** buy cars manufactured by domestic car companies.

2. 영감을 주다
- ⓥ be inspired by sth ~에 의해 영감을 받다
- It was **by** a business presentation that his idea of inventing electric cars **was inspired**.

[S] encourage

0674 manipulate
/mənípjulèit/
/머니퓰레이트/

1. 조종(조작)하다
- ◇ manipulate public opinion 여론을 조작하다
- A political party that holds radical attitudes toward the stock market is trying to manipulate public opinion for its own profit.

[S] control, influence

2. (어려운 장비나 기계 등을) (잘) 다루다, (능숙하게) 조작하다
- ◇ manipulate a computer 컴퓨터를 잘 다루다
- People can intentionally manipulate the weather by making rain fall in drought-affected areas.

[S] handle, operate

▶ manipulation (명사) 조작
◇ the manipulation of the camera 카메라 조작

0675 permit
/pərmít/

허락(허용)하다
- ⓥ permit doing sth ~하는 것을 허락하다 / permit O목적어 to do 목적어가 ~하는 것을 허락하다
- During the suspension period, he **is** not **permitted to** attend school.

[S] allow

0676 reject
/ridʒékt/

거절하다, 거부하다
- China rejects the suggestion that they started the pandemic.

[S] refuse, decline, spurn
[A] accept 받아들이다

▶ rejection (명사) 거부

0677 restrict
/ristríkt/

1. (양, 크기, 또는 범위 등을) 제한하다
- ⓥ restrict A to B: A를 B로 제한하다
- He decided to **restrict** the time allowed to play games **to** 1 hour.

[S] limit, control

2. (법률이나 규칙 등으로) 제한하다, 규제(통제)하다
- ◇ restrict the sale of sth ~의 판매를 제한하다
- They explained how to restrict access to confidential information.

[S] control, limit, hold down

0678 soak
/sóuk/

1. 적시다; 젖다, 스며들다
- ⓥ get soaked 젖다 / soak into sth ~로 스며들다
- The bed in his room **got** completely **soaked** by the rain. He had fallen asleep leaving a window open.

2. (액체 속에) 담그다
- I had him soak the T-shirt in warm water to remove the stain on it. The stain came out after 5 hours of soaking.

ⓝ soak up sth ~을 흡수하다, 빨아들이다

[S] absorb, take in sth

0679 strive
/stráiv/
/스트라이브/

노력하다, 애쓰다, 분투하다
- ⓥ strive to do sth ~하려고 노력하다, 애쓰다
- My dad is a taxi driver. He earns 200 dollars a day. He **strives to** feed his family with very little money.

[S] try, struggle, exert
[S] struggle to do sth, seek to do sth

0673 1960년대, 예를 들면, 한국 정부는 국민들에게 국내 자동차 회사에 의해 제조된 차들을 사도록 고무시켰다. / 바로 한 사업 설명회에 의해 전기 자동차를 발명하려는 그의 생각이 영감을 받았다. 0674 주식 시장에 대한 급진적인 태도를 가지고 있는 한 정당이 자신의 이익을 위하여 여론 조작을 시도하고 있다. / 사람들은 가뭄에 영향을 받는 지역에 비를 내리게 함으로써 날씨를 의도적으로 조작할 수 있다. 0675 정학 기간 동안 그는 학교에 등교하는 것이 허용되지 않는다. 0676 중국은 그들이 팬데믹을 일으켰다는 의견을 거부한다. 0677 그는 게임하는 것이 허용되는 시간을 한 시간으로 제한하기로 결정했다. / 그들은 어떻게 기밀 정보에 접근을 제한하는지를 설명했다. 0678 그의 방의 침대는 비에 완전히 젖었다. 그는 창문을 열어 둔 채 잠이 들었었다. / 나는 그에게 티셔츠에 묻은 얼룩을 없애기 위해 따듯한 물에 티셔츠를 담가 두라고 시켰다. 그 얼룩은 다섯 시간 동안 담근 후에 나왔다. 0679 우리 아버지는 택시 기사이다. 그는 하루에 200달러를 번다. 그는 매우 적은 돈으로 그의 가족들을 먹여 살리려고 노력한다.

adjective 형용사

0680 animate
/ǽnimət/
/애니멋/

살아 있는, 생물의
○ Many science fiction and fantasy books make inanimate objects, like trees, into animate beings.

S living, alive
A inanimate 무생물의, 죽은

N animated (형용사)
1) 활발한, 활기찬
◇ animated conversation / discussion 활기찬 대화/토론
2) 만화 영화의, 살아 있는 듯이 움직이는
◇ animated charts 움직이는 것처럼 보이게 만든 도표

S lively

0681 comfortable
/kʌ́mfətəbl/
/컴퍼*터블/

1. (몸이) 편안한
◇ a comfortable chair / bed 편안한 의자/침대

2. 편한, 기분 좋은
ⓤ comfortable (in) doing sth ~하는 것이 편한
○ Some Koreans may feel uncomfortable when they see Muslim women wearing head scarves on the street.
○ She became **comfortable** (in) play**ing** her piece without reading the music.

A uncomfortable 불편한

▶ comfortably (부사) 편안하게
○ They can live affluently and comfortably in their old age.

0682 consecutive
/kənsékjutiv/

연속적인
○ Recently, Seoul recorded more than 600 new cases of the virus for four consecutive days.

S sequential, successive

0683 genuine
/dʒénjuin/
/제뉴인/

1. 진짜의
○ Much of the evidence makes it hard to believe the painting is genuine.

S authentic, real, original

2. (감정 등이) 진심의(진실된), (사람 등이) 진실한(진지한)
○ He showed genuine respect for his father.

S not pretended, sincere, veracious

▶ genuinely (부사) 진심으로, 진실로, 진짜로
○ One of the qualities needed to be a genuinely good friend is honesty.

S sincerely, truly

0684 hostile
/hástl/
/하스틀/

1. 적대적인, 적의
◇ hostile to / towards the Japanese government 일본 정부에 적대적인 / hostile territory 적지
○ The inhabitants behaved toward us in a hostile way.

S antagonistic, aggressive

2. (강하게) 반대(거부)하는
ⓤ hostile to sth ~에 반대하는
○ Most people are **hostile to** the idea of the government providing financial support only for low-income families.

S antagonistic, opposed
S opposed to

▶ hostility (명사) 적개심

S animosity

0685 inconclusive
/ìnkənklúːsiv/
/인*컨클루시브/

(사실이나 증거 등이) 결정적이지 않은, 결론이 나지 않는
○ The results of the research were inconclusive.

S uncertain, vague, ambiguous
A conclusive 결정적인

0680 많은 공상 과학 소설과 판타지 책들은 나무와 같은 무생물들을 생물체로 만든다. 0681 몇몇 한국들은 거리에서 두건을 쓴 무슬림 여성을 보았을 때 불편하다고 느낄지도 모른다. / 그녀는 악보를 보지 않고 자신의 곡을 연주하는 것이 편해졌다. / 그들은 노년에 풍족하고 편안하게 살 수 있다. 0682 최근에 서울은 4일 연속 600명이 넘는 신규 바이러스 환자를 기록했다. 0683 증거의 상당 부분이 그 그림이 진짜라는 것을 믿기 어렵게 만든다. / 그는 그의 아버지에 대한 진실된 존경을 보였다. / 진짜로 좋은 친구가 되기 위해 필요한 자질 중 하나는 정직이다. 0684 주민들은 우리에게 적대적인 태도로 행동했다. / 대부분의 사람들은 정부가 단지 저소득 계층에게만 금융 지원을 제공한다는 생각에 반대한다. 0685 그 연구의 결과는 결정적이지 않았다.

0686
inconsequential
/ìnkansikwénʃəl/
/인*칸시*퀜셜/

중요하지 않은, 하찮은, 사소한
- In that year, the amount of rainfall was inconsequential.

S insignificant, trivial, minor
A consequential 중요한

0687
meticulous
/mətíkjuləs/
/머티*큘러스/

꼼꼼한, 철저한
◇ meticulous research / planning 철저한 연구/계획
- He's always meticulous in checking for grammar and spelling errors.

S thorough, careful

0688
obstinate
/ábstinət/
/압스티넛/

고집센, 집요한, 완강한
- Union General Ulysses. S. Grant encountered obstinate resistance from the Confederacy. *the Union and the Confederacy 미국 남북 전쟁 당시의 북군과 남군

S stubborn

0689
pleasant
/plézənt/
/플레*전트/

기분 좋은, 즐거운, 쾌적한
◇ a pleasant night 즐거운 밤 / a pleasant aromatic smell 기분 좋은 아로마 향
- It's pleasant to go for a walk in the park in the early evening.

A unpleasant 불쾌한

0690
puzzling
/pázliŋ/

이해하기(설명하기) 어려운, 당혹스러운
◇ a puzzling fact 당혹스러운 사실
- The producer made the puzzling film commercially successful.

S baffling, confusing

0691
slight
/sláit/

1. 작은, 약간의
ⓤ a slight increase / decrease 약간의 증가/감소
- ***A slight increase*** in your body temperature is negligible.

2. 대수롭지 않은
◇ a slight novel / film 대수롭지 않은 소설/영화

S small
A big 큰

0692
strict
/stríkt/

(규칙 등이) 엄한(엄격한), (신앙심 등이) 엄격한
◇ strict guidelines 엄격한 지침 / strict Catholics / Christians 엄격한 가톨릭 신자/기독교인
- Parents should make strict rules if they want their children to succeed because strict rules help children to develop good habits such as getting their homework done first before playing with their friends.

▶ strictly (부사)
1) 엄격하게
2) 매우 제한되게
3) 정확하게

S rigorous, stringent
A lenient (판결이나 처벌이) 관대한

S exclusively
S exactly, correctly

0693
varied
/vérid/

다양한
- The research center conducted a poll to get people's varied opinions about making public transportation free.

S diverse, various, different

adverb
부사

0694
firmly
/fɜːrmli/

1. 단단하게(단단히), 꽉
◇ be firmly attached 단단히 부착되어 있다 / fasten your seatbelt firmly 안전벨트를 꽉 매다
○ Make sure the head of the hammer is firmly attached to the handle.

[S] securely

2. 단호하게, 강하게
○ The United States is firmly in opposition to China annexing Taiwan.

[S] steadfastly

0695
previously
/ˈpriːviəsli/

예전에, 전에
◇ six months previously 6개월 전에
○ She previously worked part-time as a waitress in a bar in downtown Manhattan.

[S] before

0696
properly
/ˈprɑpərli/

적절히, 제대로, 예의 바르게
○ He always greets me first when we meet in the elevator. He behaves properly.

0697
at once
/æt wʌns/

1. 즉시
○ I didn't recognize him at once. He had changed so much.

[S] immediately, instantly

2. 동시에
○ Focus on one thing at a time. Don't try to do two things at once.

[S] simultaneously, concurrently, at one time

0694 망치의 머리가 손잡이에 단단히 부착되어 있는지 확인하십시오. / 미국은 중국이 대만을 합병하는 것을 강하게 반대하고 있다.　0695 그녀는 이전에 맨해튼 시내에 있는 한 술집에서 여종업원으로 파트타임으로 일했다.　0696 그는 우리가 엘리베이터에서 만났을 때 항상 나에게 먼저 인사를 한다. 그는 예의 바르게 행동한다.　0697 나는 그를 즉시 못 알아봤다. 그는 너무 많이 변했었다. / 한 번에 한 가지에만 집중해라. 동시에 두 가지 일을 하려고 하지 마라.

DAY 15

ANGRY ENGLISH
ACADEMIC VOCABULARY

noun 명사
- [ ] aim
- [ ] bank
- [ ] chance
- [ ] dimension
- [ ] element
- [ ] innovation
- [ ] lead
- [ ] mechanism
- [ ] peak
- [ ] prowess
- [ ] retention
- [ ] sanctuary
- [ ] scenario
- [ ] strain
- [ ] well

verb 동사
- [ ] admire
- [ ] alleviate
- [ ] benefit
- [ ] cite
- [ ] constitute
- [ ] demonstrate
- [ ] dismay
- [ ] encounter
- [ ] extend
- [ ] force
- [ ] install
- [ ] manifest
- [ ] produce
- [ ] prompt
- [ ] relish
- [ ] soothe
- [ ] subject
- [ ] withdraw

adjective 형용사
- [ ] annual
- [ ] attributable
- [ ] committed
- [ ] convenient
- [ ] definitive
- [ ] essential
- [ ] incredulous
- [ ] indecipherable
- [ ] monotonous
- [ ] obscure
- [ ] plentiful
- [ ] public
- [ ] sole
- [ ] sturdy
- [ ] vague

adverb 부사
- [ ] fortunately
- [ ] hardly
- [ ] by mistake
- [ ] in the first place

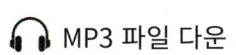 MP3 파일 다운

noun 명사

0698 aim /éim/

목표, 목적
- with the aim of (doing) sth ~의 목표(목적)를 가지고
  - **With the aim of** mak**ing** the atmosphere cleaner, the government passed a law that makes it illegal for companies to produce harmful gases.

▶
1. aimless (형용사) 목적 없는
2. aimlessly (부사) 목적 없이

[S] intention, purpose

[S] purposefully

0699 bank /bæŋk/

1. 둑, 제방, 기슭 강에 맞닿아 있는 땅
- on the bank(s) of sth ~의 기슭(둑)에서
- the banks of the Nile River 나일강 기슭
  - **On the banks of** the Gilo, which is a river full of crocodiles, stood a group of refugees who were being forced to cross the river.

3. (둑 처럼 비슷한 물건이) 길게 늘어선 것
- a bank of lights 길게 늘어서 있는 불빛들

3. (눈이나 구름의) 층, 더미
- a bank of clouds 구름층
  - He walked along a bank of snow.

[S] shore

[S] pile, heap

0700 chance /tʃæns/

1. 가능성
1) There is a chance that S주어 V동사 ~할 가능성이 있다 (=There is a chance of (S주어) Ving동명사) / There is little / no chance that S주어 V동사 가능성이 거의 없다/없다 (=There is little / no chance of (S주어) Ving동명사)
  - **There is a chance that** she will be found alive.
  (=**There is a chance of** her be**ing** found alive.)
2)
① (the) chances are that S주어 V동사 ~할 가능성이 있다
② (the) chances are good that S주어 V동사 ~할 가능성이 높다
  - **The chances are that** private collectors who discover a lot of fossils will donate them to libraries and schools.

2. 기회
① the chance (for sb) to do sth (누군가) ~할 수 있는 기회
② lose a chance to do sth ~할 수 있는 기회를 놓치다
  - I don't want to **lose a chance to** get promoted.
  (=I don't want to miss out on a promotion.)

[S] possibility

[S] (the) odds are that S주어 V동사
[S] (the) odds are good that S주어 V동사

[S] opportunity

[S] miss out on sth

0701 dimension /diménʃən/

1. 관점, 측면
- a political dimension 정치적 관점(측면)

2. 치수, 크기 dimensions
- the dimensions of the kitchen drawer 부엌 서랍의 치수 / a cast bronze statue of vast dimensions 엄청난 크기의 청동 주조 동상

3. 차원
- two dimensions 이차원
  - It's a two-dimensional shape, so if it tears in even one place, there will be a big hole in the web.

4. 규모, 범위 dimensions
- the dimensions of the problem 문제의 규모

[S] aspect

[S] size

0702 element
/éləmənt/
/엘러먼트/

1. 요소
- an element of sth ~의 요소
- Charisma is **a** key **element of** being an entrepreneur.

2. (화학) 원소
- the 3 main chemical elements: carbon, hydrogen, and oxyen 3대 주요 화학원소들: 탄소, 수소, 그리고 산소

[S] part

0703 innovation
/ìnəvéiʃən/
/이너*베이션/

혁신
- Steve Jobs made many innovations in mobile phone technology.

0704 lead
/lí:d/

1. 선두 the lead
- take the lead in sth ~에서 선두에 서다, 주도권을 잡다
- Samsung Electronics began to **take the lead in** semi-conductor technology.

2. (동물 등을 매는) 줄
- keep dogs on leads 개들을 줄에 묶어 두다

[N] lead (명사) (금속) 납
- lead poisoning 납중독
- Lead is a toxic metal.

[S] leash

0705 mechanism
/mékənìzm/

1. 장치, 구조
- the defense mechanism of the human body 신체 방어 구조
- This virus can make the defense mechanisms of the human body break down.

2. 체계, 방법
- a mechanism for doing sth ~하기 위한 방법 / a mechanism to do sth ~하는 방법
- At university my major was education, and I learned the **mechanisms to** control a classroom.

[S] means, system

0706 peak
/pí:k/

1. 절정
- the peak of sth ~의 절정 / be at one's peak 절정에 있다
- The empire reached its peak in the mid 16th century.

2. 산 꼭대기, 봉우리
- mountain peaks 산봉우리

[S] pinnacle, apex, height

[S] summit

0707 prowess
/práuis/
/프라우*이스/

(엄청난) 능력(실력)
- He must train everyday to improve his physical prowess as a golf player.

[S] great ability

0708 retention
/riténʃən/
/리텐션/

보유, 유지, 보존
- the retention of sth ~의 유지(보유)
- **The retention of** knowledge is easier for younger people than for older people.

[S] keeping

0709 sanctuary
/sǽŋktʃuèri/

1. 성역
- Still, churches are sanctuaries for the persecuted.

2. 피난처, 안식처
- find / seek sanctuary 피난처를 찾다
- Since then, Central Park has become a place of sanctuary for New Yorkers who live in the bustling city.

[S] refuge

3. 동물 보호 구역
- This place is used as a wildlife sanctuary.

[S] reserve

0710
scenario /sənériou/

(일어날지 모르는 일 등의) 시나리오(상황)
- Many people think that there is no possible scenario in which North and South Korea can unify.

S situation

0711
strain /stréin/

부담(압박), (근육 등의) 염좌 삔 것
- put a strain on sth ~에 부담을 주다
- Stress can **put a strain on** the heart.

S pressure, stress

0712
well /wél/

우물
- An elementary school in the U.S. raised money to help drill wells for people in Africa.

N will (명사) 유언

verb 동사

0713
admire /ədmáiər/

존경하다
- Good communication skills make people admire their leaders.

S esteem, honor, look up to
A look down on, despise 깔보다, 업신여기다

0714
alleviate /əlí:vièit/

(통증이나 문제점 등을) 완화하다
- Chinese herbal medicines are believed to alleviate pain.

S ease, reduce, relieve

0715
benefit /bénəfit/ /베너핏/

~에게 유리하다, ~에 이익을 주다
- No policy can benefit everyone.

N benefit from sth ~로 인해 이익을 얻다, 덕을 보다
- All citizens seem to benefit from a continuous decrease in the interest rate by the Federal Reserve. *the Federal Reserve 연방 준비은행

S be useful

0716
cite /sáit/ /사이트/

1. 인용하다
- Refer to the article cited above for more information about neuroscience.

S quote, mention

2. (법정에) 소환하다
- cite sb for sth ~의 일로 ~을 소환하다
- A police officer **cited** a man **for** careless driving instead of issuing him a ticket. *careless driving 부주의한 운전(운전 부주의)

S summon

3. 표창하다
- cite sb for sth ~에 대해 ~을 표창하다
- He **was cited for** an act of bravery.

0717
constitute /kánstitjù:t/ /칸스티튜트/

1. 여겨지다
- A sharp decrease in the number of births constitutes a serious social problem.

S be considered

2. 구성하다
- The smallest unit that constitutes a family is two people related by marriage, birth, or adoption.

S form, compose, make up

3. 설립하다
- Once Seoul, where children were able to study in better educational surroundings, began to develop rapidly, many universities were constituted.

S found, establish, set up

▶ constitution (명사) 설립, 구성, 헌법

0718
demonstrate
/démənstrèit/
/데먼*스트레이트/

1. 입증(증명)하다, 보여 주다 — show, prove
- The study demonstrates the link between obesity and adult diseases like diabetes and high blood pressure.

2. 시위하다
- ⓘ demonstrate against sth ~에 항의하는 시위를 하다
- Many small shops in Seoul have started to **demonstrate against** the government's restrictions on opening hours and the number of customers who can enter a store at one time.

0719
dismay
/disméi/

크게 놀라게 하다, 실망시키다 — disappoint
- I was dismayed when I lost my job.

0720
encounter
/inkáuntər/

1. 만나다, 마주치다 — come across
- A common mistake normally made by students is to try to understand the meaning of every word they encounter when reading passages.

2. (어려움이나 문제점에) 직면하다, 부닥치다 — meet, run into
- ◇ encounter a problem 문제점에 맞닥뜨리다
- Union General Ulysses. S. Grant encountered obstinate resistance from the Confederacy. *obstinate 완강한

0721
extend
/iksténd/

1. (도로나 철도 등을) 연장하다
- The prices of houses located near the new subway stations on the extended lines are more likely to soar.

2. 확장하다, 넓히다, 걸치다(달하다), 뻗다; 뻗어 있다 — stretch
- ◇ The extended family 대가족
- He extended his empire to countries around the Mediterranean Sea.
- Glen Canyon extends 186 miles along the Colorado River in northern Arizona.

3. (기간 등을) 연장하다 — prolong
- ◇ extend my visa 비자를 연장하다 / extend the project's deadline 프로젝트 기한을 연장하다

0722
force
/fɔːrs/

강요하다 — push; push sb to do sth
- ⓘ force sb to do sth ~에게 ~할 것을 강요하다
- Universities should not **force** students **to** study history.

0723
install
/instɔ́ːl/

1. 설치하다
- You must first install the application on your phone.

2. 취임시키다
- ⓘ be installed as sb ~로 취임하다
- He **was installed as** the first president of FTK, a non-profit independent organization that represents the interests of businesses.

0724
manifest
/mǽnifèst/
/매니*패스트/

1. (명확히) 보여 주다 — demonstrate, reveal, show
- A series of the government's policies manifest their willingness to bring the continued rise in house prices under control. *bring sth under control 억누르다(억제하다)

2. 나타나다 — appear
- ⓘ manifest oneself in / as sth ~로 나타나다
- Stress can **manifest** itself **in** a variety of physical symptoms.

▶ manifest (형용사) 명백한, 분명한 — evident, apparent

0725
produce /prədjúːs/ /프러*듀스/

만들어 내다, 생산하다
- Cars produce more emissions than trains and trains cause less pollution than cars.

S make, create

0726
prompt /práːmpt/

자극하다, 유발하다, 재촉(촉구)하다
- ⓥ prompt sb to do sth ~에게 ~할 것을 자극(재촉)하다
- His doctor warned him that he could die if he continued to gain weight, which **prompted** him **to** go on a diet.

S provoke

▶ prompt (형용사) 즉각적인

S immediate

0727
relish /réliʃ/ /렐리쉬/

즐기다, 좋아하다
- ⓥ relish the chance to do sth ~할 수 있는 기회를 즐기다 / relish doing sth ~하는 것을 즐기다
- She is relishing the idea of going to Harvard University next year.

S enjoy

0728
soothe /súːð/

1. 달래다, 진정시키다, 위로하다
- A mom is soothing her crying baby.

S calm, console 위로하다, comfort

2. (아픔이나 고통 등을) 누그러뜨리다
- This lotion helps soothe itchy skin.

S relieve, alleviate, ease

0729
subject /səbdʒékt/ /서브*젝트/

겪게 하다, 받게 하다, 드러내놓다
- Many employers **subjected** their employees **to** unfair treatment.
- ⓥ
- ① be subjected to sth ~을 당하다, 겪다, 받다
- The prisoners had **been subjected to** torture and inhumane treatment.
- ② be subjected to sth ~에 노출되다
- The pottery **was subjected to** a hot temperature to make it stronger. It was not adorned that much; for example, it was not glazed. *glaze (도자기에) 유약을 바르다

S be exposed to sth

▶ subject (형용사) ~의 지배를 받는, ~을 따르는
- Every citizen is subject to the laws that Congress enacts.

0730
withdraw /wiðdrɔ́ː/
*withdraw-withdrew-withdrawn

1. 빼내다, 인출하다
- ⓥ withdraw A from B: B에서 A를 빼내다
- You can withdraw and deposit money online without going to the bank.

S take out

2. (조직에서) 탈퇴하다, (시합에서) 빠지다
- ◇ withdraw from the EU EU에서 탈퇴하다 / withdraw from the competition 시합에서 빠지다
- Argentina will withdraw from the Organization of American States (OAS).

3. (지지, 지원 또는 말했던 것 등을) 철회하다
- He withdrew his support for the candidate Moon just 5 hours before election day.

4. (군대 등을) 철수하다
- The U.S. will soon withdraw its troops from that country.

▶ withdrawal (명사) 인출, 철수, 철회, 금단 현상(=withdrawal symptoms)

A deposit 예금(입금)

adjective
형용사

0731 annual
/ǽnjuəl/
/애뉴얼/

일년의
◇ an annual event 연중 행사 / an annual income 연봉 / annual leave 연간 휴가 (연차)
○ The company's budget is forecast on an annual basis.

S yearly

0732 attributable
/ətríbjutəbl/
/어트리*뷰터블/

기인하는
ⓤ A be attributable to B: A는 B 때문이다
○ The forest fire that broke out in Son-ja-rung, seen as a sacred place for camping by campers, **was attributable to** a careless camper who made a fire.

S A be attributed to B, A be caused by B

0733 committed
/kəmítid/
/커미*티드/

헌신적인, 열성적인, 전념하는(몰두하는)
ⓤ be committed to sth ~에 전념하다
◇ a committed member 열성 당원
○ The government of Canada **is committed to** securing 3 million COVID-19 vaccine doses to administer to its citizens. *secure 확보하다 / dose 투여량 / administer 투여하다

S dedicated
S be dedicated to sth

0734 convenient
/kənvíːniənt/

1. 편리한
◇ convenient facilities 편의 시설
○ The mobile phone is convenient for old people to use.
○ As a city becomes more developed, many convenient facilities, such as shopping malls and theaters, are built.

S useful, easy 하기 쉬운

2. 가까운
ⓤ convenient to sth ~에 가까운
○ The apartment is very **convenient to** the station.
○ The apartment is just 5 minutes from the station. It's very convenient.

0735 definitive
/difínitiv/
/디피니*티브/

최종적인, 최고의 더 이상 향상될 수 없을 정도의 완벽한
◇ a definitive judgement 최종 판결
○ A definitive agreement on the pay raise was reached after a strike by the workers.

S final

▶ definitively (부사) 확실(명확)하게, 분명하게, 최종적으로
○ We cannot definitively say why whales are being found dead on beaches in large numbers.

N definite (형용사) 확실한 ◇ a definite answer 확실한 답변

0736 essential
/isénʃəl/
/이센셜/

1. 필수적인
○ To increase sales, it is essential for companies to find a new strategy suitable for rapidly changing economic or political circumstances.

S vital, necessary, needed

2. 근본적인, 본질적인
○ The psychological definition of self-discipline is so complex that it is difficult to tell the essential difference between self-control and self-discipline.

S fundamental, basic

0737 incredulous
/inkrédʒələs/

믿기 힘든, 믿으려 하지 않는, 의심하는
○ My mother gave me an incredulous look when I told her I wanted to drop out of university and become a singer.

S suspicious, dubious
A credulous 잘 믿는, 잘 속는

0731 그 회사의 예산은 1년 단위로 예측된다. 0732 캠퍼들에 의해 캠핑의 성지로 여겨지는 선자령에서 난 산불은 모닥불을 피운 한 부주의한 캠퍼 때문이었다. 0733 캐나다 정부는 그들의 시민들에게 투여할 3백만 코로나19 백신 투여량을 확보하는 데 전념하고 있다. 0734 그 핸드폰은 노인분들이 사용하기 편리하다. / 도시가 더 발달하게 되면서 쇼핑몰과 영화관과 같은 많은 편의 시설들이 지어진다. / 그 아파트는 역에 매우 가깝다. / 그 아파트는 역에서 겨우 5분 거리에 있다. 그것은 매우 가깝다. 0735 임금 인상에 대한 최종 합의는 노동자들의 파업 이후에 이루어졌다. / 우리는 왜 고래들이 대규모로 해변에서 죽은 채로 발견되고 있는지 확실히 말할 수 없다. 0736 매출을 늘리기 위해서 기업들이 급변하는 경제 또는 정치적 상황에 적합한 새로운 전략을 찾는 것은 필수적이다. / 자기 수양에 대한 심리학적 정의는 매우 복잡하여 자제와 자기 수양의 본질적인 차이를 구별하는 것은 어렵다. 0737 내가 대학을 그만두고 가수가 되고 싶다고 어머니에게 말했을 때 어머니는 믿기 힘든 표정을 지었다.

0738
indecipherable
/ìndisáifərəbl/
/인디*사이퍼러블/

해독할 수 없는, 읽을 수 없는
- His handwriting is indecipherable.

▶ decipher (동사) 해독하다

S illegible, unreadable
A decipherable 해독 가능한

0739
monotonous
/mənátənəs/
/머나*터너스/

단조로운
- But as time passes, you will definitely become bored with the monotonous routine of life in the countryside.

▶ monotony (명사) 단조로움, 지루함

S tedious, dull, repetitive

0740
obscure
/əbskjúər/
/업*스큐어/

이해하기 힘든, 모호한
- Your essay is obscure.

S unclear, uncertain, vague
A explicit 명백한

0741
plentiful
/pléntifl/
/플렌*티플/

풍부한, 많은
- There still would have been plentiful predators to eat the sea urchins, so the sea cows would have had food.

S abundant

0742
public
/pʌ́blik/

1. 공공의, 대중의, 공적인
◇ public opinion 여론 / public transportation 대중교통 / public parks 공원 / public places 공공장소
- Almost every government in the world has the right to take private property for public use, but it must be done through legal means. *take private property 사유재산(사적 소유권)을 빼앗다
- The diversion of public funds by the President to pay for his own home caused his downfall.

2. 공개하는
ⓤ
① make sth public ~을 공개하다
- Details of how his crewmates abandoned him alive have not **been made public**.
② go public (비밀을) 공개하다; (일반인들에게 주식을) 공개(상장)하다
- After dropping out of Reed College, he and his best friend Steve Wozniak started a company in the garage of his parents' home, and the company **went public** in 1981.
- When do you want to **go public**?

N in public 사람들이 있는 데서
- In Korea, most old couples don't hold hands in public.

A private 사적인

A in private 사람들이 없는 데서

0743
sole
/sóul/

1. 유일한, 하나의
- His sole interest is to eat delicious meals.

2. 독점적인, 단독의
ⓤ have sole responsibility for sth ~에 대해 단독으로 책임지고 있다 / have sole rights to do sth ~하는 독점적인 권리를 가지고 있다
- The organization **has sole responsibility for** supervising and regulating bank operations.

▶
1. sole (명사) 발바닥, 밑창
◇ shoes with rubber soles 고무 밑창이 있는 신발
2. solely (부사) 혼자서, 오로지, 단지
- The structures were used solely for that purpose.

S only, single

S only, exclusively

0744 sturdy
/stə́ːrdi/
/스터디/

강한, 튼튼한
- Sturdy boots might afford protection to manual workers.

N stocky (형용사) 다부진

S robust, hardy

0745 vague
/véig/

애매한, 모호한
- The animal had already become extinct for reasons that remain vague.

▶ vaguely (부사) 애매모호하게

S unclear, ambiguous, imprecise

adverb 부사

0746 fortunately
/fɔ́ːrtʃənətli/
/포춰*넛리/

운좋게, 다행히
- But, fortunately, we were able to contact you on the Internet.

S luckily

0747 hardly
/háːrdli/

거의 ~않는
- He hardly eats before competitions.

N 빈도부사
- always (언제나) 100%
- usually (대개) 90%
- frequently (자주) 80%
- often (종종) 70%
- sometimes (때때로) 50%
- occasionally (이따금) 30%
- seldom (좀처럼 ~하지 않는) 15%
- rarely (거의 ~않는) 5%
- hardly (거의 ~않는) 5%
- almost never (거의 ~없는) 3%
- never (절대 ~않는) 0%

- He rarely practices before competitions.
- Out of breath, I could hardly talk.

S almost not

0748 by mistake
/bai misteik/

실수로, 잘못하여
- The soup had a unique taste after he added too much chili powder to it by mistake.

S accidently 우연히
A deliberately 일부러, on purpose 고의로

0749 in the first place
/in ðə fɜːst pleis/

처음부터, 애초에
- If I had known the well was deep, I wouldn't have jumped into it in the first place.

S from the beginning

0744 강한 부츠는 육체노동자들에게 보호를 제공할지도 모른다. 0745 그 동물은 여전히 모호한 상태로 남아 있는 이유로 이미 멸종하였다. 0746 하지만 다행히 우리는 인터넷에서 당신과 연락할 수 있었다. 0747 그는 시합전에는 거의 먹지 않는다. / 그는 대회전에 거의 연습을 하지 않는다. / 숨이 차서 거의 아무 말도 할 수 없었다. 0748 실수로 국물에 너무 많은 고춧가루를 넣은 후에 국물은 독특한 맛이 났다. 0749 만약 내가 우물이 깊다는 것을 알았다면 애초에 우물에 뛰어들지 않았을 것이다.

DAY 16
ANGRY ENGLISH
ACADEMIC VOCABULARY

noun 명사

- [ ] approach
- [ ] chip
- [ ] dispersal
- [ ] edge
- [ ] heyday
- [ ] limit
- [ ] opportunity
- [ ] portion
- [ ] provocation
- [ ] retrospect
- [ ] scale
- [ ] scapegoat
- [ ] sorrow
- [ ] story
- [ ] well-being

verb 동사

- [ ] adopt
- [ ] align
- [ ] belittle
- [ ] claim
- [ ] concede
- [ ] consider
- [ ] denote
- [ ] design
- [ ] engender
- [ ] expose
- [ ] forge
- [ ] hamstring
- [ ] intensify
- [ ] maintain
- [ ] propose
- [ ] remedy
- [ ] restore
- [ ] spare

adjective 형용사

- [ ] anonymous
- [ ] commonplace
- [ ] continual
- [ ] extreme
- [ ] faithful
- [ ] indifferent
- [ ] mounting
- [ ] noteworthy
- [ ] predictable
- [ ] specific
- [ ] ubiquitous
- [ ] undoubted
- [ ] upright
- [ ] wrong

adverb 부사

- [ ] fully
- [ ] verbally
- [ ] by means of
- [ ] needless to say

MP3 파일 다운

noun
명사

0750 approach /əpróutʃ/

1. 다가옴, 접근
   - My approach to work is to start early in the day.
2. 접근법
   - ⓤ adopt a new approach to sth ~에 대한 새로운 접근을 채택(도입)하다
   - With the new Delta variant, the government has had to **adopt a new approach to** social distancing.

0751 chip /tʃíp/

1. 조각, 부스러기
   - ◇ stone / wood chips 돌/나무 조각
   - Chips of stone to be used to pave the road were unloaded from a truck.
2. (컵 등에) 이 빠진 자국, 흠
   - This cup has a chip in it.

Ⓢ flake

0752 dispersal /dispə́:rsl/ /디스*퍼슬/

해산, 분산, 확산
- Due to COVID-19, crowd dispersal is necessary.

Ⓢ distribution, spread, scattering

0753 edge /édʒ/ /에쥐/

1. 가장자리(끝), 변두리, 경계
   - ⓤ the edge of sth ~의 가장자리
   - The birds on **the edge of** a roost usually suffer from the cold weather. *roost (닭이나 새 등이 앉는) 홰
2. 우위, 우세, 강점
   - ⓤ an edge over sb/sth ~보다 강점
   - Spending a long time working abroad will give you **an edge over** applicants with no international work experience.

Ⓢ fringe, border, perimeter 외곽, 경계

Ⓢ advantage

0754 heyday /héidèi/

전성기
- ⓤ in sb's/sth's heyday ~의 전성기 때에
- **In** its **heyday**, Liverpool, a maritime city in northwest England, was a major port.

Ⓢ prime, peak

0755 limit /límit/

제한(한도), 한계
- ◇ age limit 나이 제한 / speed limit 속도 제한 / time limit 시간제한 / credit (card) limit 신용 카드 한도
- ⓤ
- ① set a time limit (of 시간) for ~에 (얼마의) 시간제한을 두다
  - They **set a time limit of** 20 minutes **for** the test.
- ② set / impose limits on sth ~에 제한을 두다 / there is a limit on sth ~에 한도(제한)가 있다
- ③ there is a limit to sth ~에(는) 한계가 있다 / there's no limit to sth ~에(는) 한계가 없다
  - **There is a limit to** what you can learn about a foreign country from newspapers published in that country.

Ⓢ restriction 제한

0756 opportunity /ápərtjú:nəti/ /아퍼튜너티/

기회
- ⓤ an opportunity (for sb) to do sth (누가) ~할 수 있는 기회
- The TV program travels to many cities in Korea and provides **an opportunity** for obscure singers **to** sing on television. *obscure 무명의

0750 일에 대한 내 접근(방식)은 하루에 일찍 시작하는 것이다. / 새로운 델타 변종으로 정부는 사회적 거리 두기에 대한 새로운 접근법을 채택해야 했다. 0751 도로를 포장하기 위해 사용될 돌 조각들이 트럭에서 하역되었다. / 이 컵은 안에 이 빠진 자국이 있다. 0752 코로나19 때문에 군중 해산이 필수적이다. 0753 홰 가장자리에 있는 새들은 보통 추운 날씨로 고생한다. / 오랜 시간을 해외에서 일하는 데 보내는 것은 너에게 외국에서 일한 경험이 없는 지원자들보다 강점을 줄 것이다. 0754 전성기 때에, 영국의 북서쪽의 해양 도시인 리버풀은 주요 항구였다. 0755 그들은 그 테스트에 20분의 시간제한을 두었다. / 네가 한 외국에 대해 그 나라에서 발행되는 신문을 통해 그 나라에 대해 알 수 있는 것에는 한계가 있다. 0756 그 TV 프로그램은 한국의 많은 도시들을 돌아다니며 무명 가수들이 텔레비전에서 노래할 수 있는 기회를 제공한다.

0757 portion
/pɔ́ːrʃən/

1. 부분, 일부
- a portion of sth ~의 일부
- The mayor should bear **a portion of** the blame for the failure to prevent the pandemic. *bear (책임 등을) 감당하다

2. (음식) 일 인분, 양
- The portion of meat that the restaurant serves is generous.

[S] part

0758 provocation
/prάvəkeiʃən/

도발 누군가를 일부러 화나게 하거나 자극하는 행위
- a deliberate act of provocation 의도적인 도발 행위
- These days, South Korea and the United States tend to respond to North Korea's provocations with apathy. *with apathy 무관심하게

0759 retrospect
/rétrəspèkt/
/레트러*스펙트/

회상, 회고
- in retrospect (지금 과거를) 돌이켜보면
- **In retrospect**, I realized that taking that job was the wrong move. I should have gone to graduate school instead. *move 조치

0760 scale
/skéil/

1. 규모
- on a scale 규모로
- on a small / large / massive / global / national scale 소/대/엄청난/세계적/국가적 규모로
- It costs a lot to launch a full-scale investigation into the consequences of their release into the wild.

2. 저울
- He always weighs himself on the bathroom scale.

▶ scale (동사) 기어오르다
- In the end, he scaled Mount Everest.

[S] climb

0761 scapegoat
/skéipgout/

희생양
- The leader of the political party needed a scapegoat for the failure of the election.

0762 sorrow
/sárou/

슬픔, 애도
- sorrow over / at / for sth ~에 대한 슬픔 / be in sorrow 슬픔에 잠기다
- The President expressed deep **sorrow at** the destruction of the city that had been struck by a deadly earthquake.

[S] sadness, grief, unhappiness

0763 story
/stɔ́ːri/

(건물의) 층
- We live in an apartment building 28 stories high.

[S] floor

0764 well-being
/wel-bíːiŋ/

건강과 행복 (=wellbeing)
- As income rises, well-being increases.

[S] welfare 복지, 행복

verb 동사

0765 adopt
/ədápt/

1. 입양하다
   - He was born to a single mother and was later adopted by a poor family.

2. 채택(사용)하다 — **accept, start to use**
   ◇ adopt a strategy / a measure 전략/방법을 채택하다
   - It seems very likely that the Celts simply adopted the Anglo-Saxon language and made up the majority of the population.

0766 align
/əláin/

1. 일직선으로 맞추다 — **A** skew 비스듬하게 되다
   - Only car service centers can align the wheels of your car.

2. 공개적으로 지지하다
   ⓤ align oneself with sb/sth ~을 공개적으로 지지하다
   - Some newspapers **align** themselves **with** the Conservative Party.

0767 belittle
/bilítl/

하찮게 만들다, 업신여기다(무시하다), 폄하하다 — **disparage**
   - The president was belittled a lot in the press.

0768 claim
/kléim/

1. 주장하다, (권리 등을) 요구하다 — **assert, demand, ask for**
   ⓤ claim credit for sth ~에 대한 공로를 주장하다
   - He **claims credit for** inventing that expression, but we don't know for sure that his claim is true. *for sure 확실히

2. (보상금 등을) 신청(청구)하다
   - He tried to claim money from the government for damage to his property.

3. 차지하다, 얻다
   - Brazil was claimed by Portugal.

0769 concede
/kənsíːd/
/컨시드/

1. (마지못해) 인정하다 — **admit**
   ◇ concede defeat 패배를 인정하다
   - He will never concede that he lost to Joe Biden.

2. (마지못해) 내주다 — **give sth to sb**
   ⓤ concede sth to sb ~에게 ~을 내주다
   - In 1956, France **conceded** independence **to** Tunisia and Morocco.

0770 consider
/kənsídər/

1. 고려하다, 심사숙고하다 — **think about / of**
   - The car he's considering buying is the BMW X5.

2. 여기다, 생각하다 — **think of, see, believe** / **believe A to be B, think of A as B**
   ⓤ consider A (as / to be) B: A를 B로 여기다
   - The lecturer **considers** natural pesticides (to be) detrimental to birds.
   (=The lecturer believes natural pesticides to be detrimental to birds.)
   - Steve Jobs thought of him as a very talented leader.

0771 denote
/dinóut/
/디*노우트/

나타내다, 의미하다
- The word "capitalism" denotes "a free market economy."

[S] indicate, mean, signify

0772 design
/dizáin/

디자인하다, 설계하다, 계획하다, 의도하다
- Hydroelectric dams use fish ladders, which are openings designed to allow fish to pass through dams.

[S] intend

▶ designed (형용사) 의도된, 설계된
ⓒ designed to do sth ~하기 위해 의도된
- With the help of fish ladders, which are openings **designed to** allow fish to pass dams, strong species of fish like salmon ascend vertically.

[S] intended

0773 engender
/indʒéndər/
/인젠더/

(상황 등을) 유발하다, 발생시키다
◇ engender controversy 논쟁을 유발하다 / fears engendered by a pandemic 대유행에 의해 유발된 두려움들
- The Civil War engendered an economic crisis.

[S] produce

0774 expose
/ikspóuz/

(숨겨져 있던 것을) 드러내다, 노출하다, 폭로하다
- Our skin can be easily exposed to the harmful ultraviolet rays of the sun.
- The president lost all vestige of respectability when the scandal was exposed.

[S] uncover, reveal, disclose
[A] conceal 숨기다

0775 forge
/fɔ́ːrdʒ/
/포오쥐/

1. (관계 등을) 형성하다, 맺다
ⓒ forge a relationship with ~와 관계를 형성하다
- The country compares its alliance with the United States to a relationship forged in blood.

[S] form, build, establish

2. (문서 등을) 위조하다
◇ forge a document / a passport / a painting 문서/여권/그림을 위조하다
- If there were a department that teaches how to forge documents, my daughter would be a top applicant.

[S] counterfeit, falsify

▶ forgery (명사) 문서 위조, 서명 위조

0776 hamstring
/hǽmstriŋ/

좌절시키다
ⓒ be hamstrung by sth ~에 의해 무력화되다(좌절되다)
- The lame duck president feels he **is hamstrung by** Congress.
*lame duck 재선에 실패하고 임기가 끝나가는 대통령

[S] thwart, prevent

0777 intensify
/inténsifài/

강화시키다; 강화되다
- I intensified my effort to finish the project as quickly as possible.

▶ intensification (명사) 강화

[S] escalate, heighten

0778 maintain
/meintéin/

1. 유지(지속)하다
- The two countries maintained close relations even after the military coup.
- It costs money to maintain airplanes that just sit idle.

[S] sustain, preserve, perpetuate

2. 주장하다
- I maintain that South Korea's medical system is the best in the world.

[S] assert, claim, insist

▶ maintenance (명사) 유지

0771 "자본주의"라는 단어는 "자유 시장 경제"를 의미한다. 0772 수력 발전 댐은 물고기들이 댐을 통과하도록 설계된 통로인 물고기 사다리를 사용한다. / 물고기가 댐을 통과하도록 설계된 통로인 물고기 사다리의 도움으로 연어 같이 강한 종의 물고기는 수직으로 올라간다. 0773 남북 전쟁은 경제 위기를 유발했다. 0774 우리 피부는 태양의 해로운 자외선에 쉽게 노출될 수 있다. / 그 스캔들이 드러났을 때 대통령은 존경할 만한 점의 모든 자취를 잃었다. 0775 그 나라는 미국과의 동맹을 피로 맺어진 관계로 비유한다. / 만약 문서를 위조하는 방법을 가르치는 과가 있다면, 우리 딸이 수석 입학자일 것이다. 0776 그 레임덕 대통령은 자신이 의회에 의해 무력화되고 있다고 느낀다. 0777 나는 그 프로젝트를 최대한 빨리 끝내기 위한 노력을 강화했다. 0778 그 두 나라는 심지어 군사 쿠데타 이후에도 긴밀한 관계를 유지했다. / 운행하지 않고 가만히 앉아 있는 비행기들을 유지하는 데는 돈이 든다. / 나는 한국의 의료 시스템이 세계 최고라고 주장한다.

0779 propose
/prəpóuz/

(계획이나 아이디어 등을) 제안하다
- Many theories have been proposed to explain this unusual behavior.

▶ proposal (명사) 계획안, 제안
- make a proposal to do sth ~하는 제안을 하다
- The Australian government **made a proposal to** stop the spread of cane toads that had been introduced to their country.

S suggest, offer

S proposition 제안

0780 remedy
/rémədi/
/레머디/

(상황 등을) 바로잡다, 개선(교정)하다
- It is up to the government to remedy the situation.

▶ remedy (명사)
1) 치료(제) ◇ home remedies for colds 감기에 대한 가정 치료법
2) 해결책 ◇ remedies for traffic congestion 교통 혼잡에 대한 해결책

S correct, rectify, improve

S treatment, cure
S solution

0781 restore
/ristɔ́:r/

1. 회복하다, 되찾다
- The president promised to restore the economy to full employment.
- The army was brought in to restore order.

2. 복원(복구)하다
- In other words, the cost of restoring the damage that newly introduced species cause to native species would be far greater than that of doing research into controlling introduced species.

S reinstate, retrieve

0782 spare
/spéər/

1. ~의 목숨을 살려주다, 손상시키지 않다
- spare one's life 목숨을 살려주다 / be spared 손상되지 않다
- The church **was spared** from the enemy's air attacks on the region.

2. (시간 등을) 할애하다
- Thank you for sparing me your valuable time.

adjective 형용사

0783 anonymous
/ənániməs/
/어나니*머스/

익명의
- The killer was caught thanks to the testimony from an anonymous informer. *informer 제보자(내부 고발자)

▶ anonymously (부사) 익명으로
- There are good reasons to believe that opinions posted anonymously by people on the internet cause our society tremendous problems. *there are good reasons to believe that ~라고 믿는 데는 타당한 이유가 있다

S unnamed, unidentified

0784 commonplace
/kámənpleis/

(여러 장소에서 일어나는) 흔한, 평범한
- Eating kimchi with every meal is commonplace in Korea.

S ordinary, common
A rare 희귀한

0785 continual
/kəntínjuəl/

계속되는, 반복되는, 되풀이되는
◇ continual problems 반복되는 문제 / continual arguments 되풀이되는 주장
- Eventually, I escaped to my mother's house because of the continual noise from the construction site next door.

S repeating
A sporadic 산발적인

0786 extreme
/ikstríːm/
/익스트림/

1. 지나친, 과도한
- There was a flood of complaints about the TV show because of its extreme violence.

2. 극도의, 극심한, (사상 등이) 극단적인
◇ extreme weather conditions 극한 날씨 조건 / extreme views 극단적인 견해
- Elderly people are very susceptible to colds when engaging in outdoor activities in the winter. In extreme cases, a cold can even lead to pneumonia.

▶ extremely (부사) 엄청나게

0787 faithful
/féiθfl/
/페이쓰*플/

1. 충실한, 충직한, 독실한 — loyal, staunch
- I like dogs because they are faithful to their owners.

2. (원문 등에) 충실한, 정확한 — accurate, exact
◇ a faithful account 정확한 설명
- You should be faithful to the original text.

▶ faithfully (부사) 1. 충실하게 2. 정확하게 — accurately, exactly

0788 indifferent
/indífərənt/

1. 무관심한 — uninterested, apathetic
ⓒ indifferent to sb/sth ~에 무관심한
- Political apathy means being **indifferent to** politics.

2. 그저 그런 — mediocre
- The food was indifferent. It was nothing special.

▶ indifference (명사) 무관심 — apathy

0789 mounting
/máuntiŋ/

(뭔가 부정적인 것 등이) 점차 증가하는, 커지는 — growing
- Because of skyrocketing housing prices, mounting personal debts are shooting up to unmanageable levels. *shoot up 급증하다, 치솟다

0790 noteworthy
/nóutwərði/

주목할 만한 — memorable 기억할 만한, notable, remarkable
ⓒ It is noteworthy that S주어 V동사 ~는 주목할 만하다
- His remarkable achievement in writing is noteworthy.

0791 predictable
/pridíktəbl/
/프리딕*터블/

예측할 수 있는 — expected
- Typhoon Lui is slowly moving along a predicable route.

A unpredictable 예측할 수 없는

0792 specific
/spisífik/
/스피*시픽/

1. 구체적인, 명확한 — precise, exact
◇ specific examples 구체적인 예시
- Use specific reasons and examples to support your answer.

2. 특정한 — particular
- In the past, a few groups monopolized information. If someone wanted to obtain specific information, he or she had to pay for it.

0793 ubiquitous
/juːbíkwətəs/
/유비*쿼터스/

아주 흔한, 어디에나 있는(존재하는) — omnipresent, pervasive
- At first glance, the chicken shop looked like one of the ubiquitous local takeout spots in a big city, but after tasting the chicken, I was speechless because the outside was so crispy, and the inside was so tender.

0794
undoubted
/ʌndáutid/

의심할 여지가 없는, 확실한
- Their new album proved to be an undoubted success.

S indubitable, certain, definite

0795
upright
/ʎprait/

1. (자세가) 똑바른, 수직의
◇ stand upright 똑바로 서 있다 / sit upright 똑바로 앉아 있다 / walk upright 똑바로 걷다(직립 보행하다) / sitting in a upright position 똑바른 자세로 앉아 있는
- Homo sapiens is the only species of primates that walks upright all the time.

2. (사람 등이) 정직한, 청렴한
- He was an upright politician, but Ireland's economy was in crisis while he was president.

S vertical, straight, erect

0796
wrong
/rɔːŋ/

1. 잘못된, 틀린
- Wrong choices of words can convey the false impression that men are superior to women in many ways.

2. 이상(문제)이 있는
Ⓤ wrong with sth ~에 문제가 있는
- Is there anything **wrong with** the policy?
- What's **wrong with** your nose?

adverb 부사

0797
fully
/fúlli/

완전히
- Not a single theory can fully explain why such an important civilization collapsed in a single day.

S completely

0798
verbally
/vɔ́ːrbəli/
/버벌리/

말로, 구두로
- After the emergence of language, folktales were verbally passed on from one generation to another through stories and songs.
*folktales 민담

▶ verbal (형용사) 말의, 구두의

0799
by means of
/bai miːnz əv/

~에 의해, ~의 도움으로
- Deaf people communicate by means of sign language.

Ⓝ
1. via ~에 의해
- We accept only applications submitted via the Internet.
2. by way of ~을 경유하여
- We went to the U.K. by way of Tokyo.

S via

0800
needless to say
/niːdləs tu sei/

말할 필요도 없이
- Needless to say, the kids who had spent many years in the United States did better on the TOEFL test.

S as you would expect, obviously

DAY 17

ANGRY ENGLISH
ACADEMIC VOCABULARY

noun 명사
- [ ] autonomy
- [ ] charge
- [ ] dichotomy
- [ ] essence
- [ ] leap
- [ ] longevity
- [ ] pedestrian
- [ ] promise
- [ ] reverence
- [ ] scrap
- [ ] spot
- [ ] surveillance
- [ ] tenet
- [ ] wisdom

verb 동사
- [ ] admit
- [ ] alienate
- [ ] beckon
- [ ] concern
- [ ] conflict
- [ ] criticize
- [ ] deplete
- [ ] displace
- [ ] engulf
- [ ] expend
- [ ] hang
- [ ] interfere
- [ ] last
- [ ] protrude
- [ ] reminisce
- [ ] spark
- [ ] suffer
- [ ] witness

adjective 형용사
- [ ] anxious
- [ ] comparable
- [ ] crucial
- [ ] definite
- [ ] even
- [ ] inept
- [ ] mundane
- [ ] noticeable
- [ ] pre-eminent
- [ ] rational
- [ ] spectacular
- [ ] subject
- [ ] ultimate
- [ ] utmost

adverb 부사
- [ ] forward
- [ ] rapidly
- [ ] except for
- [ ] once and for all

MP3 파일 다운

noun 명사

0801 autonomy
/ɔ:tánəmi/
/오타*너미/

자치권, 자율성
- have autonomy to do sth ~할 수 있는 자치권(자율성)을 가지고 있다
- Once you turn 18 you **have autonomy to** make your own choices.

▶ autonomous (형용사) 자치의

S independence
S self-ruling

0802 charge
/tʃá:rdʒ/

1. 책임
- in charge of sth ~을 맡고 있는, 담당하는
- The department is **in charge of** teaching techniques for handling customer complaints.

2. 요금, 비용
- an admission charge 입장료 / free of charge 공짜로
- The charge for children to enter Everland is quite expensive.

3. 혐의, 비난, 고소, 고발
- be arrested on a charge of sth ~의 혐의로 체포되다
- The defendant denies the charges against him.

S allegation

4. 충전
- run out of charge 충전량이 바닥나다(떨어지다)
- Halfway through the journey, my phone **ran out of charge**.

0803 dichotomy
/daikátəmi/
/다이카*터미/

양분, 이분, 커다란 차이
- a dichotomy between theoretical knowledge and practical knowledge 이론적인 지식과 실용적인 지식 사이에서의 커다란 차이
- The book talks about the dichotomy between public and private healthcare.

0804 essence
/ésns/
/에슨스/

본질
- The essence of religion is to live an ascetic life and help people in need. *ascetic 금욕적인

N in essence 본질적으로
- The tribe, in essence, was an agricultural society that was able to feed the population.

S essentially, per se

0805 leap
/lí:p/

도약, 비약 높이 뛰어오름, 대규모 변화(상승)
- Taking a leap forward means that you are coming ever closer to achieving the things that you have set as goals.

▶ leap (동사) 도약하다

S bound

0806 longevity
/landʒévəti/
/란줴*버티/

장수, 수명
- the longevity of a battery 배터리 수명
- The longevity of a company is determined by how skilled the boss is.

N life expectancy 기대 수명

0807 pedestrian
/pədéstriən/
/퍼데*스트리언/

보행자
- A pedestrian was hit by a car.

0801 일단 네가 18살이 되면 너는 너 스스로가 선택을 할 수 있는 자율성을 갖는다. 0802 그 부서는 소비자 불만 사항을 처리하는 기술을 가르치는 일을 맡고 있다. / 에버랜드에 입장하기 위한 어린이 요금은 꽤 비싸다. / 피고는 자신에 대한 혐의를 부인한다. / 이동 중에 내 전화기 충전량이 떨어졌다. 0803 그 책은 공공 의료와 민간 의료의 차이에 대해서 얘기한다. 0804 종교의 본질은 금욕적인 삶을 살고 도움이 필요한 사람들을 돕는 것이다. / 본질적으로 그 부족은 인구를 먹여 살릴 수 있는 농업 사회였다. 0805 한 단계 더 도약한다는 것은 당신이 목표로 설정한 것들을 성취하는 데 점점 더 가까워지고 있다는 것을 의미한다. 0806 한 회사의 수명은 사장이 얼마나 유능하냐에 따라 결정된다. 0807 한 보행자가 자동차에 치였다.

0808 promise
/prámis/

1. 약속
- ⓤ make / keep / break a promise 약속을 하다/지키다/깨다
- ○ Despite his promises, my boyfriend cheated on me again. So, we broke up.

2. (전도) 유망, 가능성 (불가산) — ⓢ potential
- ⓤ show great promise as N ~로서 커다란 가능성을 보여 주다
- ○ Beth **shows great promise as** a world-class chess player.

▶ promising (형용사) 유망한
◇ a promising young man 전도가 유망한 청년

0809 reverence
/révərəns/
/레버*런스/

숭배, 존경 — ⓢ respect, veneration, worship
- ⓤ reverence for sb/sth ~에 대한 숭배
- ◇ reverence for false gods 이단 숭배
- ○ Catholics have great **reverence for** the Pope and Vatican City.

▶ revere (동사) 숭배하다 — ⓢ worship

0810 scrap
/skrǽp/

1. 조각 — ⓢ piece, fragment
- ◇ a scrap of paper / cloth 종이/천 조각
- ○ You're allowed to take notes on the colored scrap of paper that has been supplied.

2. 폐품
- ○ The old couple make a living by selling scrap metal.

3. 적은 양, 조금 — ⓢ bit, chip, flake
- ◇ a scrap of information / evidence 아주 적은 정보/증거
- ○ The police were looking for any scrap of information at the crime scene.

▶ scrap (동사) 버리다, 폐기하다 — ⓢ abandon, get rid of

0811 spot
/spát/

1. 점, 반점, 얼룩, 자국
- ◇ a spot of blood 핏자국
- ○ As the kid had the measles, his body became covered in red spots.

2. (특정한) 곳(장소), 자리
- ○ There're only spots for three.
- ⓤ on the spot 현장에서
- ○ The prisoners who escaped from the prison were killed **on the spot**.

0812 surveillance
/sərvéiləns/
/서베일*런스/

감시 — ⓢ observation, watch
- ⓤ keep 장소/사람 under surveillance 장소/사람 등을 감시하다
- ◇ surveillance cameras 감시카메라
- ○ Because of his crimes against children, the police **keep** him **under** constant **surveillance**.

0813 tenet
/ténit/
/테닛/

교리, 신념, 믿음, 원칙 — ⓢ creed, dogma 종교적 교리, principle
- ○ They support the fundamental tenets of collective ownership of the means of production.

0814 wisdom
/wízdəm/
/위즈*덤/

1. 지혜
- ○ Older people generally have more wisdom than younger people.

2. (오랜 시간에 걸쳐 쌓인) 지식
- ○ A lot of wisdom can be found in the Bible and other holy books.

0808 그의 약속에도 불구하고 내 남친은 또 바람을 피웠다. 그래서 우리는 헤어졌다. / 베스는 세계적인 체스 선수로서 큰 가능성을 보여 준다. 0809 가톨릭 신자들은 교황과 바티칸 시국에 대한 큰 존경심을 가지고 있다. 0810 당신은 제공된 색깔 있는 종이에 메모하는 것이 허용된다. / 그 노부부는 고철을 팔아서 생계를 유지한다. / 경찰은 범죄 현장에서 어떤 적은 정보라도 찾고 있었다. 0811 아이가 홍역에 걸렸을 때 그의 몸은 붉은 반점으로 덮여 있었다. / 3명이 앉을 수 있는 자리밖에 없다. / 감옥을 탈옥한 그 죄수들은 현장에서 살해되었다. 0812 아이들을 상대로 한 그의 범죄 때문에 경찰은 그를 계속 감시하고 있다. 0813 그들은 생산 수단의 공동 소유라는 근본적인 원칙을 지지한다. 0814 나이든 사람들은 일반적으로 젊은 사람들보다 더 많은 지혜를 가지고 있다. / 많은 지식들이 성경과 다른 성서에서 발견될 수 있다.

verb 동사

0815 admit
/ədmít/ or /ædmít/

1. 인정하다
- I admit that it costs a lot to build a recycling plant. But we can save money on fuel and labor because only one truck picks up all the trash from a single family at a time.

2. 자백하다, 시인하다
- admit (to) doing sth ~한 것을 자백하다
- He **admitted (to)** murder**ing** his wife.

[S] acknowledge

[S] confess
[A] deny 부인하다

0816 alienate
/éilianèit/
/에일*리어*네이트/

1. 멀어지게 만들다, 소원하게 만들다
- The government's proposal alienated many voters in their forties.

2. 소외감(이질감)을 느끼게 하다
- alienate sb from sb/sth ~을 ~에서 소외감을 느끼게 하다 / feel alienated from sth ~에서 소외감을 느끼다
- Most of the immigrants who left their homelands in search of economic prosperity still **feel alienated from** the new country they live in.

0817 beckon
/békən/

1. 손짓하여 부르다
- beckon (to) sb to do ~에게 ~하라고 손짓하여 부르다
- The immigration officer **beckoned (to)** me **to** come toward his counter.

2. 손짓하여 부르다, 유혹의 손짓을 하다
- One of the world's Seven Wonders, Cristo Redentor, a statue of Jesus Christ, beckons.

[S] signal

0818 concern
/kənsə́:rn/

1. 걱정시키다
◇ the overuse of social media that concerns many parents 많은 부모들을 걱정시키는 소셜 미디어의 남용
- It concerns many parents that their children spend too much time on social media.

2. (영화나 책 등이) ~에 관한 것이다
- The movie concerns Steve Jobs.
(=The movie is concerned with Steve Jobs.)
(=The movie is about Steve Jobs.)

3. ~에 영향을 미치다, ~에 관여(관계)하다
- All of the parties concerned had to appear in court on the day when the judge delivered his final verdict. *party 당사자
- A gradual increase in the interest rate will concern people who have already borrowed too much money from banks.

N
1. concern oneself with sth ~에 관여하다
- The Department of Defense concerns itself with war.
2. To whom it may concern (누군지 모르는) 관계자 분들께

[S] be about, be concerned with

[S] affect, involve

[S] become involved in sth

0819 conflict
/kənflíkt/

충돌하다, 상반되다, 모순되다
- conflict with sth ~와 충돌하다(상반되다)
- Your behavior always **conflicts with** all of your religious beliefs.

▶ conflicting (형용사) 모순되는

[S] clash
[S] clash with sth

[S] contradictory

0820
criticize
/krítisàiz/

비난하다
- criticize sb/sth for (doing) sth ~때문에 ~을 비난하다
- At the time he wrote his novels, many people strongly **criticized** his novels **for** being too descriptive.

- **N** critic (명사) 비평가

S censure, attack, deprecate
A praise, compliment 칭찬하다

0821
deplete
/diplí:t/

다 써 버리다, 고갈시키다
- Humans have been depleting Earth's natural resources, especially oil and coal, since the Industrial Revolution.

S use up, run out of, exhaust

0822
displace
/displéis/

1. 대신하다, 대체하다
- Many workers have been displaced by machines.

2. 쫓아내다
- After the Gold Rush, Native Americans were displaced from their land.

S replace

S expel, evict, oust

0823
engulf
/ingʌlf/
/인걸프/

완전히 에워싸다, 삼키다
- be engulfed by / in sb/sth ~에 휩싸이다
- The house **was engulfed in** flames in a few minutes.

0824
expend
/ikspénd/
/익스*펜드/

(시간, 돈, 노력 또는 에너지 등을) 쓰다
- expend energy / effort (in / on) doing sth ~하는 데 에너지/노력을 쓰다
- I **expended** a lot of time and money on build**ing** my new house in the countryside.

▶ expenditure (명사) 지출, 소비(소모)

- **N** expand (동사) 넓히다, 확장하다
- **N** extend (동사) (도로 또는 기간 등을) 연장하다

0825
hang
/hæŋ/
*hang-hung-hung

걸다(매달다); 걸리다(매달리다)
- hang A from B: A를 B에 매달다 / A hang from B: A가 B에 매달리다
- He **hung** a banner **from** a fence.
- A banner **hung from** the ceiling.
- Bats are **hanging from** the ceiling of the barn.

▶ hanging (명사) 교수형
- He will be executed by hanging which many people believe is cruel.

S suspend, dangle

0826
interfere
/ìntərfíər/

1. 간섭(개입)하다
- interfere in sth ~에 간섭(개입)하다
- I believe the church should not **interfere in** politics. Religion and politics should be separate.

2. 방해하다, 막다
- interfere with sth ~을 방해하다
- Contrary to the common belief that authoritative parents **interfere with** their children's academic success, the children of authoritative parents usually do well in school.

S meddle

0820 그가 소설을 쓸 그 당시 많은 사람들은 너무 묘사적이라고 그의 소설을 강하게 비판했다. 0821 산업 혁명 이후로 쭉 인류는 지구의 천연자원, 특히 석유와 석탄을 고갈시키고 있다. 0822 많은 노동자들이 기계에 의해 대체되었다. / 골드러시 이후에 아메리카 원주민들은 그들의 땅에서 쫓겨났다. 0823 그 집은 몇 분 만에 화염에 휩싸였다. 0824 나는 시골에서 새집을 짓는 데 많은 시간과 돈을 썼다. 0825 그는 현수막을 펜스에 걸었다. / 현수막이 천장에 매달렸다. / 박쥐들이 그 헛간의 천장에 매달려 있다. / 그는 많은 사람들이 잔인하다고 믿는 교수형에 처해질 것이다. 0826 나는 교회가 정치에 개입해서는 안 된다고 믿는다. 종교와 정치는 분리되어야 한다. / 권위적인 부모가 자녀의 학문적 성공을 방해한다는 일반적인 믿음과 반대로, 권위적인 부모의 자녀들은 대개 학교에서 공부를 잘한다.

0827 last
/læst/

1. 지속되다, 오래가다, (특정기간 동안) 계속되다
- The odor of the mosquito repellent doesn't last very long. After a few minutes it gets weaker.
- The civil war lasted four years.

2. (일정 기간 동안) 사용하기에 충분하다, 가다
- We get 5 masks per box and the box lasts about eight and a half days.
- For one thing, sea cows were big. So, a few sea cows could last Siberian natives for many months.

0828 protrude
/proutrúːd/

돌출되다, 튀어나오다
- protrude from sth ~에서 돌출되다
- Tuna do not have protruding eyes.

[S] stick out, project
[S] stick out from sth

0829 reminisce
/rémənis/

(좋은 추억담을) 나누다, 회상하다
- reminisce about sth ~에 대해 회상하다
- He **reminisced about** his years in the army.

0830 spark
/spáːrk/

촉발(유발)하다
- spark one's interest / protest ~의 관심/저항을 촉발시키다
- His travels in China **sparked** his **curiosity** about oriental medicine.

[S] provoke

0831 suffer
/sʌ́fər/

1. 고통을 받다
- The patient is still suffering even though he took a painkiller.

2. (병, 고통, 나쁜 경험 등을) 앓다(가지고 있다)
- suffer from diabetes 당뇨병을 앓다
- One of the withdrawal symptoms from which patients suffer is nausea. *withdrawal symptoms 금단 현상

[S] have diabetes

3. (부상, 손실 등을) 입다, 겪다
- suffer depression 우울증을 겪다 / suffer head injury 머리 부상을 입다 / suffer heavy loss 큰 손해를 입다 / suffer a defeat 패배를 당하다
- They are regions that are most likely to suffer water shortages.

0832 witness
/wítnis/

목격하다
- witness sb doing sth 누가 ~하는 것을 목격하다
- The boy **witnessed** his father **being** arrested by the police.

[S] observe

adjective 형용사

0833 anxious
/ǽŋkʃəs/

1. 걱정(근심)하는
- be anxious about sth ~에 대해 걱정하다 / be anxious for sb ~을 걱정하다
- I **am anxious about** my final exam. If I fail, I may have to repeat the year.
- Parents **are** always **anxious for** their kids.

[S] worried, uneasy, nervous

2. 열망(갈망)하는
- be anxious to do sth ~하는 것을 열망하다
- I **am** really **anxious to** testify at the trial, because I will have to come face-to-face with my attacker.

[S] eager, keen
[S] be eager to do sth

0827 모기 퇴치제 냄새는 오래가지 않는다. 몇 분 후에 그것은 차츰 약해진다. / 내전은 4년 동안 계속되었다. / 우리는 한 상자당 5개가 들어 있는 마스크를 구매하고 그 상자는 약 8일하고 반나절이 간다. / 한 가지 이유는 바다소들은 컸다. 그래서 몇 마리의 바다소들이 여러 달 동안 시베리아의 원주민들이 사용하기에 충분할 수 있었다. 0828 참치는 튀어나온 눈을 가지고 있지 않다. 0829 그는 군대에서 보낸 세월을 회상했다. 0830 중국에서의 그의 여행은 한의학에 대한 그의 호기심을 유발했다. 0831 그 환자는 진통제를 복용했음에도 불구하고 여전히 고통받고 있다. / 그 환자들이 앓고 있는 금단 현상 중 하나는 메스꺼움이다. / 그들은 가장 물 부족을 겪을 것 같은 지역들이다. 0832 그 소년은 그의 아버지가 경찰에 체포되는 것을 목격했다. 0833 나는 기말고사가 걱정된다. 만약 실패하면 난 한 해를 더 다녀야 할지도 모른다. / 부모들은 언제나 그들의 자식을 걱정한다. / 나는 진짜 재판에서 증언하기를 열망하는데 왜냐하면 내가 나를 공격한 가해자와 대면해야 할 것이기 때문이다.

0834 comparable
/kámpərəbl/
/캄퍼*러블/

비교할 수 있는(비슷한), 비교될 수 있는(필적하는)
- comparable to / with sb/sth ~와 비교될 수 있는(비슷한)
- The newly launched smartphone is **comparable** in size **to** the previous model.

S similar, equal, equivalent

0835 crucial
/krúːʃəl/

결정적인, 매우 중요한
- be crucial to / for sth ~에 매우 중요하다 / be crucial in / to doing sth ~하는 데 있어서 결정적이다
- Plants **are crucial to** our survival because they absorb carbon dioxide from the air and release oxygen back into the air that we breathe.

S essential, vital, pivotal 중심이 되는

0836 definite
/définət/
/데피닛/

확실한, 명확한
- be definite about ~에 대해 명확하다
- a definite answer 확실한 답변(확답)
- We all know there is a definite need to meet the world's demand for energy, so this mining method seems to be the best option for finding energy resources.

S clear, obvious, unambiguous

0837 even
/íːvn/
/이븐/

일정한, 고른, 평평한, 균등한
- an even temperature 고른 기온
- An even distribution of food can help feed the global population; we have enough food to do so.
- The roads are said to have been paved with asphalt, but the surface is still uneven.

▶ evenly (부사) 고르게, 평평하게, 균등하게

S constant, consistent
A uneven 고르지 못한(균등하지 않은)

S equally

0838 inept
/inépt/

서투른
- Many experts blamed the prime minister's inept handling of the economic downturn of 2008 for the economic collapse. *blame A for B: B의 원인을 A때문이라고 보다

S clumsy
A skillful 능숙한

0839 mundane
/mʌndéin/
/먼데인/

지루한, 평범한, 흔한, 일상적인
- a mundane task 일상적인 업무
- The most mundane job in the workplace is to print out copies of a report for a meeting and staple each set together. *print out 출력하다 / staple 스테이플로 고정시키다

S ordinary, common, boring

0840 noticeable
/nóutisəbl/

뚜렷한, 눈에 띄는, 주목할 만한
- a noticeable improvement in sth ~에서의 주목할 만한 향상
- There is a noticeable difference between the two stoves.

S marked

0841 pre-eminent
/priémənənt/
/프리*에머넌트/

중요한, 뛰어난
- Jane Austen was the pre-eminent female novelist in King George III's day.

0842 rational
/ræʃənl/
/래셔늘/

합리적인, 이성적인
- The president should make rational decisions, rather than ones based on emotions.

S reasonable
A irrational 비이성적인, 비합리적인

0843 spectacular
/spektækjulər/
/스펙*태큘러/

장관의, 멋진, 환상적인
- Freddie Mercury's performance at Band Aid was spectacular.

S breathtaking

0834 새롭게 출시된 스마트폰은 크기에서 이전 모델과 비교할 수 있다. 0835 식물은 우리의 생존에 매우 중요한데 왜냐하면 그들은 공기 중의 이산화 탄소를 흡수하고 우리가 숨쉬는 공기 중으로 산소를 다시 방출하기 때문이다. 0836 우리 모두는 에너지에 대한 세계 수요를 충족시킬 명확한 필요가 있다는 것을 알고 있어서 이 채굴 방식이 에너지 자원을 찾는 가장 최고의 선택인 것처럼 보인다. 0837 식량의 균등한 분배는 전 세계의 인구를 먹여 살리는 것을 도울 수 있다; 우리는 그렇게 할 수 있는 충분한 식량을 가지고 있다. / 그 도로는 아스팔트로 포장되었다고 하지만 표면은 여전히 고르지 않다. 0838 많은 전문가들은 그 경제 붕괴의 원인을 수상의 2008년의 경기 침체에 대한 서투른 대응 때문이라고 본다. 0839 직장에서 가장 일상적인 일은 회의용 보고서 사본을 출력해서 각각의 세트를 스테이플로 철하는 것이다. 0840 두 가스레인지 사이에는 눈에 띄는 차이가 있다. 0841 제인 오스틴은 조지 3세 시대에 뛰어난 여성 소설가였다. 0842 대통령은 감정에 기반한 결정이 아니라 이성적인 결정을 해야 한다. 0843 밴드 에이드 콘서트에서의 프레디 머큐리의 공연은 환상적이었다.

0844 subject
/sʌ́bdʒekt/

1. (규칙이나 법, 관세, 세금, 또는 벌금 등) ~의 지배를 받는, ~을 따르는
- be subject to a tax / a tariff / a fee 세금/관세/요금을 내다
- Because I was speeding I **was subject to** a $100 fine.
- Middle and high school students are subject to rules about their uniforms.
- Mining precious metals from the ocean floor is not subject to obligations imposed by international law.

2. (뭔가 안 좋은 일에) 영향을 받기 쉬운, 될 수 있는
- be subject to sth ~에 영향을 받기 쉽다
- be subject to delays 지연될 수 있다
- Everything **is subject to** death.
- Food prices **are subject to** seasonal changes.

3. ~의 (정치적) 지배하에 있는
- the Persian Empire and its subject peoples 페르시아 제국과 그들의 지배 하에 있는 민족들

0845 ultimate
/ʌ́ltimət/ /얼티멋/

1. 궁극적인, 최종적인
- the ultimate result / outcome 최종 결과
- The ultimate objective of this environmental organization is to protect the environment.

2. 최고의
- TOEFL is the ultimate English proficiency test.

▶ ultimately (부사) 마침내, 결국

[S] final, eventual

0846 utmost
/ʌ́tmoust/

최대한, 극도의
- of the utmost importance 가장 중요한(극히 중요한)
- with the utmost care 매우 조심스럽게
- Studying the effect of climate change on our environment is a matter **of the utmost importance**.

adverb 부사

0847 forward
/fɔ́ːrwərd/

앞으로
- A young woman in sportswear is leaning forward, resting her elbows on a fence.

[N]
1. look forward to doing sth ~을 고대(기대)하다
- I'm looking forward to us working together eventually.
2. crane one's neck forward to do sth ~하기 위해 목을 앞으로 길게 빼다
- She craned her neck forward so that she could see her son performing on stage.

[A] backward 뒤로, 거꾸로

0848 rapidly
/rǽpidli/

빠르게, 급속히
- The number of unemployed people is rising rapidly.

[S] very quickly

0849 except for
/iksépt fər/

~을 제외하고
- Everything is closed except for grocery stores and gas stations. People won't be able to get their hair cut for a while.

[S] save for

0850 once and for all
/wʌns ənd fər ɔːl/

최종적으로, 완전히
- The aim of the government is to once and for all eliminate poverty.

[S] finally, completely

DAY 18

ANGRY ENGLISH
ACADEMIC VOCABULARY

noun 명사
- [ ] appeal
- [ ] barge
- [ ] complacency
- [ ] devastation
- [ ] equipment
- [ ] favor
- [ ] invention
- [ ] period
- [ ] projection
- [ ] reward
- [ ] shore
- [ ] source
- [ ] witticism

verb 동사
- [ ] adorn
- [ ] aim
- [ ] bear
- [ ] clear
- [ ] conclude
- [ ] deposit
- [ ] disregard
- [ ] distinguish
- [ ] enjoy
- [ ] founder
- [ ] hasten
- [ ] intimidate
- [ ] limit
- [ ] prove
- [ ] render
- [ ] resort
- [ ] spawn
- [ ] swell

adjective 형용사
- [ ] appropriate
- [ ] competent
- [ ] curious
- [ ] external
- [ ] familiar
- [ ] inert
- [ ] maneuverable
- [ ] necessary
- [ ] preferable
- [ ] ready
- [ ] stationary
- [ ] unanimous
- [ ] undesirable
- [ ] universal

adverb 부사
- [ ] providing
- [ ] respectively
- [ ] far from
- [ ] on the spot

MP3 파일 다운

noun 명사

0851
appeal
/əpíːl/

1. 호소
   - ⓤ an appeal for sth ~에 대한 호소 / an appeal to sb to do sth ~에게 ~해 달라는 호소
   - He made **an appeal to** voters **to** help re-elect him.

2. 상소 상급 법원에 재심을 요구하는 것, 항고 2심에 상소, 상고 3심에 상소
   - In light of new evidence, she made an appeal to a court of law. *in light of sth ~을 고려하여

3. 매력
   - K-pop has a wide appeal for young fans globally.

0852
barge
/báːrdʒ/

바지선 강이나 운하에서 무거운 물건을 나르는 배
- Because cargo ships can't sail down rivers, goods are usually carried on barges instead.

0853
complacency
/kəmpléisnsi/
/컴플레이*슨시/

자기만족, 안주함 — satisfaction
- One of the issues associated with the complacency in this country is that people didn't consider a recent coronavirus surge to be serious. *surge 급증

▶ complacent (형용사) 자기만족의, 현실에 안주하는

0854
devastation
/dèvəstéiʃən/
/데버*스테이션/

파괴 — (great) destruction
- The tsunami caused widespread devastation along the coast of Japan.

0855
equipment
/ikwípmənt/

용품, 장비
- ◇ kitchen equipment 주방 용품 / camping equipment 캠핑 용품
- Equipment for removing dead trees in forests damaged by forest fires is expensive to use.

Ⓝ gear (명사) 장비
- ◇ camping gear 캠핑 장비
- Protective gear will protect manual workers' hands from being injured.

0856
favor
/féivər/

1. 찬성, 지지, 총애 — approval, support
   - ⓤ in favor of sth ~에 찬성 / gain / lose favor with sb ~에게 지지를 얻다/잃다 / fall out of favor with sb ~에게서 총애를 잃다
   - The majority of the local people voted **in favor of** the proposal.
   - Shortly after his boss lost faith in him, he **fell out of favor with** his boss and was laid off.

2. 부탁
   - Can I ask you a favor?

3. 편애
   - ⓤ show favor to sb ~을 편애하다
   - I feel like my mother **showed favor to** my little brother. She always gave him more food at dinner and didn't punish him as much as me.

0851 그는 그를 재선될 수 있게 도와 달라고 유권자들에게 호소했다. / 새로운 증거를 고려하여 그녀는 법원에 상소했다. / K-pop은 전 세계적으로 젊은 팬들에게 폭넓은 매력을 가지고 있다. 0852 화물선은 강을 따라 항해할 수 없기 때문에, 물건들은 대신에 보통 바지선으로 운반된다. 0853 이 나라에서 안주함과 관련된 문제 중 하나는 사람들이 최근의 코로나바이러스의 급증을 심각하게 여기지 않았다는 것이다. 0854 그 쓰나미는 일본 해안을 따라 광범위한 파괴를 가져왔다. 0855 산불로 피해를 입은 숲의 죽은 나무를 제거하는 장비를 사용하는 데는 돈이 많이 든다. / 보호 장비는 육체노동자의 손을 다치는 것으로부터 보호할 것이다. 0856 지역 주민의 대다수가 그 제안에 찬성하는 쪽에 투표했다. / 그의 상사가 그에 대한 믿음을 잃고 나서 곧바로 그는 그의 상사에게서 총애를 잃어서 해고되었다. / 부탁 하나만 할까? / 나는 어머니가 내 남동생을 편애했다고 느낀다. 그녀는 항상 저녁 식사 때 그에게 더 많은 음식을 주었고 그를 나만큼 많이 혼내지 않았다.

0857
invention
/invénʃən/

1. 발명 (불가산), 발명품 (가산)
- The monopoly of knowledge has been made impossible since the invention of the printing press.
- The contraceptive pill is a great invention that is the most effective method of birth control.

2. (이야기 등의) 허구
- I thought the movie was based on historical events, but it was a pure invention of the director.

0858
period
/píriəd/

기간, (개인의 또는 역사에서의) (특정) 시기
- ◇ sb's early period 초창기
- Korea went through a period of political turbulence right after declaring independence from Japan in 1945. *turbulence 격변
- The singer's early period was characterized by lively dance performances, but as she got older, she started singing more ballads.

0859
projection
/prədʒékʃən/

1. 예상(치), 전망   [S] estimate
- According to the government's projections, there will be an economic boom next year.

2. 돌출부
- The Titanic sunk because it hit a projection – identified as an iceberg – under the surface of the water.

3. (화면에) 투사(투영)

0860
reward
/riwɔ́ːrd/
/리워드/

보상, 상   [S] payment보상, prize
- ⓤ a reward for sth ~에 대한 (보)상
- ◇ rewards and punishments 상과 벌
- I was given a new bike by my parents as **a reward for** getting a perfect score on the spelling test.

0861
shore
/ʃɔ́ːr/
/쇼오/

해변(해안), 호숫가 shores
- ◇ on the shore 해변에 / two miles off shore 해안에서 2마일 떨어진
- A huge octopus washed from the sea onto the shore.
- There are a lot of beautiful plants that grow along the shores of the lake.

0862
source
/sɔ́ːrs/

원천, 원인   [S] origin, cause
- Lack of communication is a main source of conflict at work.
- We have to try to harness natural power such as wind and waves as renewable sources of energy. *harness (물이나 바람 등을) 이용(활용)하다

0863
witticism
/wítisizm/
/위티*시즘/

재담 재치 있는 말
- He is never lacking in witticism or verbal dexterity.

[N] wit (명사) 재치(기지), 재치가 있는 사람

0857 인쇄기의 발명 이래로 지식의 독점은 불가능하게 되었다. / 피임약이 산아 제한의 가장 효율적인 방법인 위대한 발명품이다. / 나는 그 영화가 역사적 사건을 토대로 만들어졌다고 생각했지만, 그것은 감독의 완전한 허구였다.   0858 한국은 1945년 일본으로부터 독립을 선언한 후에 바로 정치적 격변기를 겪었다. / 그 가수의 초창기는 활발한 댄스 공연으로 특징지어지지만 나이가 들면서 그녀는 더 많은 발라드를 부르기 시작했다.   0859 정부의 전망에 따르면 내년에는 경제 호황이 있을 것이다. / 타이타닉호는 침몰했는데 왜냐하면 그것이 수면 아래에 있던 돌출부 – 빙산으로 밝혀진 – 에 부딪혔기 때문이었다.   0860 나는 받아쓰기 시험에서 만점을 받은 것에 대한 상으로 부모님으로부터 새 자전거를 받았다.   0861 거대한 문어가 바다에서 해안으로 밀려왔다. / 호숫가를 따라 자라는 많은 아름다운 식물들이 있다.   0862 대화 부족은 직장에서 갈등의 주된 원인이다. / 우리는 바람과 파도와 같은 자연의 힘을 재생 가능한 에너지원으로 이용하려고 노력해야 한다.   0863 그는 결코 재담이나 말재주가 부족하지 않다.

verb 동사

0864 adorn
/ədɔ́ːrn/
/어돈/

장식하다
- adorn A with B: A를 B로 장식하다
- Unlike Northwestern pottery which was decorated with intricate and elaborate patterns, Southwestern pottery **was adorned with** simple paintings; for example, it was not glazed. *glaze (도자기에) 유약을 바르다

▶ adornment (명사) 장식

[S] decorate, embellish

0865 aim
/éim/

1. 목표로 하다
- aim to do sth ~하는 것을 목표로 하다
- He supported and introduced policies that **aim to** reduce the gap between the rich and poor.

[S] intend
[S] be aimed at doing sth

2. 겨냥하다(겨누다), 조준하다
◇ aim a missile at a city 미사일을 한 도시에 조준하다

▶ aim (명사) 목표(목적), 조준

0866 bear
/béər/
*bear-bore-born(borne)

1. 참다, 견디다
- bear to do sth ~을 참다
- I could not **bear to** see the animals die.

[S] stand, put up with

2. (책임 등을) 떠안다, 부담하다, 감당하다
- Consumers bear the whole cost of companies advertising their products.

3. 몸에 지니다, 소지하다
- The second amendment to the U.S. Constitution is the right to bear arms.

[S] carry

4. ~로 향하다, 가다
- Bear to the right.

▶ bearable (형용사) 참을 만한, 견딜 만한

[S] tolerable, sustainable

0867 clear
/klíər/

1. 정리하다, 치우다
◇ clear summer stock 여름 재고 상품을 치우다(싸게 팔다) / clear fields 밭을 개간하다
- It was necessary to clear fields for the crops needed to support a sudden increase in the area's population.

2. 혐의를 벗기다
- clear A of B: A에게서 B혐의를 벗기다 / be cleared of sth ~혐의를 벗다
- The lawyer **cleared** Sam **of** a false charge of murder.

0868 conclude
/kənklúːd/

1. (연설이나 모임 등을) 끝내다, 종결하다
- The investigation into his car crash in February has been concluded.

[S] end, finish

2. 결론짓다
- The committee concluded that the new product will sell well.

0869 deposit
/dipázit/

(은행 계좌 등에 돈을) 넣다
◇ deposit money 돈을 넣다
- You can withdraw and deposit money online without going to the bank.

0864 복잡하고 정교한 패턴으로 장식된 북서부의 도자기와 달리 남서부의 도자기는 단순한 그림으로 장식되었다; 예를 들면, 그것은 유약이 발라져 있지 않았다. 0865 그는 빈부 격차를 줄이는 것을 목표로 하는 정책들을 도입했고 지지했다. 0866 나는 그 동물들이 죽는 것을 도저히 볼 수가 없었다. / 소비자들은 회사들이 그들의 제품을 광고하는 모든 비용을 부담한다. / 미국 헌법의 수정 헌법 2조는 무기를 소지할 권리이다. / 오른쪽으로 가시오. 0867 그 지역의 급격한 인구 증가를 부양하기 위해 필요한 농작물을 위해 들판을 정리하는 것이 필요했다. / 그 변호사는 샘에게서 살인 누명을 벗었다. 0868 2월에 있었던 그의 자동차 사고에 대한 조사가 종결되었다. / 위원회는 그 신제품이 잘 팔릴 것이라고 결론지었다. 0869 너는 은행에 가지 않고 온라인으로 돈을 빼고 넣을 수 있다.

0870 disregard
/dìsrigá:rd/

무시하다
- The three possible explanations for the mass beaching of whales that were suggested in the article **disregard** some very important facts regarding this behavior. *mass beaching 고래들이 떼를 지어 물가에 올라와서 죽는 것

S ignore

0871 distinguish
/distíŋgwiʃ/

구별하다
- distinguish A from B: A를 B와 구별하다 / distinguish between two things 두 사물을 구별하다
- Young Korean university students who enjoy watching American television series often find it hard to **distinguish between** Korean and American culture.

S differentiate, separate, tell apart

0872 enjoy
/indʒɔ́i/

1. 즐기다
- enjoy Ving동명사 ~하는 것을 즐기다
- I **enjoy** meet**ing** people.

2. (권리, 특권, 장점 등을) 가지고 있다, 누리다
- My grandfather enjoys good health.
- Some people believe teachers should enjoy the respect that our society accords to doctors and lawyers and be paid the same amount of money as doctors and lawyers are. *accord sth to sth ~을 ~에 부여하다

S have, own, experience

0873 founder
/fáundər/

1. (계획 등이) 실패하다
- Eventually, the talks foundered.

2. (배가) 침몰하다
- A passenger ship struck a reef and foundered off the coast.

S fail

0874 hasten
/héisn/
/헤이슨/

1. 서두르다
- hasten to do sth 서둘러 ~하다
- You shouldn't **hasten to** finish this project. Please take your time.

2. 재촉하다, 앞당기다
- Civil wars following political instability hastened the fall of the Roman Empire.

S hurry, rush
S rush to do sth
S hurry, speed

0875 intimidate
/intímidèit/
/인티미*데이트/

1. 겁을 주다
- be intimidated by sth ~에 겁을 먹다
- I **was intimidated by** the idea of starting a new business.

2. 위협(협박)하다
- intimidate sb into doing sth ~을 협박하여 ~하게 하다
- In those days, political gangsters, usually members of criminal groups, **intimidated** citizens **into** vot**ing** for the parties they supported.

N intimate (형용사) 친밀한

S frighten, terrify, daunt

0876 limit
/límit/

1. (양, 수를) 제한하다
① limit sth (to sth) ~을 (~로) 제한하다
- The policy of limiting the catches of menhaden may have negative consequences for the local economy.
② be limited to sth ~에 국한되다
- A consistent increase in house prices **is limited to** big cities such as Seoul.

2. (개인이 특정 범위를 넘어서지 못하도록) 한정(제한)하다
- The Charter limited the king's power.

S restrict, check, curb

0870 지문에서 제시된 해안에서 고래들의 떼죽음에 대한 세가지 가능한 설명은 이 행동과 관련된 몇 가지 매우 중요한 사실들을 무시한다. 0871 미국 텔레비전 시리즈를 즐겨 보는 젊은 한국 대학생들은 종종 한국과 미국 문화를 구별하는 것이 어렵다고 생각한다. 0872 나는 사람들을 만나는 것을 즐긴다. / 우리 할아버지는 건강을 누린다. / 어떤 사람들은 선생님들이 우리 사회가 의사와 변호사에게 부여하는 존경을 누려야 하고 의사들과 변호사들이 받는 것과 같은 액수의 돈을 받아야 한다고 믿는다. 0873 결국 회담은 실패했다. / 한 여객선이 암초에 부딪혀 해안에서 떨어진 곳에 침몰했다. 0874 당신은 이 프로젝트를 서둘러 끝내서는 안 된다. 천천히 해라. / 정치적 불안정 이후에 일어난 내전은 로마 제국의 몰락을 재촉했다. 0875 나는 새로운 사업을 시작할 생각에 겁을 먹었다. / 그 당시에는 보통 범죄 단체의 구성원인 정치 깡패들이 시민들을 협박하여 그들이 지지하는 당에 투표하게 했다. 0876 청어의 어획량을 제한하는 정책은 지역 경제에 부정적인 결과를 가져올 수도 있다. / 집값의 지속적인 상승은 서울과 같은 대도시에 국한된다. / 그 헌장은 왕의 권력을 제한했다.

0877 prove
/prúːv/

1. 입증(증명)하다
- prove that S주어 V동사 ~을 입증하다
- The lab results disproved the theory.
- Nutritionists have **proved that** those who crave sweets can develop a sugar addiction.

[S] verify, confirm
[A] disprove 틀렸다는 것을 입증하다

2. 판명되다
- prove (to be) A형용사 / N명사 ~로 판명되다
- Their new album is **proving** to be a success.

[S] turn out

0878 render
/réndər/

(어떤 상태로) 만들다
- render sb/sth A형용사 ~을 ~상태로 만들다
- render sb/sth harmless / impossible / useless ~을 무해하게/불가능하게/쓸모없게 만들다
- Fish ladders, which are openings designed to allow fish to pass by dams, **render** hydroelectric dams harmless to river wildlife.

0879 resort
/rizɔ́ːrt/
/리조트/

(대안이 없어 뭔가 나쁜 것을 어쩔 수 없이) 하다(사용하다), 의지하다, 호소하다
- resort to sth ~에 호소하다(의지하다)
- resort to war / violence 전쟁/폭력에 호소하다
- The lecturer suggests that the Ministry of Environment should **resort to** killing all the toads in Australia, including native species.

*Ministry of Environment 환경부

0880 spawn
/spɔ́ːn/
/스폰/

(결과 등을) 낳다, 가져오다, 야기시키다
- The Industrial Revolution spawned social problems such as child labor exploitation.

[S] generate, produce, give rise to

0881 swell
/swel/
/스웰/
*swell-swelled-swollen

부어오르다, 붓다 (=swell up), (수나 양이) 늘다
- The place where he was stung by a bee is beginning to swell up.
- A 50-year-old farmer died while trying to cross a swollen river.

[A] shrink 줄어들다

adjective 형용사

0882 appropriate
/əpróupriət/
/어*프로우*프리엇/

적합한, 적절한
- appropriate for sth ~에 적합한
- The post is **appropriate for** those who have experience working abroad.
- People taking their pets to vets to receive appropriate vaccinations cannot be seen as spending too much money on their pets.

▶ appropriately (부사) 적절하게

[S] suitable
[A] inappropriate 부적합한, 부적절한

[S] suitably
[A] improperly 부적절하게

0883 competent
/kɑ́mpitənt/
/캄피턴트/

유능한, 능숙한
- I don't think our government is competent enough to solve the current issues we face.

▶ competence (명사) 능력

[S] capable, proficient, skilled
[A] incompetent 무능한

[S] ability
[A] incompetence 무능

0877 실험실 결과는 그 이론이 틀렸다는 것을 입증했다. / 영양학자들은 단 것을 갈망하는 사람들이 설탕 중독에 걸릴 수 있다는 것을 증명했다. / 그들의 새 앨범은 성공작으로 판명되고 있다. 0878 물고기가 댐을 통과하도록 설계된 통로인 물고기 사다리는 수력 발전 댐을 강에 사는 야생 동물들에게 무해하게 만든다. 0879 강의자는 환경부가 토착종을 포함한 오스트레일리아에 있는 모든 두꺼비를 죽여야 한다고 제안한다. 0880 산업 혁명은 아동 노동 착취와 같은 사회 문제를 낳았다. 0881 그가 벌에게 쏘인 곳이 부어오르기 시작하고 있다. / 한 50세의 농부가 불어난 강을 건너려고 하다가 죽었다. 0882 그 자리는 해외에서 일한 경험을 가지고 있는 사람에게 적합하다. / 사람들이 적절한 예방 접종을 받기 위해 그들의 반려동물을 수의사에 데려가는 것은 그들의 애완동물에 너무 많은 돈을 쓰는 것으로 보여질 수 없다. 0883 나는 우리 정부가 우리가 직면한 현안을 해결할 수 있을 만큼 유능하다고 생각하지 않는다.

0884
curious /kjúriəs/

호기심이 강한(많은), 궁금한
- Ⓤ curious about sth ~에 대해 궁금한
  - Of course, fans are always **curious about** where their favorite stars go and whom they meet.

S inquisitive

0885
external /ikstə́:rnl/

1. 외부의
- Plants grow in response to external stimuli.
- All animals do have parasites. But the really dangerous parasites are internal parasites.

S outside
A internal 내부의

2. 외국의, 대외적인
- The countries have to depend on external assistance for food.

0886
familiar /fəmíljər/ /퍼밀리어/

잘 알려진, 익숙한
- A familiar example of success these days is BTS.
- Ⓤ
  ① be familiar to sb ~에게 익숙(친숙)하다
  - How to calculate the ratio of π **is** not **familiar to** me. (=I don't know how to calculate the ratio of π.)
  ② be familiar with sth ~을 잘 알고 있다(~에 정통하다)
  - You need to **be familiar with** various grips to play golf well.

N familial (형용사) 가족의
◇ familial relationships 가족 관계

S recognized, well-known

S know sth well

0887
inert /inə́:rt/

불활성의 다른 물질과 반응하지 않는, 움직이지 않는
- Helium is chemically inert.

0888
maneuverable /mənú:vərəbl/ /머누*버러블/

조종할 수 있는
- Because of AI programs, airplanes are very easily maneuverable nowadays.

▶ maneuver (동사) 조종하다
- You need a lot of skill to maneuver a drone effectively, especially in windy weather.

S easily controlled

0889
necessary /nésəsèri/ /네서*세리/

필요한, 불가피한
- The protest was seen as necessary to raise awareness of the issue.
- Due to COVID-19, crowd dispersal is necessary.

S essential, inevitable

0890
preferable /préfərəbl/ /프레*퍼러블/

더 좋은, 나은, 더 적합한
- Ⓤ A be preferable to B: A가 B보다 낫다
  - Sometimes, monarchy, a form of government in which a country is ruled by a king or queen, **is preferable to** democracy in which rulers are elected by the people.

0891
ready /rédi/

준비가 된
- Ⓤ
  ① ready for sth ~의 준비가 된 / ready to do sth ~할 준비가 된
  ◇ be ready for school / church 학교/교회 갈 준비가 되다
  - Are you **ready for** school?
  - Are you **ready for** your driver's license test?
  ② get ready to do sth ~을 준비하다
  - Dad **is getting ready to** go to work.
  - She spends too much time **getting ready to** go out.
  ③ get sth ready ~을 준비하다 / get sb ready ~을 준비시키다
  ◇ get breakfast ready 아침 식사를 준비하다 / get the kids ready for school 아이들을 학교 갈 준비를 시키다

0892 stationary
/stéiʃəneri/
/스테이*셔네리/

1. 정지된, 움직이지 않는
- Other large birds that are living today, like the condor or the eagle, can remain stationary in midair for a short period of time without flapping their wings constantly to stay in the air. *in midair 하늘에, 공중에

S fixed, motionless, still
A mobile 움직이기 쉬운

2. 고정된, 변동이 없는
- The GDP growth rate is stationary.

S static

N stationery (명사) 문구 ◇ a stationery shop 문구점

0893 unanimous
/juːnǽniməs/
/유*내니머스/

만장일치의
- The jury's verdict was unanimous.

S agreed

▶ unanimously (부사) 만장일치로
- The executive committee voted unanimously to sell all its shares.

N anonymous (형용사) 익명의

0894 undesirable
/ʌ́ndizairəbl/
/언*디자이*러블/

원하지 않는, 바람직하지 못한
- The strategy of developing a new version of an existing product could have undesirable consequences for the original product.

S unwanted

0895 universal
/jùːnivə́ːrsl/
/유니버슬/

1. 보편적인
◇ a topic / subject of universal interest 보편적 관심사의 주제
- Universal Basic Income is thought to be a possible cure for poverty.

2. 만국의, 세계적인
- English is considered a universal language.

adverb 부사

0896 providing
/prəváidiŋ/

~하기만 하면 (반드시) ~ 하다 (부사절 접속사)
- You can go to university, provided that you pass your exams.

S provided

0897 respectively
/rispéktivli/
/리스펙*티블리/

각각 (앞에서 말 한 것을 언급할 때)
- On 6 and 9 August 1945, respectively, the U.S. dropped atomic bombs on the two Japanese cities of Hiroshima and Nagasaki.

N
1. respectable (형용사) 존경할 만한, 훌륭한
2. respective (형용사) 각각의
3. respectful (형용사) 공손한, 예의 바른, 존경하는

S respected
S courteous, polite

0898 far from
/faːr frəm/

1. ~하기는커녕
- Far from getting promoted, they are apprehensive about surviving in the company at every moment. *apprehensive 불안해하는, 걱정하는

2. ~과 거리가 먼
- This method of sorting various materials into one bag is far from ideal.

S not at all

0899 on the spot
/aːn ðə spaːt/

현장에서, 즉각
- The gun that he had used to murder his wife was found on the spot.

S immediately, at once

0892 콘도르나 독수리 같은 오늘날 살고 있는 다른 큰 새들은 공중에 머물러 있기 위해 계속 그들의 날개를 펄럭이지 않고 짧은 시간 동안 공중에 계속 움직이지 않고 있을 수 있다. / 국내 총생산 성장률이 고정되어 있다. 0893 배심원의 판결은 만장일치였다. / 이사회는 만장일치로 모든 주식을 매각하는 것에 투표했다. 0894 기존에 있는 제품의 새로운 버전을 개발하는 전략은 기존 제품에 원하지 않는 결과를 가져올 수도 있다. 0895 보편적 기본 소득은 가난에 대한 가능한 해결책으로 여겨진다. / 영어는 만국어로 여겨진다. 0896 너는 시험만 통과하면 대학에 갈 수 있다. 0897 1945년 8월 6일과 9일에 각각 미국은 일본의 히로시마와 나가사키 두 도시에 원자 폭탄을 투하했다. 0898 승진을 하기는커녕 그들은 매 순간 회사에서 살아남는 것에 대해 걱정한다. / 다양한 재료들을 한 봉투에 분류하는 방법은 이상적인 것과는 거리가 멀다. 0899 그가 아내를 살해하기 위해 사용했던 총이 현장에서 발견됐다.

DAY 19

ANGRY ENGLISH
ACADEMIC VOCABULARY

noun 명사

- [ ] area
- [ ] cohesion
- [ ] culprit
- [ ] demand
- [ ] flight
- [ ] flood
- [ ] generation
- [ ] harm
- [ ] life
- [ ] primacy
- [ ] risk
- [ ] specimen
- [ ] spell
- [ ] yardstick

verb 동사

- [ ] afflict
- [ ] avoid
- [ ] bar
- [ ] cluster
- [ ] conduct
- [ ] desert
- [ ] dissent
- [ ] diverge
- [ ] entail
- [ ] fuel
- [ ] hide
- [ ] lag
- [ ] provide
- [ ] replace
- [ ] speculate
- [ ] upset
- [ ] withstand
- [ ] wriggle

adjective 형용사

- [ ] approximate
- [ ] astute
- [ ] complicated
- [ ] desperate
- [ ] fanatical
- [ ] inferior
- [ ] mutual
- [ ] neat
- [ ] preoccupied
- [ ] recurrent
- [ ] steady
- [ ] subsidiary
- [ ] uncanny
- [ ] unmistakable

adverb 부사

- [ ] enough
- [ ] generally
- [ ] seemingly
- [ ] in an effort to

MP3 파일 다운

noun
명사

0900 area
/ɛ́riə/

1. 지역
   - My company is based in the area of upper New York.
2. 범위, 분야 — **S** subject, realm, range
   - The project will cost in the area of $50,000.

0901 cohesion
/kouhíːʒən/

결속, 결합 — **S** unity, bond, solidarity
- After Korea got its liberation from Japan, it quickly developed national cohesion.

0902 culprit
/kʌ́lprit/

1. 범인
   ◇ catch the culprit 범인을 체포하다
2. (문제의) 원인
   - The main culprit of road damage is heavy vehicles running on diesel.

0903 demand
/dimǽnd/

1. 요구
   ⓤ meet the demands of sth ~의 요구를 충족시키다
   - I couldn't **meet the demands of** a Master's Degree, so I gave it up.
2. 수요
   ⓤ demand for sb/sth ~에 대한 수요
   - There is a large **demand for** factory workers.

0904 flight
/fláit/

1. 비행
   ⓤ in flight 비행 중인(날고 있는)
   - You have to be very careful when you go bird watching, because it's not easy to tell an eagle from a hawk **in flight.**
2. 비행기, 항공편
   - All the flights between Seoul and Je-ju were cancelled due to the storm.
3. 도망, 탈출
   ◇ one's flight from sth ~에서의 누구의 탈출
   - In Western Europe, **rich people's flight from** the city to the countryside has caused a larger divide between the rich and the poor. *divide 차이

0905 flood
/flʌ́d/

1. 홍수
   - The city was destroyed by floods, causing the entire population to move to higher ground.
2. 쇄도 한꺼번에 많은 편지, 질문, 또는 사람 등이 나타나는 것
   - There was a flood of complaints about the TV show because of its extreme violence.

0906 generation
/dʒènəréiʃən/

1. 세대
   - Languages change from generation to generation.
2. (에너지 등의) 발생 — **S** production
   - The generation of electricity comes from coal, oil and nuclear power plants.

0900 우리회사는 뉴욕 북부 지역에 본사가 있다. / 그 프로젝트는 5만 달러 범위 안에서 비용이 들 것이다.   0901 한국이 일본으로부터 자유를 얻고 나서 한국은 빠르게 국민적 결속을 전개했다.   0902 도로 파손의 주범은 디젤로 가는 대형 차량이다.   0903 나는 석사 학위의 요구를 충족시킬 수 없어서 나는 포기했다. / 공장 노동자에 대한 큰 수요가 있다.   0904 새를 관찰하러 갈 때는 매우 조심해야 하는데 비행 중인 독수리와 매를 구별하기가 쉽지 않기 때문이다. / 서울 제주간 모든 항공편이 폭풍으로 취소되었다. / 서유럽에서 부자들의 도시에서 시골로의 탈출은 빈부 사이의 더 커다란 차이를 가져왔다.   0905 도시는 홍수로 파괴되었고, (이것이) 전체 인구를 더 높은 곳으로 이동하게 만들었다. / 지나친 폭력성 때문에 그 티브이 쇼에 대한 불만이 쇄도했다.   0906 언어는 대대로 변한다. / 전기 발생은 석탄, 석유, 원자력 발전소에서 나온다.

0907
harm
/háːrm/

해
ⓤ cause / do harm to sth ~에 해를 가하다 / inflict harm on sth ~에 해를 가하다 / do more harm than good 득보다 실이 많다
○ Another advantage of hydroelectric dams is their environmental friendliness. Hydroelectric dams do not **inflict harm on** the environment.

▶ harm (동사) 해치다

Ⓢ damage

Ⓢ hurt, damage

0908
life
/láif/

1. 삶
◇ life and death 삶과 죽음

2. 목숨
○ She said, "I'm gonna tell police there's an African-American man threatening my life."

3. 생명체, 생물 (불가산)
◇ marine life 해양 생물
○ There is life on Mars.

4. (한 사람의) 인생(삶), 생애
○ The movie is about the life of Steve Jobs, the co-founder and former CEO of Apple.

Ⓝ
1. daily life 일상 생활
2. real life 실생활
○ He is as humble in real life as he seems to be on TV.

0909
primacy
/práiməsi/
/프라이*머시/

최고 가장 중요한 것, 으뜸
ⓤ give primacy to sth ~에 우선순위를 두다
○ There is a debate in EU countries about whether they should **give primacy to** EU law or their own national laws.

0910
risk
/rísk/

위험, 위기
ⓤ
① the risk of doing sth ~할 위험
◇ the risk of getting the coronavirus 코로나에 걸릴 위험
② there is a risk of (sb/sth) doing sth / there is a risk that S주어 V동사 (누가/무엇이)~할 위험이 있다
○ If we use a paint containing special ingredients that protect buildings from the impact of acid rain, **there** will **be little risk of** acid rain caus**ing** damage to them.
③ be at risk (of (doing) sth) (~하는) 위험에 처해 있다
○ The spiders at the center of the web **are at** the greatest **risk** since predators, especially birds, can easily catch them.
④ put sb/sth at risk ~을 위험하게 하다(위험에 빠뜨리다)
○ Trump's plan to force some international students out of the U.S. would **put** the students **at risk**.

Ⓢ be in danger (of (doing) sth)

Ⓢ put sb/sth in danger

0911
specimen
/spésimən/
/스페*시먼/

견본(표본), 샘플, 예시
○ Lucy is a specimen of Australopithecus afarensis, which is an ancestor of modern humans.

Ⓢ sample, example

0907 수력 발전 댐의 또 다른 장점은 환경친화성이다. 수력 발전 댐은 환경에 해를 가하지 않는다. 0908 "나는 경찰들에게 내 목숨을 위협하는 한 흑인이 있다라고 말할 거야"라고 그녀는 말했다. / 화성에 생명체가 있다. / 그 영화는 애플의 공동 창업자이자 전직 CEO였던 스티브 잡스의 생애에 대한 영화이다. / 그는 티브이에서 보여지는 것만큼 실생활에서도 겸손하다. 0909 유럽 연합(EU) 국가들에서 그들이 유럽 연합(EU) 법에 우선순위를 두어야 하는지 아니면 자국법에 우선순위를 두어야 하는지에 대한 논쟁이 있다. 0910 만약 우리가 산성비의 영향으로부터 건물을 보호하는 특수한 성분이 포함된 페인트를 사용하면 산성비가 건물에 피해를 입힐 위험은 거의 없다. / 거미줄의 가운데에 있는 거미들은 가장 커다란 위험에 처해 있는데 왜냐하면 포식자, 특히 새들이 그들을 쉽게 잡을 수 있기 때문이다. / 미국 밖으로 일부 유학생들을 몰아내려는 트럼프의 계획은 그 학생들을 위험에 빠뜨릴 것이다. 0911 루시는 현대 인류 조상인 오스트랄로피테쿠스 아파렌시스의 표본이다.

0912
spell /spél/

1. (날씨나 특정 활동의) 기간 주로 짧은 기간
   - a brief spell 짧은 기간
   - She spent **a brief spell** as an environmental activist at Save Earth, an NGO established in India.

2. 주문, 마법
   - cast / put a spell on sb ~에게 마법을 걸다
   - The wizard **cast a spell on** the sleeping princess.

▶ spell (동사) 철자를 쓰다
   - He spelled 'true' wrongly.

[S] period

0913
yardstick /járdstik/

기준, 척도
- The yardstick of success is usually measured by a person's wealth.

---

verb 동사

0914
afflict /əflíkt/ /어*플릭트/

(정신적으로 또는 육체적으로) 고통 받게 하다, 괴롭히다
- be afflicted with sth ~로 고통받다(~에 시달리다)
- People who experience high levels of stress **are** often **afflicted with** anxiety disorders including panic disorder.

▶ affliction (명사) 고통

[S] affect sb badly

0915
avoid /əvɔ́id/

피하다
- avoid Ving 동명사
- And perhaps more importantly, workers can **avoid** gett**ing** hurt by wearing thick gloves.

[S] prevent, shun

0916
bar /báːr/

막다, 금하다
- bar O 목적어 from Ving 동명사 목적어가 ~하는 것을 막다
- Spain started to **bar** people **from** smok**ing** in enclosed public places.

[S] ban, prevent

0917
cluster /klʌ́stər/

모이다
- ◇ cluster together 함께 모이다
- At Donna's birthday party, her friends clustered around a clown to watch him do magic.

[S] gather

0918
conduct /kəndʌ́kt/

1. (특정한 활동 등을) 하다
   - conduct a survey / research / an experiment 설문 조사/연구/실험을 하다
   - Scientists took some of the gopher tortoises into a laboratory to **conduct research** on them.

2. (열, 전기, 소리 등을) 전도하다 지나가게 하다
   - Metals conduct electricity and heat well.

▶ conduct (명사) 행동

[S] carry out, do

[S] behavior

0919
desert /dizə́ːt/ /디저트/

1. 버리다
   - He deserted his daughters and young wife for another woman.

2. (군대에서) 탈영하다
   - ◇ desert from the army 탈영하다

▶ desert (명사) 사막
[N] dessert (명사) 디저트(후식)

[S] abandon, leave

0920
dissent
/disént/

의견이 다르다
- ⓥ dissent from sth ~과 의견이 다르다
- He **dissented from** the theory of plate tectonics that the lithosphere, the layer of rock consisting of the outer part of Earth, is divided into oceanic and continental plates. *lithosphere 암석권(지각)

[S] disagree, disapprove, object

0921
diverge
/divə́ːdʒ/

(길 등이) 갈라지다, (의견이) 갈리다
- The river diverges from the Canadian side.
- Opinions diverged greatly on whether the CEO would have to resign from the company after taking responsibility for the incident.

[S] deviate, depart
[A] converge 합쳐지다

0922
entail
/intéil/

필요로 하다, 수반하다
- ◇ entail some risk 위험을 수반하다
- Studying abroad often entails spending a lot of money.

[S] involve, cause, produce

0923
fuel
/fjúːəl/
/퓨얼/

1. ~에 연료를 공급하다
- Uranium, which is used to fuel nuclear plants, is very cheap.

2. (상황 등을) 촉발시키다
- The government's announcement fueled a debate on the safety of genetically modified (GM) foods.

[S] stoke, provoke

0924
hide
/háid/

감추다, 숨기다; 숨다
- A police officer was arrested for trying to hide evidence that could be used against him.

[N] hide-and-seek (명사) 숨바꼭질

[S] conceal, screen

0925
lag
/lǽg/

뒤에 처지다
- ⓥ lag behind sb ~보다 뒤처지다
- The institute did academic research into why African-American students **lag behind** their peers.

[S] trail

0926
provide
/prəváid/
/프러*바이드/

제공하다
- ⓥ
- ① provide A with B: A에게 B를 제공하다
- The large company **provides** its employees **with** better benefits than the small company.
- ② provide B for / to A: B를 A에게 제공하다
- The large company **provides** better benefits **for** its employees than the small company.

[S] furnish, supply, offer

0927
replace
/ripléis/

1. 대체하다
- ⓥ replace A with B: A를 B로 대체하다
- If you don't have olive oil, you can **replace** it **with** coconut oil.
(=If you don't have olive oil, you can use coconut oil instead of it.)
(=If you don't have olive oil, you can substitute coconut oil for it.)

2. (원래 있던 곳에) 다시 가져다 놓다
- Someone doesn't seem to have replaced the book on the shelf.

[S] substitute, swap 바꾸다
[S] use B instead of A, substitute B for A

[S] put sth back

0928
speculate
/spékjulèit/
/스페큘*레이트/

1. 추측(짐작)하다
- ⓥ speculate about sth ~에 대해 추측하다
- Netizens started to **speculate about** the reasons why the couple abruptly divorced.

2. 투기하다
- ⓥ speculate in sth ~에 투기하다
- People at that time **speculated in** everything including stocks and property, hoping to hit the jackpot.

▶ speculation (명사) 1) 추측 2) 투기

[S] guess, conjecture, hypothesize 가설을 세우다

[S] conjecture 추측

0929
upset
/ʌpsét/

1. 속상하게 만들다(하다)
- ⓥ it upset sb to do sth ~하는 것은 ~을 속상하게 한다 / it upsets sb that S 주어 V 동사 ~하는 것은 ~을 속상하게 한다 / it upsets sb when S 주어 V 동사 ~할 때 ~을 속상하게 한다
- **It upsets** me **when** I hit my ball out of bounds.

2. (기존 질서 등을) 어지럽히다, 교란시키다
- Even though the striped bass is a major predator of menhaden, eliminating this species will upset the ecological balance of the ecosystem.

[S] distress

[S] disturb

0930
withstand
/wiðstǽnd/

견디다
- The high-rise apartments on the beach were specially designed to withstand high winds and storms.

[S] survive, resist, weather

0931
wriggle
/rígl/
/리글/

꼼지락거리다, (지렁이 등이) 꿈틀거리며 나아가다
- ◇ wriggle one's toes 발가락을 꼼지락거리다
- A centipede is wriggling.

[S] wiggle

adjective 형용사

0932
approximate
/əpráksimət/
/어프락*시멋/

대략적인
- This leaflet will give you an approximate idea of what the treatment will involve.

▶ approximately (부사) 대략

[S] rough
[A] exact 정확한

[S] roughly, about, around

0933
astute
/əstú:t/
/어스튜트/

영리한
- My business partner is very astute. She has helped our company to grow to double its size in just 1 year.

▶ astutely (부사) 영리하게

[S] smart, clever
[A] unintelligent 영리하지 못한, dumb 멍청한

0934
complicated
/kámplikèitid/
/캄플리*케이티드/

복잡한, 어려운, 난해한
- I'm going to drop out of his class. His lectures are too complicated for me to follow.

▶ complicate (동사) 어렵게 만들다
- Bad weather has complicated the rescue.

[S] complex
[A] simple 단순한

0928 네티즌들은 그 커플이 갑자스럽게 이혼을 한 이유에 대해서 추측하기 시작했다. / 그 당시 사람들은 대박을 터트리기를 바라면서 주식과 부동산을 포함한 모든 것에 투기를 했다. 0929 내가 경기장 밖으로 공을 쳤을 때 나를 속상하게 한다. / 비록 줄무늬 농어가 청어의 주요 포식자이지만 이 종을 없애는 것은 생태계의 생태적 균형을 교란시킬 것이다. 0930 해변에 있는 그 고층 아파트들은 강풍과 폭풍에 견디도록 특별히 설계되었다. 0931 지네가 꿈틀거리며 나아가고 있다. 0932 이 책자는 당신에게 그 치료가 무엇을 수반하는지에 대한 대략적인 아이디어를 줄 것이다. 0933 내 동업자는 매우 영리하다. 그녀는 단지 1년 만에 우리 회사를 두 배로 성장하도록 도왔다. 0934 나는 그의 수업을 그만둘 거야. 강의가 너무 어려워서 내가 따라갈 수가 없다. / 나쁜 날씨가 구조를 어렵게 만들었다.

0935 desperate
/déspərət/
/데스*퍼럿/

1. 절망적인
- They're now in a desperate situation.

2. 절실한, 필사적인
◇ be in desperate need of help 절실한 도움을 필요로 하다
- These days, people in their thirties who are desperate to buy their own house borrow money to the hilt. *to the hilt 최대한

▶ desperately (부사) 필사적으로

[S] serious, grave

0936 fanatical
/fənǽtikl/
/퍼내*티클/

광적인, 열광적인
- Apple is one of the world's most successful companies. One key to its success is the fanatical loyalty of its customers. How does it maintain such strong brand loyalty?

[S] obsessive, enthusiastic

0937 inferior
/infíriər/

1. (~보다) 못한, 낮은, 열등한
ⓤ inferior to sb/sth ~보다 못한
- Although organic produce is gaining in popularity nowadays, it is generally **inferior to** conventionally grown fruits and vegetables.
- The low-budget film is of inferior quality.

2. 하위의, 아래의
ⓤ inferior to sth ~아래에 있는
- Federal courts are **inferior to** the Supreme Court.

[S] shoddy
[A] superior 우월한

0938 mutual
/mjúːtʃuəl/
/뮤추얼/

상호간의
- Trust and mutual respect are most important in maintaining a happy, long-lasting marriage.

[S] reciprocal

0939 neat
/níːt/

정돈된, 단정한
ⓤ neat and tidy 정돈되고 깨끗한
- Children should develop the habit of keeping their room **neat and tidy**.

[S] orderly, tidy

0940 preoccupied
/priɑːkjupaid/
/프리*아큐파이드/

몰두한, 열중한
ⓤ preoccupied with sth ~에 몰두한
- He is **preoccupied with** a woman.

▶ preoccupy (동사) 몰두시키다, 열중하게 하다, 사로잡다
- I was preoccupied by fear and hunger.

0941 recurrent
/rikə́ːrənt/
/리*커런트/

반복되는, 되풀이되는
- Betrayal of friendship is a recurrent theme in his novels.

[S] repeated, continued, periodic

0942 steady
/stédi/
/스테디/

1. 지속적인, 끊임없는, 일정한
◇ a steady flow of people into the store 매장으로 사람들의 끊임없는 유입
- Nuclear reactors, on the other hand, always produce a steady amount of power.

2. 안정된, 흔들리지 않는
- You need to keep your camera steady to take clear photos.

▶ steadily (부사) 지속적으로
◇ generate power steadily 지속적으로 전력을 발생시키다

[S] constant

[S] constantly

0943
subsidiary
/səbsídièri/
/섭*시디에리/

부차적인, 부수적인 _{추가 되는 것에 붙어 따르는}
ⓓ subsidiary to sth ~보다 덜 중요한
○ The country played only a subsidiary role in maintaining international peace and security.

▶ subsidiary (명사) 자회사(계열사)

[s] subservient
[s] less important than sth

0944
uncanny
/ʌnkǽni/

이상한, 신비로운
○ He has an uncanny ability to solve murder cases.

[s] strange, mysterious, cryptic

0945
unmistakable
/ʌnmistéikəbl/
/언*미스테이*커블/

틀림없는, 명백한, 확실한
○ The Consumer Sentiment Index (CSI) shows unmistakable signs of economic recovery. *consumer sentiment 소비자 심리

▶ unmistakably (부사) 틀림없이, 명백하게, 오해의 여지가 없이
○ I want to make it unmistakably clear that I am against you taking a job in the army. It is against my conscience.

[s] clear, obvious, certain

adverb 부사

0946
enough
/ináf/

~할 만큼 (충분히)
ⓓ 형용사/부사 enough to do sth ~할 만큼 ~한
○ A product advertising message must be strong **enough to** stay in people's minds for a long time.

0947
generally
/dʒénərəli/

1. 일반적으로
ⓓ be generally known / regarded as sb/sth 일반적으로 ~로 알려지다/여겨지다
○ Pride and Prejudice (1813) by Jane Austen **is generally regarded as** one of the most popular English novels to be adapted as a Hollywood movie.

[s] mostly, broadly, widely

2. 대개, 대체로
○ Young people are generally more physically active, so they do not easily gain weight and seldom get adult diseases.

[s] usually, on the whole, as a rule

0948
seemingly
/síːmiŋli/
/시밍리/

1. 겉보기에, 외견상으로
◇ seemingly irrelevant behavior 겉보기에 관련 없는 행동 / seemingly useless work 겉보기에 쓸모없어 보이는 일
○ He was seemingly unaware of his importance to people.

[s] apparently

2. 듣기로는, 듣자 하니
○ Seemingly, it was an impossible task, but I was able to do it.

[s] apparently

0949
in an effort to
/in ən efət tu/

~하기 위한 노력으로(노력의 일환으로)
○ The newly elected president plans to eliminate some regulations on business in an effort to boost the economy.

[s] in an attempt to

DAY 20

**ANGRY ENGLISH
ACADEMIC VOCABULARY**

noun 명사

- [ ] authority
- [ ] cliche
- [ ] credence
- [ ] degree
- [ ] end
- [ ] facet
- [ ] groove
- [ ] opposite
- [ ] problem
- [ ] rival
- [ ] shred
- [ ] speck
- [ ] tip
- [ ] work

verb 동사

- [ ] affront
- [ ] aggravate
- [ ] baffle
- [ ] coalesce
- [ ] confirm
- [ ] deserve
- [ ] deter
- [ ] disturb
- [ ] enlarge
- [ ] fragment
- [ ] hone
- [ ] impress
- [ ] issue
- [ ] languish
- [ ] pursue
- [ ] repel
- [ ] resist
- [ ] suggest

adjective 형용사

- [ ] apt
- [ ] asleep
- [ ] conceivable
- [ ] decisive
- [ ] explicit
- [ ] fascinating
- [ ] infinite
- [ ] narrow
- [ ] primary
- [ ] regular
- [ ] still
- [ ] subtle
- [ ] unbridled
- [ ] uniform

adverb 부사

- [ ] granted
- [ ] immediately
- [ ] in part
- [ ] when it comes to

🎧 MP3 파일 다운

noun
명사

0950 authority /əθɔ́ːrəti/ /어쏘*러티/

1. 권한, 지휘(권)
   - ⓥ have / exercise the authority to do sth ~할 권한을 가지고 있다/권한을 행사하다
   - She can **exercise** her **authority to** stop the law from passing.
   - Several members in authority were dismissed from the chairman's office. *office 직

2. 당국, 부
   - ◇ the health authority / the housing authority 보건 당국/국토부

0951 cliche /kliːʃéi/

진부한(식상한) 표현
- The old cliche that women should only be housewives is finally changing.

ⓢ truism, platitude, bromide

0952 credence /kríːdns/ /크리*든스/

신빙성
- ⓥ give / add / lend credence to sth ~에 신빙성을 주다
- If you try to retaliate, it will only **add credence to** the rumors. It is better to just say nothing. *retaliate 복수하다

0953 degree /digríː/

1. 정도
   - ⓥ to some degree 어느 정도
   - ◇ a high degree of skill 고도의 기술
   - I agree with you **to some degree**, but not completely.

2. (온도 단위) 도
   - ◇ 470 degrees 470도 / 25 degrees Celsius 섭씨 25도
   - Because of global warming, the temperature has risen to 39 degrees on the Celsius scale.

ⓢ to a certain degree

0954 end /énd/

끝, 종료, (이야기 등의) 결말
- They asked him a lot of questions related to the end of the story.
- ⓥ
- ① come to an end 끝나다
- There are three theories that explain why the Mayan civilization **came to an end**.
- ② bring sth to an end ~을 끝내다
- Let's **bring** this meeting **to an end** now.
- ③ meet one's end 죽다

ⓢ end
ⓢ put an end to sth
ⓢ die

0955 facet /fǽsit/

측면, 점
- After he became famous, it became totally impossible to go shopping, travel with his son, or meet his friends because paparazzi always watched him and broadcasted every facet of his private life.

Ⓝ faucet (명사) 수도꼭지
- ◇ turn on / off the faucet 수도꼭지를 틀다/잠그다
- Don't forget to turn off the faucet.

ⓢ aspect

0950 그녀는 그 법이 통과되는 것을 막을 수 있는 권한을 행사할 수 있다. / 권한을 가진 몇몇 의원들이 의장직에서 해임되었다. 0951 여자들은 가정주부만 되어야 한다는 그 오래된 식상한 표현이 마침내 변하고 있다. 0952 만약 당신이 복수하려고 하면 그것은 단지 그 소문에 신빙성만 줄 것이다. 그냥 아무 말도 하지 않는 것이 더 낫다. 0953 나는 어느 정도 당신과 동의하지만 완전히 동의하지는 않는다. / 지구 온난화 때문에 기온이 섭씨 39도까지 올라갔다. 0954 그들은 그에게 그 이야기의 결말과 관련한 많은 질문을 했다. / 왜 마야 문명이 끝났는지를 설명하는 세 가지 이론이 있다. / 이제 이 회의를 끝내자. 0955 그가 유명하게 된 후에 쇼핑을 하러 가거나, 그의 아들과 여행하기, 또는 그의 친구들을 만나는 것이 완전히 불가능해졌는데 왜냐하면 파파라치들이 언제나 그를 지켜보고 그의 사생활의 모든 측면을 방송했기 때문이다. / 수도꼭지를 잠그는 것을 잊지 마라.

0956
groove /grúːv/

1. 홈
   - surface grooves 표면 홈
   - It turned out that the lines discovered on Mars were just grooves on the surface of the planet.
2. (대중 음악) 리듬

0957
opposite /ápəzit/ /아퍼짓/

반대
- the opposite of sth ~의 반대
- Vanity is **the opposite of** modesty.

[s] antithesis

0958
problem /prábləm/

1. 질환
   - Pollution can cause respiratory problems for some people.
2. (시험) 문제
   - difficult math problems 어려운 수학 문제
   - I have five mathematical problems to do for homework.

[s] question

0959
rival /ráivl/

경쟁자
- a rival company / team 라이벌 회사/팀
- When it comes to the contest, we're rivals.

[s] competitor, contender

0960
shred /ʃréd/ /쉬레드/

1. (잘려진 얇은) 조각
   - shreds of paper 종이 조각
2. 티끌, 아주 조금
   - a shred of sth 티끌만큼의
   - I don't have **a shred of** remorse for not going to college.

0961
speck /spék/

(작은) 점, 얼룩, 자국
- a speck of dust 먼지 한 점
- Humans are just **specks of dust** in the vast universe.

[s] spot

0962
tip /típ/

(뾰족한 것의) 끝
- the tip of the iceberg 빙산의 일각
- Large ships often encountered large waves in the ocean surrounding Cape Horn, which is at the southern tip of South America.
- When the bird's wings were fully extended, the distance from tip to tip could reach up to 7 meters.

[s] end

0956 화성에서 발견된 그 선들은 단지 그 행성의 표면에 있는 홈일 뿐이라는 것이 밝혀졌다. 0957 허영심은 겸손함의 반대이다. 0958 오염은 일부 사람들에게 호흡기 질환을 일으킬 수 있다. / 나는 숙제로 해야 할 5개의 수학 문제를 가지고 있다. 0959 그 경연에 관한 한 우리는 라이벌이다. 0960 나는 대학에 가지 않은 것에 대해 티끌만큼의 후회도 가지고 있지 않다. 0961 인간은 광대한 우주의 먼지 한 점일 뿐이다. 0962 큰 배들은 남아메리카의 남쪽 끝에 있는 케이프 혼을 둘러싸고 있는 바다에서 종종 큰 파도와 마주쳤다. / 그 새의 날개가 완전히 펴졌을 때 끝에서 끝까지의 거리가 7미터까지 닿을 수 있었다.

0963 work
/wɜːrk/

1. 일
- Doing this project was really hard work.

2. (해야 할) 일
- Don't bring your work home.
- Don't take your work home.

3. 회사, 직장
ⓤ
① get to work / go to work 출근하다
② get off work / leave work 퇴근하다
- I normally take the subway to **get to work** to avoid getting stuck in traffic.
③ at work 회사에서
- Dad is **at work**.
④ get home from work 퇴근해서 귀가하다
- One day I **got home from work** and went out for dinner with my kids.

4. 작품 (가산)
◇ works by Rambrandt 램프란트 작품 / the complete works of Shakespeare 셰익스피어 전집 / several works of art 몇 가지 미술 작품 (=several art works)
- The curator guided us around the art gallery, explaining the art works to us.

verb 동사

0964 affront
/əfrʌ́nt/

모욕하다
- I felt deeply affronted by his rude remarks on my essay.

Ⓢ insult, offend

▶ affront (명사) 모욕

Ⓢ insult, indignity, humiliation

0965 aggravate
/ǽɡrəvèit/
/애그러*베이트/

1. 악화시키다
- The COVID-19 pandemic aggravated the unemployment problem.

Ⓢ exacerbate, worsen
Ⓐ improve 향상시키다

2. 화나게 하다
- His malicious lies ended up aggravating his friend.

Ⓢ irritate, annoy, anger

▶ aggravating (형용사) 짜증나게 하는, 성가신

Ⓢ irritating, annoying, vexing

0966 baffle
/bǽfl/

당황하게 만들다
- The question about his mother-in-law baffled him.

Ⓢ puzzle

▶ baffled (형용사) 당황한, 난처한

Ⓢ puzzled

0967 coalesce
/kòuəlés/

합치다
ⓤ coalesce into / with sth ~로 합쳐지다
- The two streams **coalesce into** a single river.

Ⓢ combine, fuse, amalgamate

▶ coalesced (형용사) 합쳐진
- The coalesced tribes formed a large army and were able to attack and burn the city of Rome.

Ⓢ joined

0963 이 프로젝트를 하는 것은 정말 힘든 일이었다. / 일을 집으로 가져오지 마라. / 일을 집으로 가져가지 마라. / 나는 차 막히는 것을 피하기 위해 출근하기 위해 보통 지하철을 탄다. / 아빠는 회사에 있다. / 어느 날 퇴근해서 집에 와서 아이들과 저녁을 먹으러 나갔다. / 그 큐레이터는 미술 작품을 설명해 주면서 우리에게 미술관 주변을 안내해 주었다. 0964 내 에세이에 대한 그의 무례한 말에 나는 몹시 모욕감을 느꼈다. 0965 코로나19 대유행이 실업 문제를 악화시켰다. / 그의 악의적인 거짓말이 결국 그의 친구를 화나게 했다. 0966 그의 장모에 대한 질문이 그를 당황하게 만들었다. 0967 그 두 개의 하천이 한 개의 강으로 합쳐진다. / 합쳐진 부족들은 대규모 군대를 형성하여 로마시를 공격하고 불태울 수 있었다.

0968 confirm
/kənfə́:rm/

1. 입증하다
- There's a lot of evidence confirming this pollution hypothesis.

[S] prove, affirm, corroborate
[A] refute 반박하다

2. (약속 등을) 확정(확인)하다, 승인하다
◇ confirm a booking / reservation 예약을 확인하다
- Make sure that your reservation has been confirmed.

▶ confirmation (명사) 확인
- I've not yet received confirmation of my reservation.

0969 deserve
/dizə́:rv/

누릴 자격이 있다, 받을 만하다, ~해야 마땅하다
- Every one of our kids deserves the right to attend university.
- He deserves to be punished.
- You deserve a rest after doing your homework.

[S] be worthy of

0970 deter
/ditə́:r/

막다, 좌절(단념)시키다
ⓒ deter sb/sth from Ving 동명사 ~누가 ~하는 것을 막다(단념시키다)
- The Internet sometimes **deters** users **from** com**ing** up with new and creative ideas.

[S] prevent, discourage, thwart
[A] encourage 격려하다

0971 disturb
/distə́:rb/

1. 방해하다, (제자리에 있는 것을) 흩뜨리다
- I placed a "Do Not Disturb" sign on the outside of the door and went to bed.
- They found the victim's body because the soil in the garden had been disturbed.

[S] interrupt

2. 교란시키다, 어지럽히다
- Removing bass from a lake can disturb the ecological balance of nature because bass are good predators. *bass 배스 (물고기의 종류)

0972 enlarge
/inlá:rdʒ/

1. 크게 하다, 확대하다
- Since she doesn't want to feel self-conscious about her appearance, she is considering an operation to enlarge her breasts.
*self-conscious about ~에 대해서 남의 시선을 의식하는

[S] expand

2. (지식이나 어휘 등을) 넓히다, 확장하다
- One of the easiest ways to improve your English is to enlarge your vocabulary.

▶ enlargement (명사) 확대
◇ breast enlargement surgery 가슴 확대 수술

0973 fragment
/frǽgmənt/

잘게 부수다; 잘게 부서지다, 산산조각이 되다
- The company fragmented after the founder died.

▶ fragment (명사) 파편

0974 hone
/hóun/
/호운/

1. (숫돌로 칼이나 가위 등을 날카롭게) 갈다
- These days, it is hard to find people whose job is to hone blunt knives or scissors.

[S] sharpen

2. (기술 등을) 연마하다
◇ hone one's skills 기술을 연마하다
- You should hone your reading skills if you want to get a perfect score on the SAT reading section.

[S] improve, enhance

0975 impress
/imprés/

1. 감명을 주다, 감동시키다
   - I was impressed by her presentation.

   [s] move, touch

2. (도장 등을) 찍다
   - He impressed the document with his seal.
   (=He impressed his seal on the document.)

   [s] imprint

0976 issue
/íʃuː/

1. 발표하다
   ◇ issue a report 보고서를 발표하다
   - Samson will issue a statement to the press about the tax evasion the company has been accused of.

2. 발급(지급)하다
   ⓤ issue A with B / issue B to A: A에게 B를 지급하다
   ◇ issue a passport / a visa 여권/비자를 발급하다 / issue equipment 장비를 지급하다
   - Companies **issue** their employees **with** masks for free to protect them from COVID-19.

3. 발행하다
   - The date on which the government bond was issued is printed on it.

   [s] publish

4. (영장 등을) 발부하다
   ◇ issue a writ against sb ~에게 영장을 발부하다

0977 languish
/lǽŋgwiʃ/

(불쾌한 일을 오랫동안) 겪다, (강제적으로) 머물다
- He languished in prison for the rest of his life.

0978 pursue
/pərsúː/

1. 뒤쫓다, 추적하다
   - In the process of pursuing a stolen vehicle, the police got into a car accident.

   [s] chase, run after

2. (오랜 기간 동안 목표 등을) 추구하다
   ⓤ pursue a career in the field of sth ~의 분야에서 직업을 갖다
   ◇ pursue a career as a doctor 의사로서 경력을 쌓다 / pursue a career in medicine 의학계에서 경력을 쌓다
   - These days, it seems that no one wants to become a teacher. College graduates are pursuing other careers.

0979 repel
/ripél/

물리치다, 쫓아 버리다
◇ repel an attack 공격을 물리치다
- Garlic, which contains a substance called allicin with a strong odor, is a very popular method of repelling mosquitoes.

0980 resist
/rizíst/

1. 저항하다, (병에) 견디다
   - The trees grown in research centers are not capable of resisting diseases.

   [s] fight against

2. 반대하다
   ⓤ resist doing sth ~하는 것을 반대하다
   - The Bank of Korea continued to **resist** rais**ing** the interest rate despite growing concerns about rising household debt.

   [s] oppose

3. 참다, 견디다
   ⓤ can't resist doing sth (도저히) ~을 참을 수가 없다
   ◇ resist the temptation to do sth ~하는 유혹을 참다
   - I **can't resist** golf**ing**.

   [s] withstand

▶ resistance (명사) 저항, 내성

0981 suggest
/sədʒést/

1. 제안하다
- ⓤ suggest Ving^{동명사} ~을 제안하다 / suggest that S^{주어} (should) V^{동사} ~해야 한다고 제안하다
- ○ The lecturer **suggests that** the Ministry of Environment should resort to killing all the toads in Australia, including native species.
  *Ministry of Environment 환경부
- ○ The lecturer **suggests** develop**ing** paints containing materials that will prevent acid rain from damaging buildings.

[S] recommend

2. (사실임을 넌지시) 나타내다, 시사(암시)하다
- ⓤ evidence / research / studies / data suggest (that) S^{주어} V^{동사} 증거/조사/연구/자료가 ~라는 것을 나타내다(암시하다)
- ○ This **suggests that** the stone balls served as money.

[S] indicate

adjective 형용사

0982 apt
/æpt/
/앱트/

1. 적절한, 적당한, 어울리는
- ⓤ apt for sth ~에 적절한
- ◇ an apt comment 적절한 언급
- ○ The song, "My Heart Will Go On" by Celine Dion, is very **apt for** funerals.

[S] appropriate, timely

2. ~하기 쉬운, ~하는 경향이 있는
- ⓤ be apt to do sth ~하는 경향이 있다
- ○ The leaves on this tree **are apt to** stay on the tree through the winter.

[S] inclined
[S] tend to do sth, be inclined to do sth

▶ aptly (부사) 적절하게

[S] appropriately

0983 asleep
/əslíːp/

자고 있는
- ⓤ fall asleep 잠이 들다
- ○ If they go to sleep late at night, they will **fall asleep** during class.

[N] doze off 졸다

[S] sleeping

0984 conceivable
/kənsíːvəbl/
/컨시*버블/

상상(생각)할 수 있는, 가능한
- ⓤ it is conceivable that S^{주어} V^{동사} ~하는 것은 상상할 수 있는 일이다
- ○ According to the politician, **it is conceivable that** two men can love each other. That is why same-sex marriage should be allowed.
- ○ People once thought of conquering cancer as inconceivable.

[S] possible, imaginable
[A] inconceivable 상상할 수도 없는

▶ conceivably (부사) 생각건대, 상상컨대

[S] possibly

0985 decisive
/disáisiv/
/디*사이시브/

1. 단호한
- ○ The government took decisive action to stop the disease from spreading.

[A] indecisive 우유부단한

2. 결정적인
- ○ During the harvest season, cooperating with others played a decisive role in a good harvest.

[S] crucial, critical, significant

[N] divisive (형용사) 구별하는, 불화를 일으키는

0981 강의자는 환경부가 토착종을 포함한 오스트레일리아에 있는 모든 두꺼비를 죽여야 한다고 제안한다. / 강의자는 산성비가 건물을 손상시키는 것을 막아 줄 물질을 함유한 페인트를 개발할 것을 제안한다. / 이것은 그 돌공이 돈으로 역할을 했다는 것을 나타낸다. 0982 셀린 디온의 노래 "My Heart Will Go On"은 장례식에 매우 적절하다. / 이 나무의 잎은 겨울 내내 나무에 붙어 있는 경향이 있다. 0983 만약 그들이 밤에 늦게 자면 그들은 수업 중에 잠이 들 것이다. 0984 그 정치인에 따르면, 두 남자가 서로 사랑할 수 있다는 것은 상상할 수 있는 일이다. 이것이 동성 결혼이 허용되어야 하는 이유이다. / 사람들은 한때 암을 정복하는 것은 상상할 수도 없는 일이라고 생각했다. 0985 정부는 그 질병이 퍼지는 것을 막기 위한 단호한 조치를 취했다. / 수확기 동안, 다른 사람들과 협력하는 것은 풍작에 결정적인 역할을 하였다.

0986 explicit
/iksplísit/
/익스*플리싯/

1. 명백(명확)한, 정확한
◇ explicit explanations 정확한(명확한) 설명
○ Teachers should give students explicit instructions.

2. 외설적인, 노골적인
◇ sexually explicit movies 선정적인 영화
○ For example, children can be exposed to sexually explicit content, such as pornography.

▶ explicitly (부사) 명확하게

S clear, exact

S clearly

0987 fascinating
/fǽsənèitiŋ/
/패서네이팅/

(매우) 흥미로운
○ I found it fascinating that South Koreans don't care about North Korea's constant threats.

▶ fascinated (형용사) 매료된
ⓒ fascinated by sb/sth ~에 매료된
○ I was **fascinated by** his handwriting.

S extremely interesting

0988 infinite
/ínfinət/

무한한
◇ an infinite source of energy 무한한 에너지원
○ But we don't have the technology to mine the metals in the deep sea, where there are infinite metal resources such as gold and iron.

S limitless, unlimited
A finite 제한된

0989 narrow
/nǽrou/
/내로우/

1. 좁은
○ The river is narrow.

2. 좁은, 한정된
◇ narrow-minded 속 좁은, 편협한
○ The dictionary contains a narrow range of vocabulary.

3. 아슬아슬한
◇ suffer a narrow defeat 아슬아슬한 패배를 당하다 / win a narrow victory 아슬아슬한 승리를 거두다
○ Joe Biden won a narrow victory over Donald Trump in the presidential election.

▶ narrowly (부사) 간신히
○ A couple narrowly escaped injury Saturday night when their car crashed into a van.

A wide 넓은

A broad 넓은

0990 primary
/práiməri/
/프라이메리/

1. 주된, 주요한
◇ a primary source of income 주된 소득원 / primary aim 주요 목표
○ He concludes that earthquakes cannot be a primary cause of mass whale strandings. *stranding 고래들이 물가에 올라와서 죽는 것

2. 초기의, 일차의
○ Primary cancer is the place where cancer starts growing.

S prime, main, chief

0991 regular
/régjulər/

1. 규칙적인, 주기적인
○ Regular exercise can minimize your chances of getting heart disease.

2. 정규의(정기의), 정기적인
◇ non-regular workers 비정규직 근로자들 / at regular intervals 주기적인 간격으로
○ Getting medical check-ups on a regular basis can increase people's life expectancy.

▶ regularly (부사) 정기적으로, 주기적으로

A irregular 불규칙의

A irregular 비정규의

S periodically

0992 still
/stíl/
/스틸/

가만히 있는, (물 등이) 움직이지 않는, 고요한
- ⓤ keep still 가만히 있다
  - When the butterfly is still, it looks like a dead leaf.
  - He has trouble **keeping still**.

S motionless, stationary

0993 subtle
/sʌ́tl/
/서틀/

1. 미묘한
- ◇ subtle differences 미묘한 차이
  - We can notice subtle but distinct changes in the climate in the last 10 years.

2. 교묘한, 영리한
- The journalist asked subtle questions of the politician to find out whether he was involved in the corruption.

S elusive 파악하기 어려운
A obvious 명백한

0994 unbridled
/ʌnbráidld/
/언*브라이들드/

억제되지 않은, 굴레를 벗은
- ◇ unbridled greed / ambition 억제되지 않은 탐욕/야망
  - It's unbridled greed that makes people refinance their loans when interest rates go down, and then buy another house with the margin loan. *margin 차액 / refinance one's loans 대출금을 재융자하다

▶
1. bridle (명사) 굴레
2. bridle (동사) 굴레를 씌우다

S unrestricted, uncontrolled

0995 uniform
/júːnifɔ̀ːrm/
/유니폼/

일정한, 동일한, 균일한
- Soldiers have to walk in a uniform manner.

▶
1. uniform (명사) 제복 ◇ school uniform 교복 / army uniform 군복
2. uniformly (부사) 동일하게, 한결같이

S consistent, unvarying, even

S consistently

adverb 부사

0996 granted
/grǽntid/
/그랜티드/

당연히
ⓤ
① take sth for granted ~을 당연시하다
  - Children today tend to **take** sacrifices their parents make for their success **for granted**.
② take it for granted that S주어 V동사 ~하는 것을 당연시하다
  - Children today tend to **take it for granted that** their parents should make sacrifices for their success.

0997 immediately
/imíːdiətli/

바로, 즉시
- The meerkat that had stood guard ran immediately into a burrow after making a loud noise. *stand guard 보초를 서다 / burrow 굴

S at once

0998 in part
/in paːrt/

부분적으로
- Due in part to the development of the Internet, many people don't work five days a week these days.

N in large part 대부분

S partly, partially

0999 when it comes to
/wen it kʌmz tu/

~하는 데 있어서, ~에 관한 한
- BTS are amazing when it comes to performing on stage.

0992 나비가 가만히 있을 때 그것은 마치 죽은 나뭇잎처럼 보인다. / 그는 가만히 있는 데 어려움이 있다. 0993 우리는 지난 10년간 기후의 미묘하지만 두드러진 변화를 알아차릴 수 있다. / 그 기자는 그가 그 비리에 관련되어 있었는지를 알아보기 위해서 그 정치인에게 교묘한 질문들을 했다. 0994 사람들이 이자율이 내려갈 때 그들의 대출금을 재융자하게 만들어 그 차액의 대출금으로 그 다음에 또 다른 집을 사게 만드는 것이 바로 억제되지 않은 탐욕이다. 0995 군인들은 동일한 방식으로 걸어야 한다. 0996 오늘날 아이들은 그들의 성공을 위해 부모들이 하는 희생들을 당연시하는 경향이 있다. / 오늘날 아이들은 부모가 자신의 성공을 위해 희생해야 한다는 것을 당연시하는 경향이 있다. 0997 큰 소리를 낸 후 보초를 섰던 미어켓은 바로 굴 속으로 뛰어 들어갔다. 0998 부분적으로 인터넷 발달로 인해 오늘날 많은 사람들은 주 5일 근무는 하지 않는다. 0999 무대에서 공연하는 것에 관한 한 BTS는 정말 대단하다.

INDEX

A

abide	34	alienate	145	assault	26	brace	50
abiding	20	align	137	assemble	17	bridle	26
abnormal	12	alike	38	assert	67	brief	44
abort	17	allegedly	46	assign	75	brisk	28
abound	26	alleviate	128	astute	163	browse	42
abroad	22	allow	119	asymmetric	13	bulb	65
absurd	28	ambitious	94	at once	124	bulge	34
abuse	42	ambivalent	103	attach	110	burden	18, 90
access	40, 50	amenity	32	attributable	131	burrow	82
accommodate	58	amiable	113	authority	167	by means of	141
accomplish	10	analogous	12	autonomy	143	by mistake	133
according to	88	analyze	101	available	103		
accurate	36	animate	122	avoid	161	C	
acknowledge	67	annual	131	aware	78	calligraphy	98
acquainted	44	anomaly	24	awful	52	camouflage	34
acquisition	9	anonymous	139			candidly	71
anxious	147			B		capable	20
act	75	apart	54	backbone	48	cardinal	36
actual	52	apex	65	baffle	169	care	32, 42
acute	60	appeal	151	balanced	20	cargo	48
adapt	83	appear	91	bank	126	carry	50
address	91	appearance	90	bar	161	case	56
adhere	101	appease	83	bare	13	cast	75
adjoin	110	application	98	barely	63	casual	44
adjust	119	apply	58	barge	151	category	98
admiration	48	approach	50, 135	barrier	9	cater	84
admire	128	appropriate	155	basis	24	cause	58
admit	145	approximate	163	bear	153	caution	67
adopt	137	approximately	14	beckon	145	cautious	52
adorn	153	apt	172	belittle	137	ceaseless	61
advantage	56	archive	82	benefit	128	central	69
advice	73	area	159	blame	119	certain	78
afflict	161	arouse	42	blind	86	chamber	108
affluence	108	array	34	block	10	chance	126
affront	169	as for	106	blot	92	characterize	92
aftermath	117	as is the case with	96	bode	83	charge	101, 143
aggravate	169	as of	115	body	40	chief	87
aggressive	69	as opposed to	88	bold	113	chip	135
agile	78	as such	106	bolster	67	choke	110
ahead	30	as well	96	bother	58	chunk	90
aim	126, 153	as with	115	bounds	98	circulate	120
alarming	86	asleep	172	bountiful	69	cite	128

claim	137	consider	137	design	138	efficacy	9
clarify	26	consistently	80	desperate	164	efficient	53
clear	153	constitute	128	destined	95	eject	43
cliche	167	construe	18	deter	170	element	127
cling	110	consumption	9	determine	18	elevate	51
clockwise	14	contact	18, 24	detest	27	eliminate	59
close	94	contemplate	34	devastation	151	elongate	68
clumsy	103	contend	26	devoid	13	elude	76
cluster	161	continual	139	devote	35	embark on	84
coalesce	169	contribute	42	dichotomy	143	embed	93
coax	110	contrive	50	differ	51	embody	102
cohesion	159	convenient	131	diligent	78	emerge	111
coinage	82	convey	59	dimension	126	eminent	61
coincide	92	convince	67	direction	108	eminently	88
coincident	113	correlate	84	disapprove	42	enable	120
collect	84	count	92	discard	59	encounter	129
collide	75	credence	167	discharge	68	encroach	11
combine	67	credit	48, 120	discount	76	end	167
come across	58	cremate	10	discrepancy	117	energetic	78
comfortable	122	criticize	146	discrete	61	engender	138
command	50	crucial	148	discriminate	84	engulf	146
commence	42	culprit	159	disgust	101	enjoy	154
commit	34	curious	156	disintegrate	111	enlarge	170
committed	131			dismantle	120	enough	165
common	13	**D**		dismay	129	entail	162
commonplace	139	damage	27	disparate	44	enthusiastic	95
company	117	daub	18	dispersal	135	entire	113
comparable	148	debilitate	42	displace	146	enumerate	84
compare	26	debris	9	disregard	154	epitomize	76
compel	18	decay	10	dissent	162	equip	68
competent	155	deceptive	28	distance	98	equipment	151
complacency	151	decisive	172	distinction	90	erase	59
complaint	73	decline	92	distinguish	154	especially	96
complement	101	deduce	34	distract	101	essence	143
complex	65	deem	51	disturb	170	essential	131
complicated	163	defect	48	diverge	162	etch	51
comprehend	120	defer	59	diversion	73	evade	43
concede	137	define	67	domain	65	even	148
conceivable	172	definite	148	doomed	95	eventuate	93
concern	24, 145	definitive	131	dream	56	everywhere	106
concerned	61	defy	76	drive	48, 76	exacerbate	111
conclude	153	degrade	84	drudgery	32	exaggerate	120
condition	40	degree	167	due	20	except for	149
conducive	36	delineate	92	dwarf	40	expansion	117
conduct	161	deliver	110	dwelling	16	expedition	98
confirm	170	demand	101, 159	dye	24	expend	146
conflict	98, 145	demonstrate	129			experience	40
congestion	48	denote	138	**E**		explicit	173
conscientious	28	dependable	113	eager	36	expose	138
conscious	94	deplete	146	ease	18	extend	129
consecutive	61, 122	deposit	153	echo	27	extensively	115
consent	75	desert	161	edge	135	extent	56
consequence	16	deserve	170	efface	35	external	156

extreme	140	generally	165	impress	171	invariably	38
		generation	159	impression	82	invention	152
F		genuine	122	improbable	53	involved	87
face	18	gradual	28	improve	59	isolated	78
facet	167	grand	20	improvised	61	issue	171
fade	35	granted	174	in an effort to do	165		
faithful	140	grasp	76	in part	174	**J**	
familiar	156	gratifying	70	in search of	22	joint	32
fanatical	164	groove	168	in the first place	133	judicious	21
far from	157	ground	99	in unison	80	juncture	108
fascinating	173	guarded	104	inactive	70		
favor	151			inadvertent	78	**K**	
feature	51, 108	**H**		incessant	87	keen	53
feed	68	hail	111	incidence	57		
fervent	87	halt	111	incident	117	**L**	
fiery	70	hamper	120	incidental	95	lag	162
figure	99	hamstring	138	incipient	104	languish	171
fill	85	hands-on	45	incisive	113	last	147
fire	82	hang	146	inconclusive	122	lead	127
firmly	124	haphazard	29	inconsequential	123	leap	143
fit	61	hardly	133	incorporate	68	legendary	13
fix	102	harm	160	incredulous	131	level	108
flake	65	hasten	154	incur	77	life	160
flavor	9	hatred	108	incursion	10	lifespan	73
flexibility	32	hazardous	87	indecipherable	132	limit	135, 154
flight	159	hence	22	indicate	11	logical	29
fling	120	hesitant	95	indifferent	140	longevity	143
flood	159	heyday	135	indulge	85	loop	117
force	57, 129	hide	162	inept	148	loose	45
foresight	48	high	104	inert	156		
forge	138	hindrance	90	inevitably	30	**M**	
form	11	hone	170	inferior	164	magnificent	70
fortunately	133	hope	49	infinite	173	magnitude	99
forward	149	host	9	inflict	93	mainly	46
founder	154	hostile	122	inform	102	maintain	138
fraction	16	huge	13	ingredient	16	major	62
fractious	53	hustle	35	initiative	49	malady	57
fracture	40			innate	20	maneuver	117
fragment	170	**I**		innovation	127	maneuverable	156
freak	27	iceberg	24	inordinate	29	manifest	129
fuel	162	identify	19	inquire	111	manipulate	121
full	45	idle	20	inroad	40	martial	13
fully	141	ignite	27	inspire	121	marvelous	87
fun	73	immediately	174	install	129	mean	95
function	9	immerse	35	instantaneous	37	meanwhile	54
fundamental	37	imminent	29	instead of	30	mechanism	127
furnace	90	impact	65	instrument	73	mediate	11
futile	20	impede	43	instrumental	45	mediocre	104
		imperative	13	intensify	138	mere	113
G		impervious	37	intent	62, 73	meticulous	123
gain	27	implicit	45	interfere	146	mock	111
gaze	43	implore	51	intimidate	154	monotonous	132
gear	59	imprecise	53	intolerable	70	more of	46

moreover	63	overall	29	premise	33	rebel	11
mount	102	overlap	27	preoccupation	16	recognize	52
mounting	140	overlook	35	preoccupied	164	record	41
mundane	148	override	93	present	85	recurrent	164
mutual	164	overriding	21	pretty	115	redress	60
mystery	32	overt	45	prevent	93	reduce	69
		overview	41	previously	124	reed	33
				primacy	160	refer to	77

N

		P		primary	173	refine	86
name	93			prime	79	reflect	93
narrow	102, 173	packed	21	problem	109, 168	reflection	25
natural	79	painstaking	37	proceed	111	refrain	102
neat	164	palliate	19	procure	102	regular	173
necessary	156	paramount	29	prodigious	21	reject	121
needless to say	141	pare	27	produce	130	relate	112
news	74	parity	57	proficient	37	relation	118
niche	25	particularly	88	programmed	62	relentless	21
none other than	54	pass	35	prohibit	85	relish	130
normally	71	pastime	25	project	51	remedy	139
noteworthy	140	patch	74	projection	152	reminisce	147
nothing less than	63	patient	45	promise	144	render	155
nothing more than	71	patron	49	prompt	130	repel	171
noticeable	148	pattern	82	pronounced	95	repellent	29
now that	80	peak	127	properly	124	repercussion	16
nuance	16	pedestrian	143	propose	139	repetitive	38
nuisance	109	perceptible	53	prosper	11	replace	162
		perennial	62	prosperous	105	replete	46

O

		period	152	protrude	147	reproduce	103
obliterate	11	periodic	70	prove	155	reserve	11
obscure	14, 132	permanent	79	provide	162	reservoir	10
observe	85	permit	121	providing	157	resist	171
obstinate	123	perpetual	87	provisional	114	resort	155
obvious	113	perpetually	96	provocation	136	respect	100
occasion	65	pervasive	95	prowess	127	respectively	157
occupy	77	petrified	104	public	132	response	109
occur	68	pillar	99	punctuality	118	responsibility	118
odds	33	plain	114	purpose	91	restore	139
odor	117	platform	118	pursue	171	restrict	121
offspring	10	plausible	14	pursuit	74	result from	103
on the contrary	38	pleasant	123	puzzling	123	retention	127
on the spot	157	pledge	59			retrospect	136
once and for all	149	plentiful	132			reveal	12
operate	59	portion	136	R		reverence	144
opportunity	135	pose	109	ramification	74	revert	86
opposite	168	potential	91	range	19	reward	152
optimize	51	practically	106	rank	27	rigid	53
order	16	practice	66	rapidly	149	risk	60, 160
ordinary	104	precaution	41	ratio	82	rival	105, 168
origin	74	precede	68	rational	148	robust	62
original	95	precipitate	43	reach	43, 57	roster	91
otherwise	80	predictable	140	ready	156	routine	70, 91
outnumber	43	predominate	77	realm	66	rub	43
outstanding	87	pre-eminent	148	reason	36, 49	rust	83
oval	37	preferable	156	reasonable	14		

rye	66	soothe	130	swirl	17	V	
		sorrow	136	switch	77	vague	133
S		source	152	synthesis	41	vanish	12
sacrifice	19, 109	span	57			vanity	17
sake	118	spare	139	**T**		variation	25
sanctuary	127	spark	147	tapered	105	varied	123
sap	28	spawn	155	tear	60	variety	33
satire	10	specific	140	technique	41	velocity	57
scale	136	specimen	160	tedious	29	vent	69
scapegoat	136	speck	168	telltale	38	verbally	141
scenario	128	spectacular	148	temper	119	vessel	66
scoop	74	speculate	163	tenacity	33	vestige	74
scrap	144	spell	161	tender	54	viability	83
scrupulous	96	spot	103, 144	tenet	144	vibrant	114
seal	36	spur	12	tentative	71	vicinity	10
seamless	79	stable	88	term	25	view	77, 109
search	44	startle	19	texture	17	vigor	91
secondary	21	state	109	though	46	volume	83
secrete	93	stationary	157	threat	49	voracious	105
security	17	steady	164	thus	54	vow	52
sedentary	14	stem from	77	tip	57, 168		
seemingly	165	stick	28	toil	36	**W**	
seize	52	still	174	tolerant	79	wanton	96
seldom	22	stimulate	36	trace	28, 66	wary	54
selected	114	stimulus	119	track	44	way	110
selective	29	sting	112	traverse	86	weak	71
seminal	38	store	12	treat	19	weigh	94
separate	46	story	136	trespass	12	well	128
sequential	53	strain	52, 128	trivial	88	well-being	136
series	25	strangely enough	14	troublesome	96	when it comes to	174
serve	60	strenuous	114	true	105	wholly	71
service	41	stress	69, 100	typical	114	willing	88
session	33	strict	123			win	112
severe	62	strive	121	**U**		wipe out	12
severity	49	structure	83	ubiquitous	140	wisdom	144
shatter	69	sturdy	133	ultimate	149	withdraw	130
shed	83	subject	130, 149	unanimous	157	withstand	163
sheer	70	subsidiary	165	unbridled	174	witness	147
shore	152	subtle	174	uncanny	165	witticism	152
shortcoming	91	succeeding	88	uncover	19	work	169
shortly	30	success	57	underpinning	83	wriggle	163
shred	93, 168	successor	91	undesirable	157	wrong	141
silent	114	suffer	147	undoubted	141		
sizable	105	suggest	172	uniform	174	**Y**	
skeleton	100	superb	79	universal	157	yardstick	161
slight	123	superficial	71	unleash	19		
slightly	14	superior	62	unmistakable	165	**Z**	
snatch	103	support	25	upright	141	zone	100
sneak	112	supposed	54	upset	163		
soak	121	surveillance	144	urge	33		
sole	132	sustainable	38	usually	63		
solution	66	swell	155	utility	17		
somewhat	38	swift	79	utmost	149		

앵그리 아카데믹 보카
Angry Academic Vocabulary
토플·수능·외고·특목고·텝스·IELTS·공무원

ANGRY ENGLISH
academic
VOCABULARY

WORKBOOK

CONTENTS

DAY 01	Practice Test	3
DAY 02	Practice Test	9
DAY 03	Practice Test	15
DAY 04	Practice Test	21
DAY 05	Practice Test	27
DAY 06	Practice Test	33
DAY 07	Practice Test	39
DAY 08	Practice Test	45
DAY 09	Practice Test	51
DAY 10	Practice Test	57
DAY 11	Practice Test	63
DAY 12	Practice Test	69
DAY 13	Practice Test	75
DAY 14	Practice Test	81
DAY 15	Practice Test	87
DAY 16	Practice Test	93
DAY 17	Practice Test	99
DAY 18	Practice Test	105
DAY 19	Practice Test	111
DAY 20	Practice Test	117
ANSWER		123

PRACTICE TEST (DAY 01)

A. 다음 단어의 뜻을 우리말로 쓰시오. #001

1. meditate _____
2. mediate _____
3. slightly _____
4. rebel _____
5. strangely enough _____

B. 다음 우리말을 영어로 쓰시오. #002

1. 습득 _____
2. 소비 _____
3. 전쟁의 _____
4. 박차를 가하다 _____
5. 저장하다 _____

C. 동의어를 찾아 연결하시오. #003

1. incursion · · (A) trespass
2. satire · · (B) suggest, show
3. encroach · · (C) enormous
4. indicate · · (D) raid
5. huge · · (E) book
6. reserve · · (F) naked
7. bare · · (G) sarcasm
8. flavor · · (H) taste

D. 반의어를 찾아 연결하시오. #004

1. reveal · · (A) rare
2. common · · (B) conceal
3. obscure · · (C) celebrated
4. analogy · · (D) dissimilarity

E. 문맥상 빈칸에 들어갈 가장 적절한 단어를 고르시오. #005

1. The theory of relativity formulated by Albert Einstein, who was Jewish, _____ the basis for the creation of atomic energy.
   (A) stored (B) trespassed (C) formed (D) vanished

2. The idea of applying the law everywhere is _____ because newly introduced species can be hazardous to native species everywhere.
   (A) reasonable (B) asymmetric (C) analogous (D) martial

3. Native American society was _____ of guns.
   (A) sedentary (B) huge (C) devoid (D) bare

4. You should first try to find things you have in _____ with her before you ask her out.
   (A) flavor (B) common (C) vicinity (D) abnormal

5. Alcohol can cause a whole _____ of problems that can contribute to crimes, like drunk driving.
   (A) consumption (B) barrier (C) host (D) incursion

6. _____ from the aircraft was found on the beach, weeks after the crash.
   (A) Efficacy (B) Debris (C) Satire (D) Reservoir

F. 다음 글을 읽고 밑줄 친 단어의 동의어를 고르시오. #006

1. It is <u>imperative</u> to find solutions to global warming which is most often attributed to the excessive use of fossil fuels. *be attributed to sth ~에 의해 야기되다
   (A) vital (B) outgoing (C) ominous (D) prompt

2. A large marine mammal called Steller's sea cow <u>vanished</u> for reasons that are not clear.
   (A) evacuated (B) dwindled (C) disappeared (D) congregated

3. The problem with this explanation is that using some powerful chemicals that are toxic to zebra mussels can control their numbers, but this method can also <u>wipe out</u> other native species at the same time. *zebra mussel 얼룩무늬 홍합
   (A) replace (B) exterminate (C) repel (D) debilitate

4. Without raising the average price of gasoline, governments can easily <u>accomplish</u> their goal of fuel conservation.
   (A) achieve (B) amend (C) shrink (D) exceed

5. The offspring of many birds are pushed out of the nest as soon as they are able to fly.
   (A) young   (B) inertia   (C) shortage   (D) vicinity

6. Jo Biden has a host of important domestic issues to deal with.
   (A) border   (B) shard   (C) multitude   (D) chip

7. It was difficult to clear the scattered debris from the car crash in the dense fog. *clear 치우다 / dense 짙은
   (A) dogmas   (B) pieces   (C) aspects   (D) transactions

8. The main function of the kidneys is to excrete waste products from the body. *excrete 분비하다
   (A) dichotomy   (B) dignitary   (C) role   (D) freight

9. His face that had previously appeared devoid of feeling turned lively after he met a girl. *lively 생기발랄한
   (A) void   (B) moist   (C) ensuing   (D) abiding

10. One of the main problems with historical buildings is that they may act as a barrier to sustainable urban development.
    (A) foe   (B) agent   (C) obstacle   (D) consultant

11. They are still doing tests to demonstrate the efficacy of the drug.
    (A) drudgery   (B) length   (C) effectiveness   (D) tenet

12. Rhode Island was first settled by approximately one hundred people from England.
    (A) albeit   (B) roughly   (C) consequently   (D) apparently

13. Most civilizations prospered along rivers.
    (A) harnessed   (B) flourished   (C) launched   (D) flooded

14. *PD Notebook*, an investigative journalism program, revealed a grocery store's unsafe and unsanitary conditions.
    (A) rectified   (B) interrogated   (C) proliferated   (D) disclosed

15. Birds, bats, and insects have structures, such as wings, that are analogous to one another.
    (A) sedentary   (B) asymmetric   (C) plausible   (D) similar

16. Global warming has obliterated wetlands in the US. For example, a lack of rain makes the Everglades, which is a natural region of tropical wetlands in the southern part of the state of Florida, drier.
    (A) dried   (B) drained   (C) enriched   (D) destroyed

17. As it takes years for dead trees to decompose, there is no space for new and young trees to grow.
    (A) unearth   (B) vacate   (C) decay   (D) thrive

G. 문맥상 빈칸에 들어갈 가장 적절한 단어를 찾아 넣으시오.   #007

| satire | legendary | vicinity | blocked | accomplished | offspring | debris | clockwise |

1. Ocean currents move in a _____ direction in the northern hemisphere.
2. A pack of wolves consists of the alpha couple and its _____.
3. The movie was a stinging _____ on life in America in the 1970s. *stinging 신랄한
4. A crowd of 40,000 workers gathered in the immediate _____ of the city hall to protest against the tax reform bill.
5. When the drainage pipes get _____, it will create a water leak.
6. The vague location of the treasure makes many scholars believe that King Arthur was a _____ hero.
7. As a result of the storm, the ship was wrecked just off the coast, and _____ from the ship was scattered along the shore.
8. We've _____ the sales objectives we set last year.

H. 문맥상 빈칸에 들어갈 가장 적절한 단어를 찾아 넣으시오. *같은 단어 두 번 사용 가능   #008

1.
| store | decay | huge | formed | reservoir |

To construct a dam, a large ①_____ that can ②_____ ③_____ amounts of water is also created behind the dam. When plants submerged in the ④_____ begin to ⑤_____, methane, which is a greenhouse gas, is ⑥_____. *submerge 물에 잠기게 하다

2.
| stored | flavor | slightly | formed |

When the beer is poured into a glass, a thick white froth is ①_____. It is not cold because it is made and ②_____ at room temperature. Its ③_____ is ④_____ sweet and bitter.

I. 다음 밑줄 친 우리말을 영어로 바꾸어 보기에 주어진 단어나 어구를 활용하여 또는 조건에 맞게 영작하시오. *필요시 어형을 변화할 것

#009

1. 비만은 <u>흔한 건강 문제의 전형적인 예</u>이다. *classic 전형적인

   a / a / is / classic / _____ medical problem / obesity / of / example

   _____

2. <u>새끼들은 그들의 부모에게서 물려받은 유전적 특징들을 가지고 있다.</u> *genetic trait 유전적 특징 / pass down sth ~을 물려주다

   genetic traits / have / from / _____ / their parents / passed down

   _____

3. 그는 <u>화장</u>되었고 그의 재는 고국으로 옮겨졌다.

   taken / _____ and his / to / he was / his home country / ashes were

   _____

4. 세금 징수는 정부의 공무상의 <u>기능</u>들 중 하나이다. *official 공무상의

   | 조건 | 다음 표현을 사용할 것: tax collection / of / one / the government / of |

   _____

5. 1인치는 대략 2.5센티미터(cm)와 같고, 1풋은 약 30센티미터와 동등하고, 그리고 1야드는 약 90센티미터와 같다. *equal 동등한(같은) / equivalent 동등한(같은) / equal 같다

조건	다음 표현을 사용할 것: one inch / one foot / a yard / roughly 2.5 centimeters (cm) / about 30 cm / 90 cm

6. 지진들이 고래들로 하여금 스스로 해변으로 헤엄쳐 가서 그곳에서 고립되게 만든다는 생각은 처음에는 그럴듯해 보일지 모르지만 가능성은 거의 없다. *beach (고래가) 해변으로 헤엄쳐 가서 그곳에서 고립되다 / cause 야기하다(만들다) / highly unlikely 가능성이 거의 없는

조건	다음 표현을 사용할 것: the idea / is / at first but / beach themselves might seem / highly unlikely

7. 대부분의 회사원들의 생활 방식은 앉아서 지내는데, 왜냐하면 그들은 그들 시간의 대부분을 그들의 컴퓨터 앞에서 앉아서 보내기 때문이다. *spend (시간을) 보내다

조건	다음 표현을 사용할 것: of their computers / their time / the lifestyle of most office workers / of / , as they / most / front

PRACTICE TEST (DAY 02)

A. 다음 단어의 뜻을 우리말로 쓰시오.　#010

1. contract _____
2. aboard _____
3. unleash _____
4. palliate _____
5. seldom _____

B. 다음 우리말을 영어로 쓰시오.　#011

1. 질감 _____
2. 보안, 안보 _____
3. 미묘한 차이 _____
4. 희생하다 _____
5. 주거(지), 주택 _____

C. 동의어를 찾아 연결하시오.　#012

1. compel · · (A) usefulness
2. ease · · (B) lasting
3. construe · · (C) coerce
4. utility · · (D) encumber
5. abiding · · (E) alleviate
6. burden · · (F) colossal
7. prodigious · · (G) interpret
8. packed · · (H) full

D. 반의어를 찾아 연결하시오.　#013

1. vanity · · (A) take apart
2. assemble · · (B) chaos
3. order · · (C) humble
4. grand · · (D) modesty

E. 문맥상 빈칸에 들어갈 가장 적절한 단어를 고르시오. #014

1. Synthetic fertilizers, which can be water-soluble, are made through chemical processes, whereas organic fertilizers are made from natural _____ such as manure that people can easily obtain.
   (A) barriers (B) ingredients (C) swirls (D) textures

2. Traditional retail shops _____ competition from companies selling goods online such as Gu-pang.
   (A) startle (B) construe (C) encroach (D) face

3. These days, only a small _____ of people don't go to university.
   (A) reservoir (B) vanity (C) repercussion (D) fraction

4. A recent study has _____ a genetic link between the indigenous people sampled in the study and people living in modern Germany and Denmark. *sample 표본 조사를 하다
   (A) aborted (B) obliterated (C) uncovered (D) encumbered

5. Science comic books deal with topics _____ from looking for alternative sources of energy on other planets to developing genetically modified foods.
   (A) daubing (B) ranging (C) construing (D) palliating

6. His attempts to arbitrate between the two countries proved _____. *arbitrate 중재하다
   (A) innate (B) martial (C) packed (D) futile

F. 다음 글을 읽고 밑줄 친 단어의 동의어를 고르시오. #015

1. This company has all the <u>ingredients</u> of being successful.
   (A) antecedents (B) candidates (C) parts (D) crevices

2. He <u>daubed</u> his face with charcoal so that the pig he had tried to kill couldn't see him.
   (A) decorated (B) smeared (C) veiled (D) wiped

3. All attempts to save sea turtles have proved <u>futile</u>.
   (A) pointless (B) ornate (C) lethal (D) staunch

4. Many theories have been proposed to <u>determine</u> how the stone buildings were used.
   (A) discover (B) depict (C) assess (D) cite

5. The professor missed the <u>overriding</u> factor; that is the dialect in which the poems were written.
   (A) prime (B) respectful (C) avid (D) impudent

6. You may not be able to <u>identify</u> him. He's gained so much weight.
   (A) recognize (B) intrude (C) favor (D) dislike

7. Finally, archaeologists have <u>uncovered</u> an ancient Egyptian city that was described in the manuscript.
   (A) curtailed (B) hidden (C) unearthed (D) endorsed

8. His current <u>preoccupation</u> with backpacking caused him to sell his entire comic book collection just to buy camping gear.
   (A) obsession (B) flaw (C) jurisdiction (D) domain

9. An earthquake in Po-hang, a southern part of my country, struck on December 13th in 2018. That year's college entrance exam was <u>due</u> to take place on December 16th.
   (A) postponed (B) integral (C) essential (D) scheduled

10. Humans have an <u>innate</u> ability to do mathematics.
    (A) fragmentary (B) lucrative (C) unbearable (D) inborn

11. What <u>surprised</u> me most was that she moved to our rival company.
    (A) daubed (B) unleashed (C) startled (D) palliated

12. The <u>judicious</u> use of nuclear reactors to produce electricity makes it possible for humans to protect the environment by reducing greenhouse gas emissions.
    (A) sensible (B) sedentary (C) devoid (D) vain

13. I mean, if the buildings were used as residential centers where people <u>assembled</u> to live together, then there would have had to be many fireplaces where each family could cook their daily meals, but there are very few fireplaces in the buildings.
    (A) recurred (B) commemorated (C) cooperated (D) gathered

14. Women in hunter-gatherer societies had no choice but to <u>abort</u> their babies when they had unwanted pregnancies.
    (A) end (B) retard (C) soothe (D) adopt

15. The book has sold over a million copies in its first week, <u>hence</u> making it the fastest-selling book ever.
    (A) nevertheless (B) further (C) approximately (D) therefore

16. A virus that researchers are developing could have profound <u>consequences</u> for cane toads living in other areas. *cane toad 사탕수수 두꺼비
    (A) repercussions (B) incursions (C) obstacles (D) counterparts

G. 문맥상 빈칸에 들어갈 가장 적절한 단어를 찾아 넣으시오. *필요시 어형을 변화할 것   #016

| uncover   innately   relentlessly   hence   idle   capable   contact |

1. We don't have any new job vacancies at the moment. We will _____ you in the future if anything comes up. *vacancy 빈자리, 사람이 없음
2. They actually succeeded in _____ the buried treasure.
3. I am sure robots are not able to kill people, but they are _____ of taking people's jobs.
4. The shipyard has remained _____ for two weeks because of a strike by the workers. *shipyard 조선소
5. Humans are _____ greedy, so making a lot of money is very important for all people, including professors.
6. He worked _____ to find a cure for cancer.
7. The ash formed during the volcanic explosion of Mount Toba, _____ making it difficult for the sun to heat the earth.

H. 문맥상 빈칸에 들어갈 가장 적절한 단어를 찾아 넣으시오. *필요시 어형을 변화할 것   #017

1.
| balance   cargo   unload   vessel |

Ballast water makes ① _____ more stable during a voyage and keeps them ② _____ when they ③ _____ their ④ _____. *ballast water 배의 균형을 잡기 위해 배 아래쪽 탱크에 채우는 물

2.
| flourish   inflow   allow   accommodate   search |

Not only did the sudden ① _____ of people rushing into California in ② _____ of gold lead to the development of towns that ③ _____ the gold-diggers, it also ④ _____ merchants such as Levi Strauss to ⑤_____.

I. 다음 밑줄 친 우리말을 영어로 바꾸어 보기에 주어진 단어나 어구를 활용하여 또는 조건에 맞게 영작하시오. *필요시 어형을 변화할 것

#018

1. 제임스는 그가 아직 시작도 하지 않은 내일이 <u>마감인</u> 중요한 과학 과제를 해야 한다. *work on sth ~을 (작업)하다

> work on / yet started / James / tomorrow that he / big science assignment _____ / hasn't / a / must

2. 1998년 여름에 발발한 그 화재는 그 지역 경제에 부정적인 <u>결과들을</u> 가져왔다. *break out 발발하다

> the local economy / in / for / had / that / the summer of 1998 / negative _____ / the fire / broke out

3. 그 나라에는, 범죄에서 인플레이션에 <u>걸친</u> 사회 문제들이 있다.

> in / social problems _____ / are / to / crime / inflation / that country, there / from

4. 음식에 있어서, 그에게, 맛은 <u>별로 중요하지 않다</u>.

> of / it / to / is / importance / when / food, for him, taste / _____ / comes

5. 정부는 사람들이 주식과 부동산 투자로 벌어들이는 이익에 대한 세금을 인상하기로 결심했다. *increase 인상하다 / make (돈을) 벌다

조건	다음 표현을 사용할 것: taxes / from / was / stock and property investments / the government / the profits that / on

6. 높이 솟고, 소용돌이치는 바람이 순식간에 수백 채의 집을 삼켰다. *tower 높이 솟다 / swallow 삼키다 / in no time 순식간에

조건	다음 표현을 사용할 것: of / the towering, / houses in no time / winds

7. 이 의료 기술은 유전 질환을 가지고 있는 환자를 치료하는 데 사용될 수 있다. *use 사용하다

조건	다음 표현을 사용할 것: with / a patient / this medical technology / a genetic disease

8. 문서화된 기록이 없어서, 판사는 피고인 측이 수면제를 과다 복용했다는 것을 증명할 수 없었다. *in the absence of sth ~이 없어서 / prove 증명하다 / overdose on sth ~을 과다 복용하다 / the guilty party 피고인 측

조건	① not 을 사용하지 말 것 ② 다음 표현을 사용할 것: of / that / sleeping pills / written records, the judge / had

PRACTICE TEST (DAY 03)

A. 다음 단어의 뜻을 우리말로 쓰시오.   #019

1. dye _____
2. assault _____
3. freak _____
4. pare _____
5. conscientious _____

B. 다음 우리말을 영어로 쓰시오.   #020

1. 틈새 _____
2. 빙산 _____
3. 중복되다 _____
4. 빠른, 활기찬 _____
5. 논리적인 _____

C. 동의어를 찾아 연결하시오.   #021

1. anomaly · · (A) irregularity
2. detest · · (B) loathe
3. ignite · · (C) reverberate
4. sap · · (D) misleading
5. tedious · · (E) principal
6. deceptive · · (F) boring
7. echo · · (G) weaken
8. paramount · · (H) set fire to

D. 반의어를 찾아 연결하시오.   #022

1. gradual · · (A) sluggish
2. brisk · · (B) behind
3. ahead · · (C) planned, organized
4. haphazard · · (D) sudden

E. 문맥상 빈칸에 들어갈 가장 적절한 단어를 고르시오. #023

1. There's growing _____ that invasive species will kill off the native plants in the Everglades. *Everglades 미국 남부의 습지대
   (A) texture   (B) anomaly   (C) concern   (D) debris

2. For the second year in a row, Angry University has been _____ second among the top colleges in the country.
   (A) sapped   (B) startled   (C) encroached   (D) ranked

3. As the number of people who get vaccinated against the virus gradually increases, the _____ situation is stabilizing.
   (A) overall   (B) repulsive   (C) innate   (D) devoid

4. Dad is a man who seems to bring the rain with him. It _____ rains when we go camping.
   (A) conscientiously (B) haphazardly   (C) inevitably   (D) tediously

5. Most young infants at the time died _____ after being born.
   (A) instead of   (B) tediously   (C) ahead   (D) shortly

6. Given the number of legal _____ in the book, novice readers could get lost.
   (A) terms   (B) dyes   (C) reflections   (D) pastimes

F. 다음 글을 읽고 밑줄 친 단어의 동의어를 고르시오. #024

1. A typical <u>pastime</u> of British people is to go to a pub quiz on a Sunday evening.
   (A) diversion   (B) hobby   (C) obsession   (D) allegiance

2. Tattoos have <u>gained</u> popularity in recent years among university students.
   (A) loathed   (B) arbitrated   (C) resonated   (D) attained

3. The hotel received a high rating for the <u>overall</u> quality of the facilities and services that it offered.
   (A) optimum   (B) masculine   (C) general   (D) paramount

4. Companies always <u>contend</u> that their products are better than those of their competitors.
   (A) abort   (B) maintain   (C) alleviate   (D) obliterate

5. The secret of the country's economic miracle is a policy which was a <u>series</u> of economic and political reforms that led to rapid economic growth.
   (A) hallmark   (B) grief   (C) glimpse   (D) string

6. It is incorrect to say that most residents living in areas that abound in old buildings are enthusiastic about the removal of these structures for development.
   (A) teem (B) overlook (C) mitigate (D) unleash

7. CAT scans can show a variation in brain activity. *CAT scans 전산화 단층 촬영
   (A) vanity (B) reservoir (C) offspring (D) change

8. Government support for people who are ill, old, poor, and unemployed and government regulation to prevent large companies from becoming monopolies are good examples of this.
   (A) variant (B) aid (C) modification (D) string

9. He is in such imminent danger of being fired that he has to beg his boss to keep his job.
   *beg sb to do sth ~에게 ~해 달라고 애원하다
   (A) sedentary (B) disorganized (C) painstaking (D) impending

10. The series of political scandals recently witnessed in this country is a reflection of the current government's corruption.
    (A) sarcasm (B) obstruction (C) acquisition (D) sign

11. Over many centuries of hunting, the native population could have gradually wiped out the sea cow. *wipe out sth ~을 완전히 죽이다(없애다)
    (A) slowly (B) infrequently (C) hence (D) roughly

12. The slums outside of Mumbai in India were built in a haphazard manner. The only way to fix the situation is to destroy all the buildings and start again.
    (A) exposed (B) unsystematic (C) analogous (D) plausible

13. I mean, in the future, people will not be allowed to purchase non-native species of animals. But this does not inevitably mean that the law will affect pet owners who already own these animals.
    (A) intentionally (B) remarkably (C) boundlessly (D) unavoidably

14. Body Worlds, an exhibition of dissected human bodies, is sometimes repellent to young children.
    (A) reluctant (B) appealing (C) deceitful (D) repulsive

15. The journalists persistently asked the spokesperson to clarify the party's official position on the war.
    (A) exterminate (B) elucidate (C) liken (D) disguise

16. It's so nice of you to help me with my homework instead of doing other stuff you want to do.
    (A) in return for (B) in search of (C) rather than (D) as opposed to

17. Ludicrous as their idea might have sounded, they succeeded in placing one satellite in orbit around Mars.
    (A) Inherent (B) Deviant (C) Brilliant (D) Absurd

G. 문맥상 빈칸에 들어갈 가장 적절한 단어를 찾아 넣으시오. *필요시 어형을 변화할 것   #025

| shortly | inordinately | concern | series | contract | contact | ranked | compared |

1. Physical _____ with strangers is discouraged because of COVID-19. *discourage 못하게 하다

2. To be _____ as a masterpiece, a work of art must be original, timeless, and thought provoking. *timeless 시대를 초월한 / thought provoking 생각하게 하는

3. _____ before his wife's death, he fell in love with a woman 10 years younger than him.

4. The pottery made by people who lived in the Southwest was utilitarian _____ with the decorative pottery made in the Northeast.

5. A(n) _____ large number of toilet rolls were sold at the beginning of the pandemic as people started panic buying. *panic buying 사재기

6. The law to prevent the introduction of any non-native species is of great _____ to pet owners.

7. Behind this great success in iPhone sales are a(n) _____ of advertisements that Apple has placed on social media sites.

8. Some schools use the money they receive through advertising _____ with soda companies to buy uniforms for their sports teams.

H. 문맥상 빈칸에 들어갈 가장 적절한 단어를 찾아 넣으시오.   #026

1.
| constructed | damaged | followed | measuring |

An earthquake ① _____ 7.2 on the Richter scale was ② _____ by a massive tsunami that ③ _____ the first nuclear power plant to be ④ _____ in Japan.
*Richter scale 리히터 척도(지진의 규모를 나타내는 단위)

2.
| limbs | rid | detrimental | stuck | parasites |

Fish don't have any ① _____, so the only way they can get ② _____ of the ③ _____ ④ _____ on their bodies that could be ⑤ _____ to them would be by jumping out of the water and shaking vigorously.

I. 다음 밑줄 친 우리말을 영어로 바꾸어 보기에 주어진 단어나 어구를 활용하여 또는 조건에 맞게 영작하시오. *필요시 어형을 변화할 것

#027

1. 성전이라 불리는 십자군 전쟁(the Crusades)은 기독교인들과 이슬람교도들 사이의 <u>일련의 종교 전쟁</u>이었다.

   of / Christians and Muslims / a holy war, / a / religious wars between / , called / were / _____ / the Crusades

2. 당신은 당신이 막 타려고 하는 말에 <u>굴레를 얹고</u>, 그리고 당신은 그 <u>굴레의 고삐</u>로 그것(말)을 조정한다. *put 얹다 / control 조정하다 / ride 타다 / rein 고삐

   about / with / _____ / on / it / a / to / ride, and you control / horse you're / a / you put / the reins of the _____

3. 매우 짧은 기간 내에 화석 연료 <u>대신에</u> 수소가 세계 에너지의 주요 공급원으로서 사용될 것 같지 않다. *unlikely ~일 것 같지 않은(가능성이 없는)

   time / unlikely that hydrogen fuel / is / period / will be / very short / the chief source of global energy in / it / used _____ _____ fossil fuels as / a / of

4. 그녀가 그 돈을 훔쳤다는 주장은 <u>터무니없다</u>. *steal 훔치다

조 건	다음 표현을 사용할 것: the claim / the money / that

5. 지질학적 관점에서, 지층은 바위의 층이다. *bed 지층 / layer 층

조건 다음 표현을 사용할 것: geological / a / a / of rock

6. 그 프로젝트의 성공은 정부 지원에 달려 있다. *rely on sth ~에 달려 있다

조건 다음 표현을 사용할 것: the success of the project / on government

7. 재즈의 역사는 아프리카로 거슬러 올라갈 수 있다.

조건 다음 표현을 사용할 것: can be / the history of jazz / back

8. 그 쓰나미는 일본에서 건설된 최초의 원자력 발전소를 훼손했다. *construct 건설하다

조건 다음 표현을 사용할 것: constructed in / that tsunami / nuclear power plant / first / to

PRACTICE TEST (DAY 04)

A. 다음 단어의 뜻을 우리말로 쓰시오.   #028

1. aspire to _____
2. drudgery _____
3. contemplate _____
4. abide by _____
5. fade _____

B. 다음 우리말을 영어로 쓰시오.   #029

1. 갈대 _____
2. 생활 편의 시설 _____
3. 모두, 둘 다 _____
4. 고자질쟁이 _____
5. 판단하다 _____

C. 동의어를 찾아 연결하시오.   #030

1. toil · · (A) push
2. tenacity · · (B) fundamental
3. cardinal · · (C) erase
4. painstaking · · (D) meticulous
5. hustle · · (E) persistence
6. somewhat · · (F) labor
7. efface · · (G) arrange
8. array · · (H) to some degree

D. 반의어를 찾아 연결하시오.   #031

1. stimulate · · (A) permeable
2. variety · · (B) suppress
3. impervious · · (C) inept
4. proficient · · (D) sameness

E. 문맥상 빈칸에 들어갈 가장 적절한 단어를 고르시오. #032

1. Some local authorities started to recognize the importance of the _____ of children whose parents both worked.
   (A) efficacy (B) care (C) anomaly (D) assumption

2. The victory of a ragtag group of soldiers over such a great civilization that had spanned thousands of years remains an unsolved _____. *ragtag 오합지졸의
   (A) proximity (B) mastery (C) ingredient (D) mystery

3. People will soon use up fossil fuels, gas, coal, and oil stored underground, so we need to find energy sources that are _____ and that don't pollute the environment either. *use up sth ~을 다 써버리다
   (A) sustainable (B) absurd (C) telltale (D) painstaking

4. The folk song has been _____ on from person to person.
   (A) cremated (B) unleashed (C) contemplated (D) passed

5. The _____ of your data being lost are small.
   (A) urges (B) joints (C) sessions (D) odds

6. Climate change is a _____ cause of the continuing population decline of the small, rare tree, commonly called the Florida Torreya.
   (A) fundamental (B) proficient (C) impervious (D) oval

F. 다음 글을 읽고 밑줄 친 단어의 동의어를 고르시오. #033

1. If you try the experiment yourself, you might <u>deduce</u> that the theory is wrong.
   (A) demonstrate (B) concede (C) assure (D) infer

2. There's no solid evidence that the majority of local residents living near old architecture are <u>eager</u> to remove historic buildings for development.
   (A) prone (B) reluctant (C) worried (D) anxious

3. The UN Security Council held an emergency <u>session</u> to discuss Russia's military invasion of Ukraine.
   (A) aid (B) deficiency (C) support (D) meeting

4. She was able to get the top grade because she was <u>proficient</u> in academic tasks, such as taking tests.
   (A) gainful (B) plentiful (C) skilled (D) invariable

5. Men tend to succumb to sexual urges more than women. *succumb to sb/sth ~에 굴복하다
   (A) desires (B) restrictions (C) incursions (D) repercussions

6. During the Black Death, sanitary conditions were fundamental to preventing the disease from spreading.
   (A) analogous (B) achievable (C) eccentric (D) essential

7. The fish that they caught were pulled onto the boat and killed instantaneously.
   (A) conscientiously (B) immediately (C) relentlessly (D) approximately

8. Shawn had affairs with many beautiful women until he was sent to prison for committing adultery with a famous politician's young wife. *adultery 간통
   (A) doing (B) alleviating (C) palliating (D) prosecuting

9. The mapping of the human genetic code has made determining people's backgrounds easier and much more accurate. *mapping 지도 제작
   (A) prodigious (B) equivocal (C) precise (D) grand

10. It is invariably true that people are using smartphones for everything these days.
    (A) always (B) infrequently (C) occasionally (D) undoubtedly

11. In the end, he carried out his plan to murder her. But he got arrested at the crime scene.
    (A) arbitrated (B) committed (C) erased (D) amended

12. First of all, breaking the ice is very helpful in getting to know people you are meeting for the first time.
    (A) void (B) prompt (C) conducive (D) imminent

13. To help members of the audience immerse themselves in the play, the chorus speaks in unison.
    (A) veil (B) engross (C) obliterate (D) manifest

14. UN troops deployed to Ukraine camouflaged their tanks with tree branches.
    (A) coerced (B) waned (C) disguised (D) located

15. The Student Union building offers students a variety of amenities such as a bookstore, a travel agency, and even a prayer room for Muslim students.
    (A) solicitude (B) diversity (C) repercussion (D) series

16. Susan B. Anthony (1820-1906), a leading champion of women's suffrage, devoted herself to fighting for women's rights.
    (A) dedicated (B) counted (C) palliated (D) daubed

G. 문맥상 빈칸에 들어갈 가장 적절한 단어를 찾아 넣으시오. *필요시 어형을 변화할 것 / 같은 단어 두 번 사용 가능 #034

| seminal | commit | care | pass | sealed | oval | variety |

1. The principal demanded that all food be put in _____ plastic bags.

2. Some Korean people think that women should stay home and take _____ of their kids.

3. When private collectors discover a lot of fossils, libraries and schools have more opportunities to buy fossils, and this allows the public to see a _____ of fossils.

4. The _____ crater was made by the impact of a large meteorite.

5. George Orwell's _____ works are *1984* and *Animal Farm*.

6. In cases where a person _____ a crime in a foreign country, he or she may be deported from that country.

7. She chose a book from the library and _____ it on to her sister.

8. The property that he owns now will automatically be _____ from him to his wife if he dies.

H. 문맥상 빈칸에 들어갈 가장 적절한 단어를 찾아 넣으시오. #035

1.
| native | somewhat | eradicate | poisonous |

Although using chemicals that are ① _____ to zebra mussels is known to ② _____ control their numbers, this method will ③ _____ other ④ _____ species simultaneously and devastate their populations. *zebra mussel 얼룩무늬 홍합

2.
| accused | based | innocent | premise | guilty |

The presumption of innocence is ① _____ on the basic ② _____ that any person who is ③ _____ of a crime is ④ _____ until proven ⑤ _____.

I. 다음 밑줄 친 우리말을 영어로 바꾸어 보기에 주어진 단어나 어구를 활용하여 또는 조건에 맞게 영작하시오. *필요시 어형을 변화할 것*

#036

1. 그 조개들은 당신이 그들을 먹기 전에 적어도 몇 분 동안 끓는 물에 <u>담겨</u>야 한다.

   few minutes before / at / be _____ / least a / them / the clams / boiling water for / should / you eat / in

2. 팀으로 함께 일할 때 사람들이 <u>간과</u>하는 몇 가지 문제들이 있다.

   together as / some / are / that people / team / working / problems / _____ when / a / there

3. 그 돌공 모양은 <u>계란형</u>이다.

   shape / the stone balls / _____ / in / are

4. 처음에 그들이 사용했던 아도비는 <u>둥그런</u> 모양이었다. 그러나 나중에 그것은 벽돌처럼 <u>직사각형의</u> 모양이 되었다. *adobe 아도비 점토(벽돌)

   in / _____ / was / shape; but later it / in / shape like bricks / became _____ / initially, the adobe they used

5. 아메리카 원주민들은 원뿔 형의(원뿔 모양의) 집에서 대평원에 살았다. *the Great Plains 대평원

_____ houses / native Americans / the Great Plains in / on / lived

6. 그녀는 경찰관이 되기를 갈망한다.

a police officer / to / _____ / become / she

7. 그들은 어떻게 덫으로 동물을 잡는지에 대한 지식을 다음 세대에게 건네주었다. *catch 잡다

| 조건 | 다음 표현을 사용할 것: an animal in a trap to / how / on their / the next generation / of |

8. 개인 교습 시간 중에, 외부 음식은 허용되지 않는다. *outside 외부의 / allow 허용하다 / tutor 개인 교습을 하다

| 조건 | 다음 표현을 사용할 것: during / a / tutoring / food |

9. 이 물고기의 유선형 몸 모양은 물의 저항을 줄이는 것을 도울 뿐만 아니라 좁은 지느러미와 꼬리 그리고 튀어나오지 않은 눈은 물속에서 항력을 줄이는 것을 돕는다. *reduce 줄이다 / drag 항력 / help 돕다

| 조건 | ① Not only (으)로 문장을 시작할 것
② 다음 표현을 사용할 것: the streamlined body shapes of these fish / water resistance, but their narrow fins and tails and eyes / drag in the water as well / don't / that |

PRACTICE TEST (DAY 05)

A. 다음 단어의 뜻을 우리말로 쓰시오.   #037

1. inroad　　　　＿＿＿＿＿＿＿
2. precaution　＿＿＿＿＿＿＿
3. gaze　　　　　＿＿＿＿＿＿＿
4. hands-on　　＿＿＿＿＿＿＿
5. acquainted　＿＿＿＿＿＿＿

B. 다음 우리말을 영어로 쓰시오.   #038

1. 개관, 개요　　　　＿＿＿＿＿＿＿
2. 참을성이 있는　　＿＿＿＿＿＿＿
3. 내쫓다, 탈출하다　＿＿＿＿＿＿＿
4. 기록　　　　　　　＿＿＿＿＿＿＿
5. 군대　　　　　　　＿＿＿＿＿＿＿

C. 동의어를 찾아 연결하시오.   #039

1. abuse ·   · (A) misuse
2. arouse ·   · (B) combination
3. browse ·   · (C) graze
4. commence ·   · (D) follow
5. debilitate ·   · (E) weaken
6. track ·   · (F) circumstance
7. synthesis ·   · (G) begin, start
8. condition ·   · (H) excite

D. 반의어를 찾아 연결하시오.   #040

1. commence ·   · (A) serious
2. casual ·   · (B) covert
3. full ·   · (C) empty
4. overt ·   · (D) finish

E. 문맥상 빈칸에 들어갈 가장 적절한 단어를 고르시오. #041

1. It seems plausible to say that every user can have _____ to all the information they need on the Internet.
   (A) drudgery (B) niche (C) access (D) synthesis

2. She has more _____ taking care of little kids than any other female applicant.
   (A) precaution (B) overview (C) inroad (D) experience

3. The boat tied to a dock came _____.
   (A) disparate (B) loose (C) innate (D) implicit

4. The monster in the folktale _____ had a head like that of a snake.
   (A) allegedly (B) futilely (C) overtly (D) haphazardly

5. The team leader was _____ a hindrance than a help because he would force the others to follow his ideas.
   (A) in search of (B) shortly after (C) inroads into (D) more of

6. The dam created a large _____ of water.
   (A) technique (B) body (C) precaution (D) dwarf

F. 다음 글을 읽고 밑줄 친 단어의 동의어를 고르시오. #042

1. Cracks and <u>fractures</u> in the building grew larger, until it finally collapsed.
   (A) adherents (B) drawbacks (C) delights (D) breaks

2. Too much stress <u>impedes</u> physical growth.
   (A) effaces (B) hinders (C) dilutes (D) complements

3. The sturgeon looks for its food on the bottom of the ocean. This means that it has a <u>disparate</u> mouth shape from other fish that eat flying insects.
   (A) comparable (B) dissimilar (C) parallel (D) corresponding

4. The police arrested a man who <u>allegedly</u> helped to smuggle drugs into the country.
   (A) predominantly (B) purposefully (C) supposedly (D) previously

5. Once you decide to hire an employee, you should have <u>implicit</u> trust in them.
   (A) absolute (B) sheltered (C) extensive (D) occasional

6. London is replete with art galleries and museums.
   (A) fabled	(B) familiar	(C) filled	(D) void

7. The pottery was used mainly for ornamental purposes.
   (A) supposedly	(B) chiefly	(C) innately	(D) instantaneously

8. Gandhi was instrumental in gaining India's independence from the UK.
   (A) impervious	(B) precise	(C) influential	(D) vigorous

9. Search engines such as Google or Naver help people search for information they want to get on the Internet.
   (A) look	(B) bridle	(C) smear	(D) teem

10. He identifies three principles that will help you to write a good essay. The first is making your essay as brief as possible.
    (A) analogous	(B) misleading	(C) short	(D) indifferent

11. In that store, I had the arduous task of carrying heavy things such as a huge plastic box full of 24 bottles of wine.
    (A) packed	(B) repulsive	(C) monotonous	(D) adept

12. I admit that building this type of recycling plant is more expensive than building a traditional plant but remember that a traditional plant needs separate trucks to pick up trash from a single family; for example, a truck for recycling plastic, and another truck for bottles or paper.
    (A) several	(B) seminal	(C) covert	(D) tacit

13. The technique of making glass started in Mesopotamia almost 4,000 years ago.
    (A) intention	(B) ingestion	(C) method	(D) persistence

14. The family fled from Korea to the US to escape the civil war that broke out in 1950.
    (A) trigger	(B) evade	(C) freak	(D) suppress

15. It was unfortunate that we missed the chance to climb to the top of the mountain, though it was nice for me to eat one of my Mom's home-cooked meals.
    (A) shortly after	(B) although	(C) unless	(D) hence

16. Before the Civil Rights Act of 1964 was passed, Black people in the United States were not allowed to sleep at the same hotels or eat at the same restaurants as white people. Black people had to stay in separate areas in theaters, buses, etc.
    (A) different	(B) spacious	(C) hollow	(D) dormant

G. 문맥상 빈칸에 들어갈 가장 적절한 단어를 찾아 넣으시오. *필요시 어형을 변화할 것 #043

| reach outnumber access separate care evade rub precipitate |

1. Historical studies have shown that the Celtic population vastly _____ the invading Anglo-Saxons.

2. The military coup _____ the country into chaos.

3. According to him, China had good ships and advanced sailing skills. That's why they were able to _____ the Americas long before Europeans did.

4. _____ your eyes can be harmful to your eyes.

5. In an attempt to _____ taxes, the company was incorporated in 1988.

6. Despite a word of caution from the government that they should take it seriously, they still didn't _____ about natural resources in their own country.

7. This would mean that many talented artists would be excluded from _____ to public funding for their projects.

8. When producing a car, people in the past who did not do _____ work had to cooperate with one another to make the car.

H. 문맥상 빈칸에 들어갈 가장 적절한 단어를 찾아 넣으시오. #044

1.
| collapse techniques survival livestock |

One of the reasons for the ① _____ of the Mayan civilization is that the Mayans used poor ② _____ for growing crops and raising ③ _____ so they did not have enough food for ④ _____.

2.
| tracking located damage apparatus monitor |

The introduced new animals that cause the most serious ① _____ to the ecosystem are usually large predators like lions and wolves, and these animals are at the top of the food chain. Fortunately, it is easy to ② _____ them. For example, it is not a difficult task to use some detecting and ③ _____ ④ _____ that helps to find where the species are ⑤ _____.

I. 다음 밑줄 친 우리말을 영어로 바꾸어 보기에 주어진 단어나 어구를 활용하여 또는 조건에 맞게 영작하시오. *필요시 어형을 변화할 것

#045

1. 주식 시장의 투기적 사고는 1929년 월스트리트 대폭락에 <u>원인이 되었다</u>. *speculative 투기적인

   1929 / the Wall Street Crash / thinking in / of / _____ / the stock market / speculative / to

2. 그는 엄청 그의 외모와 그가 옷을 입는 방식에 대해서 <u>신경을 쓴다</u>.

   much / way he / _____ very / his appearance and / he / about / the / dresses

3. 그의 아버지는 그에게 두 개의 나무 조각을 <u>문질러서</u> 불을 피우는 법을 가르쳐 주었다.

   to / a / him / wood together / how / two / fire by _____ / his father / make / taught / of / pieces

4. 그 저예산 영화는 독립영화라기 보다는 (오히려) 포르노 비디오<u>에</u> (더) <u>가깝다</u>.

   an / than / the low-budget film / _____ _____ a / independent movie / is / pornographic video

5. 만약 원자로가 과열되면, 그것은 방사성 폐기물이 빠져나가는 온도에 도달할 수도 있다. *overheat 과열되다 / escape 빠져나가다

if / _____ / at / the temperature / radioactive waste / could / overheats, it / which / a nuclear reactor / escapes

6. 만약 그것(it)이 일곱 난쟁이의 관점에서 쓰여진다면 Snow White(백설 공주)는 매우 다를 것이다.

조건
① Snow White (으)로 문장을 시작할 것
② 다음 표현을 사용할 것: were / from / the seven / of / very different if / written / the perspective

7. 종속 이론의 주요 인물인 캐롤 박사는 어려운 질문을 빠져나가는 것으로 유명하다. *famous 유명한 / figure 인물 / dependency theory 종속 이론 / key 주요한

조건 다음 표현을 사용할 것: Dr. Carol, a / difficult questions / in

8. 나는 한국인들이 북한의 끊임없는 위협에 신경을 쓰지 않는다는 것을 흥미롭다고 생각했다. *find 여기다(생각하다) / fascinating 흥미로운

조건 다음 표현을 사용할 것: it / North Korea's constant threats / South Koreans / don't / that

PRACTICE TEST (DAY 06)

A. 다음 단어의 뜻을 우리말로 쓰시오.   #046

1. admiration _____
2. foresight _____
3. optimize _____
4. backbone _____
5. initiative _____

B. 다음 우리말을 영어로 쓰시오.   #047

1. 매우 좋아하는 _____
2. 순차적인 _____
3. 맹세 _____
4. 그러는 동안에 _____
5. 들어 올리다, 높이다 _____

C. 동의어를 찾아 연결하시오.   #048

1. cargo ·   · (A) harshness
2. defect ·   · (B) support
3. drive ·   · (C) flaw
4. severity ·   · (D) freight
5. brace ·   · (E) succeed, invent
6. contrive ·   · (F) irritable
7. perceptible ·   · (G) noticeable
8. fractious ·   · (H) desire

D. 반의어를 찾아 연결하시오.   #049

1. tender ·   · (A) tough
2. rigid ·   · (B) flexible
3. cautious ·   · (C) likely
4. improbable ·   · (D) heedless

E. 문맥상 빈칸에 들어갈 가장 적절한 단어를 고르시오. #050

1. Due to the pandemic, the number of _____ has gone down to just around 10 people a day.
   (A) credits   (B) patrons   (C) odds   (D) backbones

2. A legitimate _____ for this concurrence is safety issues.
   (A) reed   (B) credit   (C) freight   (D) reason

3. One day, I was _____ a box of wine downstairs to put it in the storage area, and I slipped and fell down the stairs.
   (A) carrying   (B) contriving   (C) contemplating   (D) imploring

4. Authors who write fables that _____ animals often criticize people's irrational behaviors or absurdities in a humorous manner.
   (A) deduce   (B) strain   (C) brace   (D) feature

5. My dog _____ at the leash to go towards a cat.
   (A) strained   (B) impeded   (C) etched   (D) vowed

6. New technologies pose a _____ to humans; for example, many people have lost their jobs because of computers.
   (A) reason   (B) foresight   (C) defect   (D) threat

F. 다음 글을 읽고 밑줄 친 단어의 동의어를 고르시오. #051

1. <u>Patrons</u> of the website donated money to keep the website going.
   (A) Loopholes   (B) Supporters   (C) Opponents   (D) Antagonists

2. More conservative individuals <u>deem</u> spending money on the arts to be a waste of very precious resources that could be used to better safeguard the country.
   (A) detest   (B) compensate   (C) oppose   (D) consider

3. He <u>commanded</u> his men to ambush the enemy.
   (A) compelled   (B) aborted   (C) ordered   (D) encroached

4. There are some situations in which you need to be <u>cautious</u> when using this word.
   (A) instant   (B) careful   (C) constant   (D) indigenous

5. After the outbreak of the civil war in Somalia, the Korean ambassador <u>implored</u> the Government Army to guard the Korean Embassy.

   (A) criticized   (B) deplored   (C) begged   (D) praised

6. In the end, the prime minister <u>recognized</u> that Brexit was a bad idea because the U.K. economy is now shrinking. *Brexit 브렉시트(영국의 유럽 연합(EU) 탈퇴)

   (A) agitated   (B) denied   (C) repudiated   (D) acknowledged

7. Knights took an oath of allegiance to their lords. They were <u>supposed</u> to not only observe a strict set of rules enforced by their lords, but also fight and die for them.

   (A) expected   (B) enthusiastic   (C) anxious   (D) eager

8. For example, the insects mentioned in the text <u>actually</u> cause little damage to the area where they live.

   (A) painstakingly   (B) in fact   (C) on the spot   (D) arbitrarily

9. His paintings <u>feature</u> the fragile and divisive nature of human relationships. *fragile 깨지기 쉬운 / divisive 불화를 일으키는

   (A) condemn   (B) cremate   (C) portray   (D) include

10. He <u>seized</u> her by the waist and pulled her close.

    (A) grabbed   (B) emancipated   (C) startled   (D) twisted

11. Actually, zebras rest in open fields where they can more easily watch predators <u>approaching</u> them.

    (A) threatening   (B) nearing   (C) protruding   (D) snatching

12. Because their previous phone models overheated easily, customers are <u>wary</u> of their latest phone model.

    (A) cautious   (B) objective   (C) capable   (D) acceptable

13. That's why many cats, which could have prevented the spread of the plague by killing rats that <u>carried</u> the plague, were killed.

    (A) abounded   (B) infected   (C) averted   (D) transported

14. Working conditions in factories during the Industrial Revolution were really <u>awful</u>. Workplaces were filthy, unsanitary, and dangerous.

    (A) futile   (B) dreadful   (C) prodigious   (D) pre-eminent

15. Hammer the nails correctly so that they will not <u>protrude</u> from the wall. *hammer a nail 못을 박다

    (A) construe   (B) project   (C) penetrate   (D) separate

16. He pulled out his zipper lighter, felt his initials YJ <u>etched</u> on the case, and lit a cigarette.

    (A) displayed   (B) carved   (C) concealed   (D) mediated

G. 문맥상 빈칸에 들어갈 가장 적절한 단어를 찾아 넣으시오. *필요시 어형을 변화할 것 / 같은 단어 두 번 사용 가능   #052

| carry | thus | supposed | apart | none other than | access | congestion |

1. The passage describes problems associated with traffic _____, whereas the lecturer offers suggestions to ease traffic _____.

2. If the number of hospital beds dramatically increased but roads to help ambulances _____ patients in urgent need of care didn't exist, what would happen?

3. A dog's ability to smell things sets it _____ from other animals.

4. Suppressing anger saps your energy, _____ making you tired. *sap 약화시키다

5. The bubonic plague rapidly spread by fleas that were _____ by rats. *the bubonic plague 흑사병

6. I was _____ to go camping.

7. My first backpacking site was _____ Gul-up Island, a place that backpackers call one of the three sacred sites in Korea.

8. Charlie Chaplin and Adolf Hitler were born four days _____.

H. 문맥상 빈칸에 들어갈 가장 적절한 단어를 찾아 넣으시오.   #053

1.
| pull | pose | clog | threat |

Besides the major ① _____ that zebra mussels ② _____ to fish populations in their new habitats, they also ③ _____ water pipes, which is a problem for water treatment plants that ④ _____ water out of lakes through pipes. *zebra mussel 얼룩무늬 홍합

2.
| unloaded | place | filled | unsuitable | invasion | cargo |

These tanks are ① _____ with ballast water that balances ② _____ ships when they are ③ _____. So, one of the most effective ways to obstruct the ④ _____ of zebra mussels is to make the ballast tanks ⑤ _____ for their survival in the first ⑥ _____. *ballast water 배의 균형을 잡기 위해 배 아래쪽 탱크에 채우는 물 / zebra mussel 얼룩무늬 홍합

I. 다음 밑줄 친 우리말을 영어로 바꾸어 보기에 주어진 단어나 어구를 활용하여 또는 조건에 맞게 영작하시오. *필요시 어형을 변화할 것

#054

1. 일본 사람들은 자신의 진짜 감정을 드러내는 것을 싫어한다고 한다.

   their real feelings / are / Japanese people / _____ / showing / to / hate

2. 우리는 이 어려운 시기를 뚫고 회사를 이끈 사장님의 공로를 인정해야 한다. *lead 이끌다

   give / for / this difficult time / have / _____ / our boss / we / our company through / leading / to

3. 불법 이민자 수의 급격한 상승 때문에 정부는 금리를 올리는 것에 대해 신중하게 되었다.

   in / illegal immigrants / the number / _____ about / of / interest rates because / increasing / of / the government / became / the sharp rise

4. 사람들은 나중에 자신들의 집값이 오를 것이라는 희망(기대) 속에 집을 사기 시작했다.

   started / homes in / increase / the price of their homes / would later / to / that / the _____ / people / buy

5. 남자는 여자와 체온이 다르다.

| temperature from / men / body / in / women / _____ |

6. 그 거대한 플라스틱 상자는 너무 무거워서 혼자서 나를 수(옮길 수) 없었다.

| 조건 | ① The huge plastic box (으)로 문장을 시작할 것
② 다음 표현을 사용할 것: too / by myself / heavy |

7. 수소 연료 전지 차량은 가솔린으로 작동되는 자동차보다 연료를 사용하는 데 거의 두 배나 효율적이다.
*power 작동시키다

| 조건 | 다음 표현을 사용할 것: nearly / a hydrogen fuel-cell vehicle / twice / fuel as a car powered / at using / as |

8. 황급히, 그는 그가 그의 전처의 이름을 새긴 진입로 옆에 심어져 있던 키 큰 나무를 베었다. *hurriedly 황급히 / cut down sth ~을 베다 / plant 심다

| 조건 | 다음 표현을 사용할 것: a / tree planted next / his driveway on / had / his ex's name |

PRACTICE TEST (DAY 07)

A. 다음 단어의 뜻을 우리말로 쓰시오. #055

1. redress _____
2. nothing less than _____
3. intent _____
4. eminent _____
5. programmed _____

B. 다음 우리말을 영어로 쓰시오. #056

1. 즉흥의 _____
2. 복역(복무)하다 _____
3. 우연히 만나다 _____
4. 버리다 _____
5. 맹세하다 _____

C. 동의어를 찾아 연결하시오. #057

1. usually · · (A) only just
2. barely · · (B) sturdy
3. robust · · (C) separate
4. defer · · (D) procrastinate
5. consecutive · · (E) successive
6. ceaseless · · (F) more often than not
7. discrete · · (G) incessant
8. risk · · (H) venture

D. 반의어를 찾아 연결하시오. #058

1. success · · (A) minor
2. major · · (B) inequality
3. superior · · (C) inferior
4. parity · · (D) failure

E. 문맥상 빈칸에 들어갈 가장 적절한 단어를 고르시오. #059

1. House prices in Seoul increased to such an _____ that we couldn't buy any house at all.
   (A) advantage   (B) equality   (C) incidence   (D) extent

2. He is suing the Aurora Police Department for excessive _____.
   (A) force   (B) parity   (C) span   (D) malady

3. Coating the roofs and the outer walls of buildings with a protective material so that acid rain cannot seep into them could reduce economic losses _____ by acid rain. *seep (물기 등이) 스며들다
   (A) accommodated   (B) caused   (C) pledged   (D) deferred

4. He _____ his lecture to advanced-level students.
   (A) tore   (B) discarded   (C) geared   (D) came across

5. Every student goes to the library to gain knowledge related to their major and uses the computer lab to obtain useful _____ for getting employed by large companies.
   (A) velocities   (B) incidences   (C) reaches   (D) tips

6. The root system _____ several important purposes.
   (A) redresses   (B) pledges   (C) serves   (D) accommodates

F. 다음 글을 읽고 밑줄 친 단어의 동의어를 고르시오. #060

1. Queen Elizabeth ruled for the longest span of time.
   (A) period   (B) ownership   (C) milestone   (D) defect

2. I tried to erase the incident that occurred that night from my mind.
   (A) deteriorate   (B) delete   (C) embrace   (D) remind

3. After his death in 1985, his fellow botanist Joseph Fullers embarked upon many more expeditions to find out how plants survive in severe weather conditions.
   (A) implicit   (B) regular   (C) extreme   (D) moderate

4. As the companies were too lazy to invest in car engines, car design, and new product development, their products increasingly lost popularity in the world market and could not compete with other superior foreign car manufacturers.
   (A) materialistic   (B) acute   (C) better   (D) methodical

5. The chances of the United States <u>redressing</u> its trade imbalance with China are slim. *slim (가능성이) 희박한

   (A) negating (B) counteracting (C) offsetting (D) correcting

6. Doctors have observed that heavy smokers have a high <u>incidence</u> of lung cancer.

   (A) occurrence (B) drudgery (C) cure (D) amenity

7. People today want to <u>improve</u> their looks by getting plastic surgery done on their faces or bodies.

   (A) impede (B) enlarge (C) postpone (D) enhance

8. The massive influx of people moving from the countryside into big cities led to excessive land development to <u>accommodate</u> these people.

   (A) house (B) evaluate (C) connect (D) certify

9. People create false stories online to catch people's attention and leave a <u>perennial</u> impression.

   (A) brisk (B) futile (C) imperative (D) continuing

10. Be careful not to <u>tear</u> your pants on a protruding nail. *protrude 튀어나오다

    (A) demolish (B) rip (C) cripple (D) insulate

11. <u>Moreover</u>, the rapid growth of cities destroys the natural environment.

    (A) Nonetheless (B) Likewise (C) What's more (D) Meanwhile

12. Old buildings are not <u>suitable</u> for modern people's needs.

    (A) seamless (B) susceptible (C) fit (D) detrimental

13. It's a kind of material that people put in their gardens to <u>eliminate</u> weeds.

    (A) optimize (B) remove (C) contemplate (D) pursue

14. Wrong choices of words can <u>convey</u> the false impression that men are superior to women in many ways.

    (A) impart (B) explode (C) entomb (D) halt

15. Because the cost of <u>operating</u> a hydroelectric dam is relatively low, hydroelectric energy is seen as a low-cost renewable energy source.

    (A) effacing (B) functioning (C) procrastinating (D) demolishing

16. The sense of smell in dogs is believed to be more <u>acute</u> than in humans.

    (A) seminal (B) prominent (C) blunt (D) keen

17. The rocket gained <u>velocity</u> as it travelled through space. *gain 증가시키다

    (A) speed (B) volume (C) persistence (D) occurrence

G. 문맥상 빈칸에 들어갈 가장 적절한 단어를 찾아 넣으시오. *필요시 어형을 변화할 것 / 같은 단어 두 번 사용 가능   #061

| case   success   fit   dream   extent   apply   advantage |

1. When he was elected, I didn't feel that he was _____ to be the President of the United States.

2. Radio dramas have two _____ over TV dramas.

3. A _____ in point is the Wright brothers, who were American inventors.

4. As soon as Neil Armstrong succeeded in landing on the moon, humans started to dream big _____.

5. People's language skills are improved to the _____ that they practice. The more practice, the better their skills will be.

6. We don't know the exact _____ of the damage yet.

7. There are many people who have had great _____ in selling a lot of properties at high prices.

8. History is not _____ for solving the problems people face today.

9. I still remember the time when we decided to go to Korea to teach English as a second language. We had no idea where to _____.

H. 문맥상 빈칸에 들어갈 가장 적절한 단어를 찾아 넣으시오.   #062

1.
| severe   led   hardship   referred |

The 'IMF,' generally ① _____ to as an economic crisis by the Korean people, was a time of ② _____ economic ③ _____ in Korea that ④ _____ to long-term economic depression.

2.
| convey   bottom   sediment   surface   separate |

And, even if you could ① _____ precious metal resources from the ② _____ at the ③ _____ of the ocean, you would need a way to ④ _____ the metals to the ⑤ _____ of the ocean. Unfortunately, these technologies just don't exist right now.

I. 다음 밑줄 친 우리말을 영어로 바꾸어 보기에 주어진 단어나 어구를 활용하여 또는 조건에 맞게 영작하시오. *필요시 어형을 변화할 것

#063

1. 그는 경찰이 차종을 확인할 수 없을 <u>정도까지(정도로)</u> 그 차를 파괴했다. *identify 확인하다

   the model / an _____ / the car to / that / identify / the police could not / he / destroyed / such

2. 만약 그가 제때 브레이크를 <u>밟지</u> 않았더라면, 그는 그 대형 트레일러트럭과 충돌했을 것이다.

   the heavy trailer truck / not / collided / time, he would / _____ his brakes in / had / with / have / if he

3. 그 왕은 그의 부하들에게 그의 통치에 대항해 반란을 일으킨 그의 적수들을 <u>제거</u>하라고 시켰다. *have 시키다

   had / had revolted / who / the king / _____ his rivals / his rule / his men / against

4. 인터뷰 동안 당신이 <u>전달</u>할 수 있는 생각의 범위에는 한계가 있다.

   the extent of the thoughts / interview / limit / is / an / there / you can _____ during / a / to / that

5. 민주당(the Democratic Party)은 공화당(the Republican Party)을 누르고 <u>간신히</u> 선거에서 승리했다.

> _____ won / the Republican Party / the Democratic Party / the election over

6. 많은 사람들은 새로운 기술이 가져올 변화에 대해 <u>걱정한다</u>. *bring 가져오다

> 조건 다음 표현을 사용할 것: new technology / are / the changes / that / will

7. 혼자 사냥하는 새들은 무리를 지어 사냥하는 새들보다 몇 가지 중요한 <u>이점들</u>을 누린다. *enjoy (장점 등을) 누리다 / hunt 사냥하다

> 조건 다음 표현을 사용할 것: several key / over / in flocks / alone / that / that

8. 등유의 공급이 다 떨어져 가고 있어서 우리는 <u>일부러(굳이)</u> 램프에 불을 붙이진 <u>않았다</u>. *kerosene 등유 / run out 다 떨어지다 / light 불을 붙이다

> 조건 다음 표현을 사용할 것: our supply of kerosene / running out, so we / the lamp / to

PRACTICE TEST (DAY 08)

A. 다음 단어의 뜻을 우리말로 쓰시오. #064

1. apex _____
2. domain _____
3. assert _____
4. intolerable _____
5. superficial _____

B. 다음 우리말을 영어로 쓰시오. #065

1. 대형 단지 _____
2. 호밀 _____
3. 규정하다, 정의하다 _____
4. 박살나다 _____
5. 분출하다 _____

C. 동의어를 찾아 연결하시오. #066

1. occasion · · (A) boost
2. bolster · · (B) event
3. caution · · (C) include
4. incorporate · · (D) warn
5. elongate · · (E) plentiful
6. bountiful · · (F) lengthen
7. magnificent · · (G) splendid
8. candid · · (H) frank

D. 반의어를 찾아 연결하시오. #067

1. aggressive · · (A) definite
2. tentative · · (B) submissive
3. normally · · (C) follow
4. precede · · (D) abnormally

E. 문맥상 빈칸에 들어갈 가장 적절한 단어를 고르시오. #068

1. When the price of tulips reached its peak, a tulip _____ cost more than a mansion.
   *mansion 대저택
   (A) occasion (B) domain (C) bulb (D) apex

2. Bad eating habits can cause blood _____ to narrow, which results in high blood pressure.
   (A) vessels (B) vassals (C) flakes (D) traces

3. Modern farming _____ such as the use of chemicals could put animals in danger.
   (A) practices (B) realms (C) occasions (D) domains

4. In its pure state, aluminum is light but weak, but when _____ chemically with other metals, it is a strong metal.
   (A) shattered (B) elongated (C) discharged (D) combined

5. Some scientists believe that GMOs (genetically modified organisms) can increase crop yield to help _____ the world's growing population.
   (A) feed (B) incorporate (C) vent (D) precede

6. Hail can destroy crops. Cloud seeding, a process by which substances including silver iodide are sprayed into the air, can be a(n) _____ to this problem. * cloud seeding 구름씨 뿌리기(인공적으로 비나 눈을 내리게 하는 방법) / silver iodide 요오드화은
   (A) trace (B) impact (C) occasion (D) solution

F. 다음 글을 읽고 밑줄 친 단어의 동의어를 고르시오. #069

1. The negative <u>impact</u> caused by the introduction of new species often leads to a certain number of economic burdens.
   (A) vanity (B) effect (C) persistence (D) summit

2. People trust leaders who <u>acknowledge</u> the mistakes that they have made.
   (A) underscore (B) stir (C) display (D) admit

3. Management made a <u>tentative</u> agreement with employees about a raise in wages.
   (A) radical (B) suggestive (C) archetypal (D) provisional

4. The canals scientists believed to be artificially made turned out to be <u>nothing more than</u> naturally occurring channels.
   (A) only (B) occasionally (C) paradoxically (D) simultaneously

5. The British political organization <u>convinces</u> people to have conservative opinions on issues such as abortion and homosexuality.
   (A) persuades (B) implores (C) commands (D) compels

6. Adolescents can be self-centered, impulsive, and <u>aggressive</u>.
   (A) egocentric (B) abnormal (C) fragile (D) hostile

7. One of the first bubbles in history, known as Tulip Mania, <u>occurred</u> in the Netherlands in the seventeenth century. *mania 열광
   (A) outnumbered (B) commenced (C) transpired (D) smeared

8. The success of the spread of Greek culture was due to his <u>sheer</u> endeavor to create a cohesive community.
   (A) utter (B) implicit (C) remarkable (D) instinctive

9. She said that she had cleaned the kitchen, but there is no <u>trace</u> of her doing anything there.
   (A) patron (B) culmination (C) mark (D) chip

10. In ecological terms, the best way to <u>reduce</u> the number of zebra mussels is to introduce predators into the mussels' new habitats. *zebra mussel 얼룩무늬 홍합
    (A) accelerate (B) inflate (C) unearth (D) cut

11. The article <u>stressed</u> that at that time they started using bronze out of which they made tools and weapons.
    (A) proposed (B) accentuated (C) revised (D) issued

12. Most of the old people in the country work until late at night while sitting <u>inactive</u>, which means that they easily gain weight.
    (A) fatal (B) far-reaching (C) harmless (D) still

13. His paintings are <u>normally</u> of ordinary people living in a big city.
    (A) instantly (B) usually (C) incidentally (D) previously

14. The events were important in the decades <u>preceding</u> the American Civil War.
    (A) happening before (B) happening after (C) igniting (D) forecasting

15. The first <u>flakes</u> of snow showed that winter had finally arrived.
    (A) chips (B) appearances (C) menaces (D) patrons

16. This theory developed by Sigmund Freud, the father of psychoanalysis, can also be applied to other <u>realms</u> of social science.
    (A) fields (B) capacities (C) merits (D) anomalies

17. The high singing noise of the cicadas <u>coupled with</u> my wife's snoring was driving me crazy, which was why I couldn't sleep a wink.
    (A) discharged with (B) equipped with (C) combined with (D) bolstered with

G. 문맥상 빈칸에 들어갈 가장 적절한 단어를 찾아 넣으시오. *필요시 어형을 변화할 것 / 같은 단어 두 번 사용 가능 #070

| combined   fiery   acknowledge   equipped   weak   routine   discharged |

1. The fans of the team didn't want to _____ that their team had lost the championship game.
2. Rapidly rising wages _____ with rising inflation have caused many companies to increase the prices of their products.
3. When plastic products are burned, harmful gases are _____ into the air.
4. The arguments provided in your reading passage do seem logical at first, but upon closer examination, there are many _____ points.
5. The office is _____ with the latest in communications technology, including 5G.
6. His _____ temper often puts his family in a position that makes them uneasy.
7. They eat out _____.
8. Even critics _____ that the candidate raised some important points regarding healthcare.

H. 문맥상 빈칸에 들어갈 가장 적절한 단어를 찾아 넣으시오. #071

1.

| keep   weak   suspended   heavy |

Even if it could have somehow lifted off from the ground, the wings of the Argentavis Magnificens would have been too ① _____ to ② _____ its ③ _____ body ④ _____ in the air. *Argentavis Magnificens 아르헨티나에서 서식했던 인류 역사상 가장 큰 맹금

2.

| falling   solution   spraying   farmland   season |

Hail ① _____ down from clouds destroys crops. Cloud seeding – ② _____ substances including silver iodide into the air – is used as a ③ _____ to this problem. Scientists in America spent an entire ④ _____ seeding clouds in a specific area of ⑤ _____ in the country. *silver iodide 요오드화은 / cloud seeding 구름씨 뿌리기(인공적으로 비나 눈을 내리게 하는 방법)

I. 다음 밑줄 친 우리말을 영어로 바꾸어 보기에 주어진 단어나 어구를 활용하여 또는 조건에 맞게 영작하시오. *필요시 어형을 변화할 것

#072

1. 우리 어머니는 내가 더 많은 야채를 먹어야 할 필요성을 정말로 <u>강조했다</u>.

   eat / the need / more vegetables / really _____ / me to / my mother / for

2. 인터넷은 사람들이 사는 방식에 <u>영향</u>을 미친다.

   live / an / on / people / _____ / has / the way / the Internet

3. 몇몇 동물들은 겨울 동안 힘을 아끼기 위해 <u>활동하지 않은</u> 상태로 있다.

   winter months / save / _____ to / some animals / energy during / remain

4. 추울 때는, 뇌 안에 있는 <u>혈관</u>이 수축한다. *contract 수축하다

   | 조 건 | 다음 표현을 사용할 것: when / cold / is / the brain |

5. 그것은 독감<u>에 지나지 않는다(에 불과하다)</u>.

   | 조 건 | 다음 표현을 사용할 것: it's / the flu |

6. 통화 정책의 효과적인 수단 중에는 은행 금리, 즉 중앙은행들이 상업 은행들에게 돈을 빌려주는 이자율이 있다. *effective 효과적인 / instrument 수단 / lend 빌려주다 / the bank rate 은행 금리

조건	① Among the effective (으)로 문장을 시작할 것 ② 다음 표현을 사용할 것: which / is / to commercial banks / the bank rate, that is, the interest rate / of monetary policy

7. 대통령은 인구 감소에 대한 해결책을 찾기 위해 전문가들과의 대화에 참여하기 시작했다. *start 시작하다 / engage in conversations 대화에 참여하다 / find 찾다

조건	다음 표현을 사용할 것: the decline / the president / experts to / to engage in / population / in / a / to / with

8. 과거에는, 오로지 생존만이 인간이 해결해야 하는 가장 중요한 문제였다. *survival 생존 / matter 문제 / deal with sth ~을 해결하다

조건	다음 표현을 사용할 것: in the past, / had to / humans / important / that

9. 목장주들은 그들의 닭들을 빨리 살찌우기 위해 그들의 닭들에게 특별한 곡물을 먹이기 때문에, 과체중인 닭들 중 일부는 걷는 데 어려움을 겪는다. *rancher 목장주 / fatten 살찌우다 / have a hard time 어려움을 겪다

조건	① Since (으)로 문장을 시작할 것 ② 다음 표현을 사용할 것: ranchers / their chickens a special grain / them quickly, some / the overweight chickens

PRACTICE TEST (DAY 09)

A. 다음 단어의 뜻을 우리말로 쓰시오.   #073

1. tolerant _____
2. now that _____
3. incur _____
4. epitomize _____
5. patch _____

B. 다음 우리말을 영어로 쓰시오.   #074

1. 수명 _____
2. 솔기가 없는 _____
3. 반항(거역)하다 _____
4. ~에서 기인하다 _____
5. 기원 _____

C. 동의어를 찾아 연결하시오.   #075

1. intent · · (A) together
2. ramification · · (B) spoonful
3. scoop · · (C) complication
4. assign · · (D) intention
5. isolated · · (E) nimble
6. agile · · (F) see
7. view · · (G) remote
8. in unison · · (H) allocate

D. 반의어를 찾아 연결하시오.   #076

1. consent · · (A) oblivious
2. aware · · (B) temporarily
3. inadvertently · · (C) deliberately
4. permanently · · (D) refuse

E. 문맥상 빈칸에 들어갈 가장 적절한 단어를 고르시오. #077

1. Don't _____ like a child.
   (A) act (B) predominate (C) incur (D) epitomize

2. The _____ of public funds by the President to pay for his own home caused his downfall.
   (A) patch (B) diversion (C) ramification (D) instrument

3. Everyone has the right to the _____ of happiness.
   (A) vestige (B) origin (C) intent (D) pursuit

4. In the U.S., people who have the right to vote don't vote directly for the president. They _____ a vote for electors who then vote for the president. *elector (미국의) 대통령 선거인
   (A) cast (B) defy (C) occupy (D) grasp

5. There were _____ from residents that rats were in the trash cans.
   (A) intents (B) origins (C) complaints (D) instruments

6. We use 'who' in relative clauses to _____ to people.
   (A) defy (B) predominate (C) elude (D) refer

F. 다음 글을 읽고 밑줄 친 단어의 동의어를 고르시오. #078

1. The light is formed when a cloud of particles collide with gases in Earth's atmosphere.
   *a cloud of sth 자욱한
   (A) aggregate (B) crash (C) evade (D) combine

2. Dad referred to my girlfriend as a friend from college.
   (A) clarified (B) mentioned (C) considered (D) revered

3. The government took swift action to stop the disease from spreading.
   (A) immediate (B) inappropriate (C) conscientious (D) drastic

4. I want you to give me some advice on how to find information on the subject.
   (A) traits (B) craftsmen (C) pointers (D) predecessors

5. As sturgeons jump out of the water, they shake energetically. *sturgeon 철갑상어
   (A) persistently (B) vigorously (C) inadvertently (D) remarkably

6. He succeeded in escaping from the prison by using a spoon to dig a hole in the floor and climbing down through it. He also managed to underline{elude} his pursuers.

   (A) discard   (B) decimate   (C) resist   (D) escape

7. Many species in the National Everglades Park, underline{otherwise} known as the Everglades, would be extinct by now if it were not for the park.

   (A) widely   (B) commonly   (C) meantime   (D) differently

8. The kid underline{grasped} a baseball card in his hand.

   (A) boasted   (B) formulated   (C) soaked   (D) clutched

9. Livestock and poultry farming, which rely on menhaden as a source of protein, underline{predominate} in the surrounding areas. *menhaden 청어의 일종 / poultry 가금(닭이나 오리 등의 조류)

   (A) disseminate   (B) prevail   (C) originate   (D) flourish

10. As underline{instruments} of fiscal policy, the government uses taxation and government spending to influence the economy; for example, the government takes money out of the wallets of the rich through taxation and puts it into the pockets of the poor with government spending. *fiscal 재정의

    (A) remedies   (B) complications   (C) advantages   (D) methods

11. Her father's violence and abusive language underline{drove} her to leave home at a young age.

    (A) allowed   (B) impeded   (C) contrived   (D) forced

12. Gold was of underline{prime} importance to the tribe.

    (A) main   (B) replete   (C) concise   (D) negligible

13. As we all know, Steve Jobs had underline{excellent} presentation skills.

    (A) tacit   (B) superb   (C) mediocre   (D) overt

14. After underline{discounting} the price of the cookware, sales soared.

    (A) prompting   (B) cutting   (C) precipitating   (D) elevating

15. The tribes often went to war with other tribes to underline{occupy} territories.

    (A) debilitate   (B) stigmatize   (C) degrade   (D) take over

16. The poems written by the poet in the 1950s were too elusive for general readers to underline{grasp}.
    *elusive 이해하기 힘든

    (A) understand   (B) hustle   (C) recommend   (D) hail

G. 문맥상 빈칸에 들어갈 가장 적절한 단어를 찾아 넣으시오. *같은 단어 두 번 사용 가능 #079

consistently   certain   now that   vestige   otherwise

1. No _____ remained of native culture on the American East Coast.

2. As far as I'm concerned, chronic diseases and _____ types of cancer are often caused by bad eating habits.

3. Private fossil collectors pay millions of dollars to buy many fossils that would _____ be donated to museums.

4. _____ you have grown up, you should be independent of your parents and pay your own tuition.

5. He's _____ denied the alleged fact.

6. The government claimed that 83% of Israeli society supported the act, but a recent poll suggested _____.

7. The used car needs some minor repairs, but _____ it's in pretty good condition.

H. 문맥상 빈칸에 들어갈 가장 적절한 단어를 찾아 넣으시오. #080

1.
gender   unfair   clear   complaints

Many people still think of Muslim women as accepting ① _____ treatment without any ② _____, but what the photos that I took while I was in Teheran make ③ _____ is that they are struggling to promote women's rights and achieve ④ _____ equality.

2.
barrier   layer   so-called   covered   act

One of the many building designs used in city planning is a ① _____ "living roof." ② _____ with a ③ _____ of soil in which shrubs and small trees are grown, these roofs ④ _____ as a ⑤ _____ that protects the surface of the roof from the ultraviolet rays of the sun.

I. 다음 밑줄 친 우리말을 영어로 바꾸어 보기에 주어진 단어나 어구를 활용하여 또는 조건에 맞게 영작하시오. *필요시 어형을 변화할 것*

#081

1. 아주 많은 큰 물웅덩이가 있는 학교 운동장에서 축구를 하는 것은 <u>재미있을 것이다</u>.

   _____ playing / be / on the school ground with / will / football / so many big puddles / it

2. 나는 오늘 미국이 이라크를 침공했다는 <u>뉴스</u>를 들었다. *invade 침공하다

   heard / I / the _____ / that / U.S. / Iraq today / the / invaded

3. 우리 부모님은 대출을 받아야 한다. <u>그렇지 않으면</u>, 그들은 새로운 사업을 시작할 수 없을 것이다.

   new business / have / be / a / will / my parents / get / not / able / loan. _____, they / a / open / to / to

4. 지역 사회와 주민들은 마을과 도시를 개발하는 데 사용<u>되었을</u> 많은 돈을 이 오래된 건물을 유지하는 데 지불해야 한다. *pay sth for doing sth ~하는 데 ~을 지불하다 / maintain 유지하다

   these old buildings / to / maintaining / pay / would _____ be spent / local communities and residents / to / develop their towns and cities, for / a significant amount of money, which / have

5. 그를 쫓고 있는 경찰차를 따돌리기 위해, 그는 그의 얼굴을 땅에 댄 채 납작 엎드렸다. *flat 납작한

the / the police car chasing / on / flat, his face
/ him, he / in / lay / ground / order to _____ / after

6. 내가 너한테 사용하지 않을 때는 전등을 끄라고 말했지.

I / use / you / _____ when / not / told / _____ / to / in / the lights

7. 만약 특정 라면, 이를테면 매운맛 라면, 가격이 오르면, 매운맛 라면을 제조하는 그 회사는 더 많은 라면을 생산할 것이다. *go up 오르다 / manufacture 제조하다 / produce 생산하다

| 조건 | 다음 표현을 사용할 것: the company / will / more of it / instant noodle, let's say Spicy Sin, / manufacturing Spicy Sin / the price of |

8. 시청을 점거하고 있던 시위대에게 총을 쏘라는 명령을 내린 것은 (바로) 총사령관이었다. *give an order to do sth ~하라는 명령을 내리다 / shoot 쏘다

| 조건 | ① It (으)로 문장을 시작할 것
② 다음 표현을 사용할 것: had / City Hall / the chief commander who / the demonstrators who |

9. 경제학에서 공유지의 비극은 개인들이 그들 자신의 이익을 위해 공동의 자원을 착취하는 상황을 말한다.
*the tragedy of the commons 공유지의 비극 / exploit 착취하다 / common 공동의

| 조건 | 다음 표현을 사용할 것: a situation / economics / individuals / resources / their own profits / which |

PRACTICE TEST (DAY 10)

A. 다음 단어의 뜻을 우리말로 쓰시오. #082

1. archive _____
2. shed _____
3. appease _____
4. bode _____
5. cater _____

B. 다음 우리말을 영어로 쓰시오. #083

1. 조어, 신조어 _____
2. 무늬, 양식 _____
3. 녹 _____
4. 실컷 즐기다 _____
5. 서로 연관시키다 _____

C. 동의어를 찾아 연결하시오. #084

1. involved · · (A) modify
2. underpinning · · (B) embroiled
3. viability · · (C) improve
4. adapt · · (D) ardent
5. collect · · (E) mar
6. degrade · · (F) foundation
7. refine · · (G) gather
8. fervent · · (H) feasibility

D. 반의어를 찾아 연결하시오. #085

1. prohibit · · (A) preceding
2. succeeding · · (B) reluctant
3. willing · · (C) weighty
4. trivial · · (D) license

E. 문맥상 빈칸에 들어갈 가장 적절한 단어를 고르시오. #086

1. They come out of underground _____ at night to hunt, and they go back there to hide or sleep during the day.
   (A) burrows (B) underpinnings (C) rusts (D) patterns

2. The professor creates the _____ that there is little that can be done to save the Everglades. *Everglades 미국 남부의 습지대
   (A) ratio (B) impression (C) coinage (D) archive

3. The total _____ of water on Earth is around 1.3 billion km³.
   (A) structure (B) volume (C) viability (D) shed

4. It takes a long time for new species to _____ the gap left by extinct species.
   (A) fill (B) degrade (C) enumerate (D) cater

5. He was arrested for plotting to bomb the Supreme Court. At first, he didn't give the names of the conspirators who were _____ in the plot. *plot 음모(모의)하다 / conspirator 공모자
   (A) involved (B) willing (C) trivial (D) perpetual

6. He _____ the English Channel in a small boat.
   (A) indulged (B) reverted (C) embarked (D) traversed

F. 다음 글을 읽고 밑줄 친 단어의 동의어를 고르시오. #087

1. The lecturer suggests certain problems with all of the theories <u>presented</u> in the passage.
   (A) underscored (B) confirmed (C) shown (D) refuted

2. The professor who has done important work in the field of science won an <u>outstanding</u> prize in 2019 that is awarded to scientists every year.
   (A) minute (B) instantaneous (C) excellent (D) trifling

3. The cane toad, native to South Africa, was introduced to Australia, where its numbers have increased at an <u>alarming</u> rate and have had harmful effects on the local environment. *cane toad 사탕수수 두꺼비
   (A) rapid (B) frightening (C) exceeding (D) sudden

4. This method clears out dead trees that could fuel a fire, creating a safe zone, which can be easily <u>discriminated</u> when a forest fire occurs. *clear out sth ~을 치우다
   (A) differentiated (B) procrastinated (C) intermingled (D) blended

5. His kid's incessant jumping and running made his downstairs neighbor come up to complain.

   (A) occasional
   (B) sporadic
   (C) reluctant
   (D) constant

6. He recommended taking a look at TED.com. According to him, the website introduces ideas eminently worth spreading.

   (A) solely
   (B) highly
   (C) steadfastly
   (D) securely

7. While modern flying birds have the appropriate ratio of wing to body, a wing span of up to 7 meters would have made it impossible for the world's largest prehistoric bird to take off from a standing position because its wings would have hit the ground.

   (A) strength
   (B) width
   (C) feasibility
   (D) proportion

8. Single-stream recycling is hazardous. Employees at a single-stream recycling center must manually remove any broken pieces of glass and are at risk of seriously injuring their hands.

   (A) inefficient
   (B) laborious
   (C) instrumental
   (D) dangerous

9. There's an increased demand for smartphones, as shown in the preceding chapter. Now, in the succeeding chapter, I'm going to explain smartphone addiction.

   (A) current
   (B) dual
   (C) following
   (D) ephemeral

10. The restrictions that used to prohibit Black Americans from voting were finally removed as the result of the civil rights movement in the 1950s and 1960s.

    (A) abolish
    (B) outlaw
    (C) endow
    (D) detest

11. Earth was bombarded by innumerable asteroids, leaving wide depressions in the ground in their wake.

    (A) maladies
    (B) solicitudes
    (C) impressions
    (D) despairs

12. That is particularly true for me. I always cry when watching movies. *true for sb/sth ~에 해당되는

    (A) invariably
    (B) especially
    (C) inevitably
    (D) exceptionally

13. I couldn't work at home because of the perpetual noise from my neighbor's home renovation.

    (A) painstaking
    (B) splendid
    (C) intermittent
    (D) continuous

14. And finally, unlike residents living in or near industrial and financial areas, who appreciate the novelty and progressiveness of their towns, local residents living near old buildings feel that these old structures make their towns seem out-of-date.

    (A) myriads
    (B) phenomena
    (C) particles
    (D) buildings

15. It is true that the committee officially stated that he had indeed embarked on two expeditions to the North Pole in 1795 and 1797.

    (A) set out on
    (B) dropped out of
    (C) come across
    (D) relied on

16. I witnessed the members of a wolf pack fighting with another pack over territory and food. *pack 무리(떼)

    (A) alerted
    (B) appeased
    (C) ejected
    (D) observed

G. 문맥상 빈칸에 들어갈 가장 적절한 단어를 찾아 넣으시오. *필요시 어형을 변화할 것   #088

| eminently   fire   involved   fill   blind   stable   unwilling |

1. Because of the free rider problem, some team members might be _____ to work hard.
   *free rider problem 무임승차 문제

2. I like to buy domestic products. For me, they are _____ worth buying.

3. Many people are _____ to the suffering of homeless people.

4. It was very cold. I wanted to make a fire by the barn. I lit a stick with a match. The stick caught on _____.

5. The lord kept invaders at bay by digging a huge moat around the castle and _____ it with water. *lord (중세 시대) 영주 / moat 해자(성 주위로 땅을 파서 물을 채운 곳) / keep sb at bay ~을 가까이 오지 못하게 하다

6. According to him, until 1800, women gave birth to six children, on average. People at that time needed a big family either for the purpose of labor or in case some of their children died. The reason that the population was able to stay _____ rather than show a dramatic rise is that four out of six children died before they reached the age of 5.

7. Never underestimate the costs _____ in starting a new business.

H. 문맥상 빈칸에 들어갈 가장 적절한 단어를 찾아 넣으시오.   #089

1.
| incessant   form   designed   kept |

The gas is processed into a liquid ① _____ of hydrogen that must be ② _____ at a(n) ③ _____ temperature of minus 253 degrees Celsius in specially ④ _____ containers.

2.
| drive   attempt   travel   burdensome   according |

① _____ to him, if it becomes too ② _____ to constantly use expensive commodities, the first thing people will do is ③ _____ to use them economically. For example, people will not ④ _____ their cars to ⑤ _____ a short distance.

I. 다음 밑줄 친 우리말을 영어로 바꾸어 보기에 주어진 단어나 어구를 활용하여 또는 조건에 맞게 영작하시오. *필요시 어형을 변화할 것*

#090

1. 그들이 처음에 상상한 그 사회는 모두가 각자의 역량에 따라 일하는 사회였다. *envision 상상하다

   they initially envisioned / was a / which everyone would / their capacity / in / society / the society that / work _____ _____

2. 한 개인을 그의 또는 그녀의 너의 첫인상으로 판단하지 말아라.

   him or her / judge / a / of / don't / your first _____ / on / person

3. 어떤 반대도 없다면, 나는 왜 그것이 전혀 위험하지 않는지를 설명하고 싶다. *barring ~이 없다면

   to / why / all / not / barring / like / it / _____ at / is / explain / any objections, I'd

4. 결혼에 대한 양식은 일반적으로 집값과 육아 비용에 의해 결정된다. *determine 결정하다

   _____ of marriage / generally determined / house prices and childcare costs / by / are

5. 그에 따르면, 도로와 전기가 가난한 나라의 사람들의 삶을 개선하는 데 있어 병원과 학교보다 훨씬 더 중요하다고 한다. *important in doing sth ~하는 데 있어 중요한 / improve 개선시키다

조건	다음 표현을 사용할 것: the lives of people in poor countries / roads and electricity / hospitals and schools in / much

6. 사람들은 정부가 아주 잘할 수 있는 유일한 것은 단지 사람들로부터 세금을 징수하는 것이라고 믿는다. *believe 믿다

조건	다음 표현을 사용할 것: taxes / just to / the only thing the government can do very well / that

7. 성 아우구스티누스처럼, 나는 우리가 아무런 불평도 없이 그들(부당한 법)을 준수하기보다 부당한 법을 거역할 도덕적 책임을 가지고 있지 않나 생각한다. *disobey 거역하다 / I would say (that) 나는 ~하지 않나 생각한다

조건	다음 표현을 사용할 것: Like Saint Augustine, I would say one / rather / unjust laws / any complaints / them / a moral responsibility / than

PRACTICE TEST (DAY 11)

A. 다음 단어의 뜻을 우리말로 쓰시오. #091

1. reflect on _____
2. secrete _____
3. shred _____
4. blot _____
5. shortcoming _____

B. 다음 우리말을 영어로 쓰시오. #092

1. 고의적인, 악의적인 _____
2. 야심 찬 _____
3. 열렬한 _____
4. 용광로 _____
5. 큰 덩어리 _____

C. 동의어를 찾아 연결하시오. #093

1. vigor ·
2. mean ·
3. pronounced ·
4. eventuate ·
5. count ·
6. delineate ·
7. distinction ·
8. roster ·

· (A) consider
· (B) describe
· (C) vitality
· (D) cruel
· (E) definite
· (F) result
· (G) difference
· (H) list

D. 반의어를 찾아 연결하시오. #094

1. successor ·
2. incidental ·
3. hesitant ·
4. appear ·

· (A) predecessor
· (B) fade
· (C) willing
· (D) basic

E. 문맥상 빈칸에 들어갈 가장 적절한 단어를 고르시오. #095

1. Mortgage payments are their greatest financial _____. *mortgage payments 담보 대출 이자
   (A) successor (B) roster (C) furnace (D) burden

2. The scientists discovered a dinosaur fossil _____ in rock.
   (A) reflected (B) delineated (C) blotted (D) embedded

3. The animal _____ much more than an average adult sea otter. *sea otter 해달
   (A) addressed (B) weighed (C) overrode (D) eventuated

4. He is to be _____ expelled from his political party.
   (A) perpetually (B) hesitantly (C) as well (D) especially

5. His new restaurant was _____ from the start.
   (A) close (B) conscious (C) hesitant (D) doomed

6. One of my professors provided an article on the technique of _____ nuclear reactors from overheating to a scientific journal.
   (A) blotting (B) preventing (C) characterizing (D) naming

F. 다음 글을 읽고 밑줄 친 단어의 동의어를 고르시오. #096

1. The kid has the potential to become an opera singer.
   (A) parity (B) desire (C) promise (D) defect

2. The symptoms don't appear immediately.
   (A) emerge (B) matter (C) deteriorate (D) vanish

3. Consumers are increasingly conscious of organic produce.
   (A) senseless (B) aware (C) subsidiary (D) authentic

4. Other species, especially fish, have to compete with zebra mussels for plankton, an important source of food for fish.
   (A) permanently (B) otherwise (C) except for (D) particularly

5. People are not hesitant to act unethically if they can make money. *unethically 비윤리적으로
   (A) novel (B) voluntary (C) spontaneous (D) reluctant

6. As the world is becoming more globalized, the ability to speak and write in more than one language is becoming important <u>as well</u>.
   (A) also   (B) wholly   (C) overall   (D) at once

7. I was going back to Canada for a week, and it <u>coincided</u> with my friend's visit to Canada.
   (A) outweighed   (B) synchronized   (C) was acquainted   (D) disagreed

8. Recent environmental issues have threatened the ecology of wetlands. If these issues are not <u>addressed</u>, the areas may disappear.
   (A) decorated   (B) modified   (C) evaluated   (D) dealt with

9. A recent opinion poll shows that the Democratic Party's popularity has greatly <u>declined</u> because of their failure to stabilize house prices.
   (A) subjugated   (B) decreased   (C) burgeoned   (D) engulfed

10. One problem with using online encyclopedias as a primary source of information is that the <u>original</u> articles are prone to revisions by malicious hackers. *prone ~하기 쉬운 / revision 수정 / malicious 악의적인
    (A) genuine   (B) accessible   (C) marked   (D) counterfeit

11. The presidential veto can be <u>overridden</u> by Congress with a two-thirds vote in both the House and the Senate.
    (A) imposed   (B) emulated   (C) recommended   (D) canceled

12. A cynical view of human nature is <u>pervasive</u> in his early works.
    (A) inauspicious   (B) mighty   (C) isolated   (D) widespread

13. As weird as her crying <u>appeared</u>, Montag expected her to still feel the same way that he did, so it shocked him to hear that she would not see him anymore.
    (A) elongated   (B) seemed   (C) synchronized   (D) arrived

14. The government should first pay regard to the basic needs of individuals such as issues related to their livelihood; bread <u>overrides</u> ideology.
    (A) bolsters   (B) follows   (C) proceeds   (D) outweighs

15. The law to <u>prevent</u> the introduction of any non-native animals is of great concern to some pet owners because they have to worry about restrictions placed on their animal.
    (A) stop   (B) outline   (C) suspend   (D) precede

16. A widely held theory is that Siberian natives killed so many sea cows that the animals were <u>doomed</u> to extinction.
    (A) ill-fated   (B) subordinate   (C) ardent   (D) unprecedented

G. 문맥상 빈칸에 들어갈 가장 적절한 단어를 찾아 넣으시오. #097

| as well | close | routine | weigh | burden | inflict | destined | appearance |

1. The sea cow was _____ to be extinct.

2. If you don't wish to see me anymore, I'll never contact you again. I don't want to place a(n) _____ on you.

3. Another advantage of hydroelectric dams is their environmental friendliness. Hydroelectric dams do not _____ harm on the environment.

4. But as time passes, you will definitely become bored with the monotonous _____ of life in the countryside.

5. Since she doesn't want to feel self-conscious about her _____, she is considering an operation to enlarge her breasts. *self-conscious about sth ~에 대해서 남의 시선을 의식하는

6. There was so much traffic on the road that we came _____ to missing our flight at the airport.

7. This additional cost will get passed on to them _____.

8. Gulf sturgeons are fish that grow to a length of 7 feet and _____ up to 90 kilograms. They spend the winter in the Gulf of Mexico and spend the summer near coastal rivers in Florida.

H. 문맥상 빈칸에 들어갈 가장 적절한 단어를 찾아 넣으시오. #098

1.
| blaming | dying | doomed | unreasonable |

① _____ the fur traders for the extinction of the species is therefore ② _____. They may have sped up the process of sea cows ③ _____ out, but the sea cows were clearly already ④ _____.

2.
| conducting | spraying | substances | experiments | preventing |

Many countries in Asia are ① _____ a large number of different ② _____ with cloud seeding, which is a solution for ③ _____ the formation of hail by ④ _____ ⑤ _____ into the air. *cloud seeding 구름씨 뿌리기(인공적으로 비나 눈을 내리게 하는 방법)

I. 다음 밑줄 친 우리말을 영어로 바꾸어 보기에 주어진 단어나 어구를 활용하여 또는 조건에 맞게 영작하시오. *필요시 어형을 변화할 것

#099

1. 컴퓨터는 때때로 도움이 되기보다는 <u>방해</u>가 된다.

   more / help / a / are sometimes / a / of / than / _____ / computers

2. 취업을 <u>목적</u>으로 나는 영어를 다시 배우고 있다.

   English again / the _____ / learning / for / getting a job, I am / of

3. 그 아이는 음악에 큰 <u>잠재력</u>을 가지고 있다.

   great / in / the kid / music / _____ / has

4. 백신을 맞은 사람들의 수가 점진적으로 감소할 것이라는 가능성은 <u>특히</u> 정부에게 걱정스러운 일이다.
   *worrisome 걱정스러운

   people getting vaccines / the / _____ worrisome for / of / is the possibility / decline / the government / will progressively / number / that

5. 그 나라는 상환이 연기되어야 한다고 요청했지만, 국제 통화 기금(IMF)은 이를 <u>거절했다</u>. *repayment 상환 / postpone 연기하다 / request 요청

   a / request / the repayment / that / _____ it _____ / made / postponed, but the International Monetary Fund (IMF) / the country / be

6. 금융 위기는 종종 실물 경제 악화와 동시에 일어난다.

> deterioration in the real economy / with / a financial crisis / often _____

7. 발굴 과정에서 개인 화석 수집가들은 바위에 박혀 있는 화석들을 손상시킬 수 있다.

> excavation / _____ / private fossil collectors / the process / fossils / damage / rocks in / of / can / in

8. 이것은 인터넷에서 사람들이 새롭고 창의적인 아이디어를 공유하는 것을 막는다. *share 공유하다

| 조건 | 다음 표현을 사용할 것: this / new and creative ideas on |

9. 비록 그는 그 역경을 물리치려고 많이 노력했지만, 그는 사람이 살 수 없는 황무지 행성인 화성에서 굶어 죽을 운명에 처했다. *beat 물리치다 / the odds 역경 / try 노력하다 / starve to death 굶어 죽다

| 조건 | ① Much as he (으)로 문장을 시작할 것
② 다음 표현을 사용할 것: Mars, an uninhabitable wasteland planet |

10. 포드 자동차 회사(the Ford Motor Company)는 조립 라인으로부터 이익을 얻었을 뿐만 아니라 그것을 채택한 많은 다른 자동차 회사들도 역시 생산성의 상당한 증가를 경험했다. *benefit from sth ~로부터 이익을 얻다 / adopt 채택하다 / experience 경험하다

| 조건 | ① Not only (으)로 문장을 시작할 것
② 다음 표현을 사용할 것: productivity as / increase / the assembly line, but many other car companies / a / that / it / significant / in |

PRACTICE TEST (DAY 12)

A. 다음 단어의 뜻을 우리말로 쓰시오. #100

1. embody _____
2. magnitude _____
3. skeleton _____
4. adhere _____
5. mediocre _____

B. 다음 우리말을 영어로 쓰시오. #101

1. 서체 _____
2. 바르기, 살포 _____
3. 인물 _____
4. 분석하다 _____
5. 올라타다 _____

C. 동의어를 찾아 연결하시오. #102

1. compliment · · (A) go well with
2. high · · (B) thrive
3. prosper · · (C) terrified
4. complement · · (D) sicken
5. procure · · (E) obtain
6. disgust · · (F) ecstasy
7. petrified · · (G) commend
8. narrow · · (H) taper

D. 반의어를 찾아 연결하시오. #103

1. prosperous · · (A) tiny
2. sizable · · (B) unusual
3. true · · (C) poor
4. ordinary · · (D) false

E. 문맥상 빈칸에 들어갈 가장 적절한 단어를 고르시오. #104

1. Excuse me, can you stop biting your nails? It's _____ me from my studies.
   (A) procuring (B) distracting (C) embodying (D) complementing

2. I didn't go on vacation on the _____ that it is too expensive.
   (A) expeditions (B) bounds (C) pillars (D) grounds

3. I saw a _____ of smoke on the horizon, caused by the riots in the next town.
   (A) skeleton (B) pillar (C) category (D) conflict

4. With _____ to my earlier comment, I think that we should sell more stocks.
   (A) ground (B) magnitude (C) zone (D) respect

5. Companies can _____ higher prices by advertising the goods and services they produce.
   (A) snatch (B) spot (C) charge (D) compliment

6. The Crusades were a series of military _____ carried out by Christian countries to try to take control of the Holy Land from the Muslims. *expedition 원정 / the Holy Land 성지
   (A) expeditions (B) skeletons (C) zones (D) bounds

F. 다음 글을 읽고 밑줄 친 단어의 동의어를 고르시오. #105

1. Desertification <u>occurs as a result of</u> global warming.
   (A) worsens (B) results in (C) results from (D) accelerates

2. Video games <u>distract</u> children from their homework.
   (A) stimulate (B) divert (C) taper (D) buffer

3. You should try to be on good terms with your co-workers rather than sow the seeds of <u>conflict</u> among them.
   (A) strife (B) confidence (C) deference (D) closeness

4. <u>Refrain</u> from screaming and making other loud noises.
   (A) Promote (B) Duplicate (C) Guard (D) Desist

5. Parasites <u>fixed</u> on the external surface of a host are less harmful to the host than internal parasites.
   (A) repaired (B) acute (C) attached (D) communal

6. While it is true that the menhaden is an important source of protein for livestock and poultry, it is not the only <u>available</u> protein. *menhaden (물고기) 청어

   (A) addicted (B) well-off (C) nutritional (D) obtainable

7. The United States remains <u>guarded</u> over the impact of the compromise agreement made between the two Koreas.

   (A) cautious (B) lucrative (C) flexible (D) reluctant

8. For the utility of education, the chairman <u>demanded</u> that practical skills like rice cultivation be taught at schools.

   (A) acknowledged (B) required (C) notified (D) dictated

9. I do hope that someday the videos I post on my YouTube channel will allow me to make <u>practically</u> limitless amounts of money.

   (A) virtually (B) surprisingly (C) regularly (D) presumably

10. Hippies in the mid-1960s wore odd clothes and used a lot of slang words. They refused to accept all the things that they thought were <u>ordinary</u>.

    (A) eerie (B) normal (C) priceless (D) peculiar

11. The Korean demilitarized <u>zone</u> called DMZ symbolizes the division between North and South Korea. *demilitarized 비무장의

    (A) clash (B) sanctuary (C) boundary (D) region

12. When a defect was <u>spotted</u> on their assembly lines, the whole production process had to be stopped until it was corrected.

    (A) noticed (B) examined (C) amended (D) altered

13. I have reasonable <u>grounds</u> for believing that the poor cannot access some of the important information online, thereby reducing their ability to escape poverty.

    (A) fractures (B) scopes (C) doubts (D) reasons

14. In 1905 he graduated from college, and in the years that ensued, he planned an <u>expedition</u> to the North Pole.

    (A) clash (B) freight (C) exploration (D) anchor

15. They show great <u>respect</u> for former President Harrison, who committed suicide in 2009.

    (A) deference (B) vestige (C) heir (D) favor

16. The professor uses Caribbean nations, which sell raw materials cheaply to <u>wealthy</u> countries and buy expensive manufactured goods from them in return, as an example to corroborate dependence theory.

    (A) tentative (B) prosperous (C) unparalleled (D) impoverished

G. 문맥상 빈칸에 들어갈 가장 적절한 단어를 찾아 넣으시오. #106

| available   as such   rival   respect   distract   result   true   distance |

1. He walked quite a long _____ to get to a soup kitchen.

2. The World Health Organization wants developed countries to make COVID vaccines universally _____ and distribute them globally.

3. With _____ to the cost of generating energy, hydroelectric dams are cost-efficient.

4. A fractured tooth can _____ from chewing on hard foods such as nuts. *fracture 부러뜨리다

5. Kakaotalk and YouTube _____ students from their studies.

6. Literature can help in the development of intellectual stimulation, and this is particularly _____ for young people who don't read much literature.

7. For example, they add additives to kids' foods like candies to create bright white colors. _____, you should be careful to read the ingredients listed on food labels.

8. Samson has a ton of _____ companies, all competing fiercely against Samson for customers.

H. 문맥상 빈칸에 들어갈 가장 적절한 단어를 찾아 넣으시오. #107

1.
| damaged   disgust   show   allowed |

Advertisements showing the dangers of smoking should be ① _____, although sometimes these ads ② _____ images that ③ _____ people, such as lungs ④ _____ by smoking.

2.
| size   gigantic   precisely   prey   clumsy |

An interesting thing is, the ① _____ ② _____ of the wings would have made the bird too ③ _____ to catch things in the air and would have also made it difficult for the bird to catch ④ _____ on the ground ⑤ _____.

I. 다음 밑줄 친 우리말을 영어로 바꾸어 보기에 주어진 단어나 어구를 활용하여 또는 조건에 맞게 영작하시오. *필요시 어형을 변화할 것

#108

1. 그는 그녀를 만나는 것을 <u>자제했는</u>데 왜냐하면 그는 그것이 잘못되었다는 것을 알았기 때문이다.

   wrong / from / was / her, because he / _____ / it / he / knew / meeting

2. 우리 아버지는 만약 내가 자전거에서 떨어지면 크게 다칠 수도 있다는 <u>이유(근거)</u> 때문에 내가 자전거 타는 것을 그만두게 했다. *discourage 그만두게 하다

   fell / me / that I might get / off / my dad / riding a bike on / the _____ / it / discouraged / severely injured if I / from

3. 당시 의사들은 환자의 상처가 감염되는 것을 막을 수 없었는데 왜냐하면 페니실린 같은 항생제들이 아직 <u>구할 수 있는</u> 것이 아니었다. *prevent 막다

   antibiotics like penicillin / prevent / at that time, doctors / yet _____ / were / getting infected because / not / from / patients' wounds / could not

4. 미국의 많은 사람들은 마스크 의무화에 대해 <u>존중하지</u> 않는다.

   | 조건 | 다음 표현을 사용할 것: many people in America / no / the mask mandate / showed |

5. 그 독재자는 그의 권력 남용으로부터 주의(관심)를 딴 데로 돌리기 위해 스포츠를 사용했다. *use 사용하다

   조건 다음 표현을 사용할 것: the dictator / sports / the abuses of his dictatorship / attention

6. 그는 중동에서의 갈등들을 중재하려고 노력했다. *mediate 중재하다 / try 노력하다

   조건 다음 표현을 사용할 것: the Middle East

7. 고주파 음파는 더 많은 에너지를 가지고 있어서 그들은 매우 넓은 거리들을 이동할 수 있다. *large 넓은

   조건 다음 표현을 사용할 것: high-frequency sound waves /, so that / very large

8. 실험 중에 알파벳순으로 기록된 데이터도 마찬가지다. *order 순서 / experiment 실험 / record 기록하다 / alphabetical 알파벳의

   조건 다음 표현을 사용할 것: an / data recorded in / goes / order during / the same

PRACTICE TEST (DAY 13)

A. 다음 단어의 뜻을 우리말로 쓰시오.   #109

1. coax _____
2. sneak _____
3. incisive _____
4. amiable _____
5. bold _____

B. 다음 우리말을 영어로 쓰시오.   #110

1. 방, 실 _____
2. (곤충 등이) 쏘다 _____
3. 해체(분해)되다 _____
4. 단계, 시점 _____
5. 동시에 일어나는 _____

C. 동의어를 찾아 연결하시오.   #111

1. response   · (A) wealth
2. affluence   · (B) stop
3. adjoin   · (C) be next to
4. halt   · (D) go ahead
5. inquire   · (E) arduous
6. proceed   · (F) temporary
7. provisional   · (G) investigate
8. strenuous   · (H) reaction

D. 반의어를 찾아 연결하시오.   #112

1. hatred   · (A) detach
2. attach   · (B) unreliable
3. obvious   · (C) unclear
4. dependable   · (D) love

E. 문맥상 빈칸에 들어갈 가장 적절한 단어를 고르시오. #113

1. When you're out doing exercise like jogging on a day when fine dust concentration _____ are severe, you have to wear a mask. *be out doing sth 밖에서 ~하다 / concentration 농도

   (A) levels (B) poses (C) features (D) chambers

2. A drunken man in a pub _____ to death on a peanut.

   (A) stung (B) coaxed (C) adjoined (D) choked

3. Humans often fail to make rational choices. This tendency has _____ as economic bubbles in history.

   (A) emerged (B) snuck (C) halted (D) hailed

4. He was _____ as a Supreme Court judicial candidate.

   (A) selected (B) exacerbated (C) amiable (D) incisive

5. The axe has blades made of stone with grooves on the surface used to _____ the head to a wooden handle.

   (A) proceed (B) halt (C) attach (D) cling

6. Susan B. Anthony, who enthusiastically supported the abolition of slavery, was famous for _____ passionate anti-slavery speeches.

   (A) delivering (B) adjoining (C) emerging (D) disintegrating

F. 다음 글을 읽고 밑줄 친 단어의 동의어를 고르시오. #114

1. The level of blood sugar drops if you take insulin or other diabetes medications.

   (A) amount (B) blaze (C) flair (D) gulf

2. He deliberately mocks politicians by copying the way they behave and speak.

   (A) aggravates (B) reveres (C) makes fun of (D) slaughters

3. Sarcasm is typical of British humor.

   (A) apparent (B) devoid (C) aware (D) archetypal

4. One of the common design features of the orb web of the spider is its effectiveness in catching prey. Otherwise, this web design would not be so widely seen in so many different species of spider.

   (A) characteristics (B) distinctions (C) advantages (D) flaws

5. It is not easy to find someone <u>dependable</u> to take care of my kids.
   (A) alternate (B) reliable (C) barbaric (D) deserted

6. A new approach <u>emerged</u> in the late 1960s as a new anthropological means of interpretation of culture.
   (A) paid heed (B) vanished (C) suffocated (D) transpired

7. The city was destroyed by floods, causing the <u>entire</u> population to move to higher ground.
   (A) fearless (B) whole (C) minute (D) timid

8. The incident resulted in increasing <u>hatred</u> for the Japanese.
   (A) abhorrence (B) compassion (C) affection (D) collaboration

9. Height restriction laws will <u>exacerbate</u> the housing shortage problem in big cities.
   (A) aggregate (B) aggravate (C) alienate (D) encounter

10. It is quite <u>plain</u> that making those who cheat while doing their homework repeat the same grade the next year will be most effective in reducing the number of students who try to cheat.
    (A) obvious (B) meticulous (C) anomalous (D) temporary

11. The professor explained our independence from Japan and its effects on the Korean economy in <u>pretty</u> much the same way as my high school history teachers did except that the professor's lecture was more boring.
    (A) spectacularly (B) somewhat (C) fairly (D) otherwise

12. Due to the severe air pollution during the Industrial Revolution, white-colored peppered moths started to perish because they were <u>obvious</u> to predators such as birds when they tried to hide on trees blackened by pollution.
    (A) pungent (B) inimical (C) clear (D) subjected

13. If anyone could transform lead into gold, what would happen to gold? In his <u>view</u>, it would decline in value.
    (A) perspective (B) defect (C) roster (D) abhorrence

14. A leading manufacturer of cookware invented a coating material that prevents cooked foods from <u>clinging</u> to pans, and it was a substance that the company knew how to produce.
    (A) appeasing (B) blotting (C) adjoining (D) sticking

15. The boy prepared some funny stories to <u>relate</u> when he was left alone with the merchant's daughter.
    (A) enumerate (B) tell (C) formulate (D) connect

16. Warmer waters in the ocean stress corals, forcing the algae that live in their tissue and give them <u>vibrant</u> color to leave.
    (A) scrupulous (B) brilliant (C) nimble (D) drab

G. 문맥상 빈칸에 들어갈 가장 적절한 단어를 찾아 넣으시오. *필요시 어형을 변화할 것 / 같은 단어 두 번 사용 가능 #115

| relate | mere | deliver | direction | nuisance | level | way | as of |

1. Studies show that a fall in interest rates is _____ to an increase in real estate prices.
2. His car crashed into a truck that was driving in the opposite _____.
3. Reducing the _____ of fine dust in the air will cost a lot of money.
4. It's such a _____ having to recycle.
5. We need to build the tower in a _____ that doesn't block the skyline.
6. The shock wave came _____ minutes after the initial earthquake. *shock wave (지진으로 인한) 충격파
7. _____ today, all employees who work at recycling centers must wear protective equipment, like thick gloves.
8. You can have the groceries you buy _____ to your door.
9. She traveled across the country _____ lectures about equal rights for women.
10. The epic poem was written by James Lee to _____ the deeds of heroes.

H. 문맥상 빈칸에 들어갈 가장 적절한 단어를 찾아 넣으시오. #116

1.
| advancement | fact | nuisance | contacted |

The ① _____ of smartphone technology can be a ② _____ due to the ③ _____ that we can be ④ _____ by our bosses at any time in the day, or even on the weekend.

2.
| set | arise | problem | monitor | majority |

The professor admits that invasive species are a serious threat that should not be underestimated, but she also feels that the ① _____ of introduced species are not monitored after people ② _____ them free in their new environment. So she concludes that if people ③ _____ introduced species well, the ④ _____ of introduced species becoming invasive will not ⑤ _____.

I. 다음 밑줄 친 우리말을 영어로 바꾸어 보기에 주어진 단어나 어구를 활용하여 또는 조건에 맞게 영작하시오. *필요시 어형을 변화할 것

#117

1. 그는 반대쪽 <u>방향</u>을 가리켰다.

   the / he / opposite / _____ / in / pointed

2. 나는 공증인에 의해 서명된 서류를 <u>첨부</u>했다. *notary 공증인 / sign 서명하다

   the document / _____ / by / I've / the notary / signed

3. 그녀의 혈액 속의 나트륨은 정상 <u>수준</u>으로 떨어졌다. *sodium 나트륨

   _____ / the sodium / normal / in / has / to / a / dropped / her blood

4. 핵무기로 인한 파괴에 대한 우리의 이해에 대한 그의 공헌은 우리가 과학을 바라보는 <u>방식</u>을 완전히 바꾸어 놓았다.

   the / nuclear weapons / looked / caused / _____ we / our understanding / completely changed / to / the destruction / science / his contribution / by / at / of

5. 초대받지 않은 사람이 우리 집에 있다는 <u>단순한</u> 생각만으로도 나를 공포로 떨게 만든다.

   fear / someone / the _____ thought / shiver with / of / me / being in my home uninvited makes

6. 만성 스트레스와 <u>마찬가지로</u>, 지속적인 피로 증후군(CFS)는 일상 활동과 사회적 상호 작용을 방해한다.
   *chronic 만성적인 / interfere with sth ~을 방해하다

조건	다음 표현을 사용할 것: constant fatigue syndrome (CFS) / daily activities and social interactions

7. 추적 장치를 몸에 <u>부착함</u>으로써 대형 동물을 감시하는 것은 가능하다. *monitor 감시하다

조건	다음 표현을 사용할 것: it / large animals / a tracking device / their bodies / possible / to

8. 요즘 주부들은 그들이 예전에 했던 만큼 자주 식료품을 사러 밖에 나가지 않는다; 그들은 식료품을 집으로 <u>배달받을 뿐이다</u>. *go out to do sth ~하러 밖에 나가다 / often 자주

조건	다음 표현을 사용할 것: housewives nowadays / buy groceries as / they once did; they just have / their homes / their groceries / don't

9. 그 부족의 지도자들은 그들에게 <u>제물들</u>을 바침으로써 그들의 신들에게 도움을 청했다. *invoke (신에게) 도움을 청하다 / offer 바치다

조건	다음 표현을 사용할 것: the leaders of the tribe invoked / their gods / to them

10. 일부 과학자들은 유전자 변형 작물을 개발하자는 정부의 제안을 <u>높이 평가하지만</u>, 최근에 설문 조사된 과학자들의 25퍼센트는 유전자 변형 작물은 규제받지 않는 상태로 방치되면 생태계에 심각한 위협을 가할 수 있다고 말했다. *say 말하다 / survey 설문 조사하다 / develop 개발하다 / leave (어떤 상태로) 방치하다 / pose a threat 위협을 가하다 / serious 심각한 / unregulated 규제받지 않는

조건	다음 표현을 사용할 것: while some scientists / the government's proposal to / genetically modified crops (GM crops), 25 percent of scientists recently surveyed / serious / ecosystems if left / GM crops / that

PRACTICE TEST (DAY 14)

A. 다음 단어의 뜻을 우리말로 쓰시오.   #118

1. animated _____
2. comprehend _____
3. dismantle _____
4. expansion _____
5. maneuver _____

B. 다음 우리말을 영어로 쓰시오.   #119

1. 무생물의, 죽은 _____
2. 조작하다 _____
3. 성격, 성미 _____
4. 고리 _____
5. (정당의) 강령 _____

C. 동의어를 찾아 연결하시오.   #120

1. at once
2. firmly
3. consecutive
4. inconsequential
5. obstinate
6. strict
7. fling
8. permit

- (A) sequential
- (B) insignificant
- (C) allow
- (D) stubborn
- (E) steadfastly
- (F) concurrently
- (G) hurl
- (H) stringent

D. 반의어를 찾아 연결하시오.   #121

1. reject
2. slight
3. strict
4. discrepancy

- (A) lenient
- (B) big
- (C) accept
- (D) correspondence

E. 문맥상 빈칸에 들어갈 가장 적절한 단어를 고르시오. #122

1. He moved to the U.S. for the _____ of his children's education.
   (A) sake (B) aftermath (C) discrepancy (D) incident

2. Different _____ such as light and touch, are responsible for the movement of plants; for example, sunflowers crane their necks to face the sun.
   (A) maneuvers (B) stimuli (C) expansions (D) odors

3. You will find it _____ to wear those shoes because they have rubber soles with air cushions.
   (A) consecutive (B) meticulous (C) comfortable (D) obstinate

4. Many scientists _____ the fur traders for the extinction of sea cows.
   (A) blame (B) allow (C) credit (D) dismantle

5. Korean people do not expect _____ between Korea and Japan to improve.
   (A) tempers (B) platforms (C) relations (D) discrepancies

6. Luckily, the kids are having no trouble _____ to their new school.
   (A) adjusting (B) manipulating (C) striving (D) flinging

F. 다음 글을 읽고 밑줄 친 단어의 동의어를 고르시오. #123

1. His son fled from Korea to the U.S. right after the incident happened.
   (A) episode (B) fragrance (C) adversity (D) hunger

2. Bad weather hampered rescue efforts to find the missing boy.
   (A) perceived (B) hindered (C) dramatized (D) facilitated

3. Scientists in the past went to prison for proposing theories that were hostile to the teachings of the Catholic Church.
   (A) antagonistic (B) detrimental (C) baffling (D) tolerable

4. Sometimes, introducing new species can result in negative consequences, so the government is considering a law to restrict importing, buying, and selling of non-native species of animals.
   (A) curtail (B) hamper (C) control (D) retard

5. After several months of <u>meticulous</u> planning and preparation, the company decided to open a computer chip factory in Vietnam.
   (A) desperate (B) relentless (C) inimical (D) thorough

6. The receptor cells that dogs have in their noses are so keen that they can sense many different <u>odors</u>.
   (A) rostrums (B) reactions (C) smells (D) senses

7. Animals <u>adjust</u> to their surrounding environments only when it gives them some kind of advantage.
   (A) correspond (B) rely on (C) adapt (D) adopt

8. Advances in medical science have <u>enabled</u> scientists to discover drugs that could extend the human lifespan.
   (A) impelled (B) allowed (C) encouraged (D) evoked

9. If there is heavy rain, most of the rain that falls on the roof of a building covered with shrubs and small trees doesn't get <u>soaked up</u> and just stays there, causing the drainage system to become blocked.
   (A) dried (B) used up (C) exhausted (D) absorbed

10. There's a lot of evidence telling us that the claims of those who argue against the preservation of historic buildings might be somewhat <u>exaggerated</u>.
    (A) contradicted (B) underrated (C) falsified (D) overstated

11. Men in the 1960s wore suits in muted colors such as black and navy, just like businessmen today. There is only a <u>slight</u> difference in the width of the jacket lapels. *muted 밝지 않은 / lapel 접은 옷깃
    (A) pristine (B) overt (C) implicit (D) small

12. And third, while it's certainly true that foreign outsourcing is giving work that was <u>previously</u> done domestically to countries where labor costs are low, it's incorrect to say it threatens domestic employees.
    (A) steadfastly (B) elaborately (C) before (D) prohibitively

13. No one could stop the rumor that Jews had caused the plague to stop <u>circulating</u>.
    (A) concurring (B) annihilating (C) bursting (D) spreading

14. Jonathan Fuller, a main character in his novel, is a father who <u>strives</u> to survive during the Great Depression of the 1930s in the U.S.
    (A) struggles (B) saps (C) abhors (D) bothers

15. One of the most <u>puzzling</u> aspects of reading Shakespeare's plays is the archaic language.
    (A) conducive (B) baffling (C) painstaking (D) intriguing

16. The suicide bomb attack in the Afghan capital was carried out by a religiously <u>inspired</u> terrorist organization.
    (A) suppressed (B) hustled (C) encouraged (D) thwarted

G. 문맥상 빈칸에 들어갈 가장 적절한 단어를 찾아 넣으시오. *필요시 어형을 변화할 것 / 같은 단어 두 번 사용 가능 #124

| genuine | allow | credit | previously | responsibility | blame | company | hostile |

1. In recent years, many Korean people have been _____ to the Japanese government.

2. You should apologize _____ to her.

3. He wants others to be as unhappy as he is. He hates the _____ of others.

4. Germany had no choice but to take full _____ for the war and pay heavy reparations to the Allied powers. *the Allied powers 연합국

5. The optical device that Galileo constructed _____ for many new discoveries in astronomy.

6. The U.S. waged war on Spain, assuming that Spain was to _____ for the explosion of the battleship. *wage war on sb ~와 전쟁을 벌이다

7. Captain Sully is _____ with saving all the 155 passengers on board when he landed the plane in the Hudson River.

8. _____, I had worked part-time in a bar in downtown Manhattan.

9. Neurons are interconnected by junctions, called synapses, _____ them to send and receive electrical signals.

H. 문맥상 빈칸에 들어갈 가장 적절한 단어를 찾아 넣으시오. #125

1.

| build | make | manipulate | matter |

As a ① _____ of fact, real-estate developers ② _____ local public opinion and ③ _____ it seem as if most residents really want to ④ _____ new towns with modernized commercial facilities.

2.

| affect | are | restrict | contain |

Some comic books whose characters ① _____ detectives like Dick Tracy or action heroes like Batman could ② _____ harmful content such as violence and horror that may ③ _____ children. That is why governments need to ④ _____ their content.

I. 다음 밑줄 친 우리말을 영어로 바꾸어 보기에 주어진 단어나 어구를 활용하여 또는 조건에 맞게 영작하시오. *필요시 어형을 변화할 것

#126

1. 때때로 우리는 <u>불쾌한</u> 진실에 직면한다. *encounter 직면하다

   truths / sometimes we / _____ / encounter

2. 그 나라는 지진의 <u>여파</u>로 기근과 질병에 직면하고 있다.

   is / the earthquake / _____ / the country / of / facing / the / famine and disease in

3. 외국과의 무역을 금지한 그 법률은 미국인들에게 그들 자신의 제품을 생산하도록 <u>고무시켰다</u>. *Act 법률

   produce their / with / the Act, which / goods / to / own / Americans / foreign countries, _____ / prohibited trade

4. 그 법률은 정부 기관이 보유하고 있는 어떠한 정보도 개인이 볼 수 있도록 <u>허용한다</u>. *see 보다 / hold 보유하다

   | 조건 | 다음 표현을 사용할 것: that / the Act / a person / government organizations / any |

5. 콘크리트가 비가 땅속으로 스며드는 것을 막았다. *stop 막다

   조건 다음 표현을 사용할 것: the ground / the rain / the concrete / into / from

6. 그는 끈이 풀리지 않도록 케이크 상자에 끈을 단단히(꽉) 묶었다. *tie 묶다 / come loose 풀리다

   조건 다음 표현을 사용할 것: the cake box so / a string / the string wouldn't

7. 내 인생에서 내가 잊고 싶은 한 가지 사건(사고)은 내 결혼 피로연에서 완전히 취해 버린 나의 전처에 의해 일어난 소동이다. *forget 잊다 / disturbance 소동 / cause 일으키다 / completely 완전히

   조건 다음 표현을 사용할 것: an / my life that / I'd like / the disturbance caused /, at my wedding banquet / was / by my ex-wife, who

8. 현대의 피임약은 부부가 임신에 대해 걱정하지 않고 성관계를 가지는 것을 가능하게 한다. *worry about sb/sth ~에 대해 걱정하다 / have sex 성관계를 가지다 / pregnancy 임신

   조건 다음 표현을 사용할 것: modern contraceptives / couples / without

9. 비즈니스 복장은 종종 불편하다. 그래서 많은 회사들이 직원들에게 직장에서 그들이 입고 싶어 하는 것을 결정하게 해 준다. *let ~하게 해 주다 / decide 결정하다 / want 싶어 하다

   조건 다음 표현을 사용할 것: why / business clothes / what / that's / wear at work / their employees / often / many companies

PRACTICE TEST (DAY 15)

A. 다음 단어의 뜻을 우리말로 쓰시오.   #127

1. in the first place _____
2. definitive _____
3. prowess _____
4. peak _____
5. retention _____

B. 다음 우리말을 영어로 쓰시오.   #128

1. 성역 _____
2. 시위하다 _____
3. 치수, 크기 _____
4. 요소, 원소 _____
5. 믿기 힘든 _____

C. 동의어를 찾아 연결하시오.   #129

1. monotonous ·   · (A) dedicated
2. plentiful ·   · (B) console
3. indecipherable ·   · (C) dull
4. by mistake ·   · (D) summon
5. cite ·   · (E) accidently
6. soothe ·   · (F) abundant
7. committed ·   · (G) disappoint
8. dismay ·   · (H) illegible

D. 반의어를 찾아 연결하시오.   #130

1. admire ·   · (A) explicit
2. withdrawal ·   · (B) despise
3. obscure ·   · (C) deposit
4. public ·   · (D) private

E. 문맥상 빈칸에 들어갈 가장 적절한 단어를 고르시오. #131

1. The Roman Empire _____ from England to Egypt.
   (A) manifested   (B) extended   (C) prompted   (D) dismayed

2. Seoul City has mandated that citizens must wear masks on _____ transport, including buses, subways, and taxis, starting on the second of March. *mandate 명령하다
   (A) vague   (B) definitive   (C) incredulous   (D) public

3. Sometimes elderly people find it difficult to _____ programs or applications on their mobile phones.
   (A) alleviate   (B) install   (C) constitute   (D) soothe

4. One of the most important and _____ ways to strengthen the immune system is to do physical exercise.
   (A) essential   (B) incredulous   (C) indecipherable   (D) attributable

5. Her intelligence and wisdom were _____ in how she lived her life.
   (A) manifested   (B) cited   (C) withdrew   (D) subjected

6. A damaged reactor in the nuclear power plant was _____ to the earthquake.
   (A) convenient   (B) definite   (C) attributable   (D) annual

F. 다음 글을 읽고 밑줄 친 단어의 동의어를 고르시오. #132

1. Good communication skills make people admire their leaders.
   (A) esteem   (B) ensue   (C) surpass   (D) pursue

2. But in single-stream recycling, families can just throw everything away in one bag. That's very convenient. So, more families are likely to participate.
   (A) aggravating   (B) easy   (C) efficient   (D) adjacent

3. If your ears are subjected to longs periods of loud noise, hearing loss can occur.
   (A) exposed   (B) hardened   (C) impounded   (D) observed

4. The essential difference between the pottery of the Southwest and that of the Northeast is that the former served a functional purpose, and the latter served an ornamental purpose.
   (A) fundamental   (B) necessary   (C) questionable   (D) spacious

5. Free riding makes it more difficult for the group to produce efficient results. *free riding 무임승차
   (A) proliferate (B) summon (C) offset (D) create

6. The spider makes long sturdy spokes that radiate out from the center of the web. *spoke 바퀴살
   (A) steady (B) vulnerable (C) robust (D) weak

7. Apparently, a doctor's warning about the dangers of smoking prompted the leader to stop smoking.
   (A) provoked (B) contemplated (C) instructed (D) allowed

8. I relish the opportunity of working in the government.
   (A) orchestrate (B) acquire (C) overlook (D) enjoy

9. The sole purpose of the organization is to supervise and regulate banks.
   (A) fundamental (B) immune (C) only (D) sparse

10. I was able to alleviate my headache by taking some aspirin.
    (A) ease (B) highlight (C) magnify (D) exacerbate

11. Water constitutes about 71% of Earth's surface, while the other 29% consists of continents and islands.
    (A) ceases (B) makes up (C) curtails (D) concedes

12. Take Rome, for example, which was the greatest empire in European history. It extended from Spain to the Middle East.
    (A) stretched (B) esteemed (C) transformed (D) emigrated

13. Symptoms of the virus manifest themselves in a high fever 2-14 days after exposure.
    (A) credit (B) suffocate (C) disguise (D) appear

14. One of the possible reasons why the treasure might never have existed is that the supposed location of the treasure is vague.
    (A) obstinate (B) unclear (C) specific (D) mute

15. He embarked upon many more expeditions to the Arctic to find out how polar bears were surviving in the midst of the rapid decline of sea ice attributable to global warming.
    (A) adjoining to (B) convenient to (C) impeded by (D) caused by

16. The boy encountered two paths diverging in the woods.
    (A) came across (B) came up with (C) got over (D) went through

G. 문맥상 빈칸에 들어갈 가장 적절한 단어를 찾아 넣으시오. *필요시 어형을 변화할 것   #133

| extend lead mechanism sturdy well chance public bank |

1. We were lost. We arrived at a river. We found a small boat on the _____ of the river. We got in the boat.

2. Older women have a lower _____ of getting pregnant than young women.

3. Though, as of 2021, it ranked 16th highest in the world for national debt, the U.S. will remain a superpower because it has always taken the _____ in technology.

4. In Korea, most old couples don't show feelings of affection in _____.

5. The _____ in the middle of the village is running dry and will soon be abandoned so we should raise money for digging another one.

6. For example, the greatest empire in European history was Rome, and it _____ its control from Spain to the Middle East.

7. Al-Jazari appears to have been the first Islamic mechanical engineer to invent ingenious machines, many of which were automatic, including a hand washing device employing the _____ used in modern flush toilets.

8. Levi Strauss sold _____ pants to miners who came to California to dig for gold.

H. 문맥상 빈칸에 들어갈 가장 적절한 단어를 찾아 넣으시오. *필요시 어형을 변화할 것   #134

1.
| live inhabit demonstrate suggest |

There is no clear evidence to ① _____ that the English people who now ② _____ the country are descended from the tribes who ③ _____ there long before the Roman occupation, known as the Celts. Allow me to ④ _____.

2.
| dominate accept forced suggested believed |

It is widely ① _____ that teamwork will help team members come up with creative ideas. But in reality, this is not true. The reason for this is that one or two influential people in a group will ② _____ the group's decision making. Thus, group members will be ③ _____ to ④ _____ only the ideas that the leader has ⑤ _____.

I. 다음 밑줄 친 우리말을 영어로 바꾸어 보기에 주어진 단어나 어구를 활용하여 또는 조건에 맞게 영작하시오. *필요시 어형을 변화할 것* #135

1. 이 응급 처치 과정의 <u>목표</u>는 당신에게 어떻게 심폐 소생술을 올바르게 하는지를 가르치는 것이다. *first aid course 응급 처치 과정 / CPR 심폐 소생술

of / how / this first aid course / to / teach you / is / CPR correctly / do / to / the _____

2. 그는 그 비행기 추락 사고의 <u>유일한</u> 생존자이다.

the / is / survivor / _____ / the / of / crash / he / plane

3. 배낭이 바퀴가 있는 여행 가방보다 가지고 다니기에 더 <u>편리</u>하다.

more / are / carry than / _____ / backpacks / to / suitcases / wheels / with

4. 해로운 곤충들로 들끓을 수도 있는 죽은 나무들을 제거하는 것은 건강한 숲을 위해 <u>필수적</u>이다. *be infested with sth ~로 들끓다

for / that / is / dead trees / healthy forests / be infested with / removing / could / _____ / harmful bugs

5. 학생들이 많은 다양한 과목들을 들을 때, 그것은 그들에게 그들의 장단점을 발견할 수 있는 <u>기회</u>를 준다.
*discover 발견하다 / take (과목을) 듣다

조건	다음 표현을 사용할 것: many different subjects / gives them / a / it / their strengths and weaknesses

6. 비록 그 직원들은 부당한 대우를 <u>받는다고(당한다고)</u> 느꼈지만, 그들은 아무것도 하지 않았는데 왜냐하면 그들은 해고당하는 것이 두려웠기 때문이다. *unfair treatment 부당한 대우 / lay off sb ~을 해고하다 / afraid 두려워하는

조건	다음 표현을 사용할 것: being / although / the employees / felt / anything because / didn't

7. 대대수의 주민들은 범죄를 예방하기 위해 더 많은 가로등이 <u>설치될</u> 필요가 있다는 데 동의했다. *concur 동의하다 / prevent 예방하다

조건	다음 표현을 사용할 것: the vast majority of residents / that more street lights / needed / crime

8. <u>납</u>은 독성이 있는 금속이기 때문에, 만약 당신이 그것에 의해 오염된 음식을 먹으면, 심각한 건강상의 결과가 있을 수 있다. *toxic 독성이 있는 / eat 먹다 / contaminate 오염시키다 / serious 심각한

조건	다음 표현을 사용할 것: since / toxic metal, if you / health consequences / it, there / can / food contaminated

9. 마을 중앙에 마을 사람들이 식수를 얻을 수 있던 유일한 방법이었던 그 <u>우물</u>이 있었다. *get 얻다

조건	① In (으)로 문장을 시작할 것 ② 다음 표현을 사용할 것: the center of the village / , which was / the villagers / the only way / for / to / drinking water / was

PRACTICE TEST (DAY 16)

A. 다음 단어의 뜻을 우리말로 쓰시오.   #136

1. belittle _____
2. dispersal _____
3. denote _____
4. heyday _____
5. chip _____

B. 다음 우리말을 영어로 쓰시오.   #137

1. 말로, 구두로 _____
2. 도발 _____
3. 똑바른, 수직의 _____
4. 강점 _____
5. 익명의 _____

C. 동의어를 찾아 연결하시오.   #138

1. indifference · · (A) expected
2. forge · · (B) remarkable
3. predictable · · (C) omnipresent
4. ubiquitous · · (D) apathy
5. noteworthy · · (E) improve
6. hamstring · · (F) thwart
7. remedy · · (G) falsify
8. sorrow · · (H) grief

D. 반의어를 찾아 연결하시오.   #139

1. align · · (A) skew
2. expose · · (B) rare
3. continual · · (C) conceal
4. commonplace · · (D) sporadic

E. 문맥상 빈칸에 들어갈 가장 적절한 단어를 고르시오. #140

1. European kings tried to _____ new lands in the Americas.
   (A) hamstring (B) denote (C) align (D) claim

2. Several members in authority were dismissed from the chairman's office, one of whom was made the _____ for the split within the organization. *split 분열 / office 직
   (A) retrospect (B) dispersal (C) scapegoat (D) sorrow

3. A: Is there a _____ to how much money I can send to Canada in a year?
   B: There is no _____ to the amount you can transfer to a bank in a foreign country.
   (A) provocation (B) heyday (C) chip (D) limit

4. Don't miss the _____ to improve your English vocabulary.
   (A) well-being (B) opportunity (C) approach (D) dispersal

5. A financial crisis that starts in the U.S. could devastate the economy on a global _____.
   (A) sorrow (B) story (C) scale (D) scapegoat

6. Many scientists have _____ that sturgeons jump out of the water to eat the insects that fly over the water.
   (A) belittled (B) claimed (C) spared (D) engendered

F. 다음 글을 읽고 밑줄 친 단어의 동의어를 고르시오. #141

1. The buildings contain hundreds of rooms and stand three or four stories high.
   (A) parodies (B) floors (C) mounds (D) landscapes

2. Many of the nations within the Roman Empire adopted Latin as their language, but this didn't mean that their populations were replaced with ethnic Romans.
   (A) accepted (B) adjusted (C) abandoned (D) refused

3. He made his artworks out of commonplace things such as Coke bottles.
   (A) ordinary (B) noticeable (C) necessary (D) peculiar

4. Let's go over a recent genetic study of the DNA of people living in the eastern portion of England.
   (A) tribe (B) part (C) closeness (D) fringe

5. The sturgeon feeds on such things as shellfish that live on the ocean floor. So, this means that it has developed a mouth specifically underlined{designed} to suit this purpose.

   (A) deposited (B) demonstrated (C) conducted (D) intended

6. Problems engendered by the Civil War were more serious in the South than in the North.

   (A) produced (B) exacerbated (C) followed (D) accelerated

7. Iran's nuclear capabilities intensified tensions between the two nations.

   (A) heightened (B) eased (C) alleviated (D) assaulted

8. When the bird's wings were fully extended, the distance from tip to tip could reach up to 7 meters.

   (A) barely (B) completely (C) previously (D) scarcely

9. The major film studios can already take care of themselves, but what about art programs that cannot maintain themselves without financial aid?

   (A) rectify (B) synchronize (C) endow (D) preserve

10. Adam Smith was a celebrated Scottish economist who stated that developing only one specific skill leads to economic development.

    (A) particular (B) shoddy (C) staunch (D) adept

11. The two summits promised to bring a formal end to the Korean War and restore peace and security on the Korean Peninsula.

    (A) reinstate (B) demolish (C) arouse (D) esteem

12. Congress proposed some changes to the Constitution, ten of which were later ratified.

    (A) thwarted (B) vowed (C) suggested (D) rejected

13. A week-long train operators' strike made the government concede a 10% increase in salary for the workers.

    (A) summon (B) deny (C) elude (D) admit

14. However, I don't think that the reading faithfully explains vent mining. Let's look at some of the points in the reading, because honestly, they just don't make sense to me. *vent mining 심해에서 뜨거운 물이 분출되는 지역에서 채굴하는 것

    (A) genuinely (B) consistently (C) accurately (D) candidly

15. There is mounting concern about inflation.

    (A) inadvertent (B) growing (C) animate (D) dwindling

16. Yoon and Jun, both of whom have handwriting that is illegible, are considered real geniuses as writers and poets.

    (A) coined (B) referred to as (C) made up of (D) thought of

G. 문맥상 빈칸에 들어갈 가장 적절한 단어를 찾아 넣으시오. *필요시 어형을 변화할 것 #142

story   extreme   scapegoat   adopt   wrong   limit   align

1. A poor _____ boy named Steve became successful through hard work.
2. The government will only select artists who create works that _____ with their own political philosophy.
3. The government has decided to impose _____ on the amount of fish imported from Japan.
4. What many don't know is that politicians often try to find a _____ to blame for things that go wrong.
5. The stone heads are as tall as five-_____ apartment buildings.
6. It is important that _____ poverty in capitalist societies be eliminated.
7. Churches degrade themselves by doing something morally _____.

H. 문맥상 빈칸에 들어갈 가장 적절한 단어를 찾아 넣으시오. *같은 단어 두 번 사용 가능 #143

1.
considered   crossed   rude   same

At the ① _____ time, people in my country think that it's ② _____ to talk to someone who is older than you with your legs or arms ③ _____. It is also ④ _____ to be ⑤ _____ to stand with your hands on your hips in front of them.

2.
hanging   storing   noteworthy   folding   household

It is ① _____ that children can learn important lessons by helping with ② _____ tasks such as cutting the grass, ironing, chopping up vegetables for meals, washing dishes, doing the laundry, ③ _____ laundry out to dry, ④ _____ laundry and ⑤ _____ clothing in the closet.

I. 다음 밑줄 친 우리말을 영어로 바꾸어 보기에 주어진 단어나 어구를 활용하여 또는 조건에 맞게 영작하시오. *필요시 어형을 변화할 것

#144

1. 특정한 종류의 고래들은 물속에서 물체들을 찾아내기 위해 <u>설계된</u> 수중 음파 탐지기에 특히 취약하다.
   *detect 찾아내다 / sonar 수중 음파 탐지기

   > are / to / of / detect / whales / to / sonar _____ / species / particularly vulnerable / objects underwater / certain

2. <u>돌이켜보면</u>, 우리는 사람들이 1933년에 나치에 투표한 것을 <u>믿기 힘든</u> 일로 여긴다. *find 여기다(느끼다) / astonishing

   > it / people voted for the Nazis in 1933 / that / in _____, we find / astonishing

3. 침팬지는 인간 종족과 비슷한 사회 구조를 <u>완전히</u> 발달시켰다.

   > to / human tribes / have _____ / chimpanzees / similar / developed social structures

4. 오늘날 세계 인구는 약 80억 명의 이르렀고 그중 8억 명이 <u>극심한</u> 가난 속에 머물러 있다. *reach 이르다 / remain 머무르다

   > of / the world population / in / whom / reached / _____ poverty / around 8 billion people today, 800 million / has / remain

5. 당신이 주식에 투자하기 위해 쓸 수 있는 돈에는 한도가 있다. *invest 투자하다 / spend 쓰다

   조건 | 다음 표현을 사용할 것: the money you can / stocks / there's

6. 당신은 카메라 속 필름이 빛에 노출되는 시간의 길이를 셔터 스피드를 통해 조절할 수 있다. *control 조절하다

   조건 | 다음 표현을 사용할 것: the film in a camera / light through the shutter speed / the length of time that

7. 추운 지역에 사는 동물들은 꾸준한 체온을 유지하기 위해 하루에 더 많은 칼로리를 신진대사해야 한다.
   *metabolize 신진대사하다 / live 살다

   조건 | 다음 표현을 사용할 것: cold regions / a day to / many more calories / that / have / a steady body temperature

8. 수입된 영국 상품에 대한 불매 운동이 합의되었고, 그 법의 폐지를 요구하는 그들의 결의안이 투표 후에 채택되었다. *boycott against sth ~에 대한 불매 운동 / agree on sth ~을 합의하다 / resolution 결의안 / call for sth ~을 요구하다 / repeal 폐지

   조건 | 다음 표현을 사용할 것: a / imported British goods / , and their resolutions calling / the repeal of the act / after a vote

PRACTICE TEST (DAY 17)

A. 다음 단어의 뜻을 우리말로 쓰시오. #145

1. pre-eminent
2. expend
3. reminisce
4. leap
5. once and for all

B. 다음 우리말을 영어로 쓰시오. #146

1. 본질
2. 보행자
3. 양분, 이분
4. 장수, 수명
5. 비교할(될) 수 있는

C. 동의어를 찾아 연결하시오. #147

1. autonomy
2. reverence
3. scrap
4. surveillance
5. conflict
6. protrude
7. spectacular
8. tenet

- (A) observation
- (B) clash
- (C) bit
- (D) breathtaking
- (E) stick out
- (F) independence
- (G) creed
- (H) respect

D. 반의어를 찾아 연결하시오. #148

1. admit
2. criticize
3. inept
4. forward

- (A) skillful
- (B) compliment
- (C) backward
- (D) deny

E. 문맥상 빈칸에 들어갈 가장 적절한 단어를 고르시오. #149

1. Everybody thought he was a young man full of _____.
   (A) promise (B) scrap (C) pedestrian (D) dichotomy

2. The National Security Council (the NSC) which was created in 1947 is currently in _____ of the national security of the United States.
   (A) essence (B) longevity (C) tenet (D) charge

3. Due to the parking habits of the patrons of the restaurants in their neighborhood, local residents suffer from a lack of parking _____.
   (A) spots (B) tenets (C) surveillances (D) leaps

4. Every citizen in the nation was _____ to its law, with the exception of the king.
   (A) mundane (B) spectacular (C) subject (D) inept

5. He _____ her from her friends and family.
   (A) protruded (B) hung (C) alienated (D) expended

6. Emerging from a press conference, Chris Cuomo was _____ by reporters.
   (A) depleted (B) sparked (C) reminisced (D) engulfed

F. 다음 글을 읽고 밑줄 친 단어의 동의어를 고르시오. #150

1. Don't sign the contract until you get a <u>definite</u> answer to your question.
   (A) equivalent (B) compelling (C) abstract (D) clear

2. Initially, he denied a sexual relationship with his secretary, but later he <u>admitted</u> it.
   (A) assumed (B) acknowledged (C) apologized (D) repudiated

3. In the chronicle, an author called Hucheon (little Hugh) is credited with writing three poems, two of which <u>concern</u> the Arthurian legends.
   (A) revere (B) admire (C) are about (D) worry

4. The kid dressed in a white T-shirt was particularly <u>noticeable</u> in a group of his friends who were all wearing black T-shirts.
   (A) marked (B) keen (C) isolated (D) rudimentary

5. If we continue to <u>deplete</u> resources on our planet, there will be nothing left in 200 years.
   (A) boost (B) run out of (C) bolster (D) annihilate

6. Understanding the past is underlined{crucial} in handling present and future problems.
   (A) unambiguous   (B) futile   (C) essential   (D) astonishing

7. He hung a banner from a fence.
   (A) clashed   (B) scorched   (C) shredded   (D) dangled

8. This business doesn't concern you. Please leave it alone.
   (A) stunt   (B) provoke   (C) inflict   (D) involve

9. Since oil is not evenly distributed around the world, oil wars will never cease.
   (A) equally   (B) all but   (C) approximately   (D) randomly

10. The movement towards political equality was sparked by the murder of Martin Luther King.
    (A) complimented   (B) agitated   (C) subdued   (D) provoked

11. Theories in economics depend on rational behavior and choice.
    (A) consistent   (B) reasonable   (C) responsible   (D) economical

12. You shouldn't interfere in this matter. It doesn't concern you at all.
    (A) censure   (B) meddle   (C) succumb   (D) emerge

13. For example, mesquite, a shrub indigenous to America, was initially introduced to Africa for land restoration and as a source of forest products. But it started to displace native species in Africa.
    (A) encapsulate   (B) devastate   (C) replace   (D) endorse

14. The new military regime put a lot of famous people – including religious leaders, artists, writers, and professors – in prison for criticizing the regime.
    (A) censuring   (B) relishing   (C) discrediting   (D) advocating

15. Many people are anxious about COVID-19 variants that will newly emerge and prolong the pandemic indefinitely. *variant 변종
    (A) antagonistic   (B) worried   (C) strenuous   (D) eager

16. Before the global spread of the printing press, the mundane task of copying manuscripts was done by scribes. *scribe 필경자
    (A) animated   (B) mediocre   (C) intricate   (D) ordinary

17. Most students, except for university students, wear a uniform to school.
    (A) in particular   (B) save for   (C) by means of   (D) as with

18. A policeman beckoned to me to pull over. I thought I had got pulled over for speeding.
    (A) embodied   (B) signaled   (C) notified   (D) dictated

G. 문맥상 빈칸에 들어갈 가장 적절한 단어를 찾아 넣으시오. *필요시 어형을 변화할 것 / 같은 단어 두 번 사용 가능 #151

| deplete | crucial | last | witness | subject | suffer | charge | ultimately | interfere |

1. Everything seemed to go smoothly. But his marriage _____ for only four years.

2. He was proven guilty of all the _____ against him.

3. The design of a product is much more _____ to the product's success than its qualities.

4. Van Gogh would _____ become the greatest painter in history.

5. Korea was _____ to Japanese rule for about 40 years until it was freed in 1945.

6. People will soon _____ fossil fuels, gas, coal, and oil stored underground.

7. The government does not _____ in personal problems.

8. Food prices are _____ to the consequences of climate change. For example, if there is a drought, prices rise a lot.

9. Diplomats are not _____ to local laws.

10. The screen of my phone _____ irreparable damage. *irreparable 고칠 수 없는

11. It's quite common to _____ specific tasks being done by each person who specializes in a part of the entire production process.

12. People living near airports are _____ from continuous aircraft noise.

H. 문맥상 빈칸에 들어갈 가장 적절한 단어를 찾아 넣으시오. #152

1.
| spectacular | bucket | ranked | phenomena |

For decades, the aurora borealis has been ① _____ among the most ② _____ natural ③ _____ and seeing it is on the ④ _____ list of many people.

2.
| occurred | treated | taken | arrived | suffered |

When a gas explosion ① _____, a sign fell on his head. He ② _____ a serious head injury, and was ③ _____ to a nearby hospital. When he ④ _____ at the hospital, he was still conscious. He needed to have his wound ⑤ _____ before he could leave the hospital. *sign 간판

I. 다음 밑줄 친 우리말을 영어로 바꾸어 보기에 주어진 단어나 어구를 활용하여 또는 조건에 맞게 영작하시오. *필요시 어형을 변화할 것

#153

1. 잦은 충전은 배터리의 <u>수명</u>을 단축할 수도 있다. *shorten 단축하다

   could / battery / frequent charging / the _____ / a / shorten / of

2. 그의 시들은 그의 조국의 유명한 전설적인 영웅들 중 일부<u>에 관한 것이다</u>.

   the / some / his poems _____ / his country / famous legendary heroes in / of

3. 가격을 기반으로 물건을 사는 것은 <u>합리적인</u> 결정인 것 같다.

   on / their prices / buy products based / seems like / to / a _____ decision / it

4. 나는 부모님에게 내가 그 밴드를 그만둘 것이라고 <u>약속</u>을 했다.

   a _____ to / the band / made / I / my parents / I'd quit / that

5. 나는 산에서 캠핑하기에 좋은 조용한 <u>자리</u>를 찾는 데 20분 걸렸다. *take (시간 등을) 필요로 하다(걸리다)

   for / to / I / a nice quiet _____ / took / look
   / camping in the mountains / 20 minutes / for

6. 우리 행성의 천연자원을 고갈시킨 것은 (바로) 당신들, 선진국들이었다.

조건	① It was (으)로 문장을 시작할 것 ② 다음 표현을 사용할 것: you, the developed countries, / our planet's natural resources / that

---

7. 내 아들들은 산타클로스로부터 크리스마스 선물을 받기를 고대한다. *receive 받다

조건	다음 표현을 사용할 것: Christmas presents / Santa Claus

---

8. 외상 후 스트레스 장애(PTSD)을 앓고 있는 그 군인은 잠을 잘 수가 없어서 술에 더 의존했다.

조건	① 분사구문을 사용할 것 ② 다음 표현을 사용할 것: drinking / the soldier / and so relied more

PRACTICE TEST (DAY 18)

A. 다음 단어의 뜻을 우리말로 쓰시오. #154

1. inert _____
2. barge _____
3. maneuverable _____
4. witticism _____
5. distinguish _____

B. 다음 우리말을 영어로 쓰시오. #155

1. 끝내다, 종결하다 _____
2. 보편적인, 세계적인 _____
3. 호소하다 _____
4. (계좌 등에 돈을) 넣다 _____
5. 만장일치의 _____

C. 동의어를 찾아 연결하시오. #156

1. complacency ·   · (A) fail
2. devastation ·   · (B) hurry
3. founder ·   · (C) inquisitive
4. hasten ·   · (D) destruction
5. spawn ·   · (E) unwanted
6. curious ·   · (F) give rise to
7. undesirable ·   · (G) courteous
8. respectful ·   · (H) satisfaction

D. 반의어를 찾아 연결하시오. #157

1. swell ·   · (A) internal
2. external ·   · (B) shrink
3. stationary ·   · (C) incompetent
4. competent ·   · (D) mobile

E. 문맥상 빈칸에 들어갈 가장 적절한 단어를 고르시오. #158

1. _____ fields to feed growing populations in the world might lead to the destruction of animals' habitats.
   (A) Intimidating   (B) Foundering   (C) Disregarding   (D) Clearing

2. The prisoners who escaped from the prison were killed on the _____.
   (A) complacency   (B) witticism   (C) spot   (D) projection

3. Mom's away. So, I have to get our breakfast _____ instead of her.
   (A) stationary   (B) inert   (C) ready   (D) external

4. New technologies have _____ many manufacturing jobs obsolete.
   (A) rendered   (B) hastened   (C) resorted   (D) spawned

5. The government has made a(n) _____ to the public to wear face masks in public places.
   (A) favor   (B) invention   (C) appeal   (D) witticism

6. The trade fair in which more than 100 companies producing farm _____ will participate is to be held in the open air. *in the open air 야외에서
   (A) shore   (B) equipment   (C) devastation   (D) barge

F. 다음 글을 읽고 밑줄 친 단어의 동의어를 고르시오. #159

1. This method of throwing away recyclable materials in one bag without any sorting is <u>far from</u> perfect.
   (A) exceedingly   (B) not at all   (C) simultaneously   (D) honestly

2. Using radar that bats dislike <u>proved</u> highly effective in stopping them from flying near wind turbines.
   (A) dropped out   (B) wiped out   (C) weeded out   (D) turned out

3. First of all, initial research on geologically <u>appropriate</u> locations must be carried out before building the dams.
   (A) suitable   (B) aesthetic   (C) alternate   (D) antiseptic

4. The number of deaths caused by the storm will far exceed the government's <u>projections</u>.
   (A) endeavors   (B) estimates   (C) counterparts   (D) bounds

5. The idea of adorning the roof of a building with shrubs and small trees might sound attractive, but there are several problems that this type of roof causes for building owners.
   (A) embellishing   (B) strengthening   (C) bolstering   (D) supplementing

6. External parasites are not that harmful to animals so it doesn't make sense for sturgeons to have developed the behavior of jumping out of the water to get rid of external parasites.
   *sturgeon 철갑상어
   (A) Sizable   (B) Outside   (C) Shallow   (D) Undetectable

7. Like men, women surfers aim to ride the crest of a wave for as long as possible. *crest (파도 등의) 맨 위
   (A) daunt   (B) intend   (C) attain   (D) loathe

8. I mean, for instance, soybean is a source high in protein, which can be used for livestock and poultry farming.
   (A) complement   (B) estimate   (C) specimen   (D) origin

9. Although the current government's policies on the stock market might lead to an economic downturn, the policies now seem to be a necessary evil to sustain economic growth.
   (A) inevitable   (B) mammoth   (C) marvelous   (D) distinctive

10. You shouldn't disregard my advice. I gave it after a lot of research.
    (A) highlight   (B) teem   (C) baffle   (D) ignore

11. The executive committee was unanimous in its decision to sell all its shares.
    (A) agreed   (B) unambiguous   (C) discontented   (D) antagonistic

12. Participants in the weight loss program must limit the amount of carbohydrates they eat each day if they want to lose weight faster than others in the program. *participants 출연자 / weight loss program 체중 감량 프로그램
    (A) eliminate   (B) minimize   (C) diminish   (D) restrict

13. Plants are stationary, so they have to reproduce by spreading their pollen by wind.
    (A) still   (B) apathetic   (C) ubiquitous   (D) frail

14. When attempting to intimidate strangers, wolves display aggressive behaviors such as snarling, howling, and baring their teeth with their lips curling.
    (A) engender   (B) assault   (C) signal   (D) frighten

15. Nutritionists have proved that those who crave sweets can develop a sugar addiction.
    (A) counterfeited   (B) contended   (C) perpetuated   (D) verified

16. The novel portrayed the lives of ordinary people that were familiar and realistic to readers.
    (A) well-known   (B) noteworthy   (C) decipherable   (D) informative

G. 문맥상 빈칸에 들어갈 가장 적절한 단어를 찾아 넣으시오. *필요시 어형을 변화할 것 / 같은 단어 두 번 사용 가능   #160

| ready   clear   reward   shore   inert   bear   providing |

1. She spent two weeks getting her son's first birthday party _____.
2. The gas becomes _____ when combined with other substances.
3. _____ I can finish this project on time, you can get the results by next week.
4. The animal helped the boy – who had been abandoned on an island by his stepfather – reach _____.
5. The mayor should _____ a portion of the blame for the failure to prevent the pandemic.
6. If more forests were _____ to feed growing populations in the world, the amount of greenhouse gases in the atmosphere would increase substantially.
7. We have to work hard. Don't expect us to get a _____ for passing the exam. No one will praise us for it. That is the plain truth.
8. The next day, we went for a walk along the lake's _____.

H. 문맥상 빈칸에 들어갈 가장 적절한 단어를 찾아 넣으시오. *필요시 어형을 변화할 것   #161

1.
| roles   balances   limit   contain |

The Constitution of the United States ① _____ details about the ② _____ of Congress, such as how to ③ _____ the power of the President through a system of checks and ④ _____.

2.
| prove   make   create   false   help |

Many people are discovering that eye-catching photos and phrases on YouTube thumbnails ① _____ increase people's interest in YouTube channels. This has ② _____ people ③ _____ more and more eye-catching phrases that may soon ④ _____ to be ⑤ _____.

I. 다음 밑줄 친 우리말을 영어로 바꾸어 보기에 주어진 단어나 어구를 활용하여 또는 조건에 맞게 영작하시오. *필요시 어형을 변화할 것

#162

1. 물고기 사다리는 물고기가 그들의 산란지로 돌아가는 것을 도와주는 <u>발명품</u>이다. *fish ladder 물고기 사다리 / spawning grounds 산란지

   return / helps / a fish ladder / an _____ / their spawning grounds / that / fish / to / is

2. 농부가 몇몇 어린 아이들이 자신의 밭에서 수박을 훔치는 것을 보았을 때, 그는 <u>현장에서</u> 그들을 막았다.

   saw / his fields, he / from / when / watermelons / some young kids / stopped them _____ _____ _____ / the farmer / stealing

3. 몇몇 전문가들은 부모들은 아이들이 컴퓨터를 사용하는 시간을 한 시간이나 한 시간 미만으로 <u>제한해야 한</u>다고 제안한다. *an hour or less 한 시간이나 한 시간 미만으로

   that / using computers / some experts / to / spend / parents _____ / an hour or less / the time their children / recommend

4. 연료를 만들기 위해 부피가 큰 <u>장비</u>를 달까지 운반하는 것은 돈이 많이 들지 않을까? *haul 운반하다 / bulky 부피가 큰 / expensive 돈이 많이 드는

   make fuel? / be / to / wouldn't / _____ to / expensive / the / it / haul / Moon to / bulky

5. 이 기간 동안, 그리스 시인들은 그들의 시에서 영웅적인 행위를 묘사하기 시작했다. *portray 묘사하다 / begin 시작하다

조건 다음 표현을 사용할 것: to / heroic deeds / Greek / this / poems / poets

6. 정부는 비료 사용을 제한하는 법률을 통해 비료 수치를 줄일 수 있다. *reduce 줄이다

조건 다음 표현을 사용할 것: fertilizer levels / an act / fertilizer use / the government / that

7. 만약 그가 실험들을 통해 그가 믿는 것을 증명한다면, 그는 이론을 제안할 수 있다. *come up with sth (아이디어 등을) 생각(제안)하다 / believe 믿다

조건 다음 표현을 사용할 것: through / a theory / experiments

8. 인구 감소 문제의 원인(원천)은 주로 인플레이션과 실업을 포함한 경제적인 요인들에 있다. *depopulation 인구 감소 / mainly 주로 / lie in sth ~에 있다 / factor 요인

조건 다음 표현을 사용할 것: the / of / the problem of depopulation / inflation and unemployment / lies mainly in / including

PRACTICE TEST (DAY 19)

A. 다음 단어의 뜻을 우리말로 쓰시오. #163

1. afflict _____
2. fanatical _____
3. subsidiary _____
4. recurrent _____
5. dissent _____

B. 다음 우리말을 영어로 쓰시오. #164

1. 기준, 척도 _____
2. 꼼지락거리다 _____
3. 최고, 으뜸 _____
4. 세대 _____
5. 비행 _____

C. 동의어를 찾아 연결하시오. #165

1. cohesion ·　　　　　　　· (A) gather
2. bar ·　　　　　　　　　 · (B) reciprocal
3. cluster ·　　　　　　　 · (C) prevent
4. entail ·　　　　　　　　· (D) tidy
5. speculate ·　　　　　　· (E) conjecture
6. mutual ·　　　　　　　 · (F) solidarity
7. neat ·　　　　　　　　　· (G) strange
8. uncanny ·　　　　　　　· (H) involve

D. 반의어를 찾아 연결하시오. #166

1. approximate ·　　　　　· (A) converge
2. complicated ·　　　　　· (B) simple
3. diverge ·　　　　　　　· (C) exact
4. inferior ·　　　　　　　· (D) superior

E. 문맥상 빈칸에 들어갈 가장 적절한 단어를 고르시오. #167

1. Unsanitary conditions are the main _____ in the outbreak of the virus. *unsanitary 비위생적인
   (A) demand   (B) spell   (C) cohesion   (D) culprit

2. A large number of experts recommend that people _____ carbohydrates, typically bread, with more protein such as meat to lose weight.
   (A) replace   (B) lag   (C) entail   (D) speculate

3. The _____ in Europe for some spices, including pepper, that were grown in India was so great that European countries wanted to trade with that country for those items.
   (A) primacy   (B) specimen   (C) yardstick   (D) demand

4. The sorting machine at a single-stream recycling center frequently breaks glass bottles, so employees at the center who manually separate broken pieces of glass are at _____ of seriously injuring their hands.
   (A) generation   (B) flood   (C) risk   (D) flight

5. The emergency text message alert saved the _____ of millions of people.
   (A) lives   (B) risks   (C) demands   (D) floods

6. Revolutions in European societies _____ the long-established traditional system of social status.
   (A) clustered   (B) hid   (C) lagged   (D) upset

F. 다음 글을 읽고 밑줄 친 단어의 동의어를 고르시오. #168

1. The Anasazi people were astute enough to supply barren lands with water through channels.
   (A) agile   (B) clever   (C) hard-working   (D) laborious

2. The American pika can't withstand hot weather because of its thick fur.
   (A) weave   (B) manipulate   (C) trespass   (D) survive

3. The questions on the form are too complicated for someone whose first language is not English.
   (A) complex   (B) substantial   (C) explicit   (D) avid

4. Incan and Mayan societies appear to have diverged from the same tribe.
   (A) substituted   (B) gathered   (C) deviated   (D) protruded

5. Countries that use wind turbines to generate electricity need another power supply. Nuclear reactors, on the other hand, always produce a steady amount of power.
   (A) minute (B) unpredictable (C) constant (D) erratic

6. A new species always upsets the local ecological balance.
   (A) devastates (B) ruins (C) poisons (D) disturbs

7. According to him, if there were nothing to replace cigarettes with, people still would not reduce consumption.
   (A) ignite (B) swap (C) halt (D) obliterate

8. A survey conducted regarding public parks showed that 85% of the respondents were in favor of public parks.
   (A) probed (B) showed (C) investigated (D) carried out

9. They had to desert their village because of prolonged exposure to radiation from the nuclear power plant.
   (A) abandon (B) diminish (C) bury (D) unveil

10. The accident made him lag behind the group.
    (A) deviate (B) precede (C) surpass (D) trail

11. There is no doubt that the benefits of the Internet far outweigh those that public transportation could provide.
    (A) precipitate (B) inherit (C) conjecture (D) supply

12. *Pride and Prejudice* (1813) by Jane Austen is generally regarded as one of the most popular English novels to be adapted as a Hollywood movie.
    (A) specifically (B) equitably (C) securely (D) widely

13. He edited and published *Monthly Jazz* in an effort to popularize jazz music in Korea.
    (A) failure (B) unity (C) attempt (D) challenge

14. After being sentenced for tax evasion, my brother spent a short spell in prison. *tax evasion 탈세 / sentence sb for sth ~때문에 ~을 선고하다
    (A) service (B) regret (C) period (D) sentence

15. It is seemingly impossible that peace will come to Afghanistan.
    (A) anonymously (B) apparently (C) as for (D) for sure

16. Fear helped keep our ancestors alive; for example, a fear of snakes cautioned them to avoid walking at night.
    (A) shun (B) supplement (C) spot (D) defer

G. 문맥상 빈칸에 들어갈 가장 적절한 단어를 찾아 넣으시오. *필요시 어형을 변화할 것   #169

| hide | steady | area | desperate | inferior | preoccupied | withstand | conduct |

1. Torreya saplings cannot _____ adverse weather conditions. *sapling 묘목

2. Many scientists have problems with the argument that zebras use their stripes to _____ from or confuse predators.

3. Scientists _____ experiments, make observations, record and analyze data, and finally, write research papers.

4. In recent months, Wall Street has been _____ with rising interest rates.

5. Nuclear power is the most realistic means of generating power _____.

6. A total of 220 English navy ships and 660 private boats sailed across the English Channel, which lies in the _____ of the sea between Southern England and Northern France.

7. Companies that are _____ to make a profit will invest in Internet businesses, whereas they have no interest in public transportation because it is in the non-profit deficit.

8. If a new product developed by a car company turns out to be of _____ quality, the company's image will be damaged, and this will lead to a drop in sales of its cars as well as the new product. *turn out to be sth ~로 판명되다

H. 문맥상 빈칸에 들어갈 가장 적절한 단어를 찾아 넣으시오. *필요시 어형을 변화할 것   #170

1.
| changed | despite | betrayed | risk |

Many soldiers fought ① _____ the ② _____ of losing their lives, but they were not given enough compensation. Most of them felt ③ _____ by their country. They ④ _____ their minds and moved to the North.

2.
| risk | danger | leak | proximity | fuel |

Since there is a ① _____ that radioactive material that ② _____ a nuclear power plant can potentially ③ _____ out of the plant, ④ _____ to the plant would put people in ⑤ _____ of being exposed to radiation.

I. 다음 밑줄 친 우리말을 영어로 바꾸어 보기에 주어진 단어나 어구를 활용하여 또는 조건에 맞게 영작하시오. *필요시 어형을 변화할 것

#171

1. 그녀는 아프리카로 옮겼고 가난한 사람들을 도우면서 남은 <u>생애</u>를 보냈다.

   moved / poor people / the rest / she / her _____ / helping / to / Africa and spent / of

2. 살충제의 사용은 그 지역의 야생 동물에게 상당한 <u>해</u>를 끼친다.

   wildlife in the area / to / pesticides / a great deal of _____ / of / causes / the use

3. 일련의 화성으로의 우주 비행에서, 그들은 암석 <u>표본들</u>을 수집한 다음 지구로 그들을 돌려보냈다. *mission 우주 비행

   and then returned / of / to / series / them / Earth / in / collected / a / missions to Mars, they / _____ of rocks

4. 정부들은 개인의 문제에 대한 해결책들을 <u>제공</u>해 줄 수 없다.

   individual problems / cannot / to / governments / solutions / _____

5. 그에 따르면, 많은 우유를 마시는 여자들은 유방암에 걸릴 높은 <u>위험</u>을 가진다고 한다. *get breast cancer 유방암에 걸리다

   him, women / to / who / of / drink a lot of milk / getting breast cancer / according / a high _____ / have

6. 얼룩말은 큰 풀과 키 작은 나무들로 가득 찬 곳에 <u>숨지</u> 않는다.

in / filled / _____ / don't / zebras / tall grass and low trees / with / places

7. 그 동물은 <u>겉보기에</u> 무해하게 보이지만 그것은 매우 위험하다. *dangerous 위험한

조건	다음 표현을 사용할 것: harmless, but it / the animal

8. 보호 구역에서 사용되는 부족 언어들은 멸종 <u>위험에 처해 있다</u>. *tribal 부족의 / reservation 보호 구역 / extinction 멸종

조건	다음 표현을 사용할 것: languages spoken on reservations / at

9. 삼나무는 가을에 잎을 떨어뜨리는 낙엽수보다 심한 추위와 같은 악천후 조건을 <u>견딜</u> 가능성이 더 높다.
*cedar 삼나무 / be likely to do sth ~할 가능성이 높다 / shed 떨어뜨리다

조건	다음 표현을 사용할 것: cedars / adverse weather conditions such as severe cold than / which / deciduous trees / their leaves / the fall

10. 저소득층은 자신들의 가족을 먹여 살리기 위해 더 싸고, 영양적으로 <u>열등한</u> 식품을 사는 것 외에는 다른 선택의 여지가 없다. *have no other choice except to do sth ~하는 것 외에는 다른 선택의 여지가 없다 / feed 먹여 살리다 / buy 사다

조건	다음 표현을 사용할 것: low-income families / cheaper, nutritionally / their families / food

PRACTICE TEST (DAY 20)

A. 다음 단어의 뜻을 우리말로 쓰시오.   #172

1. languish _____
2. groove _____
3. speck _____
4. credence _____
5. asleep _____

B. 다음 우리말을 영어로 쓰시오.   #173

1. 권한, 지휘 _____
2. 파편 _____
3. 티끌 _____
4. 갈다, 연마하다 _____
5. 진부한 표현 _____

C. 동의어를 찾아 연결하시오.   #174

1. affront   · · (A) possible
2. apt   · · (B) uncontrolled
3. conceivable   · · (C) expand
4. explicit   · · (D) indignity
5. unbridled   · · (E) aspect
6. enlarge   · · (F) puzzle
7. facet   · · (G) clear
8. baffle   · · (H) appropriate

D. 반의어를 찾아 연결하시오.   #175

1. aggravate   · · (A) improve
2. confirm   · · (B) refute
3. deter   · · (C) obvious
4. subtle   · · (D) encourage

E. 문맥상 빈칸에 들어갈 가장 적절한 단어를 고르시오. #176

1. World War II came to a(n) _____ in Europe on May 8th, 1945.
   (A) end   (B) tip   (C) speck   (D) authority

2. Susan's mom has a heart _____.
   (A) facet   (B) credence   (C) problem   (D) faucet

3. He stood dead _____.
   (A) subtle   (B) explicit   (C) still   (D) conceivable

4. A suit made of dark cloth with _____ white vertical lines makes the wearer look taller.
   (A) narrow   (B) apt   (C) unbridled   (D) still

5. The landlord will give your deposit back to you after _____ that there is no damage to the house.
   (A) confirming   (B) repelling   (C) affronting   (D) coalescing

6. Take this money. This is not a bribe. You worked so hard. You _____ it.
   (A) deter   (B) deserve   (C) enlarge   (D) hone

F. 다음 글을 읽고 밑줄 친 단어의 동의어를 고르시오. #177

1. I told you to stay still.
   (A) stationary   (B) stationery   (C) continuous   (D) elusive

2. The theory suggests that humans are descended from ape-like species.
   (A) discloses   (B) uncovers   (C) indicates   (D) favors

3. Clipper ships often encountered large waves in the ocean surrounding Cape Horn, which is at the southern tip of South America.
   (A) country   (B) area   (C) coast   (D) end

4. Guns didn't play a very decisive role in the conquest of the Inca Empire because occasions when they were successfully fired were rare.
   (A) crucial   (B) consistent   (C) trivial   (D) frivolous

5. In the U.S., some people, especially those who make a fortune by making and selling weapons, <u>resist</u> any changes to the law that allows people to own weapons.

   (A) oppose (B) procrastinate (C) advocate (D) endorse

6. Materials such as gold and iron can be found in <u>infinite</u> supply along these thermal vents.
   *thermal vent 열수분출구(해저의 갈라진 틈으로 지열로 가열된 물이 배출되는 구멍)

   (A) minute (B) restricted (C) necessary (D) limitless

7. He was forced to resign from the board because he had told a secret that the company didn't want its <u>rivals</u> to know about.

   (A) adherents (B) rebels (C) disciples (D) contenders

8. Two streams <u>coalesce</u> into a single river.

   (A) amalgamate (B) deposit (C) exacerbate (D) flow

9. The cream the doctor gave me to relieve my rash just <u>aggravated</u> it.

   (A) put an end to (B) housed (C) insulted (D) worsened

10. Upon taking the class, he found calligraphy <u>fascinating</u>.

    (A) extremely interesting (B) most important (C) so conducive (D) very obsolete

11. The Internet sometimes <u>deters</u> users from coming up with new and creative ideas. This is because some users steal the work of someone else.

    (A) validates (B) nurtures (C) thwarts (D) pushes

12. Earthquakes could disorient whales, but suggesting them as a <u>primary</u> cause of beaching is illogical. *disorient ~의 방향 감각을 잃게 하다

    (A) feeble (B) prime (C) inevitable (D) plausible

13. Before the newspaper *The Moon* merged with *The Sun* – a newspaper with left-wing political views – it was <u>issued</u> once a week.

    (A) disregarded (B) engendered (C) published (D) freed

14. These experiments provide <u>uniform</u> data supporting the use of cloud seeding. *cloud seeding 구름씨 뿌리기(인공적으로 비나 눈을 내리게 하는 방법)

    (A) unresolved (B) unreliable (C) unrestricted (D) unvarying

15. The researchers neglected to include an important result that they had <u>confirmed</u> in the previous experiment.

    (A) confessed (B) protruded (C) anticipated (D) corroborated

16. The police follow tire tread marks <u>impressed</u> in the snow, their dogs sniffing.

    (A) imprinted (B) dangled (C) thawed (D) moved

G. 문맥상 빈칸에 들어갈 가장 적절한 단어를 찾아 넣으시오. *필요시 어형을 변화할 것 / 같은 단어 두 번 사용 가능   #178

| in part | narrow | facet | issue | impress | degree | regular |

1. The Earth is slightly tilted (23.45 _____).

2. The director was _____ by his exceptional performance at the audition for a major part in his new movie.

3. Another solution is to _____ protective equipment, like thick gloves, to make sure that employees don't cut their hands on glass.

4. Membership in this organization demands a high _____ of commitment.

5. She _____ won the election by only 45,000 votes. The next day, she became the first woman president of Korea.

6. He lost by a _____ margin.

7. Due _____ to global warming, glaciers melt. Melted glaciers lead to a rise in sea levels.

8. Another _____ of the problem concerns money. Without enough money, we can't finish this project.

9. If health insurance is not available, people will have difficulty staying healthy. For example, since many diseases such as cancer and heart disease can be detected early on, getting medical check-ups on a _____ basis can increase people's life expectancy.

H. 문맥상 빈칸에 들어갈 가장 적절한 단어를 찾아 넣으시오. *필요시 어형을 변화할 것   #179

1.
| advance | contribution | granted | nevertheless |

① _____, without his ② _____ to the development of computer science, many technological ③ _____ we now take for ④ _____ would not have been possible.

2.
| facets | necessarily | effects | differently | regions |

Some new species which have been introduced to many ① _____ of the world are believed to cause harm. However, new species do not ② _____ bring about only negative ③ _____. Rather, depending on what kind of ④ _____ you look at, the impact of the introduction of new species can be interpreted ⑤ _____.

I. 다음 밑줄 친 우리말을 영어로 바꾸어 보기에 주어진 단어나 어구를 활용하여 또는 조건에 맞게 영작하시오. *필요시 어형을 변화할 것

#180

1. 그 전쟁은 평화 조약에 의해 <u>종료</u>되었다.

   an _____ by / the war / to / was / the peace treaty / brought

2. 제인(Jane)은 언론계에서 <u>직업을 갖고</u> 싶어한다.

   journalism / _____ a _____ / hoping / in / to / Jane is

3. 나는 종종 위층에 사는 내 이웃에 의해 만들어진 소음에 의해 <u>방해를 받는다</u>.

   the noise / often _____ by / upstairs / by / made / I'm / lives / my neighbor who

4. 호랑이 나방이 포식자를 물리치는 방법은 독특하다; 그것은 그들을 <u>쫓아 버리기</u> 위해 몸에서 나온 독을 사용한다. *drive away sth ~을 물리치다

   a poison / which / them / the / unique; it uses / the method / its body to / tiger moth / is / its predators / _____ / from / by / drives away

5. 그는 감옥에 가야 마땅하다.

prison / to / _____ / to / he / go

6. 그는 벤치에 가만히 앉아 있었다.

bench / a / he / on / sat _____

7. 그 성(the castle)은 적의 공격에 매우 취약하여 그것(it)은 거의 즉시 함락되었다. *vulnerable 취약한 / capture 함락시키다

조건 | 다음 표현을 사용할 것: so / attack by enemies / that / captured almost

8. 오늘날 부모들은 그들이 그들의 자식을 위해 희생할 필요가 있다는 것을 당연시한다.

조건 | 다음 표현을 사용할 것: parents today / need / their children / sacrifices for

9. 공유지의 비극의 대표적인 사례 중 하나는 수도꼭지를 틀어 놓은 채 양치질을 함으로써 식수를 낭비하는 것이다. *representative 대표적인 / the tragedy of the commons 공유지의 비극 / example 사례 / brush 닦다

조건 | 다음 표현을 사용할 것: of / left on / is wasting drinking water by / your teeth with the

ANGRY ENGLISH
academic
VOCABULARY

ANSWERS

ANSWER (DAY 01)

#001
1. 숙고하다, 명상하다
2. 중재하다
3. 약간
4. 반항하다
5. 정말 신기하게도

#002
1. acquisition
2. consumption
3. martial
4. spur
5. store

#003
1. (D)
2. (G)
3. (A)
4. (B)
5. (C)
6. (E)
7. (F)
8. (H)

#004
1. (B)
2. (A)
3. (C)
4. (D)

#005
1. (C)
2. (A)
3. (C)
4. (B)
5. (C)
6. (B)

#006
1. (A)
2. (C)
3. (B)
4. (A)
5. (A)
6. (C)
7. (B)
8. (C)
9. (A)
10. (C)
11. (C)
12. (B)
13. (B)
14. (D)
15. (D)
16. (D)
17. (C)

#007
1. clockwise
2. offspring
3. satire
4. vicinity
5. blocked
6. legendary
7. debris
8. accomplished

#008
1.
① reservoir
② store
③ huge
④ reservoir
⑤ decay
⑥ formed

2.
① formed
② stored
③ flavor
④ slightly

#009
1. Obesity is a classic example of a <u>common</u> medical problem.
2. <u>Offspring</u> have genetic traits passed down from their parents.
3. He was <u>cremated</u> and his ashes were taken to his home country.
4. Tax collection is one of the official <u>functions</u> of the government.
5. One inch is equal to roughly 2.5 centimeters (cm), one foot is equivalent to about 30 cm, and a yard equals <u>approximately</u> 90 cm.
6. The idea that earthquakes cause whales to beach themselves might seem <u>plausible</u> at first but is highly unlikely.
7. The lifestyle of most office workers is <u>sedentary</u>, as they spend most of their time sitting in front of their computers.

ANSWER (DAY 02)

#010
1. 계약, 계약을 맺다
2. 탑승한
3. 놓아주다, 촉발시키다
4. 줄이다, 완화시키다
5. 좀처럼 ~않는

#011
1. texture
2. security
3. nuance
4. sacrifice
5. dwelling

#012
1. (C)
2. (E)
3. (G)
4. (A)
5. (B)
6. (D)
7. (F)
8. (H)

#013
1. (D)
2. (A)
3. (B)
4. (C)

#014
1. (B)
2. (D)
3. (D)
4. (C)
5. (B)
6. (D)

#015
1. (C)
2. (B)
3. (A)
4. (A)
5. (A)
6. (A)
7. (C)
8. (A)

9. (D)
10. (D)
11. (C)
12. (A)
13. (D)
14. (A)
15. (D)
16. (A)

#016
1. contact
2. uncovering
3. capable
4. idle
5. innately
6. relentlessly
7. hence

#017
1.
① vessels
② balanced
③ unload
④ cargo
2.
① inflow
② search
③ accommodated
④ allowed
⑤ flourish

#018
1. James must work on a big science assignment <u>due</u> tomorrow that he hasn't yet started.
2. The fire that broke out in the summer of 1998 had negative <u>repercussions</u> for the local economy.
3. In that country, there are social problems <u>ranging</u> from crime to inflation.
4. When it comes to food, for him, taste is of <u>secondary importance</u>.
5. The government <u>was determined to</u> increase taxes on the profits that people make from stock and property investments.
6. The towering, <u>swirling</u> winds swallowed hundreds of houses in no time.
7. This medical technology can be used to <u>treat</u> a patient with a genetic disease.
8. In the absence of written records, the judge <u>was incapable of</u> proving that the guilty party had overdosed on sleeping pills.

ANSWER (DAY 03)

#019
1. 염료
2. 폭행(공격)하다
3. 놀라게 하다
4. 벗기다, 줄이다
5. 성실한, 양심적인

#020
1. niche
2. iceberg
3. overlap
4. brisk
5. logical

#021
1. (A)
2. (B)
3. (H)
4. (G)
5. (F)
6. (D)
7. (C)
8. (E)

#022
1. (D)
2. (A)
3. (B)
4. (C)

#023
1. (C)
2. (D)
3. (A)
4. (C)
5. (D)
6. (A)

#024
1. (B)
2. (D)
3. (C)
4. (B)
5. (D)
6. (A)
7. (D)
8. (B)
9. (D)
10. (D)
11. (A)
12. (B)
13. (D)
14. (D)
15. (B)
16. (C)
17. (D)

#025
1. contact
2. ranked
3. Shortly
4. compared
5. inordinately
6. concern
7. series
8. contracts

#026
1.
① measuring
② followed
③ damaged
④ constructed
2.
① limbs
② rid
③ parasites
④ stuck
⑤ detrimental

#027
1. The Crusades, called a holy war, were a <u>series</u> of religious wars between Christians and Muslims.
2. You put a <u>bridle</u> on a horse you're about to ride, and you control it with the reins of the <u>bridle</u>.
3. It is unlikely that hydrogen fuel will be used <u>instead of</u> fossil fuels as the chief source of global energy in a very short period of time.
4. The claim that she stole the money is <u>absurd</u>.
5. In geological <u>terms</u>, a bed is a layer of rock.
6. The success of the project relies on government <u>support</u>.
7. The history of jazz can <u>be traced back to</u> Africa.
8. That tsunami <u>damaged</u> the first nuclear power plant to be constructed in Japan.

ANSWER (DAY 04)

#028
1. ~을 갈망(열망)하다
2. 힘들고 지루한 일
3. 심사숙고하다, 고려하다
4. (규칙 등을) 따르다
5. 사라지다

#029
1. reed
2. amenities
3. alike
4. telltale (=tattletale)
5. reason

#030
1. (F)
2. (E)
3. (B)
4. (D)
5. (A)
6. (H)
7. (C)
8. (G)

#031
1. (B)
2. (D)
3. (A)
4. (C)

#032
1. (B)
2. (D)
3. (A)
4. (D)
5. (D)
6. (A)

#033
1. (D)
2. (D)
3. (D)
4. (C)
5. (A)
6. (D)
7. (B)
8. (A)

9. (C)
10. (A)
11. (B)
12. (C)
13. (B)
14. (C)
15. (B)
16. (A)

#034
1. sealed
2. care
3. variety
4. oval
5. seminal
6. commits
7. passed
8. passed

#035
1.
① poisonous
② somewhat
③ eradicate
④ native

2.
① based
② premise
③ accused
④ innocent
⑤ guilty

#036
1. The clams should be <u>immersed</u> in boiling water for at least a few minutes before you eat them.
2. There are some problems that people <u>overlook</u> when working together as a team.
3. The stone balls are <u>oval</u> in shape.
4. Initially, the adobe they used was <u>round</u> in shape; but later it became <u>rectangular</u> in shape like bricks.
5. Native Americans lived on the Great Plains in <u>conical</u> houses.
6. She <u>aspires to</u> become a police officer.
7. They <u>passed</u> on their knowledge of how to catch an animal in a trap to the next generation.
8. During a tutoring <u>session</u>, outside food is not allowed.
9. Not only do the streamlined body shapes of these fish help (to) reduce water resistance, but their narrow fins and tails and eyes that don't <u>bulge</u> help (to) reduce drag in the water as well.

ANSWER (DAY 05)

#037
1. 침투, 진출
2. 예방 조치
3. 응시하다
4. 직접 해 보는
5. 익숙한

#038
1. overview
2. patient
3. eject
4. record
5. the service

#039
1. (A)
2. (H)
3. (C)
4. (G)
5. (E)
6. (D)
7. (B)
8. (F)

#040
1. (D)
2. (A)
3. (C)
4. (B)

#041
1. (C)
2. (D)
3. (B)
4. (A)
5. (D)
6. (B)

#042
1. (D)
2. (B)
3. (B)
4. (C)
5. (A)
6. (C)
7. (B)
8. (C)
9. (A)
10. (C)
11. (A)
12. (A)
13. (C)
14. (B)
15. (B)
16. (A)

#043
1. outnumbered
2. precipitated
3. reach
4. Rubbing
5. evade
6. care
7. access
8. separate

#044
1.
① collapse
② techniques
③ livestock
④ survival

2.
① damage
② monitor
③ tracking
④ apparatus
⑤ located

#045
1. Speculative thinking in the stock market <u>contributed</u> to the Wall Street Crash of 1929.
2. He <u>cares</u> very much about his appearance and the way he dresses.
3. His father taught him how to make a fire by <u>rubbing</u> two pieces of wood together.
4. The low-budget film is <u>more of</u> a pornographic video than an independent movie.
5. If a nuclear reactor overheats, it could <u>reach</u> the temperature at which radioactive waste escapes.
6. *Snow White* would be very different if it were written from the perspective of the seven <u>dwarfs</u>.
7. Dr. Carol, a key figure in dependency theory, is famous for <u>evading</u> difficult questions.
8. I found it fascinating that South Koreans don't <u>care about</u> North Korea's constant threats.

ANSWER (DAY 06)

#046
1. 존경
2. 선견지명
3. 최적화하다
4. 근간
5. 결단, 주도

#047
1. keen
2. sequential
3. vow
4. meanwhile
5. elevate

#048
1. (D)
2. (C)
3. (H)
4. (A)
5. (B)
6. (E)
7. (G)
8. (F)

#049
1. (A)
2. (B)
3. (D)
4. (C)

#050
1. (B)
2. (D)
3. (A)
4. (D)
5. (A)
6. (D)

#051
1. (B)
2. (D)
3. (C)
4. (B)
5. (C)
6. (D)
7. (A)
8. (B)
9. (D)
10. (A)
11. (B)
12. (A)
13. (D)
14. (B)
15. (B)
16. (B)

#052
1. congestion, congestion
2. access
3. apart
4. thus
5. carried
6. supposed
7. none other than
8. apart

#053
1.
① threat
② pose
③ clog
④ pull

2.
① filled
② cargo
③ unloaded
④ invasion
⑤ unsuitable
⑥ place

#054
1. Japanese people <u>are supposed to</u> hate showing their real feelings.
2. We have to give our boss <u>credit</u> for leading our company through this difficult time.
3. The government became <u>cautious</u> about increasing interest rates because of the sharp rise in the number of illegal immigrants.
4. People started to buy homes in the <u>hope</u> that the price of their homes would later increase.
5. Men <u>differ</u> in body temperature from women.
6. The huge plastic box was too heavy to <u>carry</u> by myself.
7. A hydrogen fuel-cell vehicle is nearly twice as <u>efficient</u> at using fuel as a car powered by gasoline.
8. Hurriedly, he cut down a tall tree planted next to his driveway on which he had <u>etched</u> his ex's name.

ANSWER (DAY 07)

#055
1. 바로잡다, 시정하다
2. (다름 아닌) 바로
3. 단호한, 몰두하고 있는
4. 저명한
5. 계획된

#056
1. improvised
2. serve
3. come across
4. discard
5. pledge

#057
1. (F)
2. (A)
3. (B)
4. (D)
5. (E)
6. (G)
7. (C)
8. (H)

#058
1. (D)
2. (A)
3. (C)
4. (B)

#059
1. (D)
2. (A)
3. (B)
4. (C)
5. (D)
6. (C)

#060
1. (A)
2. (B)
3. (C)
4. (C)
5. (D)
6. (A)
7. (D)
8. (A)

9. (D)
10. (B)
11. (C)
12. (C)
13. (B)
14. (A)
15. (B)
16. (D)
17. (A)

#061
1. fit
2. advantages
3. case
4. dreams
5. extent
6. extent
7. success
8. fit
9. apply

#062
1.
① referred
② severe
③ hardship
④ led
2.
① separate
② sediment
③ bottom
④ convey
⑤ surface

#063
1. He destroyed the car to such an <u>extent</u> that the police could not identify the model.
2. If he had not <u>applied</u> his brakes in time, he would have collided with the heavy trailer truck.
3. The king had his men <u>eliminate</u> his rivals who had revolted against his rule.
4. There is a limit to the extent of the thoughts that you can <u>convey</u> during an interview.
5. The Democratic Party <u>barely</u> won the election over the Republican Party.
6. Many people <u>are concerned</u> about the changes that new technology will bring.
7. Birds that hunt alone enjoy several key <u>advantages</u> over birds that hunt in flocks.
8. Our supply of kerosene was running out, so we <u>didn't bother</u> to light the lamp.

ANSWER (DAY 08)

#064
1. 꼭대기, 정상
2. 영역, 분야
3. 주장(단언)하다
4. 참을(견딜) 수 없는
5. 피상적인, 외관상의

#065
1. complex
2. rye
3. define
4. shatter
5. vent

#066
1. (B)
2. (A)
3. (D)
4. (C)
5. (F)
6. (E)
7. (G)
8. (H)

#067
1. (B)
2. (A)
3. (D)
4. (C)

#068
1. (C)
2. (A)
3. (A)
4. (D)
5. (A)
6. (D)

#069
1. (B)
2. (D)
3. (D)
4. (A)
5. (A)
6. (D)
7. (C)
8. (A)
9. (C)
10. (D)
11. (B)
12. (D)
13. (B)
14. (A)
15. (A)
16. (A)
17. (C)

#070
1. acknowledge
2. combined
3. discharged
4. weak
5. equipped
6. fiery
7. routinely
8. acknowledge

#071
1.
① weak
② keep
③ heavy
④ suspended
2.
① falling
② spraying
③ solution
④ season
⑤ farmland

#072
1. My mother really <u>stressed</u> the need for me to eat more vegetables.
2. The Internet has an <u>impact</u> on the way people live.
3. Some animals remain <u>inactive</u> to save energy during winter months.
4. When it is cold, <u>blood vessels</u> in the brain contract.
5. It's <u>nothing more than</u> the flu.
6. Among the effective instruments of monetary policy is the bank rate, that is, the interest rate at which <u>central</u> banks lend money to commercial banks.
7. The president started to engage in conversations with experts to find a <u>solution</u> to the decline in population.
8. In the past, <u>sheer</u> survival was the most important matter that humans had to deal with.
9. Since ranchers <u>feed</u> their chickens a special grain to fatten them quickly, some of the overweight chickens have a hard time walking.

ANSWER (DAY 09)

#073
1. 관대한, 너그러운
2. 이제 ~니까
3. 초래하다
4. ~의 완벽한 예시이다
5. 작은 부분, 헝겊 조각

#074
1. lifespan
2. seamless
3. defy
4. stem from
5. origin

#075
1. (D)
2. (C)
3. (B)
4. (H)
5. (G)
6. (E)
7. (F)
8. (A)

#076
1. (D)
2. (A)
3. (C)
4. (B)

#077
1. (A)
2. (B)
3. (D)
4. (A)
5. (C)
6. (D)

#078
1. (B)
2. (B)
3. (A)
4. (C)
5. (B)
6. (D)
7. (D)
8. (D)
9. (B)
10. (D)
11. (D)
12. (A)
13. (B)
14. (B)
15. (D)
16. (A)

#079
1. vestige
2. certain
3. otherwise
4. Now that
5. consistently
6. otherwise
7. otherwise

#080
1.
① unfair
② complaints
③ clear
④ gender

2.
① so-called
② Covered
③ layer
④ act
⑤ barrier

#081
1. It will be <u>fun</u> playing football on the school ground with so many big puddles.
2. I heard the <u>news</u> that the U.S. invaded Iraq today.
3. My parents have to get a loan. <u>Otherwise</u>, they will not be able to open a new business.
4. Local communities and residents have to pay a significant amount of money, which would <u>otherwise</u> be spent to develop their towns and cities, for maintaining these old buildings.
5. In order to <u>elude</u> the police car chasing after him, he lay flat, his face on the ground.
6. I told you to <u>switch</u> the lights <u>off</u> when not in use.
7. If the price of a <u>certain</u> instant noodle, let's say Spicy Sin, goes up, the company manufacturing Spicy Sin will produce more of it.
8. It was the chief commander who gave an order to shoot the demonstrators who had <u>occupied</u> City Hall.
9. The tragedy of the commons in economics <u>refers to</u> a situation in which individuals exploit common resources for their own profits.

ANSWER (DAY 10)

#082
1. 기록 보관소
2. 창고
3. 달래다
4. 징조(조짐)이다
5. 제공하다

#083
1. coinage
2. pattern
3. rust
4. indulge
5. correlate

#084
1. (B)
2. (F)
3. (H)
4. (A)
5. (G)
6. (E)
7. (C)
8. (D)

#085
1. (D)
2. (A)
3. (B)
4. (C)

#086
1. (A)
2. (B)
3. (B)
4. (A)
5. (A)
6. (D)

#087
1. (C)
2. (C)
3. (B)
4. (A)
5. (D)
6. (B)
7. (D)
8. (D)
9. (C)
10. (B)
11. (C)
12. (B)
13. (D)
14. (D)
15. (A)
16. (D)

#088
1. unwilling
2. eminently
3. blind
4. fire
5. filling
6. stable
7. involved

#089
1.
① form
② kept
③ incessant
④ designed

2.
① According
② burdensome
③ attempt
④ drive
⑤ travel

#090
1. The society that they initially envisioned was a society in which everyone would work <u>according to</u> their capacity.

2. Don't judge a person on your first <u>impression</u> of him or her.

3. Barring any objections, I'd like to explain why it is not <u>hazardous</u> at all.

4. <u>Patterns</u> of marriage are generally determined by house prices and childcare costs.

5. <u>According to</u> him, roads and electricity are much more important than hospitals and schools in improving the lives of people in poor countries.

6. People believe that the only thing the government can do very well is just to <u>collect</u> taxes from people.

7. Like Saint Augustine, I would say one has a moral responsibility to disobey unjust laws rather than <u>observe</u> them without any complaints.

ANSWER (DAY 11)

#091
1. ~을 심사숙고하다
2. 감추다
3. (잘게) 자르다(썰다)
4. 닦아 내다
5. 단점, 결함

#092
1. wanton
2. ambitious
3. enthusiastic
4. furnace
5. chunk

#093
1. (C)
2. (D)
3. (E)
4. (F)
5. (A)
6. (B)
7. (G)
8. (H)

#094
1. (A)
2. (D)
3. (C)
4. (B)

#095
1. (D)
2. (D)
3. (B)
4. (A)
5. (D)
6. (B)

#096
1. (C)
2. (A)
3. (B)
4. (D)
5. (D)
6. (A)
7. (B)
8. (D)
9. (B)
10. (A)
11. (D)
12. (D)
13. (B)
14. (D)
15. (A)
16. (A)

#097
1. destined
2. burden
3. inflict
4. routine
5. appearance
6. close
7. as well
8. weigh

#098
1.
① Blaming
② unreasonable
③ dying
④ doomed

2.
① conducting
② experiments
③ preventing
④ spraying
⑤ substances

#099
1. Computers are sometimes more of a <u>hindrance</u> than a help.
2. For the <u>purpose</u> of getting a job, I am learning English again.
3. The kid has great <u>potential</u> in music.
4. <u>Especially</u> worrisome for the government is the possibility that the number of people getting vaccines will progressively decline.
5. The country made a request that the repayment be postponed, but the International Monetary Fund (IMF) <u>turned</u> it <u>down</u>.
6. A financial crisis often <u>coincides</u> with deterioration in the real economy.
7. Private fossil collectors can damage fossils <u>embedded</u> in rocks in the process of excavation.
8. This <u>prevents</u> people from sharing new and creative ideas on the Internet.
9. Much as he tried to beat the odds, he <u>was doomed</u> to starve to death on Mars, an uninhabitable wasteland planet.
10. Not only did the Ford Motor Company benefit from the assembly line, but many other car companies that adopted it experienced a significant increase in productivity <u>as well</u>.

ANSWER (DAY 12)

#100
1. 상징하다, 포함하다
2. 크기, 규모, 중요성
3. 해골, 뼈대
4. 들러붙다
5. (지극히) 평범한

#101
1. calligraphy
2. application
3. figure
4. analyze
5. mount

#102
1. (G)
2. (F)
3. (B)
4. (A)
5. (E)
6. (D)
7. (C)
8. (H)

#103
1. (C)
2. (A)
3. (D)
4. (B)

#104
1. (B)
2. (D)
3. (B)
4. (D)
5. (C)
6. (A)

#105
1. (C)
2. (B)
3. (A)
4. (D)
5. (C)
6. (D)
7. (A)
8. (B)
9. (A)
10. (B)
11. (D)
12. (A)
13. (D)
14. (C)
15. (A)
16. (B)

#106
1. distance
2. available
3. respect
4. result
5. distract
6. true
7. As such
8. rival

#107
1.
① allowed
② show
③ disgust
④ damaged
2.
① gigantic
② size
③ clumsy
④ prey
⑤ precisely

#108
1. He <u>refrained</u> from meeting her, because he knew it was wrong.
2. My dad discouraged me from riding a bike on the <u>grounds</u> that I might get severely injured if I fell off it.
3. At that time, doctors could not prevent patients' wounds from getting infected because antibiotics like penicillin were not yet <u>available</u>.
4. Many people in America showed no <u>respect</u> for the mask mandate.
5. The dictator used sports to <u>distract</u> attention from the abuses of his dictatorship.
6. He tried to mediate <u>conflicts</u> in the Middle East.
7. High-frequency sound waves have more energy, so that they can travel very large <u>distances</u>.
8. The same <u>goes for</u> data recorded in alphabetical order during an experiment.

ANSWER (DAY 13)

#109
1. 달래다
2. 조용히 몰래 가다
3. 예리한, 날카로운
4. 상냥한, 친절한
5. 용감한, 대담한

#110
1. chamber
2. sting
3. disintegrate
4. juncture
5. coincident

#111
1. (H)
2. (A)
3. (C)
4. (B)
5. (G)
6. (D)
7. (F)
8. (E)

#112
1. (D)
2. (A)
3. (C)
4. (B)

#113
1. (A)
2. (D)
3. (A)
4. (A)
5. (C)
6. (A)

#114
1. (A)
2. (C)
3. (D)
4. (A)
5. (B)
6. (D)
7. (B)
8. (A)
9. (B)
10. (A)
11. (C)
12. (C)
13. (A)
14. (D)
15. (B)
16. (B)

#115
1. related
2. direction
3. level
4. nuisance
5. way
6. mere
7. As of
8. delivered
9. delivering
10. relate

#116
1.
① advancement
② nuisance
③ fact
④ contacted

2.
① majority
② set
③ monitor
④ problem
⑤ arise

#117
1. He pointed in the opposite <u>direction</u>.
2. I've <u>attached</u> the document signed by the notary.
3. The sodium in her blood has dropped to a normal <u>level</u>.
4. His contribution to our understanding of the destruction caused by nuclear weapons completely changed the <u>way</u> we looked at science.
5. The <u>mere</u> thought of someone being in my home uninvited makes me shiver with fear.
6. <u>As with</u> chronic stress, constant fatigue syndrome (CFS) interferes with daily activities and social interactions.
7. It is possible to monitor large animals by <u>attaching</u> a tracking device to their bodies.
8. Housewives nowadays don't go out to buy groceries as often as they once did; they just have their groceries <u>delivered</u> to their homes.
9. The leaders of the tribe invoked their gods by offering <u>sacrifices</u> to them.
10. While some scientists <u>hail</u> the government's proposal to develop genetically modified crops (GM crops), 25 percent of scientists recently surveyed said that GM crops could present a serious threat to ecosystems if left unregulated.

ANSWER (DAY 14)

#118
1. 활발한, 활기찬, 만화 영화의
2. 이해하다
3. 분해(해체)하다
4. 확장, 확대
5. 묘책, 책략

#119
1. inanimate
2. manipulate
3. temper
4. loop
5. platform

#120
1. (F)
2. (E)
3. (A)
4. (B)
5. (D)
6. (H)
7. (G)
8. (C)

#121
1. (C)
2. (B)
3. (A)
4. (D)

#122
1. (A)
2. (B)
3. (C)
4. (A)
5. (C)
6. (A)

#123
1. (A)
2. (B)
3. (A)
4. (C)
5. (D)
6. (C)
7. (C)
8. (B)
9. (D)
10. (D)
11. (D)
12. (C)
13. (D)
14. (A)
15. (B)
16. (C)

#124
1. hostile
2. genuinely
3. company
4. responsibility
5. allowed
6. blame
7. credited
8. Previously
9. allowing

#125
1.
① matter
② manipulate
③ make
④ build

2.
① are
② contain
③ affect
④ restrict

#126
1. Sometimes we encounter <u>unpleasant</u> truths.
2. The country is facing famine and disease in the <u>aftermath</u> of the earthquake.
3. The Act, which prohibited trade with foreign countries, <u>inspired</u> Americans to produce their own goods.
4. The Act <u>allows</u> a person to see any information that government organizations hold.
5. The concrete stopped the rain from <u>soaking</u> into the ground.
6. He <u>firmly</u> tied a string to the cake box so that the string wouldn't come loose.
7. An <u>incident</u> in my life that I'd like to forget is the disturbance caused by my ex-wife, who was completely drunk, at my wedding banquet.
8. Modern contraceptives <u>enable / allow</u> couples to have sex without worrying about pregnancy.
9. Business clothes are often <u>uncomfortable</u>. That's why many companies let their employees decide what they want to wear at work.

ANSWER (DAY 15)

#127
1. 애초에, 처음부터
2. 최종적인, 최고의
3. (엄청난) 능력(실력)
4. 절정, 봉우리
5. 유지, 보유

#128
1. sanctuary
2. demonstrate
3. dimensions
4. element
5. incredulous

#129
1. (C)
2. (F)
3. (H)
4. (E)
5. (D)
6. (B)
7. (A)
8. (G)

#130
1. (B)
2. (C)
3. (A)
4. (D)

#131
1. (B)
2. (D)
3. (B)
4. (A)
5. (A)
6. (C)

#132
1. (A)
2. (B)
3. (A)
4. (A)
5. (D)
6. (C)
7. (A)
8. (D)

9. (C)
10. (A)
11. (B)
12. (A)
13. (D)
14. (B)
15. (D)
16. (A)

#133
1. bank
2. chance
3. lead
4. public
5. well
6. extended
7. mechanism
8. sturdy

#134
1.
① suggest
② inhabit
③ lived
④ demonstrate

2.
① believed
② dominate
③ forced
④ accept
⑤ suggested

#135
1. The <u>aim</u> of this first aid course is to teach you how to do CPR correctly.
2. He is the <u>sole</u> survivor of the plane crash.
3. Backpacks are more <u>convenient</u> to carry than suitcases with wheels.
4. Removing dead trees that could be infested with harmful bugs is <u>essential</u> for healthy forests.
5. When students take many different subjects, it gives them a <u>chance</u> to discover their strengths and weaknesses.
6. Although the employees felt <u>subjected</u> to unfair treatment, they didn't do anything because they were afraid of being laid off.
7. The vast majority of residents concurred that more street lights needed to be <u>installed</u> to prevent crime.
8. Since <u>lead</u> is a toxic metal, if you eat food contaminated by it, there can be serious health consequences.
9. In the center of the village was the <u>well</u>, which was the only way for the villagers to get drinking water.

ANSWER (DAY 16)

#136
1. 업신여기다
2. 해산, 분산
3. 나타내다, 의미하다
4. 전성기
5. 조각, 이 빠진 자국

#137
1. verbally
2. provocation
3. upright
4. edge
5. anonymous

#138
1. (D)
2. (G)
3. (A)
4. (C)
5. (B)
6. (F)
7. (E)
8. (H)

#139
1. (A)
2. (C)
3. (D)
4. (B)

#140
1. (D)
2. (C)
3. (D)
4. (B)
5. (C)
6. (B)

#141
1. (B)
2. (A)
3. (A)
4. (B)
5. (D)
6. (A)
7. (A)
8. (B)
9. (D)
10. (A)
11. (A)
12. (C)
13. (D)
14. (C)
15. (B)
16. (D)

#142
1. adopted
2. align
3. limits
4. scapegoat
5. story
6. extreme
7. wrong

#143
1.
① same
② rude
③ crossed
④ considered
⑤ rude

2.
① noteworthy
② household
③ hanging
④ folding
⑤ storing

#144
1. Certain species of whales are particularly vulnerable to sonar <u>designed</u> to detect objects underwater.
2. <u>In retrospect</u>, we find it astonishing that people voted for the Nazis in 1933.
3. Chimpanzees have <u>fully</u> developed social structures similar to human tribes.
4. The world population has reached around 8 billion people today, 800 million of whom remain in <u>extreme</u> poverty.
5. There's a <u>limit</u> on the money you can spend to invest in stocks.
6. You can control the length of time that the film in a camera is <u>exposed</u> to light through the shutter speed.
7. Animals that live in cold regions have to metabolize many more calories a day to <u>maintain</u> a steady body temperature.
8. A boycott against imported British goods was agreed on, and their resolutions calling for the repeal of the act were <u>adopted</u> after a vote.

ANSWER (DAY 17)

#145
1. 중요한, 뛰어난
2. 쓰다
3. 회상하다
4. 도약
5. 최종적으로, 완전히

#146
1. essence
2. pedestrian
3. dichotomy
4. longevity
5. comparable

#147
1. (F)
2. (H)
3. (C)
4. (A)
5. (B)
6. (E)
7. (D)
8. (G)

#148
1. (D)
2. (B)
3. (A)
4. (C)

#149
1. (A)
2. (D)
3. (A)
4. (C)
5. (C)
6. (D)

#150
1. (D)
2. (B)
3. (C)
4. (A)
5. (B)
6. (C)
7. (D)
8. (D)

9. (A)
10. (D)
11. (B)
12. (B)
13. (C)
14. (A)
15. (B)
16. (D)
17. (B)
18. (B)

#151
1. lasted
2. charges
3. crucial
4. ultimately
5. subject
6. deplete
7. interfere
8. subject
9. subject
10. suffered
11. witness
12. suffering

#152
1.
① ranked
② spectacular
③ phenomena
④ bucket

2.
① occurred
② suffered
③ taken
④ arrived
⑤ treated

#153
1. Frequent charging could shorten the <u>longevity</u> of a battery.
2. His poems <u>concern</u> some of the famous legendary heroes in his country.
3. It seems like a <u>rational</u> decision to buy products based on their prices.
4. I made a <u>promise</u> to my parents that I'd quit the band.
5. I took 20 minutes to look for a nice quiet <u>spot</u> for camping in the mountains.
6. It was you, the developed countries, that <u>depleted</u> our planet's natural resources.
7. My sons <u>look forward to</u> receiving Christmas presents from Santa Claus.
8. The soldier <u>suffering from</u> PTSD couldn't sleep and so relied more on drinking.

ANSWER (DAY 18)

#154
1. 불활성의
2. 바지선
3. 조종할 수 있는
4. 재담
5. 구별하다

#155
1. conclude
2. universal
3. resort
4. deposit
5. unanimous

#156
1. (H)
2. (D)
3. (A)
4. (B)
5. (F)
6. (C)
7. (E)
8. (G)

#157
1. (B)
2. (A)
3. (D)
4. (C)

#158
1. (D)
2. (C)
3. (C)
4. (A)
5. (C)
6. (B)

#159
1. (B)
2. (D)
3. (A)
4. (B)
5. (A)
6. (B)
7. (B)
8. (D)

9. (A)
10. (D)
11. (A)
12. (D)
13. (A)
14. (D)
15. (D)
16. (A)

#160
1. ready
2. inert
3. Providing
4. shore
5. bear
6. cleared
7. reward
8. shores
9. shores

#161
1.
① contains
② roles
③ limit
④ balances
2.
① help
② made
③ create
④ prove
⑤ false

#162
1. A fish ladder is an <u>invention</u> that helps fish return to their spawning grounds.
2. When the farmer saw some young kids stealing watermelons from his fields, he stopped them <u>on the spot</u>.
3. Some experts recommend that parents <u>limit</u> the time their children spend using computers to an hour or less.
4. Wouldn't it be expensive to haul bulky <u>equipment</u> to the Moon to make fuel?
5. During this <u>period</u>, Greek poets began to portray heroic deeds in their poems.
6. The government can reduce fertilizer levels through an act that <u>limits</u> fertilizer use.
7. If he <u>proves</u> what he believes through experiments, he can come up with a theory.
8. The <u>source</u> of the problem of depopulation lies mainly in economic factors including inflation and unemployment.

ANSWER (DAY 19)

#163
1. 괴롭히다
2. 광적인, 열광적인
3. 부차적인, 부수적인, 계열사
4. 반복되는, 되풀이되는
5. 의견이 다르다

#164
1. yardstick
2. wriggle
3. primacy
4. generation
5. flight

#165
1. (F)
2. (C)
3. (A)
4. (H)
5. (E)
6. (B)
7. (D)
8. (G)

#166
1. (C)
2. (B)
3. (A)
4. (D)

#167
1. (D)
2. (A)
3. (D)
4. (C)
5. (A)
6. (D)

#168
1. (B)
2. (D)
3. (A)
4. (C)
5. (C)
6. (D)
7. (B)
8. (D)
9. (A)
10. (D)
11. (D)
12. (D)
13. (C)
14. (C)
15. (B)
16. (A)

#169
1. withstand
2. hide
3. conduct
4. preoccupied
5. steadily
6. area
7. desperate
8. inferior

#170
1.
① despite
② risk
③ betrayed
④ changed

2.
① risk
② fuels
③ leak
④ proximity
⑤ danger

#171
1. She moved to Africa and spent the rest of her <u>life</u> helping poor people.
2. The use of pesticides causes a great deal of <u>harm</u> to wildlife in the area.
3. In a series of missions to Mars, they collected <u>specimens</u> of rocks and then returned them to Earth.
4. Governments cannot <u>provide</u> solutions to individual problems.
5. According to him, women who drink a lot of milk have a high <u>risk</u> of getting breast cancer.
6. Zebras don't <u>hide</u> in places filled with tall grass and low trees.
7. The animal is <u>seemingly</u> harmless, but it is very dangerous.
8. Tribal languages spoken on reservations <u>are at risk of</u> extinction.
9. Cedars are more likely to <u>withstand</u> adverse weather conditions such as severe cold than deciduous trees which shed their leaves in the fall.
10. Low-income families have no other choice except to buy cheaper, nutritionally <u>inferior</u> food to feed their families.

ANSWER (DAY 20)

#172
1. 겪다, 머물다
2. 홈, 리듬
3. 점, 얼룩, 자국
4. 신빙성
5. 자고 있는

#173
1. authority
2. fragment
3. shred
4. hone
5. cliche

#174
1. (D)
2. (H)
3. (A)
4. (G)
5. (B)
6. (C)
7. (E)
8. (F)

#175
1. (A)
2. (B)
3. (D)
4. (C)

#176
1. (A)
2. (C)
3. (C)
4. (A)
5. (A)
6. (B)

#177
1. (A)
2. (C)
3. (D)
4. (A)
5. (A)
6. (D)
7. (D)
8. (A)
9. (D)
10. (A)
11. (C)
12. (B)
13. (C)
14. (D)
15. (D)
16. (A)

#178
1. degrees
2. impressed
3. issue
4. degree
5. narrowly
6. narrow
7. in part
8. facet
9. regular

#179
1.
① Nevertheless
② contribution
③ advances
④ granted

2.
① regions
② necessarily
③ effects
④ facets
⑤ differently

#180
1. The war was brought to an <u>end</u> by the peace treaty.
2. Jane is hoping to <u>pursue</u> a <u>career</u> in journalism.
3. I'<u>m</u> often <u>disturbed</u> by the noise made by my neighbor who lives upstairs.
4. The method by which the tiger moth drives away its predators is unique; it uses a poison from its body to <u>repel</u> them.
5. He <u>deserves</u> to go to prison.
6. He sat <u>still</u> on a bench.
7. The castle was so vulnerable to attack by enemies that it was captured almost <u>immediately</u>.
8. Parents today <u>take it for granted that</u> they need to make sacrifices for their children.
9. One of the representative examples of the tragedy of the commons is wasting drinking water by brushing your teeth with the <u>faucet</u> left on.

앵그리 아카데믹 보카
Angry Academic Vocabulary
토플·수능·외고·특목고·텝스·IELTS·공무원